'England's darling'

Manchester University Press

'England's darling'

The Victorian cult of Alfred the Great

JOANNE PARKER

Manchester University Press

Manchester and New York

distributed exclusively in the USA by Palgrave

Copyright © Joanne Parker 2007

The right of Joanne Parker to be identified as the author of this work has been asserted by her in accordance with the Copyright, Designs and Patents Act 1988.

Published by Manchester University Press
Oxford Road, Manchester M13 9NR, UK
and Room 400, 175 Fifth Avenue, New York, NY 10010, USA
www.manchesteruniversitypress.co.uk

Distributed exclusively in the USA by
Palgrave, 175 Fifth Avenue, New York,
NY 10010, USA

Distributed exclusively in Canada by
UBC Press, University of British Columbia, 2029 West Mall,
Vancouver, BC, Canada V6T 1Z2

British Library Cataloguing-in-Publication Data
A catalogue record for this book is available from the British Library

Library of Congress Cataloging-in-Publication Data applied for

ISBN 978 0 7190 7356 4   hardback

First published 2007

16 15 14 13 12 11 10 09 08 07   10 9 8 7 6 5 4 3 2 1

Typeset by Servis Filmsetting Limited, Manchester
Printed in Great Britain
by Biddles Ltd, King's Lynn

Contents

List of Illustrations

Preface: The king who burnt the cakes

It was whilst Alfred was in hiding, disguised as a poor peasant, that he knocked one day at the door of a lonely hut in the marshes and asked for shelter. A peasant woman opened the door, and taking pity on Alfred, told him that he could come in and rest. She was baking some cakes, and asked Alfred to see that they did not burn, whilst she went to the well. But Alfred was thinking about how to beat the Danes, so he forgot all about the cakes, which were soon burnt to cinders. When the women returned and found her cakes ruined, she was naturally angry, and not knowing Alfred was the king, she scolded him bitterly and even, as some of the stories tell, beat him with her broomstick.[1]

What is popularly known of King Alfred today? Possibly that he was Saxon and fought the Danes. Perhaps that a statue of him stands in Winchester. And maybe people have some vague recollection of the legend above – that Alfred burnt the cakes – although how and where this happened and, more importantly, whose cakes they were, remains – for most people – shrouded in mystery.

In the nineteenth century, the situation was very different. In 1852, Alfred's life could be described as 'the favourite story in English nurseries', and between 1800 and 1901, a cult of the Saxon king developed in Britain, with at least four statues of Alfred erected; more than twenty-five paintings of him completed; and over a hundred popular 'Alfredian' texts published – including poems, plays, novels and histories, as well as children's books. The authors of these works ranged from canonical figures such as William Wordsworth, Charles Dickens and Thomas Hughes, to devoted amateurs like John Fitchett (who spent forty years writing a 1,500-page epic about the Saxon king, a work which is possibly the longest poem in the English language). Rewriting Alfred's life was not purely a male preserve: Victorian women writers also celebrated the king, often in texts that provided a distinct, domestic focus upon his reign, and commonly in 'improving' texts for juvenile readers. And besides English authors, Alfredian texts were produced by writers from Scotland, America, Australia and India.

This book sets out to answer the questions that must arise in the face of such remarkable nineteenth-century enthusiasm for a ninth-century king who ruled only a portion of Southern England. What was it about Alfred's life that rendered him such an appealing figure? From what sources did the

Victorians derive their images of the Saxon king, and how did they rewrite and reshape these? And, finally, why did the Saxon king's reputation decline so sharply in the decades after 1901? This book begins by focusing upon what was probably the apex of Victorian Alfredianism: the grand 1901 commemoration of the king's death – held in Winchester over four days, but organised over several years by a national committee including Rudyard Kipling, Thomas Hardy and Arthur Conan Doyle. Chapters Two and Three provide the background to this event – both in terms of the wider cultural movements which provided the context for a cult of King Alfred to develop, and also in the sense of the Alfredian tradition which the nineteenth century inherited.

The intersection of the cult of Alfred with nineteenth-century British politics is the subject of Chapter Four, which focuses particularly upon the role that Alfredianism played in debate about the future of the monarchy. Chapter Five considers how the Saxon king was enlisted to vindicate and ennoble those institutions of which Victorian Britain was most proud – notably its navy, law-code, constitution and empire. It examines conceptions of ninth-century Wessex as a time of immense cultural change – the mirror-image of the nineteenth century. And it reviews Victorian appropriations of Alfred's reign as a prestigious starting point for myths of national progress. Chapter Six focuses upon more domestic narratives – the use of Alfred, by Victorian authors, to exemplify moral values, and the rewriting of his life as a parable of error and redemption. Finally, the crucial question of Alfred's decline in fame is addressed in Chapter Seven, which surveys the diminished interest in the Saxon king after 1901.

The current study began life as just one chapter in a wide survey of different figures from British history who achieved the status of national icons in nineteenth-century culture. It quickly became apparent, however, that the extent of the Victorian fascination with Alfred demanded a full-length study of its own. The recent interest in the formation of British national identity, which has arisen partly as a result of limited devolution of the countries that made up the Union at the close of the twentieth century, also makes a study of nineteenth-century Alfredianism particularly pertinent. Alfred was central to the nineteenth-century formation of a British national identity rooted in English history – a theme which underpins much of this study, but is focused on explicitly in Chapter Three (which considers the use of the Saxon king in relation to the 1801 Act of Union) and Chapter Six (which looks at Alfredianism and the rise of Victorian racialism).

Perhaps precisely because King Alfred is no longer as prominent as Robin Hood or King Arthur in popular culture, nineteenth-century interest in him has received little scholarly attention, compared with the many excellent studies published in recent years of Arthuriana or the outlaw tradition. The current study sets out to rectify this neglect. It builds, however, on the work of several notable scholars of Anglo-Saxonism. First and foremost is Simon Keynes who, with Michael Lapidge, edited the translations of Asser's *Life of*

King Alfred and the *Life of Saint Neot*, without which the current study would have been impossible. Keynes's invaluable paper on 'The Cult of King Alfred', published as a special edition of *Anglo-Saxon England*, also furnished much of the background research on the development of interest in Alfred from the ninth century to the end of the eighteenth, on which this study is founded. And, in particular, it is indebted to his analysis of the development of Alfredian fine art, and his primary investigative work on Alfred's importance to the University of Oxford.

Keynes's paper leaves the story of Alfred's reception history where the present one takes it up – with what he terms the 'overwhelming' quantity of Alfrediana produced during Victoria's reign. Other studies have examined some of this corpus. Clare Simmons's 1990 book, *Reversing the Conquest: History and Myth in Nineteenth-Century British Literature*, contains a very helpful analysis of the association of Alfred with Queen Victoria in the late nineteenth century – in the context of an equally valuable, broader examination of depictions of Normans and Saxons in nineteenth-century British literature. Like Keynes, Simmons also examines the development of Alfredianism before 1800, and for this reason provides an essential basis for the current study. More recently, Barbara Yorke has produced two excellent short papers on Alfredianism to mark the eleven-hundredth anniversary of Alfred's death in 1999 – one a survey of Alfred's role in political history from the sixteenth to the nineteenth century, and the other an invaluable account of the 1901 commemorations for Alfred which took place in Winchester. The current author owes a debt to her local archival research.

Other recent works which have provided inspiration to the current study of Alfredianism include Lynda Pratt's short paper on the early-nineteenth-century Alfredian epics produced by Henry James Pye and Joseph Cottle; the essays in Allen Frantzen and John Niles's 1997 *Anglo-Saxonism and the Construction of Social Identity* – particularly Suzanne Hagedorn's useful paper, 'Received Wisdom: The Reception History of Alfred's Preface to the Pastoral Care'; and David Sturdy's 1995 history of Alfred, which contains a concluding survey chapter on 'Alfred in Later Centuries'. Eric Stanley's 1981 article 'The Glorification of Alfred King of Wessex', also remains a useful introduction to eighteenth and nineteenth-century Alfrediana – although it focuses upon only a small number of texts (ten from the eighteenth century and eight from the nineteenth) and concludes sombrely that 'if Alfred fared badly in poetry, especially epic poetry, he fared even worse in drama, especially poetic drama'.[2]

Similar lamentations have been voiced before and since by other critics surveying the Alfredian tradition. The current study, however, does not presume either to disparage the literary quality of nineteenth-century Alfredian texts, or to propose them as equal in merit to the central works of Victorian Arthurianism. What it does aim to do, however, is to provide a broad account of the nineteenth-century cult of King Alfred; to reveal the rich cultural interest of this corpus of texts as a whole; and in so doing, to redress a misleading modern emphasis on Arthur and the Victorians, address a genuine gap in the current literature on nineteenth-century medievalism, and contribute to our continual redrawing of the Victorian cultural map.

Notes

1 Lawrence Du Garde Peach, *King Alfred the Great*, p. 20 – a Ladybird History Book.
2 Stanley, 'The Glorification of Alfred King of Wessex', p. 116.

Acknowledgements

I would like to thank the British Academy, the AHRC and the Joseph Wright Trust for the research funding which allowed the completion of this project. I am also grateful for permissions to reproduce images from the National Portrait Gallery, the Victoria and Albert Museum, the British Museum, the British Library, Tate London, University College Oxford, the Parker Library in Cambridge, the British Film Institute, the Laing Art Gallery, the Courtauld Institute of Art, the Mary Evans Picture Library and MGM films.

Many thanks are due to my doctoral supervisors, Andrew Wawn and Richard Salmon at the University of Leeds, for help with the thesis which grew into this book, and to Mark Hurst for support during its completion. I am also forever grateful to Ronald Hutton at the University of Bristol for generously allowing me space and encouragement to continue working on this project alongside new post-doctoral research. Early drafts of the book were read by Geraldine Barnes, Nick Groom, Mark Hurst, Ronald Hutton, Stephen Knight and Tom Shippey, who corrected errors and provided much valuable advice. Information for the book was also generously contributed by John Clark, Jane Cunningham, Louise D'Arcens, Richard Evans, Davyth Hicks, Jim Jackaman, Gail Marshall, Marilyn Michalowicz, Lorna Sage, Christine Thyis, Chris Williams, and the members of the Regional History Centre at the University of the West of England. Finally, I would like to thank my family for their help and encouragement, and Nick – for the care and attention he has given both to this book and its author.

For Leonard, Rosemary and Helen Parker

1

The day of a thousand years: Alfred and the Victorian mania for commemoration

They called it 'the day of a thousand years'. By noon on Friday 20 September 1901, in spite of inclement weather, thousands of spectators were crowded into the centre of Winchester or perched aloft on any available rooftop. A public holiday had been declared in the city, flags fluttered from every tower, and bunting rustled from windows and balconies. At the city's West Gate a grand procession was forming – composed of British ambassadors from every corner of the Empire; prominent academics from English-speaking universities worldwide; lord mayors and distinguished clergy from across the country; and military units fresh from the Boer War, including detachments of the Lancashire Fusiliers, the Gordon Highlanders and the Royal Portsmouth Naval Brigade (see Figure 1). These assembled dignitaries solemnly processed through Winchester's streets to the Broadway, and at 12.17 the guns of the Royal Field Artillery fired, the city's cathedral and church bells pealed, and applause erupted as the former prime minister Lord Rosebery unveiled the majestic thirteen-foot-high statue of a ninth-century Anglo-Saxon king (for a photograph of the event, see Figure 2).[1]

The obvious question is who was being celebrated in such grand style and why? And on one level this is simple to answer. The monarch was Alfred the Great, king of Wessex from 870 to 899; the occasion was the (wrongly calculated) thousandth anniversary of his death; and Winchester's role arose from the fact that the city had been the place of his death, his burial place and (allegedly) his capital. We need to ask, though, exactly what those assembled thought they were commemorating in the figure of this Saxon king – in effect, were they all there to celebrate the same Alfred? And King Alfred's Millenary goes only so far in explaining how a provincial city could muster a distinguished pantheon of internationally significant guests, or why reporters from all the national papers, and from America, France and Germany were in attendance. To begin to understand these issues, it is necessary to step back to the earliest planning of the event.

Preparations for the Millenary

In October 1897, during a lecture at the Birmingham and Midland Institute, the historian Frederic Harrison suggested that a statue of Alfred

1 'The Naval Brigade', part of the procession through Winchester to the Alfred statue (published in Bowker's 1902 record of the commemorations)

2 'The Unveiling Ceremony' (photograph of Winchester's statue being unveiled by Rosebery, published in Bowker's 1902 record of the commemorations)

should be erected in or near Winchester to mark the millennium of the king's death. Hailing Alfred as 'the model Englishman', he suggested that the erection of a statue of the king would be 'an occasion to call for representation of every side of our national life . . . Soldiers, sailors, scholars, churchmen, missionaries, teachers, councillors, judges, prelates, artists, craftsmen, discoverers – chiefs and people – all alike might gather to do honour to the royal genius who loved them all, who breathed into them all his inspiration'.[2] At this time, Harrison was leader of the British Positivists – followers of Auguste Comte, who believed that the lives of historical heroes should provide the inspiration for modern social change – so his reasons for wishing to raise Alfred's public profile were probably political. Certainly, Alfred had been one of only a handful of English heroes to have appeared in Comte's Positivist calendar.[3] And in Harrison's own *New Calendar of the Lives of Great Men*, published in 1888, he had drawn attention to the approach of the Saxon king's Millenary and had expressed his hope that a 'fitting celebration' might be held in 1901 to commemorate Alfred.[4]

Harrison's appeal was not the first call for a statue of Alfred in Winchester. Many years earlier, in 1829, a Winchester magazine called the *Crypt* had contained an article entitled 'A King Alfred monument', which lamented the want of some 'magnificent and visible monument' to the Saxon king, urging that the nation should erect one immediately, and even going so far as to suggest a suitable inscription.[5] While this suggestion seems to have passed by unremarked, Harrison's proposal was reported in *The Times*, where it caught the attention of the energetic, twenty-seven-year-old Mayor of

Winchester, Alfred Bowker. Bowker broached the question of erecting a memorial to King Alfred in Winchester at the city's Mayoral Banquet on 9 November, and by 20 November *The Times* could advertise to the nation Winchester's willingness to host an Alfred Millenary – stressing that although the event would take place in the provinces it should nevertheless be a 'national celebration . . . universally recognized'.[6]

Bowker was obviously aware from an early stage that Winchester's claim on the Alfred Millenary might be contested, so he worked hard to promote the city's Alfredian connections. His first tactic was to arrange for the novelist, popular historian and champion of the working classes, Walter Besant, to give a lecture on the life of the king at the Guildhall in Winchester, ensuring that this received national press coverage. Besant's speech attracted a huge crowd – indeed, the doors had to be closed on queues of disappointed people still outside the building – and it was careful to strike a populist chord. He praised Thomas Hardy for having lately revived the use of the term 'Wessex' – 'the name of Alfred's country, well-nigh forgotten except by scholars' – and having thus forged a sense of continuity between Alfred's ninth-century kingdom and contemporary culture, went on to stress that a monument to Alfred must be set up in Winchester 'and not in London or in Westminster, or anywhere else. Here lies the dust of his ancestors, and of the kings his successors . . . In this city Alfred received instruction from St Swithun'.[7]

Besant also presented an Alfred commemoration as the natural epilogue to the Jubilee celebrations that had taken place in 1897, relating how:

> Last year – on that memorable day when we were all drunk with the visible glory and the greatness of the Empire – there arose in the minds of many a feeling that we ought to teach the people the meaning of what we saw set forth in that procession – the meaning of our Empire; not only what it is, but how it came – through whose creation, by whose foundation. Now so much is Alfred the founder that every ship in our navy might have his name, every school his bust, every Guildhall his statue. He is everywhere. But he is invisible. But the people do not know him. The boys do not learn about him. There is nothing to show him. We want a monument to Alfred, if only to make the people learn and remember the origin of our Empire, if only that his noble example may be kept before us, to stimulate and to inspire and to encourage.[8]

Bowker's next move was to call a planning meeting for interested parties at the Mansion House in Winchester the following March, complete with a feast of golden plovers and ptarmigan to impress invited dignitaries. By now, Bowker and Frederic Harrison were working together on the planning of the Alfred Millenary. While Bowker's primary concern was to keep the commemorations in Winchester, however, Harrison, was anxious that the event should not become provincial, and so should be organised by a national committee. To this end he had spoken in London in January of 1898 – a lecture reported at length by *The Times* – arguing that the Alfred commemoration should be 'done royally, in a form at once magnificent and national' and that it should not be 'a private concern. It should be taken out of the hands of self-nominated committees and self-advertising busybodies, and be taken in hand by the Government of the nation under the sanction of Parliament'. He had also suggested that if an Alfred mausoleum were to be built in Winchester it might sensibly replace Westminster Abbey, now 'crowded to excess' with tombs, as the nation's 'Campo Sancto' and the resting place of 'the noblest sons of England'.[9]

It is likely that it was at Harrison's urging, then, that those invited to the meeting included the Archbishop of Canterbury, the Bishop of London, and the Lord Mayor of London – the latter of whom was nominated as the chairman of the Alfred committee, although Bowker and Harrison seem to have remained the real driving forces. Other figures of national import also seem to have been approached by Harrison. Expressions of support were read at the meeting from Cardinal Vaughan, the Duke of Wellington, Sir Edward Burne Jones, Henry Irving and John Ruskin, while the climax of the evening seems to have been the reading aloud of a letter from Queen Victoria, expressing her approval of the proposed commemoration.

With such heavyweight backers, an Alfred millennial commemoration of some sort began to look like a certainty, although rumblings of opposition began to surround Winchester's pivotal role in this. At the Mansion House meeting, Lord Wantage drew attention to King Alfred's close association with Berkshire, arguing for a key role for his own town in the celebrations, while the Lord Mayor of London stressed Alfred's connection to that city, arguing that:

> London is a great city, and it was the work of Alfred; Alfred built its walls after they had all been demolished . . . It was to London that Alfred looked as the starting point of that commerce which has now grown to be alike the wonder and the admiration of the world. It has been in London that the seed which he sowed of the principles of local self-government has found its home in our great civic guilds. . . . It may be worth serious consideration whether, at all events besides Winchester, London should not be a place that should have a worthy memorial.[10]

In the following month, a pamphlet was also published which argued for Dorset's importance to the king, claiming that Alfred had spent more time in Sherborne than in Winchester, and providing a comprehensive list to demonstrate that more of his family were buried in Dorset than in Wiltshire. Its author W.B. Wildman had clearly been following Bowker's campaign closely, since his rather venomous pamphlet attacked both the initial report of Winchester's plans for the Alfred Millenary (published in *The Times* the previous November) and also Besant's speech in Winchester.[11] Some grumbling about Winchester's monopolisation of the event was clearly still current the following year, when the Right Hon. G. Shaw-Lefevre spoke at a planning meeting for the Alfred Millenary, claiming, with a generous dose of exaggeration, that:

It was with Winchester that Alfred was mainly connected; it was, in fact, his home; he was educated – or at least so a credible tradition averred – at Winchester by their great bishop and Saint, St Swithun; it was from Winchester he directed his military operations; it was, no doubt, at Winchester he organised the fleet with which he defeated the Danes in Southampton Water; it was at Winchester he established his Court after the peace was made.[12]

There was still some discontent by the January of 1901, when *The Times* published a letter from a J.G. James, calling for 'Athelney, the most sacred spot within these Isles for Englishmen' to be included in the approaching Millenary celebrations and arguing that 'Alfred is associated with Athelney in the national imagination as he is not associated even with Winchester'.[13] By that stage, however, the central role of Bowker's Winchester in the celebration had become assured. Wildman also argued that Alfred had died not in 901, as Bowker and Harrison were claiming, but in 900.[14] His was not the only voice to contest the proposed timing of the Millenary celebrations. A heated debate over the date of Alfred's death ran in the *English Historical Review* in the early months of 1898, with W.H. Stevenson arguing against other contributors for the correct date of 899. In the end, Bowker's committee announced that although they acknowledged there to be much uncertainty over the correct date, they would opt for the 'traditional' one of 901. Such brushing aside of recent historical debate as 'pedantry' was to characterise much of the commemoration, but in fact the organising committee had little choice – they needed more than a year to plan a commemoration on the scale they were envisaging.[15]

The list of members on that Alfred Millenary committee now reads rather like a 'who's who' of late Victorian England – and perhaps demonstrates as well as anything else that King Alfred, by the end of the nineteenth century, was not merely a subject of interest in the environs of Winchester. Among its number were the actor Henry Irving; the historians Walter Skeat and Lord John Acton; the antiquary Sir John Lubbock (Lord Avebury); and the Poet Laureate Alfred Austin. Cultural officials included the President of the Royal Academy, and the directors of the National Portrait Gallery and the British Museum. There were political figures from both Conservative and Liberal parties, including Herbert Gladstone (son of William), the Lord Chief Justice, and the Speaker of the House of Commons. And the literary world was well represented by the presence of Rudyard Kipling, Thomas Hardy, Rider Haggard, Edmund Gosse and Arthur Conan Doyle.

Conan Doyle – soon to be known as one of the greatest advocates of British overseas policy, after the 1900 publication of *The Great Boer War* – spoke at length at the second major planning meeting for the commemoration in 1899. Describing Alfred as an already celebrated monarch 'to whom all this land, and in a sense all this empire, is one stupendous monument', he argued that:

What we are really commemorating is not merely the anniversary of the death of King Alfred but the greatness of those institutions which he founded. This anniversary may be said to indicate the thousandth milestone in the majestic journey of our race . . . From that, the greatest of English kings, to this the greatest of British queens, there extends that unbroken record, the longest which the modern world can show.[16]

A forward-thinking sympathiser of racial intermarriage, divorce and Irish independence, Doyle was cautious to distance himself from the sort of conservative nostalgia associated with medievalist writers like Charlotte Yonge, stressing that 'I think in nations as in individuals looking back too much is not a good thing; it is usually the first sign of age'. Nevertheless, he allowed that 'this is a unique occasion when we may look back on that long stretch of time and see what lessons it has to teach us. To pause now and to glance back during one year at the records of a thousand years can only brace us in those days of trial which may still be coming upon us'. And he echoed the positivist stance in suggesting that if the patron saint of England were to be 'decided in our modern democratic fashion, St. Alfred of Wessex, I am sure, would be the sage and hero whom we should select'.[17]

Doyle's speech sounded many notes that would be re-echoed throughout the planning and execution of the Alfred Millenary: the significance of the 1,000-year gap between Alfred and Victoria; the appropriateness of canonising the Saxon king; and the uses of Alfred as an exemplar from the past and an inspiration for the present. This latter point was reiterated at the same meeting by the Chief Rabbi, who 'could conceive nothing more inspiring, nothing more stimulating, no better preparation for the fulfilment of civic duties than to study deeply the life and to profit by the illustrious example of King Alfred'. Along with Cardinal Vaughan, the rabbi had been invited to join the committee in the name of religious inclusiveness. The commemoration was intended to be embraced by all 'without distinction of creed, race, nation or party'.[18] Thus, care was taken to ensure that the leaders of the Conservative and Liberal parties, Lord Salisbury and Lord Rosebery, contributed identical donations of £50 to the Millenary fund.

Other contributors to the Alfred commemoration included mayors from across England, various national businesses – including the cordwainers, the clothworkers, and most of the major railway companies – and both Eton and Harrow schools. Beyond the bounds of the British Isles, contributions came from India and North America. Despite this undoubted national – even international – interest, however, the fact that the event was to be held in Winchester meant that much of the expense had to be met locally. Bowker therefore wrote to all the local clergy urging them to make their own contributions, but also to collect donations from their parishioners, and in this way sufficient funds were raised to plan the erection of a statue.[19] Early on in the planning of the Millenary, it had been agreed that it would also be desirable to open a museum of early English history in Winchester, as part of the Alfred commemoration. Initially, this was planned for the supposed

site of the Saxon king's palace at Wolvesey Castle. This, however, was on
twenty-five-year lease to the Bishop of Winchester and he proved reluctant
to hand over the ruined castle and its surrounding land, and vehemently
opposed to the building of any museum in such close proximity to the Palace
of Wolvesey – which was still used for ecclesiastical business. A protracted
dispute simmered between the bishop and the lord mayors of London and
Winchester, a controversy which was serialised in the letters' section of *The
Times* between May of 1899 and January 1901.[20] The bishop seems to have
been the victor – if only by force of intractability. The site of Hyde Abbey
was bought instead of Wolvesey, along with some adjoining land to be used
as a public park. As the donations made to the Alfred fund were unable to
cover this, however, the purchase had to be covered by the local council. This
provoked much local opposition from those concerned about a rise in their
rates, and the coining of the epithet 'Bowker's Bog' for the land when it
became apparent that after all the wrangling over Wolvesey, sufficient
funding would never be found to construct any museum.[21] The proposal to
erect an Alfred statue also faced some initial opposition. Leonard Cust,
Director of the National Portrait Gallery, argued that it would be impossible to produce an authentic representation of a man for whom no accurate
contemporary portraiture existed, and that a different form of sculpture
where the artist might have 'a free hand in the design' would be more appropriate.[22] The majority of board members, however, evidently wished for the
closest equivalent to a portrait in stone, because the sculptor eventually
chosen to create Winchester's Alfred statue was Hamo Thornycroft, perhaps
the leading exponent of the naturalistic and anti-classical movement that had
become known as the 'New Sculpture', and the son of Thomas Thornycroft,
whose sculptural group, *Alfred the Great Encouraged to the Pursuit of
Learning by His Mother* had been criticised on the grounds of its excessive
realism. The younger Thornycroft was paid £5,000 for the Alfred statue –
to include the cost of materials – and signed a contract which stipulated only
that the statue must be 'colossal' (at least 'thirteen feet six inches from the
top of his crown to the soles of his feet') but otherwise gave the sculptor free
rein.[23] Winchester had no intention, it seems, of memorialising its claim to
glory on a subtle scale. The unusually large size of the cast caused problems
at the foundry in Frome, however. And the enormous dimensions of
Winchester's Alfred again caused difficulties when it came to raising the
statue upon its plinth. A rope snapped as the Saxon king was being hoisted,
the contractor was injured, part of the plinth sliced off, and King Alfred
received an undignified crack on the nose.[24] Such problems resulted in the
commemorations being postponed – from the summer of 1901 to late
September – though it was evidently not deemed worth waiting until 26
October, known to be the date of Alfred's actual death. Fair weather, it
seems, counted for more than historical precision.

It would be wrong, though, to imagine that the Winchester commemoration was an entirely populist event. Early on in the planning, the Alfred

Millenary committee decided that 'the usual forms of festive celebration, such as feasting and fireworks, would but ill suffice to honour the memory of one who accomplished so much for the advancement and education of his people, and it was therefore decided, after deliberation, to hold a meeting of representatives of learned societies from all lands where the English-speaking race predominates'.[25] Hence dignitaries from British universities were invited to the September commemoration and, further afield, from the universities of Adelaide, Sydney, Tasmania, Toronto, Calcutta, Madras, Bombay, Yale, Harvard and California.

The celebrations

For the Millenary guests, proceedings began on Tuesday 17 September, with a tour around the British Museum in London. Throughout the summer, the museum had held an exhibition of manuscripts and articles dating approximately to the time of King Alfred. The Winchester delegates were guided around by Frederic Harrison who, setting the tone for the excesses of patriotism which the visitors were to encounter over the coming days, described his feelings on first touching the Alfred Jewel as 'akin to those of a medieval Christian kissing a fragment of the True Cross'.[26] The Wednesday and Thursday were set aside for visits to historical sites in Winchester itself. The choice of locations indicates that the programme owed as much to civic pride as to Alfredianism. As a reporter from *The Times* wryly observed, Winchester College, for instance, had no ostensible connection with King Alfred.[27] It was also difficult to identify the precise relevance to Alfred of the Wednesday afternoon performance of Tennyson's *Beckett* in Winchester Cathedral, by Sir Henry Irving. The original intention had apparently been to have a reading of something more relevant to the commemoration, but no work on Alfred himself was deemed of sufficient literary merit for the occasion – and *Beckett* was one of Irving's specialities, and at least medieval in subject.

However, other events were more closely connected to Alfred – including the trips to Hyde Abbey, Wolvesey Castle and Winchester's West Gate, and the talk on Alfred's coinage given on the Thursday afternoon by Sir John Evans. The Thursday evening, immediately preceding the main day of celebrations, saw a mayoral reception at the Guildhall in Winchester. Palms, exotic blooms and animal skins gave the setting a veneer of imperial grandeur, while guests were entertained by a series of tableaux showing well-known scenes from Alfred's life (see Figure 3). These depicted both historical and popular, legendary incidents – though emendations were made, owing to the large number of women keen to play a part. The tableau of Alfred's battle at Ashdown, for instance, was much enlivened by a large posse of Saxon ladies and nuns tending the wounded. As *The Times* enthused, Alfred's life was depicted not as it appeared in scholarly histories, but 'as most of us love to know it'.[28]

3 Tableau of Alfred learning to read (performed as part of the Winchester
commemorations and published in Bowker's 1902 volume, *The
King Alfred Millenary*)

The climax of the celebrations, though, was on the Friday, when a public
holiday was declared in Winchester. The official record of the proceedings,
published a year later, was of course scrupulous in ironing out any hitches.
These included the minor scuffle (brilliantly parodied by a cartoonist in the
Illustrated London News) over the order of precedence of the dignitaries in
the grand procession, the improvisation necessary (due to high winds) to keep
the Alfred statue covered until the official unveiling, and Lord Rosebery's difficulties in making himself heard above such stormy weather conditions.[29] The
statue was originally to be unveiled by the Prince of Wales – a less-sectarian
choice and more in line with the committee's professed aim of cultural inclusiveness. Since he was prevented from participating by the death of Victoria,
however, a retired Liberal prime minister made a popular second choice.

Rosebery's speech was widely praised in the national press. Invoking
Alfred as 'one who by common consent represents the highest type of kingship and the highest type of Englishman', he asked the assembled crowds
around the Alfred statue:

What, indeed, is the secret of his fame, of his hold on the imagination of
mankind? It is, in the first place, a question of personality. He has stamped his
character on the cold annals of humanity. How is that done? We cannot tell. We
know only that two homely tales of his life – the story of his mother's book and
that of the neatherd's hut – have become part of our folk-lore. . . . his life has

those romantic elements which fascinate successive generations. . . . we behold in his career the highest and best type of the qualities which we cherish in our national character.

Turning then to Alfred's role as monarch, Rosebery continued, 'He was a king, a true king, the guide, the leader, the father of his people. . . . He was the captain of their enterprise, their industrial foreman, their schoolmaster, their lay bishop, their general, their admiral, their legislator'. And, drawing attention to Alfred's practical achievements, he conjured the crowd to imagine a seer leading the Saxon king up a mountain to see in a vision his modest fortress at London developed into 'a world-capital and a world-mart':

> Suppose that . . . the seer had brought him to a palace where the descendants of his Witan conduct a system of government which . . . is the parent of most constitutions in the civilised world . . . Suppose that he could have seen in an unending procession the various nations which own the free fatherhood of the British Crown . . . Suppose in a word, that he could have beheld, as in an unfolded tapestry, the varying but superb fortunes of that indomitable race by whose cradle he had watched: would he not have seen in himself one of those predestined beings, greater than the great, who seem unconsciously to fashion the destinies and mark the milestones of the world?[30]

An exemplary character; an ideal ruler; and the originator of those institutions that would make Britain great – these, the keynotes of Rosebery's speech, were sounded over and over during the Alfred Millenary, and represented the crescendo of themes which had been modulating throughout the nineteenth century. Rosebery's emphasis on Empire would also have been a familiar tune to those assembled. Alfredianism had been used to justify aggressive imperial and commercial expansion for much of the century – portraying it as an inescapable facet of the 'indomitable' British 'national character'. It was lent particular resonance on this occasion, though, owing to the country's ongoing involvement in the second Boer War. Indeed, the unveiling of the Alfred statue was immediately followed by the presenting of service medals to the Imperial Yeomanry and Hants Volunteers, freshly returned from the conflict.

The public unveiling in Winchester's Broadway was followed by a luncheon in the Guildhall to which over 400 guests had been invited, including an entire two tables occupied by the reporters who were to help make the Millenary an occasion not just of local, but of national interest. The courses were punctuated by volleys of all-encompassing toasts which linked Alfred with almost every class of person present. 'Alfred and the English civil and municipal life', 'Alfred and the literature and learning of the Anglo-Saxon race', and 'Alfred and the Royal Navy and the other forces of the Crown' were just three among these. There was also, of course 'Alfred and King Edward VII' – the latter of whom, it was declared, 'represents the oldest monarchy in the world, and counts thirty-three generations in lineal descent from the great King Alfred'. The Archbishop of Canterbury, proclaiming in his address that 'it would be difficult in all history to find any two sovereigns who had done so much for their respective countries, who had shown such an aptitude for the duties of monarchy, and had exhibited such examples of lofty devotion to high duties. The deceased Victoria was even more closely linked to Alfred by the Archbishop of Canterbury, who proclaimed in his address that 'it would be difficult in all history to find any two sovereigns who had done so much for their respective countries, who had shown such an aptitude for the duties of monarchy, and had exhibited such examples of lofty devotion to high duties'. And a commemorative rose-bowl, presented to the City of Winchester from the Keswick School of Industrial Arts, was received with much enthusiasm as touching evidence of the 'widespread interest evinced in the commemoration' among all classes, even in the North.[31]

Rosebery spoke again at the luncheon, once more alluding to Alfred's relevance to the British imperial venture and to the ongoing conflict in the Transvaal, asking:

> Does it not show a great sign of the times? A quarter of a century ago there was not the same passion for raising memorials of our historic heroes. How does that come about? How is it that we have now gone back a thousand years to find a great hero with whom we may associate something of English grandeur, and the origin of much that makes England powerful. Is it not the growing sense of British Empire, the increased feeling not for bastard, but for real Imperialism? With a present not always cheerful, with a remote past so small and yet so pregnant, we dignify and sanctify our own aspirations by referring them to the historic past.[32]

On this occasion, though, Rosebery chose to mitigate such declamation with an Alfredian joke:

> A young girl coming away from the library is greeted by another at the foot of the steps: 'Hello, Florry, what are you doing here?' Florry (in discontented accents): 'Papa sent me to find out about King Alfred'. The other girl: 'Alfred! What about him?' Florry: 'Papa asked us at tea last night what was all this about King Alfred and his millinery. Not one of us could tell him, and he sent me here to find out'. The other replied, 'Oh! You stupid, why it's the drapery round his statue of course'.[33]

A touch of humour was also allowed to lighten the address given by Bowker to 2,000 schoolchildren in front of the Alfred statue that afternoon. After being presented with commemorative medals, they were instructed to:

> Learn a lesson from the great man whose statue has been put up amongst us and unveiled this morning. You cannot do better throughout your lives than act up to the desire expressed in the excellent motto which the king ever had before him, and which he caused to be committed to writing. It was that throughout his life he sought to live worthily that he might leave to those coming after him his memory in good works.

Their spirits were probably lifted rather higher, however, by being instructed 'not to imitate Alfred in neglecting the cakes', before being set loose on a free feast of sweet treats.[34]

At 4.00 p.m. that afternoon a commemorative service was held in Winchester Cathedral. Queues had been forming for two hours prior to the event, and when the doors finally opened there was some danger that those who had been waiting longest would be crushed by the mass of bodies behind them. Indeed, demand for seats greatly surpassed what was available – aggrieved ticket-holders found their places taken by others who could not be shifted, while hundreds who had not booked tickets were left outside. For those excluded, however, various amusements were on offer during the afternoon: performing dogs, acrobatic clowns, dancing on the tight wire, old English sports, climbing the greasy pole, and 'similar observances of ancient custom', while the roasting of a whole, huge ox apparently attracted endless spectators before it was distributed to some 650 of the 'deserving poor'. The day ended with elaborate illuminations, for which the city of Winchester had already earned something of a reputation. As well as the official show in the Abbey Gardens, many local shopkeepers also produced displays: Hamo Thornycroft was particularly impressed by one in a shop window showing an illuminated shrine of St Swithun and a miniature statue of King Alfred, both constructed out of 'Silesia lining'.[35]

Despite a few minor hitches, then, the event was a roaring success for Bowker and Winchester. While the *Friend* spoke in glowing terms of Rosebery's ability to make himself heard over both the crowd and strong wind, *The Times* devoted its leading article to the Millenary, praising the former prime minister's 'brilliant eulogy', and enthusing that:

> The ancient and renowned city of Winchester has done honour to itself in worthily honouring the greatest of her sons . . . the citizens of Winchester of all ranks and classes threw themselves into the effort . . . The fine group of buildings, ruined or intact, which give Winchester its peculiar character . . . witnessed a movement of popular feeling still more significant than the crowd of guests from every country where the English language is spoken'.[36]

In Winchester, there were calls for Bowker to be knighted – though these were never answered. And Thornycroft's statue was also well received. A correspondent for *The Times* called it 'an Alfred breathing life and radiating energy'.[37] Particularly appreciated was the way in which the figure held its sword so that the hilt formed a cross – effectively recalling the religious principles that had underpinned Alfred's wars. Before the unveiling there had been fears that the statue might prove too triumphantly militaristic, but the final design with its religious subtext was so admired that it was subsequently emulated in several First World War memorials.[38]

There was some controversy over Thornycroft's choice of a bearded Alfred – one school of thought considered the Alfred Jewel and the coins from Alfred's reign with their clean-shaven figures to be the best guide to the king's appearance. Indeed, the very afternoon before the unveiling of the statue, Sir John Evans had told Winchester's delegates that although Thornycroft had doubtless sought inspiration for his statue from elsewhere than ninth-century currency, there was nevertheless one important point on which the coins were unanimous – 'they all represent the king without a beard'.[39] The organising committee on the whole, however, seems to have been more than satisfied with the statue. Frederic Harrison hailed it as 'the grandest thing in these Isles, if not in Europe'. However, he also added rather wryly, 'I only wish that I could think Alfred ever to have been such an athletic warrior'. And alluding to the diminutive and reputedly wife-beaten hero of the Second Afghan War, mused, 'I fear he was more like Lord Roberts'.[40]

After the commemorations

The echoes of Winchester's Alfred Millenary continued to sound in the weeks and months following the commemoration. On 25 September, the Somerset Archaeological and Natural History Society organised a special excursion and lectures in 'Alfred's Country', and on 26 October (the actual date of Alfred's death) the Somerset men of London enjoyed a commemorative dinner. Two days later, thousands of people gathered in Portsmouth to watch as the Countess of Lathom launched the Royal Navy's new armoured cruiser, built at a cost of one million pounds – the *HMS King Alfred* (see Figure 4 for the invitation card to this event). And later in 1901, inspired by the Winchester commemoration, the Bishop of Bristol unveiled a brass memorial plaque at the parish church of Wedmore in Somerset, the gift of Mr E.H. Dickinson, Member of Parliament for the area. It belatedly commemorated what was claimed to be the exact site upon which Alfred and Guthrum had, in 878, entered into the compact known as 'The Peace of Wedmore', and it had clearly been motivated in part by local jealousy over Winchester's monopolisation of Alfred – *The Times* reported that in the Bishop's unveiling speech, he asserted that the great work of Alfred's life 'no matter what claims Wiltshire, Berkshire and Winchester had – was planned, devised, and carried out in the Somerset marshes'.[41] The reverberations of the Winchester celebration spread not just through those areas constituting Alfred's old kingdom of Wessex. On the actual date of the Saxon king's death, commemorations took place in New York, and in 1902 London belatedly received the Alfred memorial that many had believed the capital should have had in preference to Winchester, when a large bronze and red alabaster medallion of Alfred's head, decked for the occasion with fresh flowers from Kew Gardens, was unveiled before a 'huge crowd' in the church of St Nicholas Cole-Abbey.[42]

Peripheral events connected to the Millenary also took place in the run-up to the main celebrations. On 17 September, the devout Anglo-Catholic Richard Jackson presented a plaque in memory of Alfred to the Sir Henry

4 Invitation card to the launch of the *HMS King Alfred* (reproduced in Bowker's
1902 volume, *The King Alfred Millenary*)

Tate free library in Brixton (presumably associating Tate with the Saxon king
– both being benefactors and educators of the people) and in June of 1901,
the National Home Reading Union chose to hold their summer assembly in
Winchester in order to associate their gathering with the Millenary anniversary of Alfred. During their stay they were given lectures on the subjects of
'Alfred as a Man of Letters, 'Alfred as Statesman and Lawgiver' and 'Links
between Alfred and Ourselves'. They were also addressed by the Dean of Ely,
who used Alfred's life to criticise Britain's treatment of the Boers, arguing
that the Saxon king's statesmanship was not only in advance of his own day,
but put the country's contemporary administration to shame – demonstrating that Alfred could be engaged to critique the empire just as effectively (if
more rarely) as to celebrate and justify it.[43]

The Winchester Millenary also spawned a rash of Alfredian literature –
both in expectation of the event, and in its wake. The first production was a
collection of essays, edited by Alfred Bowker himself and published in 1899,
with the specific aim of 'diffusing, as widely as possible, public knowledge
of the king's life and work. This being the sole object, it became essential that
the book should not be costly, but within the reach of all'.[44] The volume
included chapters by Frederic Harrison; the Bishop of Bristol, Charles
Oman; and the eminent Anglo-Saxonist John Earle. It was prefaced by a
short poem, 'The Spotless King', contributed by the Poet Laureate Alfred

Austin, and had an introduction by Walter Besant. Besant's own more populist *Story of King Alfred* was also published early in 1901 with a view to disseminating 'the right understanding' of the coming celebration. It had been inspired, he avowed, by his lecture on Alfred to a packed Guildhall in Winchester in 1898. On that occasion, touched to identify so many working people in his audience, he determined to write a life of the Saxon king for 'the Board Schools . . . the Continuation Classes . . . those who spend their evenings over books from the free libraries' (all institutions of which he was an active supporter).[45] In line with this desire, it was sold (posthumously, for Besant died early in June of 1901) for just a shilling. *The Times* reviewed the slim volume favourably as unpretentious, full of anecdote, and one of the best monuments produced to Alfred's memory, promising that it would 'captivate any generous lad'.[46]

National newspapers and the periodical press were full of Alfred in his Millenary year. This interest began to emerge around the time of the first planning meetings for the event, which, as we have seen, were covered by *The Times*. In 1898 the *Positivist Review* and the *English Historical Review* looked forward enthusiastically to the Millenary, while the *Leisure Hour* carried poems on Alfred. The following year, those publications to contain articles on the Saxon king included the *Antiquary*, the *National Review* and the *Englishwoman*. This was but a foreshadowing of 1901 and 1902, however, when Alfred and Alfredian subjects featured in *Macmillan's Magazine*, the *Cornhill Magazine*, the *Independent*, the *English Illustrated Magazine*, the *Gentleman's Magazine*, *Century Magazine*, *Great Thoughts*, and the *Critic*. The Saxon king's life was also considered of relevance to the readers of the *Homiletic Review*, the *Author*, and the *Parents' Review*. More than thirty articles on the planning, execution and aftermath of the Winchester Millenary appeared in *The Times* alone in 1901, and the Millenary proceedings were also reviewed in the *Telegraph*, the *Spectator* and the *Antiquary*, as well as in many local newspapers.

Immediately following the success of the commemorations, many of the daily newspapers and the weekly and monthly journals also carried pull-out guides to Alfred. Schools around Britain were encouraged to study the Saxon's reign and to assist them in this a short, informative pamphlet was produced by Mr Hearnshaw of the Hartley Institute in Southampton, while in Winchester itself an illustrated, printed sheet entitled 'What Alfred Did' was produced for popular consumption.[47] Also geared to increase juvenile enthusiasm for Alfred were two novels inspired by the Millenary and published the following year: G. Manville Fenn's charming story of Alfred's childhood, *The King's Sons*, and Tom Bevan's thrilling *A Lion of Wessex*. And the Millenary quickly inspired two Alfredian plays (by Edmund Hill and T. Fisher), while a further two also appeared early in 1902.

In the wake of the Winchester Millenary, many writers enlisted Alfred to their cause, capitalising on the sense of a seminal anniversary: whether that was the historian George Eayrs, entitling his history of Britain *Alfred to*

Victoria: Hands Across a Thousand Years; the philologist, Walter Skeat, speaking on the subject of 'The King's English, from Alfred to Edward VII'; Arthur McIlroy using Alfred's Millenary to promote cultural unity between Britain and America; or Herbert Thurston's incendiary article 'King Alfred the Idolator', published in the October 1901 edition of the *Month*. This latter angrily highlighted the irony in having celebrated Alfred – a Roman Catholic monarch – in Winchester, just months before requiring the new King of England to denounce the Church of Rome in his Protestant Declaration before parliament.[48]

Throughout 1901, lectures on Alfred took place around Britain. These were not perhaps, as Bowker boasted, 'too numerous to render any attempt at enumeration possible'.[49] But certainly, Alfred and his anniversary were the subject of many papers presented to antiquarian and historical societies in areas of the country beyond those possessing any local Alfredian heritage. The Saxon king was also chosen as the subject of the scholarly Ford lectures, given at the University of Oxford during the Michaelmas Term of 1901, which were presented by Professor Charles Plummer. Plummer was careful to distance himself from the recent enthusiasm for all things Alfredian: indeed, his lectures seem to have been calculated to counter much of popularisation of Alfred which had been central to the Winchester celebrations. He introduced them with a damning indictment of the publications produced for the event – criticising Bowker for having made Alfred 'a Broad-Churchman with agnostic proclivities', and Dugald Macfayden for writing a history which presented the Saxon as 'a nineteenth-century radical with a touch of the nonconformist conscience'. He also complained bitterly (and with a particular swipe towards Walter Besant):

> The fact is, there has been, if I may borrow a phrase from the Stock Exchange, a boom in all things Alfredian lately; and the literary speculator has rushed in to make his profit. Along with a few persons who are real authorities on the subjects with which they deal, eminent men in other departments of literature and life are engaged to play the parts which the ducal chairman and aristocratic director play in the flotation of a company. They may not know very much about the business in hand, but their names look well on a prospectus. The result is not very creditable to English scholarship.[50]

The Winchester commemorations were, indeed, unscholarly and popular in emphasis, as Plummer protested. Their aim was more to inspire and appeal widely than to educate deeply. In his lunch-time address at the city's Guildhall, Rosebery had mocked those pedants who spelt Alfred's name with a diphthong (as Ælfred).[51] While the celebrations engendered much popular, apocryphal, and downright fictitious Alfredian works, however, they also inspired scholarly research and publication. Two separate editions of the proverbs supposedly written by Alfred were inspired by the event, as well as histories of the Saxon king by Frederick Harrison, Warwick Draper, W.H. Stevenson, and – not least – Plummer himself. In his record of the Winchester commemorations, published – with photographs – in 1902, Bowker stated that one of the celebration's aims was to stimulate 'research by experts into our earlier history. . . . In times past King Alfred to the great body of the people was a dim and unrealised figure . . . a name rather than a personage who once enjoyed actual existence. In the future, as a result of the erection of the national colossal statue, all teachers will make the study of Alfred more real'.[52]

Alfredian tourism

Bowker also stated in his official record of the Alfred Millenary that one of its aims had been that of 'immediately and directly benefiting the city of Winchester'.[53] He asked, 'Is it too much to hope that in the days to come Winchester, with its beautiful buildings and historic interest, will become the pilgrimage city of the Anglo-Saxon?'[54] The notion of an Alfredian pilgrimage had been touted before – in 1790, by the Winchester divine and antiquary John Milner who, appalled at building work under way on the site of Hyde Abbey, protested that the location should be a place of pilgrimage for all Englishmen, 'like disciples of Mahomet going to Mecca'.[55] And Bowker's religious imagery also recalled that used by Frederic Harrison who (as discussed above) had the previous year compared the Alfred Jewel to a Christian relic. In the Lord Mayor's case, however, the reference to pilgrimage should be read not just in terms of providing an alternative to Christian belief in the narrative of historical progress, but rather in relation to the lucrative industry built upon pilgrims in the Middle Ages. Indeed, Bowker elsewhere explicitly stated his hope that the '*prosperity*' of Winchester would engage the sympathy of 'the English-speaking race'.[56]

What Bowker was aspiring to capitalise upon was the taste that developed during the nineteenth century for visiting historical sites around Britain. This burgeoned with the development of the railways between 1824 and 1848, opening to the middle classes the possibilities of leisure travel. So, for example, in 1843, on his summer tour to the Isle of Wight, using the South Western Railway, Thomas Roscoe was able to stop off in Winchester to visit the remains of Hyde Abbey, 'in which, before the high altar, were interred the remains of the first promulgator of our famed British constitution, Alfred the Great'.[57]

The fashion for historical tourism around Britain had its roots much earlier – in the late eighteenth and early nineteenth century, among the well-heeled élite for whom cultural travel around continental Europe suddenly became a risky undertaking because of the 1789 Revolution and the subsequent war between Britain and Napoleonic France.[58] The attraction of domestic tourism as an alternative was further heightened by the patriotic pride arising from the success of Britain's Empire and industry, which encouraged interest in the origins of that accomplishment, and consequently in the relics of the country's past. Such a desire to trace native origins seems to have inspired Richard Fenton's *Tour in Quest of Genealogy*, published in 1811 in the form of a *Series of Letters to a Friend in Dublin*.

As part of his search for a sense of historically rooted identity, Fenton visited the Alfred Tower, erected in 1772 at Stourhead by Henry Hoare to commemorate the spot at which it was supposed Alfred had mustered his troops before the Battle of Edington. In describing this, he invested the visit with much the sense of religious awe which Bowker was later to hope would inspire visitors to Winchester, relating that, 'At approaching this illustrious monument, I felt an awful veneration, little short of sacred'. He and his companion trod with 'awful reverence' before the 'votive fabric' of the tower, and he even claimed to have witnessed something akin to a transport of religious ecstasy on the 'sacred spot', watching as his companion Jones rolled his eyes in 'a fine frenzy' before breaking into rapturous, impromptu verse:

> Whoe'er thou art who dar'st approach this pile,
> And feelest not thy bosom all on flame,
> Boast as thou wilt alliance with this isle,
> Renounce thy title to a Briton's name.[59]

The account doubtless owes much to the Romantic theory of the sublime, and to the late eighteenth-century enthusiasm for the figure of the bard, but it also encapsulates – albeit in an over-dramatised form – that desire to intimately connect with the past which was to become such a driving force behind the rise of the historical novel, the growth of historical tourism, and the cult of Alfred in the Victorian period.

Some visitors to Alfredian sites were not content merely to imbibe the atmosphere of the location. Amongst the nineteenth-century's historical tourists were the amateur antiquaries who multiplied exponentially during the period – excavating barrows and uprooting megaliths across the country. In 1866 one of their number, a John Mellor, visited the site of Hyde Abbey and began to dig, determined to find the bones of Alfred the Great. He unearthed five skeletons, of which he deduced that four were Alfred, his Queen, and two of their sons. His other finds included a silver sceptre and 'a plate of lead, with the king's name upon it' – which was later discovered to have been forged by a local blacksmith (though whether Mellor was the commissioner or the dupe of this item remains unknown).[60] At any rate, his dig at Hyde Abbey was severely criticised, on the grounds of morality and decency, in the pages of both the *Hampshire Chronicle* and the *Gentleman's Magazine*, and his suggestion that the bones should be given a grand re-interment was ignored – they were buried under a plain slab in the grounds of St Bartholomew's Church, close to Hyde Abbey.[61] Mellor himself next made his way to Somerset, in search of Athelney – the place where Alfred was sequestered from his enemies for three months. There he claimed to find several Saxon articles, but did not manage to gain permission to unearth a monument which he had been told covered 'the very hearthstone upon which the poor king let the cakes burn', and under which he had been assured a treasure lay buried, hidden by Alfred himself.[62]

Alfred's ninth-century kingdom of Wessex incorporated the Victorian counties of Somerset, Wiltshire, Berkshire and Devon. Throughout the nineteenth century, the inhabitants of each of these four counties seem to have been proud of any local Alfredian connections, and keen to publicise them. The Devon city of Exeter, for instance, had been the site of many attempted Danish invasions prevented by Alfred. From 1801 until 1894, therefore, the Saxon king appeared as a symbol of protective power on the fire-marks of all Exeter buildings insured by the West of England Fire Insurance company, and between 1815 and 1831 his connection with the city was further memorialised in the name of the local newspaper: the *Alfred, West of England Journal and General Advertiser*.[63] Alfredian associations were particularly impressed upon visitors to those areas that could claim some connection with the Saxon king. While on a quest through Somerset for Alfred's hidden fortress of Athelney, in the first decade of the nineteenth century, the antiquary John Whitaker had his suspicions that he was on the right track, confirmed by the sight of an inn named 'Alfred's Head'. On entering this he discovered the tradition to be 'very prevalent' among the drinkers there that King Alfred had taken shelter from the Danes in their immediate neighbourhood, and he became convinced that he had indeed found Alfred's retreat when he discovered a farmhouse with the name 'Athelney', whose inhabitants claimed that the Saxon king had resided in their very dairy.[64]

Likewise, in 1826, on a circuitous route from London to the York Festival, the travel writer known as 'The London Hermit' visited another 'Alfred's Head' – this time an inn in Wantage which claimed to be 'the very house' of Alfred's birth – in which the writer sat and wrote in his journal, contemplating that he was 'on the very spot where Alfred the Great has written and contemplated before'.[65] While in the South-West, the Hermit seems to have determined on pursuing an Alfredian trail. He also visited 'Alfred's Castle' in Berkshire – a 'rude, rotund rampart of earth' – which he was told marked the site of the Saxon king's battle at Ashdown (but is actually an Iron Age hill-fort, first associated with the Saxon king in the eighteenth century). And he stopped at Devizes to view some recently discovered cannon-balls there, which he was assured had been fired at the Battle of Edington by Alfred's Danish enemy Guthrum. There is small wonder, then, that he complained of the 'perplexing shroud' that seemed to hang over 'each tradition of Alfred the Great, and each supposed relict of his toils' – although he blamed this confusion not on the tall tales of West Country locals, but on the machinations of 'Danish and Norman policy'.[66]

Following the seven-mile trajectory of the cannon-balls, the Hermit next made his way to the Wiltshire village of Edington – which actually was the site of a battle fought by Alfred in 878. There he visited 'Dane Lay', reputedly the summer camp of Alfred's enemy; Picket Hill, 'where tradition says the attack of the English commenced'; and a white chalk horse carved into the hillside above the village of Westbury, which he was informed had been created by Alfred's Saxon army to celebrate their defeat of the Danes. From this he extrapolated that the large number of white horses in the area must each have been fashioned by a separate garrison of Alfred's army to celebrate similar victories – including the white chalk horse at Uffington, which he later visited with 'feelings of awe and anticipation' (though he left feeling somewhat disappointed by its artistic merit).[67]

The Westbury white horse actually dates from the late seventeenth century, and most of the other white horses in the surrounding area were created somewhat later than that. Only the Uffington horse is older – now known to date as far back as the pre-Roman Iron Age, or even the late Bronze Age. The first writer to link the horse to Alfred was the antiquary Francis Wise, who claimed in his 1738 *Observations on the White Horse and other Antiquities in Berkshire* that the figure was carved to commemorate the Battle of Ashdown, fought by Alfred on the Berkshire Downs in 871. Wise's theory probably drew on an older, oral tradition from the Uffington area, however, and the Hermit may also have learnt of the theory from local residents. Certainly, one Uffington inhabitant in the mid-nineteenth century took a keen interest in the possible connection between Alfred and the local chalk horse – the popular novelist and historian Thomas Hughes.

The hero of Hughes's widely popular 1857 *Tom Brown's Schooldays* was born (like the author) in the shadow of the Uffington white horse, and the first chapter of the book, while ostensibly setting the scene for Tom's childhood, serves also to promote the area's heritage – and particularly its claims to Alfredian associations. It describes how, after Alfred's battle at Ashdown, the king came to Uffington, and:

> that there might never be wanting a sign and memorial to the countryside, carved out on the northern side of the chalk hill, under the camp, where it is almost precipitous, the great Saxon white horse, which he who will may see from the railway.[68]

Hughes encouraged his young readers to forsake European travels, instead offering the site of Ashdown as a native place of pilgrimage:

> A sacred ground for Englishmen, more sacred than all but one or two fields where their bones lie whitening. For this is the actual place where our Alfred won his great battle, the battle of Ashdown ('Aescendum' in the chronicles) which broke the Danish power, and made England a Christian land.[69]

Growing up 'in Alfred's own county', viewing himself as 'a citizen of the noblest Saxon kingdom of Wessex', and 'having been from childhood familiar with the spots which history and tradition associate with some of the most critical events of the great King's life', it is perhaps not surprising that Hughes also produced a life of Alfred in 1869 – which became one of the key texts in popularising the Saxon king.[70] In this, too, he was keen to promote the sense of proximity to Alfred that could be experienced in his local area – claiming to have seen with his own eyes the exact thorn tree at which the Saxon king's Battle of Ashdown began, explaining that Reading racecourse 'must have been within the Danish lines', and stressing that 'any reader who has travelled on the Great Western Railway' must have crossed the 'very spot' where the Danes were entrenched. He further alleged that in his own Berkshire childhood, the peasants of Uffington still spoke a dialect which could have been easily understood by 'the churls who fought at Ashdown with Alfred'.[71]

In relation to the Alfredian claims of other areas, however, Hughes was distinctly more sceptical. Mentioning the 'Somersetshire tradition' that the Alfred Tower at Stourton marked the place at which a beacon was lit to gather the Saxon troops before the Battle of Edington, he rather snidely stressed that it should be noted that the collector of that tradition, J.A. Giles, was 'himself a Somersetshire man'. Although he conceded that Giles's claim was 'worth mentioning', he stressed that 'local traditions cannot be much relied upon for events which took place a thousand years ago'. Giles was praised by Hughes, however, for having 'established the claims of Edington', a Wiltshire village, as the location of Alfred's Battle of Edington – so putting an end to 'much doubt amongst antiquaries as to the site'.[72] The Wiltshire village of Edington was indeed the site of Alfred's most famous battle.[73] However, while scholars in the mid-nineteenth century may have felt that the matter was settled, the location of the Battle of Edington continued to be the subject of lively dispute in popular culture until the end of the century – a disagreement that probably has its closest modern parallel in the contest between Yorkshire and Nottinghamshire for ownership of Robin Hood.

The problem arose from the fact that there are two modern villages called Edington – one in Wiltshire, and the other in Somerset – and the inhabitants of each area were keen to claim Alfred for their own Edington. Walter Besant (who was of course part of the committee organising Winchester's Alfred Millenary) promoted Wiltshire's claim. In his popular history of Alfred, he assured readers that at the Wiltshire village of Edington it was still possible to view 'a camp covering twenty-three acres of ground called Bratton Castle' (actually an Iron Age fort) which he claimed was 'the entrenchment to which the Danes retreated after the battle of Ethandune'.[74] By contrast, in the 1899 novel *King Alfred's Viking*, the Somerset novelist Charles Whistler opted for his local contender, though he admitted that 'much controversy has raged over the sites . . . owing probably to the duplication of names in the district'.[75] Rather less even-handed was the Somerset historian Mrs C.G. Boger. Discussing the location of the Battle of Edington in her pointedly titled article 'King Alfred in Somerset' she asserted, 'We do not know for certain the exact spot . . . but all agree that it was not in Wiltshire'.[76]

Earlier anniversaries

The long contest to be the area most closely associated with Alfred was effectively won when the 1901 Millenary took place in Winchester, forever yoking the Saxon king's name to that of the city. Bowker's achievement is all the more remarkable when it is considered that until then Winchester was not particularly prominent on the Alfredian tourist trail. And it is more remarkable still when it is taken into account that his was not the first millennial celebration of King Alfred. On 7 August 1878 the drawing up of Alfred's 'Treaty of Wedmore' (marking the end of the king's wars against Guthrum) was celebrated in the village of Wedmore with a series of scholarly lectures in the village hall, a luncheon, and various 'out-of-door amusements'.[77] And in 1849, a celebration was planned to mark the thousandth anniversary of Alfred's birth in the Berkshire city where he was born – Wantage.

There seems to have been some expectation in 1848 that Alfred's birth would be marked the following year: certainly the artist Alfred Stevens painted *King Alfred and his Mother* in preparation for the event. However, it was not until 1849 itself that the prolific poet and novelist Martin Farquhar Tupper, while dining at a friend's house in Soho, began to ruminate seriously upon the idea of an Alfredian commemoration. This was in mid-July; the anniversary of Alfred's birth was 25 October. Tupper then had precious little time in which to plan and prepare for what he intended to be a major national event. However, this was a man who through the 1840s and 1850s would have more than thirty books published, and whose second volume of poetry, *Proverbial Philosophy*, written in 1837, had run to thirty-eight editions by 1860 – so he lacked neither the energy nor the celebrity for such a coup. He commissioned the architect George Adam Burn to design an 'Alfred Memorial' statue to be erected in Wantage as part of the celebrations, and composed two poems to promote the idea of erecting such a memorial. One was the sonnet 'Alfred', which demanded:

Where is thy Tomb among us? Where the spot
Ennobled by some record of thy worth,
True father of thy country? have we lost
All love of thee? hath England then forgot
Her patriot-prince, her lawgiver, her sage?

The other was the longer ballad, *Alfred, Born at Wantage*, which roused readers:

Come, every trueborn Englishman! Come Anglo-Saxons all!
I wake a tune to-day to take and hold your hearts in thrall;
I sing the King, the Saxon king, the glorious and the great,
The root and spring of everything we love in Church and State.
'Tis just a thousand years to-day, Oh! Years are swift and brief,
Since erst uprose in majesty the daystar of our Chief,
Since Wantage bred a wondrous child, whom God hath made the Cause,
Of half the best we boast in British liberties and laws.[78]

The erection of a statue required funding, however. Tupper began his one-man campaign by circulating a prospectus to the great and good of the land, encouraging them to both participate in and financially support the Millenary. Unlike Bowker's similar appeal fifty years later, however, it met with little enthusiasm. On 7 September, therefore (anticipating Bowker's stratagem of interesting the national press) he wrote a long, passionate and deeply patriotic letter on the subject of King Alfred to the editor of *The Times*. It was never published. 'Was this a letter to be rejected?' he scrawled in frustration across the top of his draft.[79] With insufficient financial interest, Burn's statue was never to leave the drawing-board. Tupper's next aim was for Alfred's birth to be nationally marked by the creation of a new honour. His poem, 'The Order of Alfred', reflects bitterly upon the failure of the statue appeal, naming himself as Alfred's 'faithful Abdiel, *if thine only one*' (alluding to God's faithful seraph in Milton's *Paradise Lost*) and protesting:

Yea! For his greatness, faintly seen from far,
Is as the glimmering greatness of a star
Which common ignorance, with vacant stare,
Sees as a petty spangle shining there!
. . . Forgetful Britain! Haste, redeem the day,
Before this grand occasion dies away:
There yet is time one trophied Praise to rear
To Alfred's honour on his thousandth year,
Better than statues . . .
Stablish, O Queen! A new found honour here,
King Alfred's Order on his Thousandth Year,
For peaceful merit of whatever kind,
The duteous martyr, or the master-mind,
For keen invention, and for high-toned art,
For every excellence of head and heart,
For wit and wisdom, holiness and skill,
For Man's and Woman's God-devoted will,
For all things wise, and generous, and good,
Stablish this seal of England's gratitude!
Let Alfred's badge – his collar, baton, star,
Decorate Worth, more worth than that of War.[80]

Forgetful Britain did not respond to the call. Part of Tupper's problem was sheer bad luck – his campaign tragically coincided with a cholera outbreak which overshadowed interest in any long-dead Saxon king.[81] But Martin Farquhar Tupper was also, it seems, a man born before his time. King Alfred, although he was already a subject of interest for some writers, was not yet the national hero that he would become in the second half of the nineteenth century. In John Mitchell Kemble's popular *Saxons in England*, published in the same year as the millennial anniversary of Alfred's birth, the Saxon king is barely mentioned – an omission that would be unthinkable in any history of the ninth century published around the anniversary of Alfred's death.

Tupper seems to have been close to abandoning his plans for any Alfredian anniversary celebration. Around this time, however, he found an ally who encouraged and assisted him to at least persevere with his plans for a celebration in Wantage, cheering him with the following letter:

> You began the move: you prepared the way, and kept on until you were out of breath. My breath will soon be gone too: therefore get ready to catch the torch when I drop it. I assure you that the steam is well up in Wantage, and we do not want men to flinch.[82]

The author of the heartening missive was the Anglo-Saxonist J.A. Giles, who had just published a life of Alfred and therefore had some vested interest in encouraging commemoration of the king. Together, he and Tupper seem to have determined that the most fruitful approach would be to concentrate their efforts upon those who might have a sense of geographical connection with King Alfred. A poster campaign was therefore launched in Wantage and the surrounding area, with signs announcing:

> To all good men and true, of Wantage and its neighbourhood. A great and unprecedented honour is thrust upon you: on Thursday, the 25th, will be commemorated, in his native town, KING ALFRED'S 1000TH BIRTHDAY. . . . KING ALFRED is known to all the world as, perhaps, the Greatest Man – Certainly the Best King – that ever lived; and in his Institutions, Character and Fame is still and ever immortal amongst us.

Wantage's inhabitants were rather strictly advised:

> From all parts of England your countrymen, together with some foreigners and American kinsmen, are expected to flock to this Patriotic Celebration: and you need not be reminded how kindly, nor how warmly you will welcome the Guests who seek Wantage on so happy an occasion. . . . It is recommended to the Inhabitants of WANTAGE, that, in honour of their ILLUSTRIOUS TOWNS-MAN, they decorate their streets and houses with flags, oak boughs, and such other tokens of patriotic feeling as they can muster; also, that they wear their holiday apparel, and the ALFRED MEDAL; quantities of which, at a very cheap cost, will be in the town on Wednesday.[83] [See Figure 5.]

The inhabitants of Wantage may not have emptied their pockets for a statue, but they did turn up in force to take part in the Alfred celebrations. Crowds of 20,000 gathered in the city, where they enjoyed traditional games, an ox roast, and lectures on Alfred's life and character in the town hall and at the site of the legendary 'King Alfred's Well'. For Tupper, however, the highlight of the day was surely the procession through Wantage to a commemorative church service. As thousands of people, accompanied by musicians, wound their way through the city's streets, their voices chorused together to sing the words of a specially composed ditty: 'The Day of a Thousand Years' written – of course – by Martin Farquhar Tupper:

> Anglo-Saxons! In love are we met
> To honour a name we can never forget!

TO ALL
Good Men & True,
OF WANTAGE
AND ITS NEIGHBOURHOOD.

A GREAT AND UNPRECEDENTED HONOUR IS THRUST UPON YOU:

ON THURSDAY, THE 25th, WILL BE COMMEMORATED, IN HIS NATIVE TOWN

KING ALFRED'S 1000th BIRTHDAY

From all parts of England your Countrymen, together with some Foreigners and American Kinsmen, are expected to Flock to this PATRIOTIC CELEBRATION: and you need not be reminded how kindly, nor how warmly you will welcome the Guests who seek out WANTAGE on so happy an occasion. KING ALFRED is known to all the world as, perhaps, the Greatest Man,—Certainly the Best King,—that ever lived: and in his Institutions, Character, and Fame is still and ever immortal amongst us. Let us ALL now endeavour to do him, and our country, due honour on this THOUSANDTH ANNIVERSARY: commencing, as we ought, by the solemn and grateful service of GOD, after these thousand years of mercies and prosperities; and thence proceeding, as we gladly may, to the cheerful festivities of our JUBILEE.

COMMON SENSE and GOOD FEELING are never wanting to ENGLISHMEN: let these keep Order and Good Humour better than Special Constables and Police.

It is recommended to the Inhabitants of WANTAGE, that, in honour of their ILLUSTRIOUS Townsman, they Decorate their STREETS and HOUSES with FLAGS, OAK BOUGHS, and such other tokens of patriotic feeling as they can muster; also, that they wear their holiday apparel, and the ALFRED MEDAL;—quantities of which, at a very cheap cost, will be in the town on Wednesday.

Right Spirit, Good humour, & Energy are everything!

Men of Berkshire, of all grades! you will not be wanting to yourselves on so glorious an occasion.

The Committee appointed to manage the arrangements of the Jubilee, respectfully beg attention to the following recommendation, viz.—That all persons in Business, in Wantage, close their Shops, and give those in their employ a holiday on this occasion. An OX will be roasted near the Town, by the aid of Mr. Charles Hart's Steam Engine, in order that those engaged may afterwards participate in the Festivities. In addition to the distribution of Meat, some Bread will be also given, particularly to those indigent Poor of Wantage in the receipt of Relief.

5 Martin Farquhar Tupper's poster advertising the 1849 Wantage anniversary

Father, and Founder, and King of a race
. . . Alfred the Wise, and the Good, and the Great![84]

Indeed, Wantage's celebration was perceived as sufficiently successful for the event to be emulated a month later by the city of Liverpool, which invited Tupper to give a lecture and no doubt gratified him greatly with a large assembly which gave his Alfred song a second airing.[85] Tupper seems to have quickly recovered from his discouragement over the failure of the statue appeal. On the evening of the Wantage commemorations, he sat down to dinner with a group of antiquaries and scholars, including Giles, and planned the ambitious *Jubilee Edition of the Whole Works of King Alfred the Great*, edited by Giles, published three years later and dedicated to Queen Victoria, for which he himself translated the (misattributed) *Proverbs of Alfred* into modern English.[86]

Tupper also wrote *Alfred: A Patriotic Play* in the immediate aftermath of the 1849 celebrations. It was not staged until 1860, and then only briefly in Manchester. However, the two sonnets 'Alfred's Children', and 'Alfred's Memorial', which he composed as reflections on the anniversary, were more successful – being published first as part of the successful *Ballads for the Times* in 1851, and then again, in 1860, in Tupper, *Three Hundred Sonnets* (London, 1860). The latter poem is representative of both in its mixed tone of reverence and self-congratulation:

> Alfred! I stand in thought before thee now,
> And to thy throne in duteous homage bow,
> After a thousand years! My soul is glad,
> Thus to have roused to thankful thoughts of thee,
> From this dull mist of modern base and bad,
> The world of Englishmen.[87]

The two sonnets were published as a pair under the title 'The Alfred Medals', perhaps in allusion to the pair of commemorative Alfred medals which were minted for the anniversary. These were both designed by Tupper. Each featured a head of King Alfred based on the portrait of him in Matthew Paris's mid-thirteenth-century *Major Chronicle* (see Figure 6). On the obverse of the medal, which was 'issued in a public way' (sold to the inhabitants of Wantage), was a dove and the words 'The British Empire, United States, and Anglo-Saxons everywhere'. Around its edge ran the legend, 'Ælfred and his children, 1849'. The other medal was privately issued to a privileged set of subscribers whom Tupper considered intellectual, and on the obverse of this were the emblems of England and North America, signifying Tupper's hope that the figure of Alfred might act as a unifying force for Anglo-American relations.[88]

A medal was also minted for the 1901 Millenary, designed by R.C. Jackson, to be distributed to Winchester's schoolchildren. It also bore a head of Alfred – but this was based not on a late medieval portrait, but an image upon a ninth-century coin. In an article for the *Westminster Review*, Jackson stressed the difference between his medal and those designed by Tupper. He had, he urged, 'read almost every genuine antiquarian work' and 'many manuscripts in public collections' in designing an image intended to have 'the stamp of Truth upon it'. Referring to Tupper's medals, he boasted: 'I do not give you a debased portrait of our king of the thirteenth century, as seen in the medal of my friend's designing, I give you an exact copy of the portraiture of King Alfred which his moneyer placed upon the coinage of the king by "authority" '.[89] Jackson's coin, then, was self-consciously more

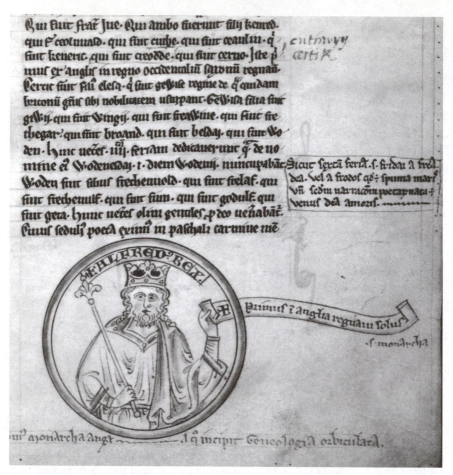

6 The earliest certain drawing of Alfred, by Matthew Paris (in his *Chronica Majora*, part I, ed. by Nigel Wilkins)

scholarly than its forerunner of fifty years earlier, and this relationship neatly exemplifies the stress upon authenticity and historical accuracy which gradually became a greater part of Alfredianism in the second half of the nineteenth century.

This development is also seen in the difference in emphasis between Victorian Britain's two King Alfred statues. The Winchester monument, designed by Hamo Thornycroft, was designed in collaboration with the historian Frederick Harrison: Alfred's physical appearance was based upon depictions of Anglo-Saxon rulers in contemporary manuscripts, and the details of his costume were carefully reproduced. By contrast, the statue of Alfred that was belatedly erected in Wantage in 1877 (designed and sculpted by Count Gleichen – a cousin of Queen Victoria) was made in the image of the local landowner who funded its erection, Colonel Robert Lloyd-Lindsay

– later Lord Wantage.[90] Lloyd-Lindsay seems to have been motivated by more than vanity – rather, he felt a particular empathy with Alfred, on the grounds that both men fought against ill-health for many years and each was educated as a mature student.[91] Such personal identification with King Alfred as a man (as distinct from respect for him as a king) became an increasingly dominant part of Alfredianism as the cult gained momentum in the second half of the nineteenth century.

Like the Winchester statue, the Wantage Alfred became a focus for local pride, appearing as the town's emblem on official documents, seals and souvenirs.[92] But its installation attracted little more attention in the newspapers and periodical press than the disappointing response to Tupper's statue-less commemoration of 1849. The acceleration of public interest in Alfred – from the unmarked 999th anniversary of his birth in 1801; to the Wantage celebration organised almost single-handedly by Tupper in 1849; to the Alfred Millenary committee's week-long extravaganza in 1901 – has been sketched in this introductory chapter. Although the celebrations are fascinating in themselves, however, it is necessary to look at the Alfredian literature and art, which was produced increasingly in the decades between such events, in order to fully understand exactly how Alfred's image developed through the nineteenth century and what the Saxon king meant to the crowds at each commemoration. This will be the concern of the main body of this study – though in considering such material, the Alfredian anniversaries, and particularly the Winchester Millenary, will be returned to repeatedly as representing the climax of many different interests and fashions within the cult of Alfred.

In considering the Alfredian anniversaries in isolation, it might also be easy to misinterpret the nineteenth-century cult of King Alfred as an interest confined to his old kingdom of Wessex. As this introduction should have begun to indicate, however, this was far from being the case. Although during the second half of the nineteenth century, Alfredianism had its nucleus in Winchester and the surrounding country, from there it was to radiate across England. Had this not been the situation, then the Winchester commemoration would not have been financed by contributions from across the country, reported so extensively in the national press, or repeatedly described by reviewers as a national event. Just as King Arthur could be both Celtic and English in the Victorian age, so Alfred managed to be simultaneously a local hero and a national icon, while the millennial anniversary of his death took on the rare aspect of a provincial event which fascinated the country. Indeed, it is perhaps the very uniqueness of a location outside London forming the centre of a pervasive, national interest which has thus far caused the nineteenth-century cult of Alfred to be overlooked in contemporary surveys of Victorian England. Therefore another aim of the main body of this study will be to further reveal King Alfred's appeal to a broad spectrum of artists, writers and readers who ranged well beyond the bounds of Wessex.

Notes

NB Where a reference is cited without an author or editor, it is listed in the Select Bibliography under the first significant word of the title, rather than under 'Anon.'.

1 *The Times* (21 Sep. 1901), p. 10; Bowker, *The King Alfred Millenary*, pp. 104–106.
2 *The Times* (20 Nov. 1897), p. 10.
3 Yorke, *The King Alfred Millenary*, p. 1.
4 Bowker, *The King Alfred Millenary*, p. 4.
5 Bowker, *The King Alfred Millenary*, p. 3.
6 *The Times* (20 Nov. 1897), p. 10.
7 Bowker, *The King Alfred Millenary*, p. 9.
8 Bowker, *The King Alfred Millenary*, p. 7.
9 *The Times* (17 Jan. 1898), p. 11.
10 Bowker, *The King Alfred Millenary*, p. 23.
11 Wildman, *King Alfred's Boyhood*, pp. 1–7.
12 Bowker, *The King Alfred Millenary*, p. 26.
13 *The Times* (29 Jan. 1901), p. 12.
14 Wildman, *King Alfred's Boyhood*, p. 1.
15 Yorke, *The King Alfred Millenary*, p. 3.
16 Bowker, *The King Alfred Millenary*, p. 20.
17 Bowker, *The King Alfred Millenary*, pp. 20–21.
18 Bowker, *The King Alfred Millenary*, pp. 22–23.
19 Yorke, *The King Alfred Millenary*, p. 9.
20 See, for instance, *The Times* (14 May 1899), p. 10; (17 Jan. 1901), p. 6.
21 Yorke, *The King Alfred Millenary*, p. 9.
22 *The Times* (11 March 1899), p. 11.
23 Yorke, *The King Alfred Millenary*, p. 10.
24 Yorke, *The King Alfred Millenary*, p. 9.
25 Bowker, *The King Alfred Millenary*, p. 47.
26 *The Times* (18 Sep. 1901), p. 10.
27 *The Times* (19 Sep. 1901), p. 8.
28 *The Times* (20 Sep. 1901), p. 4.
29 Yorke, *The King Alfred Millenary*, pp. 11–12, 15.
30 *The Times* (21 Sep. 1901), p. 10.
31 *The Times* (21 Sep. 1901), p. 10; Bowker, *The King Alfred Millenary*, pp. 113, 117.
32 *The Times* (21 Sep. 1901), p. 10.
33 *The Times* (21 Sep. 1901), p. 10.
34 Bowker, *The King Alfred Millenary*, p. 128; *The Times* (21 Sep. 1901), p. 10.
35 Bowker, *The King Alfred Millenary*, p. 133; Yorke, *The King Alfred Millenary*, p. 16.
36 *The Times* (19 Sep. 1901), p. 8.
37 *The Times* (21 Sep. 1901), p. 10.
38 Yorke, *The King Alfred Millenary*, p. 12.
39 Bowker, *The King Alfred Millenary*, p. 88.
40 On Roberts, see the *Oxford Dictionary of National Biography*, hereafter *ODNB*. On Harrison's speech, see Yorke, *The King Alfred Millenary*, p. 11.
41 *The Times* (31 Dec. 1901), p. 9.

42 *The Times* (10 Dec. 1902), p. 9.
43 Yorke, *The King Alfred Millenary*, p. 20.
44 Bowker, *Alfred the Great*, p. ix.
45 Besant, *The Story of King Alfred*, pp. 10–12.
46 *The Times* (22 Aug. 1901), p. 5. On Besant, see *ODNB*.
47 Yorke, *The King Alfred Millenary*, p. 18.
48 Thurston, 'King Alfred the Idolator', p. 423.
49 Bowker, *The King Alfred Millenary*, p. 41.
50 Plummer, *The Life and Times of Alfred the Great*, pp. 6, 8.
51 Yorke, *The King Alfred Millenary*, p. 18.
52 Bowker, *The King Alfred Millenary*, p. 186.
53 Bowker, *The King Alfred Millenary*, p. 187.
54 Bowker, *The King Alfred Millenary*, p. 188.
55 Milner, *The History of Winchester*, p. 374; Keynes, 'The Cult of King Alfred the Great', p. 325.
56 Bowker, *The King Alfred Millenary*, p. 187.
57 Roscoe, *Summer Tour to the Isle of Wight*, p. 98.
58 Dellheim, *The Face of the Past*, p. 39.
59 Fenton, *Tour in Quest of Genealogy*, p. 198.
60 Mellor, *The Curious Particulars Relating to King Alfred's Death and Burial*, pp. 12–22.
61 Extracts reproduced in Bogan, 'Where is Alfred Buried?', pp. 28–31.
62 Mellor, *The Curious Particulars Relating to King Alfred's Death and Burial*, p. 20.
63 On *The Alfred*, see Langenfelt, *Historic Origins of the Eight Hours Day*, pp. 119–122.
64 Whitaker, *The Life of Saint Neot*, p. 246.
65 *The London Hermit's Tour*, p. 20.
66 *The London Hermit's Tour*, pp. 35, 46, 88.
67 *The London Hermit's Tour*, pp. 32, 89, 90, 95.
68 Hughes, *Tom Brown's Schooldays*, p. 24.
69 Hughes, *Tom Brown's Schooldays*, p. 23.
70 Hughes, *Alfred the Great*, p. 28.
71 Hughes, *Tom Brown's Schooldays*, pp. 76, 71, 15.
72 Hughes, *Tom Brown's Schooldays*, pp. 115, 116.
73 Keynes and Lapidge, *Alfred the Great*, p. 22.
74 Besant, *The Story of King Alfred*, p. 107.
75 Whistler, *King Alfred's Viking*, p. iv.
76 Boger, 'Alfred, King in Somerset', p. 63.
77 Keynes, 'The Cult of King Alfred the Great', p. 347.
78 Tupper, 'Alfred', p. 297; Tupper, 'Alfred, Born at Wantage', p. 249, both in *Ballads for the Times*.
79 Hudson, *Martin Tupper*, p. 92.
80 Tupper, 'The Order of Alfred', in *Ballads for the Times*, pp. 252–256.
81 See Hudson, *Martin Tupper*, p. 42.
82 Hudson, *Martin Tupper*, p. 93.
83 Hudson, *Martin Tupper*, endpapers.
84 Tupper 'The Day of a Thousand Years', in *Ballads for the Times*, p. 257.
85 Hudson, *Martin Tupper*, p. 96.

86 Janet L. Nelson, 'Myths of the Dark Ages', p. 147.
87 Tupper, 'Alfred's Memorial', in *Ballads for the Times*, p. 259.
88 For a description of the medals, see Jackson, 'The Alfred Medal of 1901', p. 676. On Tupper's interest in Anglo-American relations, his 1851 trip to America, and his supper at the White House, see the *ODNB*.
89 Jackson, 'The Alfred Medal of 1901', p. 677.
90 Keynes, 'The Cult of King Alfred the Great', p. 347.
91 Yorke, unpublished paper at the King Alfred conference, Winchester, 1999.
92 'Alfred the Great: London's Forgotten King', exhibition at the Museum of London, September 1999.

2

Medievalism, Anglo-Saxonism and the nineteenth century

Before it is possible to understand the particular appeal of Alfred to nineteenth-century Britain, it is necessary to have some idea of the broader cultural contexts in which the cult of the Saxon king germinated. As part of the Alfred Millenary commemorations in 1901, the historian Frederic Harrison – as was discussed in Chapter One – gave a speech at the British Museum. During this he asserted, 'if ours was the age of progress, it was also the age of history'.[1] The Victorian mania for Alfred was initially just part of a pervasive nineteenth-century fascination with the past. This originated in the eighteenth-century interest in fallen civilisations, following the discovery of Herculaneum in 1738 and Pompeii a decade later, and the appearance of Edward Gibbon's *History of the Decline and Fall of the Roman Empire*, published in parts from 1776. Then, in the nineteenth century, theories arose about more general – and dramatic – exterminations in world history. In 1830, Charles Lyell published his *Principles of Geology*, stating that the earth had been shaped by a series of natural catastrophes, and by the mid-nineteenth century palaeontologists had discovered enough dinosaur bones and fossils to begin publishing theories about sudden extinction. Such developments encouraged anxiety about mass extermination on a popular level – John Ruskin complained that he could hear the cadence of geologists' hammers at the end of every verse of the Bible.[2] Then, in 1859, Charles Darwin published his *On the Origin of Species* – an evolutionary model which was quickly applied to the rise and fall of nations – engendering more specific fears about the future of Britain's economic and political pre-eminence in the world. Such uncertainty about the future led to a natural turning away from national identities based upon impending destiny, and towards self-definition in terms of past progress.[3]

The terrifying speed of social, political and cultural change in the nineteenth century – whether that meant revolutions across Europe, the introduction of railways and mechanised agriculture in Britain, or shifting roles in the family – also caused the emergence of a sense of loss and dislocation from the past, which fed an unprecedented historical curiosity.[4] Past periods of social turbulence, in particular, often became foci of interest – used as a means of obliquely discussing current problems, and viewed as a source of reassurance, inspiration and didacticism for the present.[5] In his record of the

1901 Alfred Millenary, its principal organiser Alfred Bowker asserted that
'those who take an interest in our historic past are more likely to make the
best of the present, and so contribute most to the future of the race and
the world'. And, at a planning meeting for the event, Arthur Conan Doyle
spoke of the 'lessons [history] has to teach us', which could 'brace us in those
days of trial which may still be coming upon us', going on to relate an anecdote of how:

> In a recent crisis of our foreign affairs, a huge ladder had been erected for dec-
> orative purposes against the Nelson Column in Trafalgar Square. 'What are you
> doing?' asked one of the crowd. 'Doing?' said another, 'they're a-getting of him
> down; they'll be wantin' him soon'.

'So with our national ideals, our memories of great men', Doyle concluded
sagely – 'in times of peace, when all is well, they tower above our heads as
objects of admiration, beautiful if unpractical, but in times of trouble we
may have to get them down'.[6]

Doyle's story about the Nelson statue introduces another factor which fed
into the Victorian fascination with history – the role of fine art. The late eighteenth and the nineteenth century saw works of art brought into the public
arena – first through the establishment of artistic societies which staged
annual exhibitions, and then by the opening of national art galleries.[7] In
1768, the Royal Academy of Art was established, and in 1824 the National
Gallery opened, followed by the establishment of a Royal Institution in
Scotland in 1826, and the opening of the Scottish Academy of Art the following year. As public institutions, the galleries demanded works of national
interest and so led to a new vogue for producing paintings not of private
estates, but of historical scenes. The impact of this development upon the
popular appeal of the past should not be under-estimated. For many
members of the public it would have breathed an entirely new life into
history, as the first occasion upon which they had been presented with large-
scale, colourful images of distant centuries. Furthermore, the invention of
lithography and other methods of reproducing images meant that it was
increasingly possible to publish affordable illustrated histories, which found
their way not just into private libraries, but into living rooms.[8]

Medievalism

One historical period, above all, proved a popular subject in the art galleries
and exhibitions of the nineteenth century – Britain's medieval age. This preference constituted part of a widespread rejection of classical antiquity in
favour of native history, a process which began in the late eighteenth century
as an attempt to trace cultural roots and from thence to discover the secret of
Britain's current achievements. It was manifested in a new fascination with the
physical remains of past ages in Britain's landscape; in an enthusiasm to document and preserve ancient traditions; and in a fresh interest in translating

and editing early native manuscripts.[9] The new focus of interest spawned the publication of a rash of national histories – most notably and influentially David Hume's 1754-62 *History of England* – and these, in their turn, facilitated the composition of historical literature and art. In the nineteenth century, national pride in the phenomenal success of Britain's Empire, and the desire to legitimate that colonialism with a long and glorious heritage, gave further impetus to the study of early native history, as did the emergence of middle-class writers like the bookseller Joseph Cottle (the 1801 author of an Alfredian epic), who had often not been classically educated and thus eschewed the subjects of ancient Greece and Rome as the preserve of a corrupt and over-privileged upper class.[10]

The medieval became the period of British history most commonly trumpeted as equivalent in prestige to the classical, partly because it was simply the earliest age to be fully documented. In the increasingly industrialised nineteenth-century landscape, however, the pastoralism of the medieval period also added to its appeal.[11] In his 1843 novel, *Forest Days*, G.P.R. James, for instance, looked back to the thirteenth century, lamenting:

> I cannot help grieving when I look back to a time when wide forests waved their green boughs over many of the richest manufacturing districts of Great Britain, and the lair of the fawn and the burrow of the coney were found, where now appear the fabric and the mill.[12]

As many recent studies have discussed, the perception that Gothic church architecture had an inherently organic form added to this view of the medieval as a time when people had existed in close harmony with nature.[13]

By the increasingly secular early nineteenth century, the omnipresence of the Catholic church in the medieval period meant that it was also looked back upon as a golden age of faith by religious writers concerned that the values of capitalism and utilitarianism were replacing those of Christianity. Similarly, the many social problems that accompanied the advent of industrial capitalism meant that the feudal system of the Middle Ages came to be hailed as an ideal political system by Tory polemicists. In his 1843 novel *Past and Present*, Thomas Carlyle contrasted the welfare of the poor in the twelfth and nineteenth centuries, calling for a return to the paternalism, mutual reciprocity, and chivalric values of loyalty, duty, and adherence to tradition, which he imagined to have dominated twelfth-century society. And, in the same decade (largely in response to the political revolutions of the 1840s), the Young England political movement attempted to translate medieval feudalism into a programme of practical politics.[14] A little later, socialist thinkers were also drawn to aspects of medieval society – specifically to the guild system which, for art-critics like John Ruskin and designers such as William Morris, had fostered crafts superior to those of the industrial world.[15]

Even this very brief survey of nineteenth-century medievalism should indicate that as an ideology it was a many-headed creature – with different facets of medieval life and different periods before the Renaissance utilised for divergent political agendas. It was also manifested in a wide range of forms. Its dominance in the art-world has already been alluded to. To provide a case in point, however, in the 1840s, a series of competitions was held to find artwork for the Houses of Parliament. Artists were at liberty to choose any theme 'from British history, or from the works of Spenser, Shakespeare, or Milton', but over a third (in total around eighty) chose medieval subjects, including Canute, Chaucer, Edward I, and St Augustine.[16] The Houses of Parliament, which were to house these works, had themselves been rebuilt in a medieval style in 1836, after being destroyed by fire in 1831; similar neo-Gothic designs were used in the construction of town halls, hospitals, and railway stations around the country (most notably St Pancras station); and between 1818 and 1900, seventy-five per cent of the new churches in England were built on a Gothic rather than a classical model.[17]

Real medieval buildings also enjoyed new popularity, with a growth in tourism to castles, abbeys and cathedrals, from the 1840s. And religious practice also took on an increasingly medieval character. The Oxford Movement introduced to Anglicanism the rituals and ornament of the Catholic church of the High Middle Ages, as part of a project to inject a progressively more secular society with a lost sense of faith and mystery.[18] And after the passing of the Catholic Emancipation Act in 1829, the Catholic Church itself attracted growing numbers of converts from those seeking a religious experience more connected with the medieval past. Even Victorian domesticity began to look more medieval. Tennyson's uncle, who added a moat, drawbridge and portcullis to his home, was part of a venerable minority, but the medieval-style textiles produced by William Morris's company decorated many affluent drawing rooms. And while the fashion for marrying in chain-mail was only briefly popular, fancy-dress balls with multiple Maid Marians and Gueneveres were not unusual, and the mid-Victorian craze for large beards began as a conscious attempt to assume a medieval appearance.[19]

Nineteenth-century literary medievalism developed against this broad cultural backdrop and was in itself nearly as varied – encompassing the light-hearted social satire of Thomas Love Peacock's *Maid Marian* and other comic novellas, Dante Gabriel Rossetti's pseudo-medieval devotional verse, and the translated sagas of William Morris. Then there were the historical novels produced by Sir Walter Scott, Charles Kingsley and Edward Bulwer-Lytton (set in the feudal, late medieval age, and at the end of the Saxon period), which at the time of their publication were often received as histories. And there was Alfred Tennyson's moralised rewriting of Malory's fifteenth-century *Morte D'Arthur*, in his 1859-85 *Idylls of the King*.

King Arthur makes an interesting point of reference in considering the nineteenth-century cult of Alfred. As has been widely documented in recent studies, it was in the nineteenth century that the legendary Celtic monarch (like the Saxon Alfred) found widespread popularity: indeed, before 1800, few major writers or artists had shown interest in him for 300 years.[20] And, throughout the Victorian period, boats, racehorses and children were named for both monarchs, while tourists flocked to Glastonbury and Tintagel for their Arthurian associations, just as they visited the sites of Alfred's birth, death and most glorious battles. In the form inherited by the nineteenth century, the medieval sources for each king shared certain characteristics: Malory's Arthur and Asser's Alfred had both followed unusual routes to kingship, brought union and order to conflict-torn states, resisted colonising forces, and at some point in their career suffered defeat at the hands of an enemy. Both lives also incorporated legendary elements, and each had a moral dimension whereby the doom that had befallen the protagonist was presented as the consequence of either folly or sinfulness.

Nineteenth-century images of Arthur closely paralleled the ways in which (as the rest of this study will discuss in greater depth) Alfred was rewritten by Victorian authors. Both figures were acclaimed as the paradigm of a perceived national character. While an 1849 article in *Sharpe's London Journal* could describe Arthur as 'the beautiful incarnation of all the best characteristics of our nation', Charles Dickens's 1852 *Child's History of England* could claim that in Alfred 'all the best points in the national character were . . . first shown'. Each also became associated with 'Englishness': for the playwright J. Comyn Carr, Arthur was 'England's chosen lord', while in an 1896 play by Alfred Austin, King Alfred is 'the greatest of Englishmen'.[21] Austin also united the two figures into an apparently seamless English history in another play, *The Passing of Merlin*, in which he presented Alfred as Arthur's direct heir, and Queen Victoria as the descendant of both. And the two figures were also used by other writers throughout the nineteenth century to celebrate not just Victoria, but other contemporary figures, including Wellington and George III.

According to a recent study of Arthurianism, 'Each age has found in the Arthurian stories the means of expressing something of its own ideals and anxieties'.[22] In the nineteenth century, this was equally true of both Arthur and Alfred. As Chapter Four of this study will discuss, Alfred, like Arthur, was used to discuss the need for a responsible monarchy – particularly in the politically volatile 1830s. So, just as in J.F. Pennie's 1832 play, *The Dragon King* (in J.F. Pennie, *Britain's Historical Drama: A Series of National Tragedies*), Arthur must be cautioned that his country 'claims thy thoughts, thy powers,/ Before all private wrong', in James Sheridan Knowles's 1831 play, *Alfred the Great*, Alfred must tell his captive wife: 'Paramount of all/ My public function! Husband – father – friend/ All titles, and all ties are merg'd in that!'[23]

Both kings were also celebrated in the nineteenth century as having established proto-unions of the British Isles, and as having anticipated British imperialism. And they proved equally malleable political symbols, capable of being invoked by opposing parties. For Edward Bulwer-Lytton and George Lewes Newnham Collingwood, they were spokesmen for strictly hierarchical, paternalist regimes. Bulwer-Lytton's Arthur asserts 'Harmonious Order needs its music scale; The Equal were the discord of the All', while Collingwood's Alfred bluntly proclaims, 'God has filled the globe/ With inequalities'.[24] But, on the other hand, Alfred's council and Arthur's Round Table (where all the knights had 'equally good seats, so that they would work for the Table, rather than each one for his own seat') were both hailed as prototypes for a democratically elected parliament.[25]

There was certainly some sense in which the two figures were in competition for the nation's affection. Few authors celebrated both, and those whose allegiance was with Alfred often stressed his superiority to Arthur. Thomas Hughes argued that while Arthur was great, Alfred was certainly 'a greater king'; while Katie Magnus told her juvenile readers that 'Alfred's reign was in truth what . . . King Arthur meant his to be' – implying that where Arthur had failed, Alfred had found success.[26] In particular, of course, Arthur's debatable historicity came in for snide comment from the Alfredian camp. Bowker, in his record of the Alfred Millenary, dismissed Arthur as a 'dim and unrealised figure', while, in his *The Story of King Alfred*, Walter Besant commented that the defeated Britons had 'consoled themselves with the legends of King Arthur . . . for the defeats which cooped them up in Wales and Cornwall' – adding loftily, 'There was no King Arthur among the Saxons'.[27]

It impossible to judge how much direct borrowing there was from one tradition to another – whether, for instance, Victorian authors claimed an Arthurian origin for the navy in response to the Alfredian claims which had been made since the early eighteenth century. In most cases the two national icons were probably just independently associated with identical prominent concerns – in which case, if considered together, they can reveal much about those issues which most occupied the nineteenth-century public. Likewise, the ways in which depictions of the two kings seem to have converged during the nineteenth century may be deeply revealing of contemporary taste and opinion. Between 1800 and 1901, Alfred noticeably acquired some of the vital components which Victorian Arthurianists seem to have found most attractive in Malory – namely a magical or mystical element; a fellowship of good men bound by loyalty to their king; and a juicy love interest. Arthur, on the other hand (as Stephanie Barczewski has recently observed) became markedly less 'Celtic': in an 1868 poem by Thomas Westwood, his enemies are not invading Saxons, but (like Alfred's) Viking; in Tennyson's *Idylls of the King* he is 'fair beyond the race of Britons'; and in Bulwer-Lytton's *King Arthur* he is of 'Saxon character' despite his 'Celtic Origin'. Barczewski reads such attempts to transform Arthur from Celt to Saxon in relation to the negative stereotyping of the 'Celtic' races of Britain's periphery which dominated popular English culture for much of the nineteenth century, as a response to mass immigrations of Irish into England; the strong Scottish and Irish presence in government and imperial office; and generalised anxieties about the stability of the union. She also relates the shift to the high prestige which Anglo-Saxon history acquired during the Victorian period.[28] This was also of crucial importance to the development of a cult of Alfred.

Anglo-Saxonism

Arguably the most pervasive aspect of nineteenth-century medievalism was Anglo-Saxonism – the study and celebration of the Anglo-Saxon period. The origins of the interest are often traced to the publication in 1799 of Sharon Turner's *History of the Anglo-Saxons* – the first extended attempt to dispel the negative, Norman-derived images of Saxons as ruthless invaders and barbarians which had biased British authors against Anglo-Saxon subjects from the twelfth to the eighteenth century.[29] As Turner stated in the introduction to the third edition of his hugely successful text, when he began work on the history, 'the subject of the Anglo-Saxon antiquities had been nearly forgotten by the British public'.[30] Significant as Turner's work was, however (and it had run to six editions by 1836), it is also true that his history appeared at an opportune moment. The publication in 1765 of Thomas Percy's *Reliques of Ancient English Poetry* had already created an appetite in Britain for native heritage. Thus, both Percy and Turner should be viewed as having contributed to the new interest in Anglo-Saxon subjects, an interest which engendered among other texts: an edition of *Beowulf* in 1820; James Ingram's edition of the *Saxon Chronicle* in 1823; and Francis Palgrave's 1832 *History of Saxon England*.

Moreover, although Turner was interested in the Saxons, he had little regard for the historical value of Saxon sources. It was therefore not until 1849, when J.M. Kemble's *The Saxons in England* had replaced Turner as the standard history of the period – using Saxon instead of Norman manuscripts as source material – that a wave of Anglo-Saxon editions began to appear.[31] These included Joseph Stevenson's monumental multi-volume series of translated chronicles, *The Church Historians of England*, which was published in the 1850s, and J.A. Giles's accessible *Six Old English Chronicles*, published in 1878, which included a modern English translation of *Asser's Life of King Alfred*. The new accessibility of reliable Anglo-Saxon source materials prompted a spate of popular histories dealing with the period, such as Stubbs's 1866 *Constitutional History*, Freeman's 1867 *History of the Norman Conquest*, and Green's 1881 *A Short History of the English People*. And these, in their turn, became the source material for popular artists and authors who could now produce historically informed Anglo-Saxonist works. Thus, among the medieval subjects painted for the Westminster competitions previously mentioned, were thirty-four on Anglo-Saxon subjects which were presumably considered to represent dramatic moments in the nation's history. These included Edith's discovery of the body of King Harold; the death of Edward the Martyr; the conversion of the English to Christianity; and several Alfredian scenes which will be discussed later.[32]

Nineteenth-century Anglo-Saxonism should also be traced, however, to the interest in the Saxons as early democrats – an interest that arose in Britain in the late seventeenth century around the time of the 'Glorious

Revolution' among radicals like the Digger, Gerard Winstanley.[33] Drawing
upon the association in Tacitus's *Germania* of the ancient Germanic peoples
with an unusual degree of personal liberty, the Diggers developed the notion
of the 'Norman Yoke' – according to which the Normans on their arrival
in England had replaced democratic institutions with feudalism; native
Christianity with Roman Catholicism; and trial-by-jury with trial-by-ordeal.
Their descendants, so the argument went, now constituted the aristocracy
and continued their oppression of the Saxons in the person of the lower and
middle classes. Calls for drastic voting and property reform could therefore
be justified on the grounds that they represented merely the restitution of
ancient rights.[34]

The notion of the Norman Yoke was revived in the late eighteenth and
early nineteenth century by radicals such as Thomas Paine and Major John
Cartwright calling for constitutional reform.[35] It was drawn upon again in
the 1840s by Whigs campaigning for the abolition of the House of Lords,
who argued that whereas the House of Commons was of 'honest' Saxon
descent, the forebears of the Lords had been Norman usurpers and they
should now, therefore, relinquish their ill-gotten privileges.[36] And, as late as
1885, an article by Arthur Arnold in the *Contemporary Review* endeavoured
to calculate the sum owed by the Norman aristocracy to the Saxon middle
classes for the land they had wrongfully held since 1066 – including com-
pound interest.[37] After the passage of the 1832 Reform Act, however, Anglo-
Saxonism gradually became less aligned with left-wing politics and class
conflict. Instead of the aristocracy, the descendants of the Normans came to
be identified with the modern French – a shift which has also been related to
'collective anxiety in the face of the revolutionary wars on the continent',
and which resulted in a spate of novels likening the Norman Conquest to the
threat of contemporary cultural invasion from Napoleonic France.[38]

Alongside this shift, a new view of the Norman Conquest also evolved in
the work of writers like Sir Francis Palgrave, which argued not that the
Normans had displaced Saxon institutions, but rather that they had made
little real impact upon Saxon society, and England's laws, institutions and
ways of life had continued more or less undisturbed for over a thousand
years.[39] This reinterpretation of the Norman influence upon English history
swiftly became dominant in England, owing to a disinclination to identify
anything but linear progress in the nation's past. The view was also rein-
forced by the anti-French sentiment that had been instigated by decades of
Anglo-French wars – and which had created a strong antipathy to attribut-
ing any component of modern England's success to Norman (in other words,
broadly French) ancestry.[40] Instead, it was preferable to celebrate modern
English culture, institutions and ethnicity as essentially Saxon.[41] In his 1840
inaugural lecture as Professor of Modern History at Oxford, Thomas Arnold
proclaimed that 'modern history' should begin with study of the Anglo-
Saxon period 'for it treats of a life which was then and is not yet extin-
guished', while Martin Farquhar Tupper began his 1849 poem 'Alfred, Born

at Wantage' by addressing his contemporary Britons as 'Anglo-Saxons all', and the historian J. Lorimer asserted in 1852 that 'the roots of our liberty, of our laws, of our language . . . are all to be traced to Saxon times'.[42]

This view of the English as Anglo-Saxons was strengthened in the second half of the nineteenth century by advances in language theory. In 1861, the philologist Max Müller gave a series of lectures at the Royal Institution in London, in which he demonstrated that the English language was essentially Teutonic and Saxon.[43] His findings were quickly appropriated by nationalists to bolster the view that English culture and institutions were also Germanic, and as final proof that there was an uninterrupted racial continuity between the Anglo-Saxons of the ninth century and the English-speaking nations of the nineteenth.[44] This belief was manifested in the scholarly use of the terms 'English' and 'Old English' from the 1870s to describe the inhabitants and language of pre-Norman England, and its increasing popular acceptance was signified by the growing general use of 'Anglo-Saxon' as a synonym for 'English' in both Britain and the United States.[45] After the death of President McKinley in 1901, the Bishop of Winchester spoke of the sorrow felt by 'both branches of the Anglo-Saxon race' and, later that year in New York, General Rockwell predicted that 'the Anglo-Saxons' would become 'if they are not already, the dominant race of the world'.[46] Rockwell also claimed that 'self-reliance' was an inherent quality of the Anglo-Saxon in any age. By the 1860s, in Victorian society, there was a dominant belief in the racial determination of character, and therefore Müller's conclusions also engendered attempts to identify an intrinsic 'Anglo-Saxon' nature, distinguishing modern English-speakers from other nationalities – particularly the speakers of Romance languages. This led to increased interest in analysing the character of prominent pre-Conquest figures (such as Alfred), in whom racial traits might be exemplified.[47]

Queen Victoria also came to be celebrated in the late nineteenth century in terms of an Anglo-Saxon racial 'type'.[48] 'Our own Queen Victoria', Sir Henry Maine proclaimed in 1897, 'has in her veins the blood of Cerdic of Wessex, the fierce Teutonic chief, out of whose dignity English kingship grew . . . she is the most perfect representative of Teutonic royalty'.[49] The presence of a Germanic royal family in Britain was another major contributory factor to the development of nineteenth-century Anglo-Saxonism. From the reign of George I, Royalist scholars tried to counter widespread British antipathy to a foreign monarch on the throne by encouraging interest in Britain's Anglo-Saxon rulers and promoting the notion of racial descent from them to the Hanoverian succession.[50] This continued throughout the eighteenth and early nineteenth centuries, and intensified during Victoria's reign with the increasing prestige of Saxon history. By the middle of the century, it was widely accepted that Queen Victoria represented the rightful return of Saxon blood to Britain's throne after many years of Norman usurpation.[51] She came to represent, as Claire Simmons has argued, 'the symbolic reversal of the Conquest'.[52] A Saxon identity was also created for

Victoria's initially unpopular German consort Albert, in order to allay suspicions about his influence over affairs of state.[53] And the notion of Britain's
royal family as Saxon was finally cemented by the commemorative statue
commissioned for Windsor Chapel in 1892 – which presented Victoria as a
Saxon queen and Albert as a ninth-century king making his last farewell.[54]

Towards the close of Victoria's reign, as Alfredianism reached its apex, the
queen was identified not just as Saxon but more specifically as the heir of
King Alfred. At the 1899 planning meeting for the Winchester Millenary, the
Bishop of London declared that 'the blood of Alfred still ran in the veins of
her Most Gracious Majesty Queen Victoria', and the same year Frederick
Pollock praised Victoria's acquisition of Hindustani as an act 'in the spirit of
her great ancestor' Alfred, who had learned Latin as an adult.[55] Victoria's
identity became even more closely associated with Alfred, following her
death in the same year as Winchester's Alfred Millenary. In his 1901 tract,
God Save King Alfred, the Reverend Edward Gilliat proclaimed that while
Alfred had 'united Anglekin in England', Victoria had 'united a wider
Anglekin the world over'.[56] At the Winchester luncheon, the Archbishop of
Canterbury maintained that it would be 'difficult in all history to find any
two sovereigns who had done so much for their respective countries, who
had shown such an aptitude for the duties of monarchy, and had exhibited
such examples of lofty devotion to high duties'.[57] And, the following year,
Charles Plummer, looking back upon the coincidence, predicted:

> Will not the historian of the future see a certain sad appropriateness in the fact
> that the Queen should have died in the year which is to celebrate the Millenary
> of this, the greatest of her ancestors, the one whom she so much resembled in
> her unswerving loyalty to duty, her constant labour for the good of her people,
> her unfaltering allegiance to truth.[58]

This association of Alfred and Victoria through the supposed correspondence of their deaths raises one final and influential factor which set the stage
for a cult of King Alfred in the nineteenth century: the Victorian mania for commemorating anniversaries. It was in Victoria's reign that the jubilee celebration
became a grand event of national significance; personal anniversaries became
commonly recognised; and commemoration of historical incidents became
widespread. Thomas Gill's 1858 volume *The Anniversaries*, containing commemorative poems to be read on each day of the year, is just one product of
the fashion which was also manifested in the periodical press – in 1897, for
instance, every single edition of the *Cornhill Magazine* carried an 'anniversary
study' of a significant event, ranging from the execution of Charles I to the
Battle of Marston Moor. The fact that the ninth-century Alfred offered
authors, artists and events organisers a set of millennial anniversaries to commemorate therefore rendered him a particularly appealing figure for rewriting.

The 1,000-year interval between Alfred and the nineteenth century also
meant that he provided a neat starting point for cultural histories: A. McIlroy
entitled his 1896 article on the English language 'Alfred the Great and One

Thousand Years of English', while George Eayrs called his 1902 study of the English monarchy *Alfred to Victoria: Hands Across a Thousand Years*. It equally made his reign a highly evocative period to be compared with or contrasted to the present. Throughout the nineteenth century, writers with a range of political interests juxtaposed the Saxon king with George IV, William IV, Victoria and William Pitt, while the invasion of Alfred's kingdom was likened to the Napoleonic wars, the Turkish invasion of Greece and the Czechoslovakian struggles against Austria, and its inventions hailed as anticipating the 1851 Great Exhibition.[59]

There were, however, several kings who ruled in England in the ninth century, and among whose achievements significance might be found by any Victorian historian with a keen eye for providence, pattern and reassuring progress. Between 825 and 830, Alfred's grandfather Egbert succeeded in gaining overlordship of the whole of Southern England, Northumberland and Wales, anticipating Alfredian projects of unification (as well as the 1801 Act of Union). In 851, Alfred's father and eldest brother won a monumental defeat over an army of invading Vikings, a victory which was allegedly the greatest slaughter of Danes in Britain that century. Neither of them, however, attracted anything like the adulation accorded in the nineteenth century to their descendant Alfred. This chapter has outlined the general conditions and contexts which allowed the cult of an Anglo-Saxon king to flourish in nineteenth-century England. What it has not fully answered, however, is the question of why that Saxon king was Alfred. The answer to this seems to reside in the sheer amount and variety of source materials available for his life – a body of Anglo-Saxon, late medieval and early modern texts that made Alfred the most documented secular character in pre-Conquest English history. This trove of biography, history and legend will be the subject of the next chapter.

Notes

1 Bowker, *The King Alfred Millenary*, p. 39.
2 Ruskin, 'Letter to Henry Ackland', p. 115.
3 See Gilmour, *The Victorian Period*, p. 25.
4 See Mitchell, *Picturing the Past*, p. 2.
5 See Gilmour, *The Victorian Period*, p. 31
6 Bowker, *The King Alfred Millenary*, pp. 186, 21, 20.
7 For a full account of this development, see Keynes, 'The Cult of King Alfred the Great', pp. 296–303.
8 See Mitchell, *Picturing the Past*, p. 2.
9 See Dellheim, *The Face of the Past*, p. 28.
10 For a fuller discussion of this subject, see Simmons, *Reversing the Conquest*, p. 59; Sanderson, *Education, Economic Change and Society in England*, p. 43; Ball, *Educating the People*, pp. 172–180.
11 See Dellheim, *The Face of the Past*, p. 37.
12 James, *Forest Days*, pp. 1–2.

13 See Morris, *The Image of the Middle Ages*, p. 36; Dellheim, *The Face of the Past*, p. 44; Chandler, *A Dream of Order*, p. 9.
14 Chandler, *A Dream of Order*, pp. 158–182.
15 Chandler, *A Dream of Order*, pp. 184–230; Morris, *The Image of the Middle Ages*, pp. 103–125.
16 See Hunt, *The Book of Art*.
17 Dellheim, *The Face of the Past*, pp. 1–6.
18 On historical tourism, see Dellheim, *The Face of the Past*, p. 39; on religious medievalism, see Morris, *The Image of the Middle Ages*, pp. 134–143.
19 On medievalist costume, see Barczewski, *Myth and National Identity*, pp. 54–55.
20 Heighway, 'A Few Words Upon Beards', pp. 611–614. On Arthur and the Victorians, see Bryden, *Reinventing King Arthur*.
21 Dickens, *A Child's History of England*, p. 23; Austin, *England's Darling*, p. vii. On Arthur, see Barczewski, *Myth and National Identity*, pp. 36, 38.
22 Taylor and Brewer, *The Return of King Arthur*, p. 219.
23 Knowles, *Alfred the Great*, p. 70. On Arthur, see Barczewski, *Myth and National Identity*, p. 93.
24 Quoted in Barczewski, *Myth and National Identity*, p. 85; Collingwood, *Alfred the Great*, p. 110.
25 Magnus, *First Makers of England*, p. 37. On beliefs surrounding Alfred's council, see Chapter Four of this volume.
26 Magnus, *First Makers of England*, p. 90.
27 Bowker, *The King Alfred Millenary*, p. 186; Besant, *The Story of King Alfred*, p. 52.
28 See Barczewski, *Myth and National Identity*, pp. 37, 39–40.
29 See Frantzen and Niles, *Anglo-Saxonism and the Construction of Social Identity*, p. 7.
30 Turner, *History of the Anglo-Saxons*, 3rd edn (1820), p. i.
31 See White, 'Changing Views of the Adventus Saxonum', pp. 585–588.
32 See Hunt, *The Book of Art*.
33 See Winstanley, *The Law of Freedom and Other Writings*, pp. 280–299.
34 Simmons, *Reversing the Conquest*, pp. 32, 16.
35 Simmons, *Reversing the Conquest*, pp. 3, 34, 141
36 See, for instance, 'The Anglo-Normans', p. 468.
37 Arnold, 'The Indebtedness of the Landed Gentry', pp. 225–232.
38 See Melman, 'Claiming the Nation's Past', p. 583.
39 Palgrave, 'The Conquest and the Conqueror', p. 291. See also Troup, 'Our Anglo-Saxon Empire', p. 687; Freeman, *Old English History*, p. xiii.
40 For examples of nineteenth-century British Francophobia, see Gibson, 'Some Characteristics of the Normans', pp. 506–513; and Hardman, 'French Conquerors and Colonists', pp. 20–32.
41 See, for instance, Besant, *The Story of King Alfred*, p. 120, and the articles in the periodical *The Anglo Saxon*, especially the editor's letter in the first issue.
42 Arnold, *Introductory Lectures on Modern History*, p. 24; Tupper, *Alfred*, p. 249; Lorimer, 'King Alfred', p. 145.
43 Simmons, *Reversing the Conquest*, pp. 180–181; Simmons, 'Iron-worded Proof', 209.
44 See, for instance, Freeman, *Old English History*, p. xiii.
45 On this subject, see Simmons, *Reversing the Conquest*, pp. 182–184; Simmons, 'Iron-worded Proof', p. 210.

46 Bowker, *The King Alfred Millenary*, p. 118; Rockwell, quoted in Yorke, *The King Alfred Millenary*, p. 20.

47 Simmons, *Reversing the Conquest*, p. 12.

48 Simmons, *Reversing the Conquest*, p. 185.

49 Quoted in Lilly, 'British Monarchy and Modern Democracy', p. 859.

50 For an overview of this, see Lilly, 'British Monarchy and Modern Democracy', p. 860. For an early example of pro-Hanoverian rhetoric, see for instance the dedication to George I in Elstob, *The Rudiments of Grammar*.

51 Victoria is defended in these terms in Lilly, 'British Monarchy and Modern Democracy', p. 859; Wolff, 'The Early Ancestors of our Queen', pp. 740–757.

52 Simmons, *Reversing the Conquest*, p. 175.

53 On the initial suspicion surrounding Albert, see Hill, 'The Future of the English Monarchy', p. 188. In *Alfred the Great in Athelnay* (p. i) Canning identifies Albert with King Alfred.

54 Pevsner, *The Buildings of England: Berkshire*, pp. 283–284.

55 Bowker, *The King Alfred Millenary*, p. 13; Pollock, 'Alfred the Great', p. 270. See also Gilliat, *God Save King Alfred*, p. vi.

56 Gilliat, *God Save King Alfred*, p. vi.

57 Bowker, *The King Alfred Millenary*, p. 117.

58 Plummer, *The Life and Times of Alfred the Great*, p. 210. See also Magnus, *First Makers of England*, p. 83.

59 See Plummer, *The Life and Times of Alfred the Great*, p. 210; Tupper, 'Alfred: Born at Wantage', in *Ballads for the Times*, p. 249; Knowles, *Alfred the Great*, p. i; Knight, *Alfred: A Romance in Rhyme*, p. 357; Matthews, *Harlequin Alfred the Great*, p. 21. Alfred was used to symbolise the Czech struggle against the Hapsburgs in Dvořák's 1870 opera, *Alfred*.

3

Turning a king into a hero: nine hundred years of pre-Victorian reinvention

'What is the secret of his fame, of his hold on the imagination of mankind?' Lord Rosebery demanded, as he stood at the feet of Winchester's newly revealed statue of King Alfred, addressing the crowds assembled for the unveiling ceremony. Answering his own question, the retired prime minister continued: 'In the first place . . . he has stamped his character on the cold annals of humanity'.[1] It was in the Victorian age that Alfred became a cult figure, but, as Rosebery's diagnosis implies, there could have been no nine-teenth-century Alfredianism if, in the first place, the Saxon king had not appeared as an impressive and engaging figure in a large body of annals, chronicles and other documents which could inspire Victorian authors, artists and popular historians. In order to properly understand why and how the Victorian cult of King Alfred developed, it is therefore necessary to survey those materials – to consider the most venerable ancestors of the Victorian Alfred, from the ninth century to 1800.

The *Anglo-Saxon Chronicle*

The mythologising that turned Alfred into a hero began in his own lifetime. The earliest source that Victorian Alfredianists could turn to for informa-tion about the king was the *Anglo-Saxon Chronicle* – a collection of annals about the British Isles spanning the period from the landing of Julius Caesar to the twelfth century. This chronicle was probably first issued in late 892 or early 893. It may have been completed on the instructions of Alfred – possibly to inspire a sense of unity at a time of Viking invasion – but there is no certain evidence for this.[2] In an age of frequent and destruc-tive pagan invasion, it was Anglo-Saxon practice to have copies of any important manuscript held in multiple locations. Today, therefore, the work is more accurately known as the *Anglo-Saxon Chronicles*, since what actually survives is not a single, original composition but a number of later versions, copied (maybe at second or third hand, or even further removed from the 'original') in different locations and at different times. These share the same core content (of events up to 891), but each also contains its own additions and continuations – often with a distinct bias towards local interests.

The first printed edition of the *Anglo-Saxon Chronicle* was published in 1643 and based on just one variant, but a composite edition based on three manuscripts was published half a century later in 1692, edited by Edward Gibson. It was not until 1823 that a composite *Anglo-Saxon Chronicle* appeared, translated into modern English by James Ingram. This proved to be the first of numerous translations published during the nineteenth century – including the editions produced in 1842 by Thomas Wright, in 1854 by Joseph Stevenson, and in 1861 by Benjamin Thorpe. The text was also paraphrased and quoted in popular histories and was confidently cited as the primary and most reliable authority for Alfred's life by every Victorian writer who wished to present him or herself as a serious historian of the king.[3]

So what did the *Anglo-Saxon Chronicle* tell the Victorians about King Alfred? The first entry referring to him is for the year 853 (when he was probably four years old) and briefly states that Alfred's father, King Æthelwulf of Wessex, sent him to Rome to be consecrated and confirmed by the Pope. When we next hear of Alfred he is fifteen years older, his father and three eldest brothers (Æthelstan, Æthelberht and Æthelbald) have already died, and alongside his only surviving brother King Æthelred he is helping Burhred of Mercia to withstand a Danish invasion. In 870, Æthelred is killed, and Alfred becomes king of Wessex. For the next seven years, the *Chronicle* relates a series of battles that Alfred fought against the Danes, and short-lived peace-treaties that he forged with them. Then, in the entry for 878, it describes how the Danes overcame Alfred, forcing him into hiding in a woody and swampy part of Somerset for three months, accompanied by only a small force. He built a fortification there and began a series of guerrilla attacks, before mustering his troops seven weeks after Easter and defeating the Danes at the Battle of Edington.

The defeated Danes vowed to leave the country and, as a token of this, thirty of them agreed to be baptised as Christians, including their leader Guthrum, who became Alfred's godson. In the 880s, the *Chronicle* tells us that Alfred fought other Danish armies (including some at sea), sent alms to Rome, and mourned the death of his sister. Then, in 893, two Danish armies invaded Alfred's kingdom simultaneously, while those Danes already settled in Northumbria and East Anglia (who had signed peace treaties with Alfred) attacked the coast of Devon. Alfred overcame these invaders and captured the wife and children of the Danish leader Haesten – a campaign that is described in unusually close detail.

The *Chronicle* tells us that the Saxon king continued to be plagued by seaborne Danish raiding armies from Northumbria and East Anglia throughout the 890s, and in 896 ordered longboats built to oppose them. That year, Alfred enjoyed his first naval victory over the Danes, off the coast of Devon. The final entry concerning Alfred is for 899 (or 901 – the dates throughout the *Chronicle* vary from version to version). It states very simply that he died on 26 October 899, to be succeeded by his son Edward.[4]

The tone of the *Anglo-Saxon Chronicle* is businesslike and brief throughout. Although particular attention is paid to some of Alfred's great victories (such as the defeat of Haesten), he appears as just one in a string of rulers, and the entries concerning Alfred and Wessex are interspersed with accounts of what was taking place at the same time among the Franks, the Bretons, the Mercians, and so on. While the *Chronicle* usefully provided Victorian Alfredianists with dates, places and a host of Æthel-somethings who had been Alfred's key followers, it provided the imaginative writers of future generations with virtually no indication of the king's personal life or character. That need, however, was fulfilled by an almost contemporary but very different Anglo-Saxon source.

Asser's *Life of Alfred the Great*

For nineteenth-century audiences, *The Life of King Alfred*, beyond any other early source, was what set Alfred the Great apart from other Anglo-Saxon monarchs. Biography became a popular genre in the nineteenth century, and this was essentially a biography – the only one written about a pre-Conquest English king, and the first to be written in England about any lay subject.

It was probably written shortly after the *Anglo-Saxon Chronicle*, in 893, by a monk (or perhaps bishop) called Asser, from St Davids in Wales. Just as the *Anglo-Saxon Chronicle* may have been intended to promote unification, the composition of the *Life of King Alfred* could have been politically motivated: in its case, as a document to be disseminated in Wales to cement Alfred's recently acquired overlordship of the country by promoting the English king's achievements and personal qualities.[5] Hence the late twentieth-century accusation that it is the earliest example of spin-doctoring.[6]

Certainly, the *Life of King Alfred* makes no claims to objectivity. On the contrary, the author presents himself as the friend, teacher and confidant of Alfred. The *Life* falls roughly into three sections: the first, which is based on the *Anglo-Saxon Chronicle* (with additions about Alfred's childhood, family and health) covers the king's life up to 887; this is followed by a short section which describes how Asser was called to Alfred's court, and taught the king to read and translate; and the rest of the work is then an unchronological, first-person account of Alfred's reign, interests and character.[7] The text ends abruptly, without recording Alfred's victories over the Danes in the 890s or his death – omissions that are particularly perplexing, given that Asser outlived Alfred by around ten years.

There is, however, a school of thought which argues that the *Life* is not Asser's work. This position has most recently (and notoriously) been adopted by Alfred P. Smyth, who suggests that the work is a forgery written around AD 1,000 (a century after Alfred's death) by the Huntingdonshire monk Byrthferth. Such doubts about the *Life*'s authenticity are not merely the product of a sceptical modern culture – they were first articulated in the nineteenth century. In 1842, the historian Thomas Wright presented a paper to the Society of Antiquaries, in which he suggested that the *Life* had been forged in the late tenth or eleventh century, highlighting the contradictions and legendary elements in the text, as well as mistakes in its Latin tenses, as the grounds for his suspicions.[8] His voice of dissension never gained popular currency in Victorian Britain. It might have urged a scholarly Anglo-Saxonist like Edward Freeman to assent in his 1871 history for children that 'we cannot put the same trust in the book called Asser as we do in the Chronicle . . . it seems hardly possible that all of it can have been written by Asser'. But still he concluded: 'it is most likely that it is Asser's book, only with some things put in afterwards by somebody else, as often happened'.[9] And, as far as less scholarly writers like Thomas Hughes were concerned, Asser was without doubt the most reliable source for subjects such as Alfred's childhood, because upon those matters its author had clearly had 'the King's own authority'.[10]

For the majority of nineteenth-century Alfredianists who trusted Asser implicitly, then, the *Life of King Alfred* was a rare and intimate insight into the life of an Anglo-Saxon king, a work that could be plundered like an archaeological hoard. In the *Life*, novelists could find information about Alfred's character: that he was a keen huntsman, liked learning poems by heart, and was very devout; that he was better looking and better mannered than his brothers; and that he was a keen learner – when his mother offered a book as a prize to whichever of her young sons could learn to read it first, Alfred was the winner, despite being the youngest.

The *Life* also provided the Victorian Alfredianist with information about Alfred's family background. Unlike the *Anglo-Saxon Chronicle*, it mentions his queen and her parents (although it does not provide her name), as well as the names and fortunes of his three daughters and two sons. There was also juicier material to fire the Victorian imagination: the fact that during Alfred's childhood, his brother Æthelbald had scandalously married his father's widow; as well as the near disaster caused during the reign of another brother, Æthelred, who lingered at his prayers for so long that Alfred had to go into battle without him.

Asser's *Life* even provided information about Alfred's state of health. It relates that during his youth, the young prince was unable to abstain from carnal desire and prayed that he might be afflicted by some illness which would strengthen his self-restraint. He was rewarded with piles. However, the pain of these eventually drove him to pray that the ailment might be switched for something less agonizing and, shortly after his wedding, Alfred was struck down by different, mysterious pain which plagued him for the rest of his life.

Most importantly perhaps, for Victorian historians, and for those who wished to adopt a historical figure in support of contemporary political or social campaigns, Asser's *Life of King Alfred* contains a wealth of information about Alfred's achievements and ideals. It explains that Alfred was a great advocate of learning and education: he had his own children educated, as well as those of his nobles. Deploring the poor state of learning in Britain, he invited numerous learned men (including Asser) to his court; his ealdormen, reeves and thegns were given the choice of learning to read or giving up their offices; and, under Asser's tutelage, Alfred himself miraculously learned to read and translate Latin all on the same day.

According to the *Life*, Alfred was also an inventor – devising time candles and lanterns to allow him to allot exactly half of his time to God's service. And not only was his own time scrupulously organised, but his court ran like clockwork, and his country's resistance to the Danes was so successful that in the 880s many Welsh princes sought overlordship from Alfred. The *Life* also asserts that the Saxon king spearheaded a programme of restoration and development: he re-established London, rebuilt other towns, and had new monasteries built. And, finally, it suggests that he was a committed believer in justice – sitting in on judicial hearings and, when necessary, investigating appeals against unfair judgements.[11]

By the Victorian period, this rich trove of information was readily available: Asser's *Life of King Alfred* was first printed in 1574; further Latin editions appeared in 1602 and 1722; and modern English versions were published in 1848 (in J.A. Giles's *Life and Times of Alfred the Great*), 1854 (in Joseph Stevenson's series, *The Church Historians of England*) and 1878 (again edited by Giles, as part of his *Six Old English Chronicles*). While many popular novelists and poets might not have read these learned editions, they would still have been familiar with the paraphrases and quotations of Asser that began to fill popular histories once the text itself had appeared in print.[12] The *Life of King Alfred* that the nineteenth century knew, however, was not the text that can be read in modern paperback today, for the Victorian editions were based upon the 1574 text, and that in its turn was reliant upon the transcription of an eleventh-century manuscript of Asser by Matthew Parker.

Matthew Parker and the *Annals of Asser*

Matthew Parker was one of Britain's first scholars of the medieval period and, in the 1560s and 1570s, his household – run like 'a cross between a Tudor university and a medieval scriptorium' – produced many of the first editions of medieval chronicles.[13] His project, however, was not merely to disseminate and preserve the often fragmentary 'ancient Monuments of the learned Men of our Nation' that passed through his hands, but to complete them, by conflating texts with others that seemed to him to be related.[14] Thus, in 1571, thanking a friend for the loan of a manuscript, he reciprocated, 'I send the same story to your lordship in print, somewhat more enlarged with such old copies as I had of other of my friends, praying for your lordship to accept it in good part'.[15]

In the case of Asser's *Life*, which Parker (or one of his editorial assistants – perhaps the Essex antiquary John Jocelyn) transcribed and printed in 1574, an eleventh-century manuscript of the text was conflated with the twelfth-century *Annals of St Neots* [*sic* – now more accurately known as the *East Anglian Chronicle*].[16] This document in its turn was a conflation, but what interested the Parker editorial team was the material that it contained from the early eleventh-century *Life of St Neot*, which relates how King Alfred in his early years was a sinful king who was warned by his relative Neot to change his ways or face punishment – which came in the form of his temporary defeat by the Danes.[17] More influentially for the mythologising of Alfred over the next three hundred years, it also told the story of how, during his three months in hiding in 878, the Saxon king visited the home of a herdsman – where he was asked to keep an eye on the baking bread of the man's wife. Distracted from the task (either because he was tending his weapons, or because he was meditating on holy scripture, depending on the version) the unfortunate king allowed the cakes to burn, and was soundly scolded.[18]

The tale of the sinful Alfred and his disastrous baking efforts was printed as an integral part of Asser's text in the 1602 and 1722 editions of the *Life*, and in every nineteenth-century translation. The 1848 volume edited by Henry Petrie enclosed the story within square brackets, and W.H. Stevenson's 1904 edition differentiated it more distinctly by printing it in small italics. But, as Charles Plummer grumbled in his 1901 Ford lectures on Alfred, such provisions were not sufficient to stop popular authors (or even some early nineteenth-century historians, like Sharon Turner) from treating the passages 'as if they were part of the original Asser'.[19]

Parker's interpolation has earned him much censure since the mid-nineteenth century.[20] In 1857, the German historian Reinhold Pauli mused sceptically whether it was introduced 'purposely or from oversight'.[21] Recently, though, scholars have been more forgiving. Simon Keynes's study of the early mythologising of Alfred suggests that Parker's additions were inserted 'in good faith', in the belief that they were Asser's work, while Alfred Smyth has proposed that the manuscript which Parker used may have already contained interpolated material.[22] This latter suggestion can never be verified, however, for, on 23 October 1731, the manuscript which Parker had transcribed – and the only surviving copy of Asser's text – was lost, when the library of Sir Robert Cotton (its new owner) was ravaged by fire, destroying 114 of his priceless volumes.

Had it not been for Parker's efforts, then, *Asser's Life of King Alfred* might never have survived to the nineteenth century. His interest in the manuscript, however, was not a purely disinterested concern for preservation. Parker was Archbishop of Canterbury at the time when the *Life* was transcribed, and in many cases the manuscripts which he selected for 'completion' and printing were those which could be used to justify the doctrinal position of the recently established Anglican Church. Asser appealed to Parker as a member of an early, native 'British' church which he believed had wielded some independence from Rome. Moreover, his *Life* presented Alfred as a king who had pre-empted (and so could vindicate) the Anglican practice of translating Latin scripture into the vernacular.[23] This point was emphasised in Parker's edition of the *Life* by appending to the text an example of Alfred's own work – the prose and verse prefaces to his Old English translation of Pope Gregory's *Pastoral Care*.

According to the eleventh-century *Life of St Neot* (which, it will be remembered, depicts Alfred as a sinful king forced into exile as a penance), while the repentant Alfred was on Athelney, St Neot (by then dead) appeared to him in a dream, promising to help him in the forthcoming battle. The next day, forces from all over England joined the king at Ecbriht's Stone. They moved to Edington and, the night before the battle, Neot appeared again to Alfred in a vision, promising to lead the Christians to victory in person.[24]

This story of Neot's mystical appearances to Alfred was not included in the *Annals of Saint Neot* (which was interpolated into Asser's *Life* by Matthew Parker). Nineteenth-century writers would not therefore have encountered the tale in modern editions of Asser. Perhaps for this reason, despite its Merlinesque resonances, the story appears in only a small number of nineteenth-century literary texts, notably those that were written by authors with a keen interest in religious matters.[25] Such writers were perhaps aware of the story of Alfred's visions of Neot as a result of having read John Whitaker's 1809 edition of *The Life of St Neot*.[26] Ironically, however, in his commentary on the *Life*, Whitaker himself derides the notion that Neot appeared to Alfred as a vision, arguing that if the saint appeared to the king at all it was in a simple dream, and that Neot certainly could not have appeared on the field at Edington, 'for one decisive reason, because Alfred was not asleep when he fought the battle'.[27]

The notion that Neot was Alfred's brother apparently originates in a now lost manuscript of the *Life of St Neot*, which is sceptically referred to in John Leland's fifteenth-century *Itinerary* and in the work of several influential seventeenth- and eighteenth-century historians.[28] It was not until 1809, however – in Whitaker's edition of the *Life of St Neot* – that it was suggested that Æthelstan and Neot might be identical.[29]

Alfred's surviving writings

Few early English monarchs have left to posterity any significant collection of their own writings and scholarship. Alfred was one of the exceptions. In the nineteenth century, Alfredianists could consult his Anglo-Saxon translations of Pope Gregory's *Pastoral Care*, Boethius's *Consolation of Philosophy*, Augustine's *Soliloquies* and the *Psalter*[30]. Besides simply deducing Alfred's interests from the choice of texts that he rendered into his native tongue, Alfredianists could also, more importantly, glimpse the Saxon king's character through his very free translation of some of these texts, and they could discern his own voice and opinions yet more clearly in the prefaces that he wrote for many of them. In the Preface to the *Pastoral Care*, for instance, Alfred expresses his regret for the decline of learning in England; his conviction of the importance of translation into the vernacular; and his eagerness to have the youth of his country educated.[31] In the Preface to his *Consolations of Philosophy* he alludes to his health problems, and in his recasting of the classical text as an explicitly Christian work he expresses a desire and a deep respect for wisdom, a wish 'to live worthily', and an appreciation of the value of friendship. Alfred's rendering of Augustine's *Soliloquies* into Anglo-Saxon was perhaps his freest translation, and in this he reveals a strong Christian faith in the immortality of the soul, and the high value that he placed upon wisdom, reason and the Christian virtues of 'faith, hope, and charity'. The king's writings could thus be used both to corroborate and to augment what Asser states about Alfred's character and concerns.

As well as Alfred's writings, Victorian Alfredianists could also refer to his law-code – a compilation of biblical and older Saxon legislation with laws of Alfred's own design. In this, he expresses a conservative reluctance to depart significantly from the laws of his predecessors; a firm belief in familial and communal responsibility for crime; and an abhorrence for oath-breaking and treason – as well as setting out a sliding scale of punishments for crime, reliant upon the social class of the victim. Alfred's will and charters could also be consulted for clues about the king's affairs, as could the treaty drawn up in 878 between Alfred and Guthrum, which defines the boundaries between Wessex and the Viking-ruled Danelaw, and outlines the legal relations that were to exist between the two countries – particularly with regard to the defence and accusation of criminals.

Both Alfred's own writings and the other documentation concerning his reign could be consulted in translated editions by the mid-nineteenth century. The king's translation of the *Pastoral Care*, of course, was translated and printed as early as 1574 by Matthew Parker; the law-code was first published in 1720 and was translated into English in 1840; Alfred's will was published in translation in 1788; and his translation of Boethius in 1829. The remaining documents all appeared in translation as part of J.A. Giles's definitive 1852 edition, *The Whole Works of King Alfred the Great* – along with several texts that had little to do with the king, such as the misnamed Middle English poem, *The Proverbs of Alfred*.

The eleventh to thirteenth centuries

The eleventh, twelfth and thirteenth centuries seem to have seen a modest renaissance of interest in Alfred – perhaps owing to an anxiety to forge a legitimate ancestry for Anglo-Norman rule, which could be neatly constructed via Alfred's kinship with Matilda, the wife of William I (a.k.a. 'the Conqueror'). Apart from the spurious attribution of poetry to Alfred, the period also produced a number of chroniclers who chose to elaborate the Saxon king's biography, and their mythopoesis proved to be influential upon nineteenth-century Alfredianism.

Among the earliest of these was Simeon of Durham, who claimed in his eleventh-century *History of Saint Cuthbert* that during Alfred's time in hiding, Cuthbert appeared to him in a dream, ordering the king to engage the Danes in battle at the time and place which he specified. Alfred followed the saint's instructions, and of course won a great victory. It is not necessary to search very far for Simeon's reasons for forging such an unlikely relationship between a Northern saint and a Southern king. Cuthbert was bishop of Lindisfarne, so the Durham-based writer would have been keen to apportion additional prestige to such a local saint by connecting him to an exalted monarch. The

History of Saint Cuthbert was published and translated several times during the eighteenth and nineteenth centuries.[32] Its story of Alfred and Cuthbert was also reiterated (and elaborated) in the early twelfth-century *History of the Kings of England* by William of Malmesbury. In the Malmesbury version of Simeon's story, Cuthbert appears to the sleeping Alfred while his men are all away fishing, and as a token that his promises of coming victory are true, predicts – correctly, as it of course turns out – that although the rivers are frozen, Alfred's fishermen will return with a huge catch.

The Malmesbury chronicle was published as early as 1596, by Sir Henry Saville; was translated into English in 1815; and subsequently appeared in three more translated editions during the nineteenth century. So it was well-known and easily available to the authors of Victorian Alfrediana. Besides its elaboration of the Cuthbert narrative, Malmesbury's history also contributed several other stories to the Alfredian tradition, stories that were to prove influential in the nineteenth century. One was its explanation that Alfred was left with no alternative but to go into hiding in 878, because the leaders of Wessex's neighbouring kingdoms each 'chose rather to resist the enemy within his own territories, than to assist his neighbours in their difficulties' – a moralistic addition that should perhaps be related to twelfth-century Britain's turbulent internal politics, and to the proto-unionist ambitions of Henry II.[33]

Among the other elements that Malmesbury contributed to the Alfredian tradition were two claims concerning crime and its prevention. The first stated that Alfred:

> Diffused such peace throughout the country, that he ordered that golden bracelets, which might mock the eager desires of the passengers while no one durst take them away, should be hung up on the public causeways, where the roads crossed each other.

The other asserted that the Saxon king had instituted hundreds and tithings (local groups of 100 and 10 men respectively)

> so that every Englishman, living according to the law, must be a member of both. If any one was accused of a crime, he was obliged immediately to produce persons from his hundred and tything to become his surety; and whosoever was unable to find such surety must dread the severity of the laws.[34]

In the case of the golden bracelet story, Malmesbury seems merely to have appropriated a traditional tale for Alfred – Bede had made the same claim about the crime-free reign of Edwy of Northumberland in his 731 history of English Christianity, and had also asserted that the same was true of Rollo the Norman's time.[35] The claim about hundreds and tithings, however, seems to have been William of Malmesbury's own creation. He might have developed the notion from some general references to communal liability in Alfred's laws and in 'The Treaty between Alfred and Guthrum',[36] but the underlying reasons for his claim were probably contemporary. During the twelfth century, when he was writing, a system of frankpledge – or communal liability for criminal behaviour – was introduced into England. This was widely considered to be the descendant of the ancient system of tithings. So, by citing the respected Alfred as the founder of hundreds and tithings, the Norman historian may have been promoting acceptance of the new system.

Both of William of Malmesbury's claims about the prevention of crime in Alfred's Wessex interested nineteenth-century Alfredianists. This was also true of his claim that Alfred was a great warrior, who rallied his troops in battle by dazzling displays of single combat; his assertion that the Saxon king translated 'the greater part of the Roman authors', including Bede and Orosius; and his tale that Alfred's grandson Æthelstan (who became king in 924) was the illegitimate product of his father's single night with a beautiful shepherdess.[37]

The most influential of William of Malmsbury's Alfredian tales in the nineteenth century, however, was the narrative which related how, during his time on Athelney, Alfred:

> hazarded an experiment of consummate art. Accompanied only by one of his faithful adherents, he entered the tent of the Danish king under the disguise of a mimic; and being admitted, in his assumed capacity of jester, to every corner of the banqueting-room, there was no object of secrecy that he did not minutely attend to both with eyes and ears. Remaining there several days, till he had satisfied his mind on every matter which he wished to know, he returned to Adelingai; and assembling his companions, pointed out the indolence of the enemy, and the easiness of their defeat.[38]

This – along with Malmesbury's other claims – was regarded by most popular nineteenth-century Alfredianists as the account of a reliable authority.[39] It provided the subject of one of the most striking Victorian paintings of Alfred, and a nail-biting chapter in numerous novels – either in the form which it takes in the *History of the Kings of England*, or in the slightly modified forms that it assumed in two fifteenth-century chronicle histories.

Fourteenth- and fifteenth-century chronicles

The fourteenth and fifteenth centuries saw Alfred get tangled up in minstrelsy, morality and university rivalry. It was in the early fifteenth-century *Book of Hyde* and the mid-fifteenth-century *History of Ingulf* (now more accurately known as the *History of Crowland*) that Malmesbury's story of Alfred in the Danish camp was subtly rewritten. The author of the *Book of Hyde* changed Alfred's disguise from a jester to a minstrel – perhaps because this was more courtly and thus considered more appropriate. The *History of Ingulf* (a monastic hoax, purporting authorship by an eleventh-century monk) then followed this lead but stated, more specifically, that Alfred was dressed as a harper.[40] This latter development may represent an amalgamation of two separate stories both found in William of Malmesbury's *History of the Kings of England* – the story of Alfred disguising himself as a jester;

and the tale of Analaf, the son of Sihctric, who in 924 disguised himself as a harper to gain access to King Æthelstan's camp.[41]

Both the *History of Ingulf* and the *Book of Hyde* were published in an English translation in 1854 by Joseph Stevenson, as part of his monumental, multi-volume edition, *The Church Historians of England*. The *History of Ingulf* had first appeared in print in a Latin edition by Henry Saville in 1596, and it was also published in English a further two times during the nineteenth century, when its true date of origin was discovered. It contributed two other innovations to the Alfredian tradition, which – like Alfred's harp – seem to be modifications or elaborations of stories from William of Malmesbury. The first is Ingulf's claim that Alfred invented the English system of shires – apparently a development of William of Malmesbury's claim that the Saxon king invented the smaller legislative units of hundreds and tithings. The second is the tale that, during Alfred's reign, 'if a traveller had in the evening lost a sum of money, however large, in the fields or highways, even if he did not return for a month afterwards, he would be sure to find it entire and untouched' – a story which was perhaps inspired by William of Malmesbury's golden bracelet tale.[42]

Another Alfredian tale found in William of Malmesbury's *History of the Kings of England* – about Alfred's encounter with St Cuthbert – was elaborated and moralised in the fourteenth century by Ralph Higden. In Higden's *Polychronicon*, the story becomes a parable – Cuthbert appears to Alfred not just in a dream but in broad daylight, dressed as a pilgrim who begs the king for food. Alfred, we are told, had only one loaf and a little wine but he told his servant to give half to the poor man. The beggar thanked him and vanished suddenly and, when the bare pantry was next inventoried, the half loaf of bread and the remaining wine had miraculously become whole again. That night, Cuthbert appeared to Alfred in a dream, promising victory as a reward for the king's generosity.[43]

The *Polychronicon* also provided the origin of what was to become one of the most notorious of Alfredian myths – the claim that the Saxon king established the University of Oxford. According to Higden, 'On the advice of Neot the abbot, whom he visited often, Alfred was the first person to establish a common school at Oxford teaching diverse arts and sciences.'[44] This notion was swiftly accepted by the Fellows of Oxford University, since it seemed to happily prove their institution to possess a more venerable founder and to be of greater antiquity than its arch-rival the University of Cambridge.[45] A succession of Oxford scholars restated and elaborated the claim.[46] Among them was the fifteenth-century author of *The Book of Hyde*, who added that Neot and Grimbald became the first Oxford readers in theology, Asser the first reader in grammar and rhetoric, and so forth.[47] Another was William Camden.

Sometime in the 1590s, Camden was sent a passage about Alfred and Oxford – a passage which claimed to have been copied from a manuscript of Asser's *Life*. The 'extract' described how a dispute about teaching methods had erupted at Oxford between Grimbald (whom Alfred had invited from France to help with the revival of learning in England) and the 'old scholars' who were already established there. Alfred visited Oxford, settled the quarrel, and Grimbald retired – hurt – to Winchester. It thus effectively proved that the University of Oxford had not been founded but rather *restored* by King Alfred, making that institution predate the recently claimed seventh-century founding of Cambridge University. Camden included the passage in his 1600 edition of *Britannia* – a survey of the history, antiquities and geography of the British Isles. More importantly, however, he also took the liberty of inserting it into his 1603 edition of Matthew Parker's translation of the *Life of King Alfred* – from where it was reproduced in Robert Powell's 1634 history *The Life of Alfred, or Alvred*, as well as in a number of influential nineteenth-century editions of Asser.[48]

The *Polychronicon* itself was translated into English in 1398 by John Trevisa; was first printed by William Caxton in 1480; and was published in a multi-volume edition between 1865 and 1886. Part of the reason why its claim about Oxford University and its version of Alfred's visitation from Cuthbert were to become quite so influential during the nineteenth century, however, was that these stories were also paraphrased in the oft-republished and long-influential *Life of Alfred the Great* by Sir John Spelman.

Sir John Spelman

John Spelman's career included a stint in Parliament (representative for Worcester in 1626); a post as the first Cambridge lecturer in Old English; and the authorship of four religious and political tracts during the Civil-War-plagued 1640s (arguing from a moderate Royalist and a conformist Protestant position).[49] He can hardly have guessed that his most enduring legacy to English cultural history was to be his biography of an Anglo-Saxon king, for although it seems to have earned him a knighthood and the favour of Charles I, his *Life of Alfred the Great* was not published until 1678 – thirty-five years after his death – and then only in a Latin translation. In fact, it was not until 1709 – sixty-six years after Spelman had died – that his original English text finally made its way into print.

Despite this tardy and undramatic debut on to England's bookshelves, however, Spelman's *Life of Alfred the Great* was second only to Asser's *Life* as a source for the Victorian cult of King Alfred, and for this reason his name will resonate through the central chapters of this study. Alfredian myth made its way into other seventeenth-century histories: John Speed's 1611 *History of Great Britaine*, for instance, included accounts of Alfred burning a 'Cake of Dow', disguising himself as a minstrel, dividing England into shires, and establishing Oxford University. But Spelman's text was the first real biography of the Saxon king written since the ninth century.

More importantly, it was also the earliest serious attempt to enlist Alfred for political ends. Robert Powell's less-than-subtly titled *Life of Alfred . . . Together with a Parallell* [*sic*] *of our Soveraigne Lord, King Charles* (1634)

had already attempted to gain for the king some reflected glory from his illustrious Saxon forebear. However, Spelman's use of King Alfred had more specific and developed aims. His *Life of Alfred the Great* was completed during
the English Civil War, while he was serving in the Royalist camp at Oxford.
The text is divided into three books – the first concerning Alfred's 'wars and
troublesome reign'. No contemporary parallels are explicitly drawn, but,
with its account of Alfred's final triumph over the Danes – after initial defeat
– it was clearly intended as a source of comfort and inspiration to Charles
and his Royalist supporters.

The second book details Alfred's 'laws and government' and stresses, above
all, that Alfred 'often heard the Opinion of his Council, whom, though they
were not yet known by that Name, yet may we properly call his Council of
State.[50] In his political tracts, Spelman identified himself as 'a wel-wisher both
to the king and parliament', arguing that 'the composite forme' was 'the only
firme and durable forme' of government, whereas 'Of the three powers,
regall, aristocraticall or popular, any of them prevailing so far as to be wholly
free from being qualified or tempered by some operation of the other two,
corrupted the legitimate forme into a tyrannicall'.[51] For Spelman, then, the
monarch's authority had to be subject to limitations. And he identified a forerunner of his political ideal in the reign of Alfred the Great. This idea was
probably underpinned by a reference to 'the councillors of the West Saxons'
and two references to 'assemblies' being held, in Alfred's will.[52] But Spelman's
main source for the notion seems to have been the late thirteenth-century
Mirror of Justices, which he (and his antiquarian father, Henry Spelman,
before him) mistakenly believed to be a pre-Conquest text. This states that:

> For the good estate of his realm King Alfred caused his counts to assemble, and
> ordained as a perpetual usage that twice a year or more often if need should be
> in time of peace, they should assemble at London to hold parliament.[53]

Spelman did qualify his presentation of Alfred as a limited monarch by
stressing that Alfred's assembly was not 'of one and the same Form and
Solemnity with our later Parliaments'. However, he also described that
meeting as 'an assembling of the *Representative* Body of the State'.[54] In so
doing, he probably did not intend to imply that Alfred's government was
democratically elected. However, his choice of wording did not escape the
notice of later writers, but set loose a whisper about constitutionalism that
was to swell into a resounding chorus by the nineteenth century.

As preparation for writing his biography of Alfred, Spelman consulted a
wide range of manuscript and print sources, particularly those held in the
ill-fated library of Robert Cotton. He examined, for instance, Cotton's
manuscript of Asser's *Life*, in order to establish whether Camden's claim
that Alfred had refounded Oxford University had any authenticity. As a
Cambridge man, he was doubtless delighted to report back that Alfred had
certainly not done so, but might have *founded* the institution (sometime after
the establishment of a university in Cambridge).[55]

Another document which Spelman consulted was Alfred's introduction to his translation of Gregory's *Pastoral Care* (either in manuscript form or printed as an appendix to Parker's edition of Asser's *Life*). Here Alfred states his desire that:

all free-born young men now in England who have the means to apply themselves to it, may be set to learning (as long as they are not useful for some other employment) until the time that they can read English writings properly.[56]

Spelman's paraphrase of this passage reads 'In sundry Parts of the Kingdom (as it seemeth) he erected Schools for Youth, ordaining . . . that every Freeman of Ability sufficient should bring up their Children to Learning'.[57] Not only did Spelman leap from Alfred's *desire* to have his country's youth educated to the conclusion that he must have actually *established* schools, he also entirely ignored the Saxon king's proviso that only those youths *not useful for some other employment* should be educated – which, in practice, would be rather a small and privileged minority in the ninth century. His image of Alfred as an educator, however, was only the first shoot of what would prove to be a strong branch of the Victorian cult of Alfred.

John Spelman's mis-reading (or perhaps just enthusiastic over-reading) of source material also seems to have given birth to another Alfredian myth. Part of Alfred's 878 treaty with Guthrum states 'And if anyone accuses a king's thegn of manslaughter, if he dares to clear himself he is to do it with twelve king's thegns'.[58] Clearly, the 'twelve king's thegns' in this passage are acting as witnesses to the accused's character or recent activity. That figure of twelve, however – exactly the same number of men as is required for a modern jury – seems to have seized Spelman's imagination. Certainly, it is difficult to see what other basis he might have had for his claim that Alfred created 'the Law of Tryal by the Verdict of 12 of our Peers or Equals' – although the context for that claim is easier to make out.[59] Shortly before he wrote his biography, there had been fierce antiquarian debate about whether trial by jury had a Norman or a pre-Norman origin.[60] In Alfred's writings, Spelman seems to have believed that he had finally found the answer.

Oversight, distortion and exaggeration – an unkindly eye might identify these running throughout John Spelman's *Life of Alfred the Great*; for example, Spelman's Saxon king does not hide on Athelney for three months, but for 'well nigh a full year'. He does not just design longboats that are 'swifter and more stable and also higher' than the Danish fleet (*Anglo-Saxon Chronicle*, AD 896), rather he is 'the first that put to sea such a Navy as was awful unto Strangers, begun the first Mastery of the Seas'.[61]

Much of this rewriting can best be understood by considering the late seventeenth-century context in which Spelman was writing: the British navy, for instance, had become a source of great national pride by that time, but there remained little consensus as to who could be celebrated as its glorious founder. Likewise, to understand why Spelman's Alfred does not merely send alms to a shrine in India (*Anglo-Saxon Chronicle*, AD 883), but has his mariners bring back 'a fair return of precious Stones, Perfumes, and other Eastern Rarities', one should probably consider the commercial success and prestige of the East India Company in the late seventeenth century.[62]

Spelman was not the first to present an Alfred distorted through the lens of his own times – William of Malmesbury had already imagined a Saxon king who upheld twelfth-century chivalric ideals. But without the Stuart historian's intensive remoulding of Alfred for the seventeenth century, the Victorians would have inherited a figure far less readily malleable to their own needs and interests. One of Spelman's claims, an assertion that was to particularly seize the imagination of later Alfredianists was his claim that Alfred became 'sole Sovereign of the whole Island' – effectively implying that he acted as overlord to all of England, all of Scotland, and the entirety of Wales.[63] This seems to be a corruption of Asser's statement that Alfred ruled 'all the Christians of the island of Britain'. Of course, what it (either deliberately or short-sightedly) overlooks is the fact that Asser's statement does not preclude the existence of other, pagan sovereigns on the British mainland – those who ruled the Danelaw in the ninth century, for instance. For Spelman, however, writing just thirty-nine years after the English and Scottish crowns had first been joined, and sixty-five years before the English and Scottish parliaments were to be united, the concept of Alfred as 'sole sovereign' enticingly demonstrated that Union was an ancient and natural state of affairs.[64]

No matter how great Alfred's achievements had been, however, for some reason nobody was keen to publish Spelman's biography when it was completed in 1642. Perhaps the work might have found its way into print at Oxford had Spelman only endorsed Camden's claims about that institution's early foundation – but, as things were, the *Life of Alfred the Great* had to bide its time, awaiting a political sea-change. That alteration came in the form of the restoration of the monarchy, in 1660. Spelman's *Life of Alfred the Great* was, in a sense, the perfect Restoration text – the biography of a king, yet one which stressed that monarch's reliance upon his council of state. So in 1676, when Obadiah Walker became the master of University College Oxford, and needed a means of raising funds for building work on the college's chapel and library, he must have come across Spelman's unpublished text like a forgotten jewel. Walker realised that publicising the achievements of Alfred and his connection with the college might encourage potential benefactors to contribute to its upkeep. The biography was therefore translated into Latin (complete with notes defending Camden's claim that Alfred *re*founded Oxford), and was printed at the college's expense, with a dedication to Charles II in a preface which likened the two monarchs – just as Robert Powell had connected Alfred to Charles's father, and a stream of later texts was to compare the Saxon king to Hanoverian sovereigns.

Walker's plan seems to have been successful. At any rate, without his campaign to publicise Alfred's refounding of Oxford, using Spelman's biography, it is likely that the 'Alfred Jewel' found in a Somerset field in 1693 would not have been donated to the university upon its owner's demise in 1698.

Thereafter – the real value of claiming Alfred as founder having been fully appreciated – there was a localised wave of enthusiasm for the Saxon king in the Oxford colleges. Alfredian stained-glass and statuary was commissioned. A fresh enthusiasm arose for translating Alfred's writings. And, in 1709, another Oxford academic, Thomas Hearne, published Spelman's *Life of Alfred the Great* in its original English – finally making available to less scholarly readers a text that was to remain the only widely known biography of Alfred until well into the Victorian age.[65]

Alfred in the eighteenth century

During the eighteenth century, Alfredianism began to develop in ways that would establish the foundations for a fully fledged cult of King Alfred in the Victorian age. Many of the texts mentioned in the following section will therefore become increasingly familiar to the reader, being frequently cited as the geneses of nineteenth-century uses of Alfred in the main body of this study. It was during this period that the figure of Alfred found a life beyond the scholarly and ecclesiastical world and in the realm of popular culture.[66] It was also at this time that the Saxon king first became intimately associated with the Hanoverian line – following the precedent set by Spelman, who had allied Alfred with the reigning monarch of his own period: Charles I. And it was between 1709 and 1801 that the malleability and versatility of King Alfred began to emerge, as the Saxon king was refracted, as if in a hall of mirrors, into multiple Alfreds – some the embodiment of royal virtue, but others the heroes of radical, oppositional politics.

At the root of almost all this new Alfrediana was Spelman's *Life*, influencing texts either directly, or obliquely – via influential histories like Paul Rapin's 1724 *History of England* (composed in French, but translated into English in 1731) which celebrated Spelman as its 'principle [*sic*] Guide' and followed him in depicting an Alfred who disguises himself as a minstrel, founds Oxford University, and divides England into shires.[67] Rapin's keen eye also seems to have been among several to note and bring attention to that use of the word 'representative' in Spelman's life. His history relates ''tis still warmly disputed whether the people had a right to send their representatives' to Alfred's assembly.[68] The section on Alfred in Hume's weighty *The History of England* (republished numerous times during the eighteenth and nineteenth centuries) was also squarely based upon Spelman's history. It reiterates his arguments about Alfred's invention of juries and foundation of Oxford, as well as relating the stories about the king's minstrel disguise and burning of the cakes (though the stories about Alfred and the two saints, Cuthbert and Neot, are omitted). And Alexander Bicknell produced his *The Life of Alfred the Great* as an attempt to make Spelman's 'antique style and circumlocution . . . more intelligible and entertaining to the generality of Readers'.[69]

Rapin's history was dedicated to George I, Britain's first Hanoverian monarch. Supporters of the Hanoverian royal family (which faced much animosity in the eighteenth century, as a foreign imposition) soon realised the obvious advantages to be gained from celebrating the *Saxon* king as a venerable ancestor of Britain's new *Germanic* sovereigns, and many enlisted Alfred to their cause. One of the earliest to do so was Richard Blackmore, in his 1723 *Alfred: An Epick Poem*. Blackmore had already written an Arthurian poem in tribute to the Hanoverians, for which he had been soundly ridiculed.[70] His Alfredian follow-up celebrated George I as 'a second Saviour to dispel Britannia's fears . . . from the old Seats, whence Alfred's Fathers came', and celebrated George II for his 'Glory and Heroick Fame' in battle.[71] Above all, though, it was interested in likening Alfred to Prince Frederick – the short-lived son of George II and father to the future George III – who, at the time of the poem's publication, was still living in Hanover.

Taking as its point of departure Asser's account of the young Alfred's trip to Rome, Blackmore's poem weaves an elaborate and neo-classical tale of adventure in which a young and inexperienced Alfred embarks on a 'Grand Tour' of foreign nations in order to study their various types of government. As part of this ninth-century odyssey, he observes the 'fruits of liberty' in enlightened Tunisia, a tyrannical king in Navarre, and the ruins of a degenerate democracy in Italy. He intercedes between seditious subjects and a spendthrift monarch in Hesperia, is seduced in Sicily and is invited to become king of Libya. Like the hero of any self-respecting epic, he also visits heaven and hell (where he observes treasonous statesmen and corrupt judges toasting) and narrowly escapes various attempts by Lucifer to cut short his rite-of-passage by summoning storms and awakening volcanoes. Blackmore's Alfred returns to Britain replete with wisdom – and just in time to disguise himself as a minstrel, marry the daughter of his defeated Danish foe and assume the throne.

Recent scholarship has argued that 'critics have yet to discover a redeeming feature in the twelve tedious cantos of rhyming couplets' that make up *Alfred: An Epick Poem*.[72] However, read in the context of pro-Hanoverian propaganda, the poem is fascinating in its attempt to make the foreign Frederick a more acceptable prospect to his potential subjects. The poem was also clearly intended as a didactic work for the benefit of the prince himself – demonstrating to him the value and antiquity of the British system of constitutional monarchy. During his adventures, Blackmore's Alfred visits a hermit who predicts Britain's future. Frederick is represented as the climax of the country's destiny. He will be 'a Genius just and bright, No less the People's than the Court's Delight' – but only as long as he allows his mind to be formed following the example of Alfred, who ruled in conjunction with an assembly.[73]

Frederick did, indeed, become the people's delight after his arrival in Britain in December 1728. Blackmore's poem was to be the last Alfredian text to celebrate the prince alongside George II, however. Relations between Frederick and his father grew antagonistic during the early 1730s. This culminated in the prince's exclusion from court in 1737, and his increasing alliance with a dissident political movement. This movement called itself 'patriotism', and was critical of both the huge national debt generated by the government of Robert Walpole, and the prevalence under him and George II of 'placemen' – public offices created for the friends of ministers.[74] One of the movement's chief spokesmen was Henry, Lord Bolingbroke. His 1738 *Letters on the Spirit of Patriotism* hypothesised that:

> A patriot king will neither neglect, nor sacrifice his country's interest. No other interest, neither a foreign nor a domestic, neither a public nor a private, will influence his conduct in government. He will not multiply taxes wantonly, nor keep up those unnecessarily which necessity has laid, that he may keep up legions of tax-gatherers. He will not continue national debts by all sorts of political and other profusion; nor, more wickedly still, by a settled purpose of oppressing and impoverishing the people, that he may with greater ease corrupt some, and govern the whole, according to the dictates of his passions and arbitrary will. . . . The wealth of the nation he will most justly esteem to be his wealth, the power his power, the security and the honour, his security and honour.[75]

Bolingbroke looked to Frederick to become the incarnation of this ideal upon his accession to the throne, while his followers (among them Voltaire) identified King Alfred as one of the best examples of a 'patriot king' from the past. When Richard Temple, the first Viscount Cobham, had a series of busts made for his 'Temple of Worthies' in the mid-1730s (with the subjects chosen to illustrate his political opposition to Walpole), Alfred was one of the worthies chosen – the inscription beneath his bust proclaiming that he had 'crush'd Corruption, guarded Liberty, and was the Founder of the English Constitution'.[76]

In 1735, Frederick himself commissioned a bust of Alfred by the sculptor Michael Rysback for his own 'temple' in the gardens of Carlton House. It was a good year for Rysback – in the same year, George II's wife Queen Caroline also commissioned him to produce a series of busts of kings and queens, beginning with Alfred and ending with her husband, for the library at St James's Palace.[77] It is difficult not to view the coincidence in the light of a competition to win a lasting identification with Alfred for either Frederick or his father. If this was so, then Frederick emerged the victor. In the following decade, Alfred became firmly aligned with the patriot cause. In 1742, when William Hogarth painted a portrait of the unconventional heiress and art patroness Mary Edwards, depicting her as a heroine of patriotism, either the painter or subject decided that a bust of King Alfred should be strategically positioned behind her. And, until the late eighteenth century, it remained a convention to hail Alfred as a 'patriot king' – even after Frederick's death, when patriotism evolved into a more radical political movement. Robert Holmes's 1778 ode to Alfred ends 'Hail, British Alfred, *patriot* King, Great Father of thy people, Hail!', while Alexander Bicknell gave his 1788 Alfredian play the title *The Patriot King*.[78]

Frederick himself became the Hanoverian figurehead most intimately associated with Alfred (excepting perhaps Victoria, in the last years of her reign). His master-stroke in achieving this was commissioning David Mallet and James Thomson to produce a drama, *Alfred: A Masque*, to be performed at

Frederick's Berkshire house Cliveden on 1 August 1740 – the anniversary date of the succession of the Hanoverian line to the British throne. The play begins with Alfred already in hiding; ends as he is inspired to engage the Danes; omits the indecorous burning of the cakes; and has Alfred's right-hand man undertake the disguised mission to the Danish camp – on the grounds that 'the public weal' depends upon Alfred himself avoiding danger. It is, then, a very brief work, but is remarkable for three reasons. Firstly, for the obvious analogy developed between Alfred and Frederick: the Saxon king – taking shelter in a rural cottage and patiently anticipating the time when he will 'shelter industry', 'deal out justice' and establish 'liberty and laws' – is clearly intended to prefigure the Hanoverian prince banished to the counties but awaiting his chance to rescue England from ministerial corruption.[79]

Secondly, Mallet and Thomson's play was the first text to make romance a central interest in Alfred's story. Thereafter, in eighteenth-century texts (and, later, in many nineteenth-century works) Alfred would spend much time wilting under the effects of (apparently) unrequited love, gallantly rescuing damsels from the clutches of dastardly pagans and fretting over whether lover or country should be prioritised among his concerns.[80] Such romanticising of Alfred's biography was clearly not always received without question, however. When John Home published his *Alfred: A Tragedy*, he prefaced it with an indignant defence of his use of romance motifs, which suggests that this tendency had been sharply criticised. 'Is it improbable that a young hero was in love?' he demanded:

> Is it inconsistent to represent the person, who was a Legislator when advanced in years, as a lover in his youth? Does it degrade the character of a hero to suppose, that he was in love with the princess whom he afterward married? . . . an imaginary idea has been formed of the character of Alfred as an old mortified, ascetic sage, of spirit too sublime and ethereal to descend to human passions or human actions. But the real as well as the dramatic Alfred was a young hero.[81]

Finally, and most importantly, Mallet and Thomson's play is noteworthy today for the 'Grand Ode in Honour of Great Britain' with which both it, and the 1754 oratorio based upon it, conclude. The words should be familiar – detached from their original context, they have remained well-known to the present, as the song 'Rule, Britannia':

> When Britain first, at Heaven's Command,
> Arose from out the Azure Main;
> This was the Charter of the Land,
> And guardian Angels sung this Strain:
> Rule Britannia, rule the Waves;
> Britains never will be slaves.[82]

In the 1740 text, the song is accompanied by a shadow-play of Alfred's ships conquering those of the Danes. In terms of the development of the Alfredian myth, this marked the first popularisation of Spelman's claim that Alfred created the navy – lines from 'Rule Britannia' were to be quoted in many nineteenth-century Alfredian plays and poems.[83] The ditty also represented the beginning of Alfred's role as a hero of *British*, rather than merely English, history – the part he was to play in the process, discussed recently by Colin Kidd, by which the English past came to 'stand proxy' for those of Britain's Celtic peripheries.[84] Indeed, by 1767, Alfred's identity as a British rather than merely an English king was sufficiently established for a bust of him, made for the Salisbury estate of the Earl of Radnor, to be engraved with the title 'Brittanic Alfred'.[85]

After the premature death of Frederick in 1751, there were some isolated attempts to realign Alfred with the ruling Hanoverian monarchy. This was not always done with much subtlety or probability. The anonymous 1753 play, *Alfred the Great: Deliverer of his Country* ends with King Alfred proclaiming:

Let all my subjects at their Homes with Chear,
The first of August keep, in every Year;
From Age to Age, may they continue free;
And this be still the Day, mark'd out for Liberty.[86]

Or, put more simply, they should all observe the anniversary (nine-hundred years in the future) of George I's accession to the British throne.

As the patriot movement became increasingly radical, however, so Alfred became associated more with political dissent than with celebration of royalty. Hume's 1762 *The History of England* hailed the Saxon's 'liberal' institutions. Obadiah Hulme's polemical 1771 *A Historical Essay on the English Constitution* credited Alfred with instituting a democratic system of government (which had then been unlawfully destroyed by the tyrannical Normans). And, in 1777, Major John Cartwright's *The Legislative Rights of the Commonality Vindicated* called for equal political representation and annual elections, arguing that King Alfred, faced with the same inequalities, would have provided 'such a remedy as we now propose'.[87] By the mid-1770s, Alfred had become so closely identified with oppositional politics that the republican author Catherine Macaulay named her Bath home 'Alfred House' and had a bust of the Saxon king 'nodding o'er the patriotic portal' of her door.[88] As the central chapters of this study will discuss in detail, such political uses of Alfred were to continue into the nineteenth century, and would feed influentially into the Victorian cult of Alfred.

One 1770s radical rewriting of Alfred, in particular, seems to have not only influenced later literature, but to have impacted dramatically upon political life. Albrecht von Haller's 1773 *Life of King Alfred* was allegedly among the works which hastened the 1789 French Revolution. Conversely, the shock-waves of the revolution can be identified in late eighteenth-century (and even in nineteenth-century) Alfredian texts. John Penn's 1792 play, *The Battle of Eddington: Or, British Liberty* was dedicated to that proponent of parliamentary reform, William Pitt the Younger. The word 'liberty' chimes through its pages like the bell of the Bastille, and Alfred opens his assembly announcing:

Now by freedom's laws,
Must the whole people send to that assembly,
The objects of its choice, to speak its will,
And independently maintain its rights.

(However, he also sagely warns his people that 'no sad excesses in a state are worse than anarchy's'.[89])

In the late 1780s and early 1790s, Alfred again resumed the role which he had filled during George II's reign (for instance in Blackmore's epic) as a pattern for princes – though, in this later period, following Alfred's use by patriot politics, such texts tended to contain more warning and censure than celebration. In Anne Fuller's 1789 novel *The Son of Ethelwolf*, a young Alfred realises the importance of putting statesmanship before lovemaking and learns about the responsibility that should come with power. In the course of a rather prolonged disguised visit to the Danish camp, he observes the pandemonium that passionate jealousy over women causes among his enemies, and during his time in hiding stays in not one but *several* rustic cottages, where he is prompted to recognise the 'unequal and unjust distribution' that afflicts his country, and to swear 'be it the care of Alfred to reverse it'.[90]

Fuller's novel was dedicated to George, Prince of Wales, at a time when there had been much consternation about the prospect of the dissolute prince acting as regent during George III's illness. The preface to the novel expresses relief at the recent recovery of the king, but Fuller's choice of title – presenting Alfred as his father's son – suggests that she intended to impress upon her readers the importance of remembering that Prince George, however apparently unpromising as royalty, remained his father's son, and was perhaps only in need of learning, like Alfred, the necessary lessons of youth. More politically radical was the 1792 *Lessons to a Young Prince* by the Welsh revolutionary David Williams, which was likewise dedicated and addressed to the future George IV. This credited Alfred with having 'organised the free parts of the community into a political constitution, the best imagined and most effectual that has hitherto been exhibited in the world' – bolstering its argument with diagrams representing Alfred's constitution; the English government of 1790; the constitution of the American states and the constitution of revolutionary France (see Figure 7).[91]

Fuller's *Son of Ethelwolf* was the first Alfredian novel to be written (just as the first Alfredian drama and epic poetry were produced in the eighteenth century). As such, it introduced many features which became common in nineteenth-century Alfredianism, and will therefore be referred to frequently as an early point of reference throughout the rest of this study. One such trait was the melodramatic images of bacchanalian, oath-swearing Vikings performing gory Odinic rites which added a touch of spice to the novel, having been previously popularised by (and probably appropriated from) Thomas Percy's 1770 translation of Mallet's *Northern Antiquities: Or A Description of the Manners, Customs, Religions and Laws of the Ancient Danes, and other Northern Nations*. Such images recurred throughout nineteenth-century

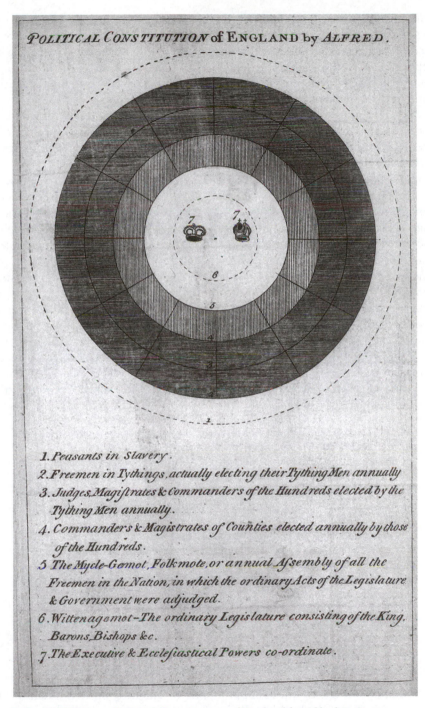

POLITICAL CONSTITUTION of ENGLAND by ALFRED.

1. Peasants in Slavery.
2. Freemen in Tythings, actually electing their Tything Men annually
3. Judges, Magistrates & Commanders of the Hundreds elected by the Tything Men annually.
4. Commanders & Magistrates of Counties elected annually by those of the Hundreds.
5 The Mycle-Gemot, Folkmote, or annual Assembly of all the Freemen in the Nation, in which the ordinary Acts of the Legislature & Government were adjudged.
6. Wittenagemot–The ordinary Legislature consisting of the King, Barons, Bishops &c.
7. The Executive & Ecclesiastical Powers co-ordinate.

7 David Williams, *Political Constitution of England by Alfred* (in *Lessons to a Young Prince*, 1790)

Alfredianism. Like an exemplary Gothic novel of its period, *The Son of Ethelwolf* also begins on a stormy night. Alfred was likewise given a Gothic setting in Ebenezer Rhodes's Alfredian play published the same year, which opens in 'A Gothic castle surrounded with oaks. At a distance the setting sun'.[92] Both texts prefigure the way in which Alfredianism was to interact with other genres in the nineteenth century.

At the opposite extreme from Rhodes's play, with its duels, draconian fathers and damsels in fear of dishonour, the eighteenth century also injected neo-classicism into Alfredianism. In Alexander Bicknell's play, *The Patriot King*, Alfred is 'Like Mars himself', and in Robert Holmes's 1778 *Alfred: An Ode*, the Saxon king's 'Chiefs of Science' (oblivious to the chill of a Wessex winter) wear 'Stoles of White' and play 'Lyres of Gold'.[93] Such allusions and images were intended to endow Alfred with greater dignity and prestige in an age when Graeco-Roman literature, language and society were widely accepted as cultural benchmarks. As the eighteenth century blossomed into the nineteenth, this tendency gradually fell from favour, as national pride increased and the Romantic movement engendered a renewed zeal for native heritage. While it remained dominant, however, neo-classicism was expressed in Alfredian literature, painting and statuary, and it became extinct not suddenly, but through a gradual attrition by which Alfred was first 'like Mars', then 'greater' than classical heroes, and finally just a great Saxon king.

There is some evidence to suggest that Alfred enjoyed currency on a popular level, as well as in courtly and political circles during the eighteenth century. This is the back-story to the West Country folk song 'Twankidillo', traditionally a blacksmith's song, as recorded by Sabine Baring-Gould:

> On 17 March when Alfred was King, he called together the Seven trades and declared his intention of making that tradesman king of all the trades who could get on best without the help of the others. Each was to bring a specimen of his work. The blacksmith brought a hammer and a horseshoe. The tailor brought a new coat, the baker his peel and a loaf, the shoemaker an awl. The carpenter his saw, the butcher his chopper, the mason his chisel. The tailor's coat was so fine that the king pronounced the tailor king of all trades. The blacksmith was very angry and went away and threw away his tools. Now the king wanted his horse shoeing and one trade after another ran short of tools. So all came to the forge on 23 November (St Clements Day) but no blacksmith was there. So they broke open the shop and each tried to do what he wanted – the king to shoe his horse, the baker to mend his peel, the butcher to sharpen his chopper, the mason to point his chisel. But the horse kicked, the fire would not burn and all began knocking each other about. Then in came St Clement with the blacksmith on his arm and the blacksmith shod the horse, pointed the chisel, mended the peel, sharpened the chopper, etc. Then the king made him prince and from that day this has been the blacksmith's song.[94]

Although not collected until 1883, the song was taken from an old fellow 'in deep decline', and the healths to 'King George' in its final verse also suggest an eighteenth-century origin.

Certainly, by the mid-eighteenth century, Alfred was sufficiently established as a popular native hero for the young Thomas Chatterton to consider invoking him in a letter to Horace Walpole, defending the authenticity of the Rowley papers (forgeries by Chatterton claiming to be the work of a fictitious fifteenth-century poet, Thomas Rowley). Chatterton's second draft of the letter, dated April 1769, proclaimed 'However Barbarous the Saxons may be calld [*sic*] by our Modern Virtuosos; it is certain, we are indebted to Alfred and other Saxon Kings for the wisest of our Laws and in part for the British Constitution'.[95] This version of the letter was never sent, but, a year earlier, Chatterton had imagined an Alfred who had long possessed patriotic appeal, when in composing the second version of the Rowley epic, *Battle of Hastings*, he had depicted a Saxon leader, Leofwine, addressing his troops before the Battle of Hastings, and commanding them to:

> Thinke of brave Ælfridus, yclept the grete,
> From porte to porte the red-haird Dane he chasd,
> The Danes, with whomme not lyoncels could mate,
> Who made of peopled reaulms a barren waste;
> Think how at once by you Norwegia bled
> Whilst dethe and victorie for magystrie bested.[96]

Thomas Chatterton also claimed Alfredian associations for his local area – Bristol. He identified Brislington, two miles south-east of Bristol centre, with the town where Alfred had defeated the Danish leader Haesten, and in his 1768 *Discorse on Brystowe* claimed that the walls and castle of Bristol itself had been constructed on the instructions of 'Edwarde Sonne of Alfrydus Magnus'.[97] In the same year, Chatterton also had the fictitious Rowley assert in a forged letter that when Edward's Chapel was built in Bristol, in 1203, there was discovered 'ynne a Ston Coffenne a Brassen Rynge onne the whyche was ycorvelled a Fygure for the Name of Alfredde sette wythe a Redde Ston whyche ynne darke nete dyd sheene'.[98]

Chatterton's claim doubtless drew upon the discovery near Oxford of the Alfred Jewel, seventy-five years earlier. It may also have helped fuel the various claims to have discovered Alfred's tomb, claims which began to be made during the late eighteenth century.[99] The first of these arose twenty years after the publication of the Rowley letter, in 1788, when the site of Hyde Abbey in Winchester was purchased by the county authorities for the construction of a gaol. At this time, three coffins were allegedly discovered, containing bones and the remains of garments. The discovery was clearly not immediately deemed significant, for news of it was not published until 1798, when Henry Howard – an officer stationed at Winchester, and an amateur antiquarian – determined to discover the whereabouts of Alfred's tomb. He interviewed a Mr Page, keeper of the new gaol, learned of the discovery during its construction, and triumphantly concluded that the graves must have been those of Alfred, Ealhswith and Edward. His discovery was published in *Archaeologia* later that year. While in Winchester, Howard also purchased a

stone inscribed 'Ælfred rex dccclxxxi', which the Catholic divine and antiquarian John Milner claimed to have found during the construction of the gaol
at Hyde Abbey. Its letter-forms could date from any period between the
twelfth and the eighteenth century, but certainly not from the ninth. Howard
took this relic home as a souvenir to Corby Castle, in Cumberland, imbuing
the family pile with a little displaced Alfredian glory.[100] It was in the eighteenth
century that pride in Alfred as a local hero was first expressed ostentatiously
(although, according to William of Malmesbury, even as early as the twelfth
century, the Winchester locals would point out locations with Alfredian associations to the passing traveller). Jubilees were seldom marked in the eighteenth century, so it is perhaps unsurprising that none of the nine-hundredth
Alfredian anniversaries were marked – neither his birth in 1749, nor his accession in 1771, nor his death in 1801. In 1762, however, the wealthy banker
Henry Hoare was inspired by the accession of George III (whom he viewed as
the first Hanoverian monarch to be truly British), and by Voltaire's account of
King Alfred, to erect a monument on Kingsettle Hill, part of his Wiltshire
estate, which was presumed to be the place where Alfred's West Saxon forces
had assembled before attacking the Danes in 878. Building began in 1769, and
by 1772 Hoare's estate was watched over by a 160-foot tower topped by a
ten-foot statue of Alfred. An inscription proclaimed: 'Alfred the Great AD 879
on this summit erected his standard against the Danish invaders. To him we
owe the origin of juries, the establishment of a militia, the creation of a naval
force. Alfred, the light of a benighted age, was a philosopher and a Christian;
the father of his people, the founder of the English monarchy and liberty'.[101]
Plans to erect a monument on the presumed site of the monastery that Alfred
erected on Athelney also began to be hatched, in 1798, by John Slade, pro-
prietor of Athelney and lord of the manor of North Petherton – although a
monument was not erected until 1801. And local pride was also expressed
during the eighteenth century in the designation of Alfredian associations to
a whole range of antiquities, including a roadside rock at Kingston Lisle in the
Vale of the White Horse, which sometime in the 1700s became known as 'King
Alfred's blowing stone', and a primitive tripod table at Burrowbridge in
Somerset, which around the same time gained the reputation of being the table
at which Alfred had sat to eat the burnt cakes.

Alfredian artwork

As well as beginning to flourish in the public and literary worlds by the end
of the eighteenth century, Alfred was also becoming an established subject
of fine art. Excluding the possibility that the stylised faces on ninth-century
coins and on the Alfred Jewel are those of the Saxon king, the earliest surviving images of Alfred occur in Matthew Paris's *Major Chronicle* (*c.* 1250),
where he is depicted as a curly-haired and bearded figure, wearing a crown,
and bearing a fleur-de-lys-topped sceptre and a banner declaring him first
sole ruler of England (see Figure 6).[102] From the date of this image, four cen-

8 Portrait of Alfred (commissioned by Thomas Walker, Master of University
College, Oxford, in 1661–62).

turies passed before an artist again attempted to portray King Alfred. In
1661, as part of the enthusiasm to promote an Alfredian origin for
University College, Oxford, Thomas Walker – Master of the college – commissioned a portrait of the Saxon king (see Figure 8). In this distinctive representation, Alfred has a beard, furrowed brow and grave eyes. Indeed, the
image's downcast gaze and restoration date have led Simon Keynes to
suggest recently that it might in fact be 'a projection back into the distant
past of the popular image of the late King Charles I'.[103]

Whether this is true or not, the picture proved to be the origin of much Alfredian iconography in both the eighteenth and nineteenth centuries. It was engraved for the 1678 Latin edition of Spelman's *Life*, and was also engraved by George Vertue, in 1722, as the frontispiece to Francis Wise's edition of Asser (see Figure 9). In Vertue's engraving, however, although Alfred's brow remains lined, the king is not weighed down by the burden of his responsibilities – he looks up and ahead, and his mouth is firmly set, triumphant over difficulty. The portrait is also accompanied by a set of symbolic accessories – a bow and arrows, harp, captured raven standard, books, compasses and a scroll, and it is framed by miniature tableaux of his foray into the Danish camp, the launch of his new fleet of ships, and a battle – presumably his 878 victory at Edington. This version of the University College portrait was also used for the 1732 folio edition of Rapin's *History of England*. Thereafter, its firm, bearded visage became the dominant image of Alfred in the eighteenth century, while its tableau anticipated, and fed into the development of, Alfredian historical painting.

Historical painting – the depiction of significant or dramatic scenes from the past, as opposed to merely portraiture of historical kings – first became popular in Britain in the mid-eighteenth century, and flourished until the middle of the nineteenth.[104] Its development seems to have been encouraged by the formation of professional bodies for artists – the Society of Arts (later the Royal Society of Arts) was established in 1753; the Society of Artists of Great Britain (later the Incorporated Society of Artists) was formed in 1760; the Free Society of Artists (an offshoot of the Society of Arts) was launched in 1761; and the Royal Academy splintered from the Incorporated Society of Artists in 1768. Sponsoring regular exhibitions, such organisations provided artists with the opportunity to exhibit their work to the general public and thus encouraged the depiction of subjects of 'national' rather than personal interest. Furthermore, many of the exhibitions were also competitions and, once the public taste for historical painting had become apparent, prizes were sometimes offered specifically for scenes from British history.

Alfred's debut in these exhibitions was made in 1764, when Mason Chamberlin the Elder exhibited his *King Alfred in a Cottage; Large as Life*. Chamberlin's strapping, bare-footed Alfred sits before the neatherd's fire, holding his bow and staring meditatively into the middle-distance with the far-sighted eyes of the Vertue engraving – transcending his immediate and humble surroundings in which a shrewish wife points angrily to the charred remains of a loaf while her husband leers foolishly on, watched by his dog. At the king's feet lie arrows and a sword, and also – adding a surprisingly scholarly touch – a quire of the King's handbook into which, Asser tells us, he copied passages of holy scripture.

Chamberlin's subject of Alfred in the neatherd's cottage was to prove one of the most enduringly popular Alfredian themes for historical painters during both the eighteenth and the early nineteenth centuries, and his composition of the scene was little altered in future incarnations – the paintings

9 George Vertue, *Portrait of King Alfred the Great* (made and engraved for the 1732 folio edition of Rapin's *History of England*)

10 David Wilkie, *Alfred Reprimanded by the Neatherd's Wife* (1806, from an engraving published in 1828)

of Alfred burning the cakes produced by Edward Edwards in 1776, Francis Wheatley in 1792, David Wilkie in 1806, and Richard Morton Paye the following year all share a pointing, head-scarfed wife looking decidedly vexed; a skulking pet; and a ruined loaf; and depict Alfred as a calm, bearded figure holding a bow (see, for instance, Wilkie's image in Figure 10).

Part of the reason for the enduring influence of Chamberlin's image undoubtedly lies in the fact that the picture was engraved and disseminated for popular consumption as a furniture print, suitable for framing and hanging on living-room walls. This is also true of another Alfredian painting that appeared in the early years of the exhibitions – Benjamin West's 1779 *Alfred the Great dividing his Loaf with a Pilgrim*, in which Alfred offers food to the disguised Cuthbert.[105] With the breaking of bread as its subject, compounded by Alfred's now traditionally hirsute appearance, it should maybe come as little surprise that West chose to invest the image with a strikingly Christ-like appearance, which may well have influenced some nineteenth-century works. West, an American who seven years earlier had begun calling himself 'Historical Painter to the King', was a favourite of George III, and his painting's possible relationship to the naming of the monarch's ninth son, born the following year, as 'Prince Alfred' is also enticing. At any rate, the coincidence of names may have won West the commission, four years later, to paint the boy in heaven after his premature death.

West's work was begun in 1778, so, given that the episode allegedly took place in 878, it might be concluded that the painting represents one of the earliest examples of Alfrediana inspired by the muse of historical commemoration.[106] However, it might equally have been inspired by the publication a year earlier of Alexander Bicknell's *Life of Alfred the Great*. Certainly, in the eighteenth century, fascinating intertextualities seem to have existed between written and illustrative Alfrediana, and these continued through to the nineteenth century. Rapin's identification of the Earl of Devon's capture of the raven standard as the seminal turning point in Alfred's fortunes in 878 (and his fabrication of a scene in which the king received the inspiring news of this victory) inspired both Nicholas Blakey (in 1750) and Samuel Wale (in 1770) to paint the fictitious scene. When Wale's painting was engraved in 1771 for Montague's *New and Universal History of England*, the capture of the raven banner was misattributed to Alfred himself. The mistake was rectified two years later, when the picture was re-engraved, but not, it seems, before it had inspired John Home to credit Alfred with the capture in his *Alfred: A Tragedy*.[107]

Illustrative histories like Montague's *New and Universal History of England* provided one of the most important markets for historical painters in the mid-eighteenth century, and also an influential means by which the public became accustomed to the idea of 'seeing' the past.[108] One of the first was the sixth edition of Lockman's *History of England*. Published in 1747, it was squarely aimed at the bottom end of the market, but was illustrated by a set of thirty drawings, including 'Pope Adrian the IId crowns King Alfred at Rome'. Many more illustrated histories appeared in the 1760s and 1770s, and a sense of Alfred's growing importance through the eighteenth century may be gained by observing his prominence in these. Mortimer's *New History of England* (1764–66), for instance, contained 'Alfred makes a Collection of Laws, and divides the kingdom into counties', which appeared again in Montague's 1771 *New and Universal History of England* (along with the taking of the Danish Standard), and a third time in Sydney's 1773 *New and Complete History of England*, as one of three Alfredian subjects (the other two being the Danish standard, and 'Alfred, disguised in the character of a harper, viewing the Danish camp').

All three of these illustrations were the work of Samuel Wale, one of the most productive and highly regarded illustrators of history in the eighteenth century, and thus inevitably also one of the most prolific painters of Alfred. More work remains to be done on the question of Wale's relationship with the authors and publisher of these histories: it is not yet clear whether the choice of illustrations was his own, determined by the text, or prescribed by the subscribers or publisher. However, the images certainly seem to have helped determine what would become the most iconic and oft-revisited Alfredian tableau in both the eighteenth and the nineteenth century. Alfred disguised as a harper in the Danish camp was attempted by Edward Edwards in the late eighteenth century; as well as by Thomas Stothard (whose 1802 Alfred plays before a remarkably swarthy Guthrum, with turban-wearing attendants); and by Robert Smirke, for Camden's *Imperial History of England*, in 1810.[109]

Wale's image of Alfred with a heavy tome of laws to hand was revisited on a grand scale in 1774, as part of a set of enormous murals made by James Barry for the Great Room at the Adelphi – the new Strand premises of the Society of Arts. The six paintings that made up the set were intended to illustrate 'The Progress of Human Culture', and an accompanying book explained the significance and symbolism of each. The last of the set was entitled *Elizium, or the State of Final Retribution* and depicted a gathering in Elysium of 128 worthies regarded by the artist as representative of the 'cultivators and benefactors of mankind'. In the centre of the composition, indicating both his general stature by this time and his significance in the world of historical art, was Alfred – as Barry's book explained, 'the deliverer of his country, the founder of its navy, its laws, juries, arts and letters, with his Dom book in one hand . . . leaning on the shoulder of that greatest and best of lawgivers, William Penn'.[110]

The young Alfred in Rome, one of Wale's earliest compositions, was visited again in 1792 by Richard Westall. Westall's *Prince Alfred before Pope Leo III*, showing the anointing of Alfred as a curly-haired boy, was engraved and published for Robert Bowyer's *Complete History of England* – the most ambitious of eighteenth-century projects to illustrate English history. Bowyer had commissioned a number of distinguished artists to produce paintings illustrative of seminal passages in David Hume's *The History of England*, for a new edition of that work. The lavish finished product, which was sold by subscription, boasted that it was 'the most superb publication, without exception, in Europe', and comprised enough illustrations to fill one of six volumes. Ten pictures dealt with the Anglo-Saxon period, and of these three were scenes from Alfred's life – plus a portrait of him, for good measure, based upon the 'original picture in the University College at Oxford', placed above a vignette showing the king supervising the building of the university.[111] The other Alfredian works were a version of *Alfred in the House of the Neatherd* by Francis Wheatley, and Henry Singleton's rather original *Alfred liberating the family of Hastings* (an Anglicisation of the Danish 'Haesten'). The prominence afforded to Alfred suggests the position that he held in the national consciousness by the end of the eighteenth century, while the choice of tableaux provides some idea of which aspects of his character were then central to enthusiasm for the Saxon king: his magnanimity and humanity, support of scholarship, triumph over adversity, and the notion that his reign was ordained by God.

Westall's choice of subject also suggests a sentimental interest in the early and domestic details of Alfred's biography. This note was struck again in his 1799 painting *Queen Judith reciting to Alfred the Great, when a child, the songs of the bards* – an intimate and fictional scene in which Alfred, as a young boy with nut-brown hair and rosy cheeks, kneels rapt at the feet of his stepmother, as she tells him tales about his ancestors (see Figure 11). The painting's themes of the beneficial influence of motherhood, and Alfred's thirst for knowledge, appealed strongly to nineteenth-century Alfredianists –

11 Richard Westall, *Queen Judith Reciting to Alfred the Great, when a Child, the Songs of the Bards* (1799)

both writers and artists. In 1801, the Poet Laureate Henry James Pye added a note to his description of Alfred's childhood, asserting that the future king 'first caught the spirit of poetry and heroism from hearing his stepmother recite poems on the heroic actions of his ancestors. There is an excellent picture on the subject by Westall'.[112] Westall's composition almost certainly influenced the 1844 painting by Philip Salter – *Queen Judith and the children of Ethelwulph* – and probably also Alfred Stevens's 1848 painting *King*

Alfred and his Mother. And, in 1859, Sarah Stickney Ellis devoted an entire chapter of her conduct manual, *The Mothers of Great Men*, to Westall's image of the nurturing stepmother Judith.

Westall's images of the young Alfred, then, may be taken as representative of the way in which, as the eighteenth century gave way to the nineteenth, Alfred grew from a political legend to a romantic and personal ideal. 'Alfred the legislator', 'Alfred the champion of liberty' and 'Alfred the responsible monarch' were to reappear and develop in the nineteenth century as time, place and politics demanded. But alongside these figures would also emerge as iconic images 'Alfred the exemplary child', 'Alfred the benevolent husband and father', and 'Alfred the self-made man'. Both of these twin and complementary strands of Victorian Alfredianism will be the subject of the next three chapters.

Notes

1 *The Times* (21 Sep. 1901), p. 10.
2 *The Anglo-Saxon Chronicles*, p. xviii.
3 See, for instance, Plummer, *The Life and Times of Alfred the Great*, p. 11. Plummer argued not only that Alfred had commissioned the *Chronicle*, but that he had personally dictated much of its content to his scribes.
4 *The Anglo-Saxon Chronicles*, pp. 64–93.
5 Keynes and Lapidge, *Alfred the Great*, p. 41.
6 Yorke, 'The Most Perfect Man in History?', p. 9.
7 A tripartite division identified in Keynes and Lapidge, *Alfred the Great*, p. 57.
8 Cited in Smyth, *The Medieval Life of King Alfred the Great*, p. 58.
9 Freeman, *Old English History*, p. 103. Mild doubts are also voiced in Plummer, *The Life and Times of Alfred the Great*, p. 16.
10 Hughes, *Alfred the Great*, p. 34.
11 Keynes and Lapidge, *Alfred the Great*, pp. 66–110.
12 For instance, in Spelman's *Life of King Alfred*, and Rapin's *History of England*.
13 Smyth, *The Medieval Life of King Alfred the Great*, p. 85.
14 Keynes, 'The Cult of King Alfred the Great', p. 240.
15 Smyth, *The Medieval Life of King Alfred the Great*, p. 86.
16 Smyth, *The Medieval Life of King Alfred the Great*, pp. 86–87.
17 It also relates that Neot appeared to Alfred in a dream, during his three months in hiding, promising him victory – but this was not included in the *Annals of St Neots*.
18 See Keynes and Lapidge, *Alfred the Great*, p. 199, for a translation. For the Latin text and an English paraphrase of the *Life of Saint Neot*, see *The Annals of St Neots with Vita Prima Sancti Neoti*, pp. 112–142, lxxv–lxxvii. All future references will be to these editions. For a full discussion of the variants in the story, see Chapter Four of this volume.
19 Plummer, *The Life and Times of Alfred the Great*, p. 22. See Turner, *The History of the Anglo-Saxons*, p. 331.
20 See Plummer, *The Life and Times of Alfred the Great*, p. 24; Draper, *Alfred the Great: A Sketch and Seven Studies*, p. 133.
21 Pauli, *The Life of Alfred the Great*, p. 4.
22 Keynes 'The Cult of King Alfred the Great', p. 245.

23 Smyth, *The Medieval Life of King Alfred the Great*, p. 88.

24 This account is printed in Latin and paraphrased in English in *The Annals of St Neots*, pp. 127–128, lxxvi–lxxvii. The *Life*'s story is reiterated in Roger of Wendover's thirteenth-century *Flowers of History*, p. 211, with the exception that Neot is still alive when he advises Alfred on Athelney.

25 See, for instance, Stewart, *Stories about Alfred the Great*, p. 38. (Stewart was clearly interested in questions of religion: her other works include *Stories of the Seven Virtues* (1848); *Life in the Cloister* (1865); and *The Seven Lights of the Sanctuary: Or, Tales Explanatory of the Holy Sacraments* (1851).)

26 Whitaker, *The Life of Saint Neot*, p. 269.

27 Whitaker, *The Life of Saint Neot*, p. 262. This rational, scientific view of the Neot vision was perhaps influenced by the work of early psychologists like Franz Mesmer (1734–1815).

28 See Smith, the editor of Leland, *The Itinerary of John Leland*, p. 118; Speed, *The History of Great Britaine*, p. 368; Spelman, *The Life of Alfred the Great*, p. 56; Rapin, *The History of England*, p. 104.

29 According to Whitaker, a window in the church of St Neot depicts Neot renouncing the world, beneath an inscription which states, 'Here he delivered his crown to his younger brother'. For Whitaker, this proved Neot's identity with Æthelstan (see Whitaker, *The Life of Saint Neot*, p. 73).

30 These were all published, for instance, in Giles (ed.), *The Whole Works of King Alfred the Great*.

31 See Keynes and Lapidge, *Alfred the Great*, pp. 124–126 for a translation of Pope Gregory's *Pastoral Care*; pp. 127–130 for Boethius's *Consolations of Philosophy*; pp. 138–152 for Augustine's *Soliloquies*; pp. 163–170 for the 'Laws of King Alfred'; and pp. 171–181 for 'The Treaty between Alfred and Guthrum'. All future references will be to this edition.

32 Simeon's *History of Saint Cuthbert* was published in 1732. This edition was reprinted twice during the nineteenth century. Simeon's text was also translated into English in Stevenson, *The Church Historians of England*.

33 William of Malmesbury, *History of the Kings of England*, p. 9. *The History of the Kings of England* was available in print from 1596.

34 William of Malmesbury, *History of the Kings of England*, p. 104.

35 Pauli, *The Life of Alfred the Great* (1857), p. 142.

36 See Anon. [maybe Alfred himself], 'The Treaty Between Alfred and Guthrum', pp. 167, 171.

37 William of Malmesbury, *The History of the Kings of England*, p. 106.

38 William of Malmesbury, *The History of the Kings of England*, p. 101.

39 See, for instance, Draper, *Alfred the Great*, p. 129; Hughes, *Alfred the Great*, p. 275; and Kelsey, *Alfred of Wessex*, I, p. liii.

40 *The Book of Hyde*, p. 509; *The History of Ingulf*, p. 603. On the Ingulf hoax, see Keynes, 'The Cult of King Alfred the Great', p. 242.

41 William of Malmesbury, *The History of the Kings of England*, pp. 101, 114.

42 *The History of Ingulf*, p. 605. The notion about shires could have developed from Henry of Huntingdon's *English History*, which claims that it was the kings of Wessex who first divided England into shires (see Keynes, 'The Cult of King Alfred the Great', p. 232).

43 Higden, *The Polychronicon*, p. 373 [spelling and syntax modernised by the present author].

44 Higden, *The Polychronicon*, p. 355 [spelling and syntax modernised by the present author].

45 In about 1380, the Fellows of University College used the claim in an appeal for help to Richard II (see Keynes, 'The Cult of King Alfred the Great', p. 236).

46 Higden's story was elaborated by the anonymous author of the early fifteenth-century *Book of Hyde* (p. 507); and by John Rous in his late fifteenth-century *History of the English Kings* (see Miles, *King Alfred in Literature*, p. 36).

47 *The Book of Hyde*, p. 507.

48 See Camden, *Britannia*, p. 272. Keynes ('The Cult of King Alfred the Great', p. 245) claims that Camden inserted the passage 'in good faith'. Joseph Stevenson and J.A. Giles, for instance, followed Camden in including the passage in their editions of Asser.

49 *ODNB*.

50 Spelman, *The Life of Alfred the Great*, p. 156.

51 Spelman, *Certain Considerations*, p. 18.

52 *The Will of King Alfred*, in Keynes and Lapidge, *Alfred the Great*, pp. 174–175. All future references will be to this edition.

53 *The Mirror of Justices*, p. 8.

54 Spelman, *The Life of Alfred the Great*, p. 157.

55 Spelman, *The Life of Alfred the Great*, p. 171. It must be noted, however, that Spelman's text was not published until after his death and was edited first by Obadiah Walker, and then by Thomas Hearne. Both were Oxford men and each added notes to the text, defending Camden's claims about Oxford (see Keynes, 'The Cult of King Alfred the Great', pp. 268–269).

56 Pope Gregory, *Pastoral Care*, p. 126.

57 Spelman, *The Life of Alfred the Great*, p. 143.

58 'The Treaty Between Alfred and Guthrum', p. 171.

59 Spelman, *The Life of Alfred the Great*, p. 106.

60 Keynes, 'The Cult of King Alfred the Great', p. 249.

61 Spelman, *The Life of Alfred the Great*, pp. 58, 150.

62 Spelman, *The Life of Alfred the Great*, p. 152.

63 Spelman, *The Life of Alfred the Great*, p. 92.

64 On Spelman, see *ODNB*.

65 Simmons, *Reversing the Conquest*, p. 40.

66 Although the anonymous 1578 popular ballad, 'The Shepherd and the King, and of Gillian the Shepherd's Wife, with her Churlish Answers: Being Full of Mirth and Merry Pastime', enticingly suggests that an oral Alfredian mythology could have survived on a popular level from the Middle Ages (*The Roxburgh Ballads*, I: ii, p. 504).

67 Keynes, 'The Cult of King Alfred the Great', p. 273.

68 Rapin, *The History of England*, p. 114.

69 Bicknell, *The Life of Alfred the Great*, p. iii.

70 MacDougall, *Racial Myth*, pp. 25–26.

71 Blackmore, *Alfred: An Epick Poem*, pp. 289–290.

72 Simmons, *Reversing the Conquest*, p. 27.

73 Blackmore, *Alfred: An Epick Poem*, p. 292.

74 Sambrook, *The Eighteenth Century*, pp. 85–88.

75 Bolingbroke, *Letters on the Spirit of Patriotism*, pp. 190–191.

76 Keynes, 'The Cult of King Alfred the Great', p. 280; Sambrook, *The Eighteenth Century*, p. 88.
77 Keynes, 'The Cult of King Alfred the Great', p. 277.
78 Holmes, *Alfred: An Ode* (1778); Bicknell, *The Patriot King* (1788).
79 Mallet and Thomson, *Alfred: A Masque*, pp. 13, 19.
80 Fuller, *The Son of Ethelwolf*, p. 193; Home, *Alfred: A Tragedy*, p. 14; Mallet and Thomson, *Alfred: A Masque*, p. 25.
81 Home, *Alfred: A Tragedy*, pp. vii, ix.
82 Mallet and Thomson, *Alfred: A Masque*, p. 42.
83 Lonsdale, *Sketch of Alfred the Great*, p. 7, ends with the celebratory line, 'Britannia rules the waves!'.
84 Kidd, *Subverting Scotland's Past*, pp. 209–210.
85 Keynes, 'The Cult of King Alfred the Great', p. 321.
86 *Alfred the Great: Deliverer of his Country*, p. 69.
87 Hume, *The History of England*, pp. 65–66; Hulme, *An Historical Essay on the English Constitution*, pp. 22–33; Cartwright, *Legislative Rights of the Commonality Vindicated*, p. 159.
88 Keynes, 'The Cult of King Alfred the Great', p. 286.
89 Penn, *The Battle of Eddington*, pp. 104, 39.
90 Fuller, *The Son of Ethelwolf*, p. 25.
91 Williams, *Lessons to a Young Prince*, p. 42.
92 Rhodes, *Alfred: An Historical Tragedy*, p. 9.
93 Holmes, *Alfred: An Ode*, p. 5; Bicknell, *The Patriot King*, p. 8.
94 Baring-Gould, *Folk Songs of the West Country*, p. 101.
95 Chatterton, *The Complete Works*, p. 273.
96 Chatterton, *The Complete Works*, p. 72.
97 Chatterton, *The Complete Works*, pp. 882, 102.
98 Chatterton, *The Complete Works*, p. 141.
99 On nineteenth-century claims to have discovered Alfred's tomb see Chapter One of this volume.
100 Keynes, 'The Cult of King Alfred the Great', pp. 325–326; Yorke, *The King Alfred Millenary in Winchester*, p. 4.
101 Keynes, 'The Cult of King Alfred the Great', p. 322.
102 Matthew Paris's *Major Chronicle* (*c.* 1250), figure 6.
103 Keynes, 'The Cult of King Alfred the Great', p. 262.
104 Roy Strong, *And When Did You Last See Your Father?*, p. 13.
105 William Hamilton revisited this subject in 1783.
106 See, for instance, Keynes, 'The Cult of King Alfred the Great', p. 301.
107 See Home, *Alfred: A Tragedy*, p. 4.
108 Strong, *And When Did You Last See Your Father?*, p. 20.
109 Edwards's picture no longer seems to exist, but is mentioned in a sale-catalogue of his house contents in 1807.
110 Keynes, 'The Cult of King Alfred the Great', pp. 301–302.
111 Keynes, 'The Cult of King Alfred the Great', pp. 315–316.
112 Pye, *Alfred: An Epic Poem*, p. 132.

4

The hero as king: Alfred and nineteenth-century politics

Addressing the crowds gathered in Winchester for the unveiling of the Alfred statue, Lord Roseberry announced that 'a thousand years ago there died in this city one who by common consent represents the highest type of kingship'. Alfred was, he said, 'a king, a true king, the guide, the leader, the father of his people'. And in his record of the Winchester Millenary, published the following year, Alfred Bowker also hailed King Alfred as a paradigm of the monarchy, enthusing 'When we commemorate the great Saxon king, benefactor of our race, we feel brought home to us the possibilities of kingship'.[1]

Types of kings, roles of kings, responsibilities of kings – the nineteenth century saw remarkable levels of doubt and debate about the future sovereignty of Britain. There had, of course, been opposition to George I and George II in the eighteenth century. But that was largely expressed as hostility to individual, unpopular monarchs. The shock of the French Revolution in 1789, however, not only intensified the critical scrutiny of Britain's sovereigns, but cast doubt on the continuance of the very institution of the monarchy itself. This was by no means a short-lived anxiety: as late as 1873, H.H.M. Herbert could write of the 1789 Revolution as a drama which continued to excite 'intense' British interest.[2] And the concern which it engendered was also refreshed during the nineteenth century by a series of further political events in Europe: revolutions in 1830, the establishment of further republics in 1848, and the defeat of Napoleon III in 1871.[3] Throughout the nineteenth century, events in Britain also encouraged discussion about the role and future of the monarchy. The continuing presence of a Germanic royal family continued to cause some resentment, while the coronation of Victoria – a young girl – gave rise to fears that the country would be weakly governed, and then (after she had married a German husband) to fresh anxieties about foreign interests behind the British throne. This subsided with Albert's premature death in 1861, but was quickly replaced by criticism of Victoria's protracted period of reclusive mourning.[4]

As the future of the monarchy began to seem less certain, the possible ways in which it might evolve in order to survive were investigated, and the positive qualities which kingship alone could offer were identified and advocated by those in favour of retaining the institution in some form – whether they were neo-feudalist, simply Royalist, or a self-styled 'republican conservative' in search of a compromise between republicanism and absolute monarchy. The most influential of the latter was Thomas Carlyle. On 22 May 1840, Carlyle gave a lecture entitled 'The Hero as King' (later to form part of his book, *On Heroes and Hero Worship and the Heroic in History*) in which he argued for the necessity of a strong, worthy monarchy to heal 'a sick world'.[5] Dismissing the French Revolution as 'the product of entire sceptical blindness', he asserted:

> This is the history of all rebellions, French Revolutions, social explosions in ancient or modern times. You have put the too Unable Man at the head of affairs! The too ignoble, unvaliant, fatuous man!' . . . We have had so many forgeries, we will now trust nothing, so many base plated coins passing in the market, the belief has now become common that no gold any longer exists – and even that we can do very well without gold![6]

For Carlyle, the 'true gold' king should be 'the ablest man' in a country – also 'the truest-hearted, justest, the Noblest Man: what he tells us to do must be precisely the wisest, fittest, that we could anywhere or anyhow learn'. Such a king should be a 'commander over men', a 'governor and captain'; forever inspiring 'brotherly love' in those around him; his chief virtues 'courage and the faculty to do'. Only a king like this could resist the contemporary threat of political revolution. And he also, Carlyle added, needed to be a 'great silent man . . . silently thinking, silently working' – a figure who could fulfil the roles of priest and teacher.[7]

Carlyle's vision of the hero king who would put an end to the threat of republicanism was influential upon several major Victorian thinkers. And many of those who built upon his thesis looked to the British past for examples of heroic kingship which might be held up as models for the future. Alfred became, perhaps, the historical king most commonly appealed to – equalled only by the legendary figure of Arthur. It is acknowledged that the contribution of Tennyson's Arthurian epic, *Idylls of the King*, to the preservation of the monarchy in nineteenth-century Britain was significant, and it has been similarly argued that Sir Walter Scott's 'services, direct and indirect, towards repressing the revolutionary propensities of his age were vast'.[8] But it is equally true that the cult of Alfred may have contributed to the survival of constitutional monarchy in Victorian Britain. Alfredian texts, then, can provide valuable insights into nineteenth-century Britain's anxieties about constitutional change; its values and priorities in relation to sovereigns; and the strategies that were used in the effort to retain a monarchy.

Carlyle's sustained importance to the Victorian cult of Alfred is perhaps best demonstrated by his direct and pervasive influence upon a writer working many years after him – Thomas Hughes. Hughes's 1869 biography of Alfred, as discussed in an earlier chapter, became one of the most important nineteenth-century texts in promoting the cult of Alfred in the popular sphere. *Alfred the Great* begins by explicitly positioning itself in relation to

Carlyle. The book's first chapter, entitled 'Of Kings and Kingship' quotes at length from 'The Hero as King':

> We come now to the last type of heroism, that which we call Kingship, the Commander over men, he to whose will our wills are to be subordinated, and loyally surrender themselves and find their welfare in doing so, may be reckoned the most important of great men. In all sections of English life the God-made king is needed, pressingly demanded in most, in some cannot longer without peril as of conflagration be dispensed with.

Calling Carlyle a 'teacher, prophet, seer', and crediting him with having 'in many ways moved more deeply than any other the hearts of this generation', Hughes demanded:

> Has not the conscience of England responded to these words? Have not most of us felt that in some shape . . . what Mr Carlyle calls 'kingship' is, in fact, our great need; that without it our modern life . . . is a poor and mean thing, ever getting poorer and meaner. Yes, this cry, to which Mr Carlyle first gave voice in our day, has been going up from all sections of English society these many years, in sad, fierce, or plaintive accents.[9]

Like Carlyle, Hughes was alarmed by and responded to the revolutions in continental Europe – in his case, specifically, the events of 1848. 'Twenty years ago', he wrote, 'the framework of society went all to pieces over the greater part of Christendom, and the kings just ran away or abdicated, and the people, left pretty much to themselves, in some places made blind work of it. Solvent and well-regulated society caught a glimpse of that same "big black democracy", the monster, the Frankenstein'. A second edition of the book was published in 1874, three years after the defeat of Napoleon III and the founding of the third French Republic. Its new preface discussed these recent events, stating that they had 'forced on those who think on such subjects at all, the practical need of examining once more the principles upon which society, and the life of nations, rest'. Louis Napoleon, it continued, had demonstrated the worthlessness of 'government by the majority' as a solution to social ills – the political situation in France now resembled 'the hurly-burly of driving cloud and heaving sea, in which as yet no trace of firm land is visible'.[10] Hughes believed that the progress of 'big black democracy' in Britain too was inevitable – a view perhaps strengthened by the passing of the 1867 Reform Act which, by giving the vote to large numbers of working-class men, significantly increased Tory anxieties about the possibility of a British revolution.[11] He was convinced, however, that a monarch who had true sympathy with the masses, who was both their representative and the ablest one among them, might not be incompatible with this. Such qualities he averred were 'gathered up in him whose life we must now try to follow: "England's herdsman", "England's darling", "England's comfort" as he is styled by the old chroniclers' – Alfred. King Alfred, he believed, fitted all the criteria of 'Mr. Carlyle's test' for a hero king. So Hughes's decision to write a biography of Alfred was an explicitly political action. 'This life of the typical English king is here offered, not to historical students, but to ordinary English readers', he stated in the preface to the 1874 edition:

> The writer . . . as a politician, both in and out of the House of Commons . . . has had to examine himself for many years the actual ground upon which the political life of the English nation stands, that he might solve for his own individual guidance, according to the best light he could get, the most practical of all questions for a public man – what leader should he support? . . . He has learnt to look upon the Saxon king as the true representative of the nation.[12]

Alfred's predecessors

Hughes believed that the kings of the West Saxons were always 'the first man in fight, in council, in worship, in the chase' – a model of ideal kingship which he contrasted with the execrable figure of Burhred, the 'titular king of the Mercians', who 'made belief to rule', but when the Danes invaded his country he determined to 'get away as swiftly as possible, as many so-called kings have done before him and since'.[13] More often, however, nineteenth-century writers used Alfred's West Saxon predecessors as foils for his own perfect kingship – specifically his elder brother Æthelred and his father Æthelwulf.

In the *Anglo-Saxon Chronicle*, Alfred's father is presented as a brave, active and successful warrior: his major battles against the Danes at Carrum and at Aclea are noted, and we are informed that in the latter conflict he 'made the greatest slaughter of a heathen raiding-army that we have ever heard tell of up to this present day'.[14] Likewise, both the *Chronicle* and Asser relate that in 853:

> Burgred, king of the Mercians, sent messengers to Æthelwulf, king of the West Saxons, asking him for help, so that he could subject to his authority the inland Welsh. . . . As soon as King Æthelwulf had received his embassy, he assembled an army and went with King Burgred to Wales, where immediately on entry he devastated that race and reduced it to Burgred's authority[15]

This positive image of Æthelwulf was incorporated into the edition of Camden's *Britannia* published in 1695, and was subsequently adopted by most eighteenth-century Alfredian authors.[16] In striking contrast, however, in many nineteenth-century texts, Æthelwulf is a cowardly figure. The historian Reinhold Pauli, in his 1857 *Life of Alfred the Great*, for instance, described him as 'little equal to the difficult task of protecting a flourishing country', and both he and the novelist G.A. Henty dubbed him 'the weak prince'. Worse still, Gordon Stables, in his 1898 novel *'Twixt Daydawn and Light*, damningly asserted:

> Ethelwulf himself seldom commanded an army corps in person. He thought it far safer to command by proxy, while he himself sat nursing a bunion in front of a roaring fire. . . . I do not look upon King Ethelwulf as a man the English can possibly be proud of.[17]

The concern here that monarchs should be martial leaders can be related to Carlyle's dictum that a king should be 'a Hero, a true Governor and Captain'.[18] And it is also worth bearing in mind that Stables was a vehemently militaristic writer who had probably sympathised with the criticism that had been voiced more than once during Victoria's reign about her seeming reticence to engage in war. So such dramatic juxtaposition of Alfred and Æthelwulf as militaristic and pacifistic leaders can be read as a nostalgic desire for Britain's next monarch – Edward VII – to revive a militaristic model of kingship.

The switch of emphasis in Stable's depiction of Æthelwulf is so dramatic, however, that it is also worth tracing whence it was derived, in order to better understand its relationship to nineteenth-century concerns about the monarchy. It is possible that a passage in Asser may have contributed to Æthelwulf's Victorian image. This relates how in 855, when Alfred's elder brother Æthelbald attempted to seize Æthelwulf's kingdom while the latter was on his way back from Rome, 'in order that . . . civil strife . . . might not become more horrible and cruel as each day passed, the previously united kingdom was divided between father and son through the indescribable forbearance of the father'.[19] The passage clearly approves of Æthelwulf's 'indescribable forbearance' in submitting to his son, and in fact it goes on to describe the king's course of action as demonstrative of his 'wise counsel'.[20] In the nineteenth century, however, so much cultural investment was made in promoting the union of Great Britain that having divided a previously united kingdom would almost inevitably have detracted from a monarch's reputation. Indeed, it is interesting to note that in J.A. Giles's 1878 translation of Asser, Æthelwulf's 'wise counsel' was ambiguously translated as 'unspeakable clemency'.[21]

The fact that Æthelwulf's kingdom was divided as the consequence of a trip to Rome might also have detracted from his image in the nineteenth century, since it was at this time that Richard I began to be explicitly criticised as an absent monarch who had gone on crusade at the expense of his own kingdom's welfare.[22] But it seems to have been the more general issue of Æthelwulf's religious faith which ultimately led to his re-imaging in the nineteenth century. The *Anglo-Saxon Chronicle* relates that Alfred's father remained in Rome for twelve months in 855, and that in that year he also 'conveyed by charter the tenth part of his land throughout all his kingdom to the praise of God and his own eternal salvation'.[23] Asser's *Life* adds that 'From the first flower of his youth he was keen to care for [his soul] in all respects'.[24] It was probably a late medieval text, however, which determined Æthelwulf's fate as anti-hero in the nineteenth century – Roger of Hoveden's twelfth-century *Annalium Pars Prior*, in which it is claimed that the young Æthelwulf became Bishop of Winchester, 'But on the death of his father, Egbert, *being compelled by necessity*, he was made king'.[25] A reluctant king was the antithesis of Carlylean notions of the hero; an ordained monarch did not sit well with the anti-monasticism dominant in nineteenth-century

British culture; and such an explicitly Roman Catholic sovereign could only be an embarrassment after the 1701 Act of Settlement had dictated that that religion should make any individual 'forever incapable to inherit, possess, or enjoy the crown and government' of England.[26] By 1777, therefore, Alexander Bicknell was to claim that Æthelwulf made a poor king because he had contracted 'an habitual propensity to indolence and inactivity during his confinement in the cloister'.[27] And, as late as 1900, such negative images of the king were still current, with the children's novelist Eva March Tappan condemning Æthelwulf for having taken money, 'much needed in his own kingdom', and wasted it in Rome.[28]

The influence of the church upon rulers is a concern that emerges clearly from nineteenth-century Alfredian texts. In particular, one event in Alfred's life was used to investigate this anxiety – the Battle of Ashdown, at which he fought as regent beside his brother King Æthelred. In his *Life of King Alfred*, Asser writes of this conflict:

> Alfred and his men reached the battlefield sooner and in better order: for his brother, King Æthelred, was still in his tent at prayer, hearing Mass and declaring firmly that he would not leave that place alive before the priest had finished Mass, and that he would not forsake divine service for that of men; and he did what he said. The faith of the Christian king counted for much with the Lord, as shall be shown more clearly in what follows. . . . since the king was still lingering in prayer, and the Vikings were ready and had reached the battlefield more quickly, Alfred (then heir apparent) could not oppose the enemy battle-lines any longer without either retreating from the battlefield or attacking the enemy forces before his brother's arrival on the scene. He finally deployed the Christian forces against the hostile armies . . . (even though the king had not yet come) . . . acting courageously, like a wild boar, supported by divine counsel and strengthened by divine help.[29]

The depiction of Æthelred in this passage is intrinsically ambiguous: read one way, the claim that Æthelred's faith 'counted for much with the Lord' seems to vindicate the king's piety; read another way, however, Asser's claim that Alfred 'could not oppose the enemy battle-lines any longer without either retreating from the battlefield or attacking the enemy forces' suggests that Æthelred was selfish and negligent, while the claim that Alfred reached the battle 'sooner and in better order' implies that he was the better leader.

Faced with this ambiguity, later writers could choose whether to credit Æthelred or Alfred for the victory at Ashdown. In the late medieval period, monastic chroniclers (perhaps unsurprisingly) gave the credit to the pious king. Both the early fourteenth-century *Chronicle of Pierre de Langtoft* (edited by Thomas Wright) and William of Malmesbury's twelfth-century *History of the Kings of England* criticised Alfred for his 'impetuousness'.[30] On the other hand, however, William Camden, writing in the sixteenth century, claimed to have read an unidentified 'old Poet' who had presented Æthelred's behaviour at Ashdown as less creditable than that of Alfred.[31] He incorporated this claim into *Britannia*, and from there it found its way into Spelman's history of Alfred.[32]

The nineteenth-century Alfredianist, then, could opt to follow either the late medieval chroniclers or Camden and Spelman in depicting the dynamics of Ashdown, or they could leave the issue uncertain, as in Asser's *Life*. Only one author chose to side with the otherwise very influential Malmesbury. In his 1845 *Lives of Alfred the Great, Sir Thomas More and John Evelyn*, the anonymous 'J.F.R.' referred to Alfred as 'the too precipitate prince', and claimed that Æthelred's 'faith in the God of battles' had won the day.[33] 'J.F.R.' was devoutly Christian however – his life of Alfred appeared in a volume alongside a biography of the Catholic martyr Sir Thomas More – so this emphasis is not surprising. A few other writers were clearly aware of and hesitated over this interpretation of events – opting finally to leave the issue ambiguous. Among them was Florence Attenborough, in whose 1902 play, *Alfred the Great*, the dilemma of contradictory interpretations is dramatised. Discovering that Æthelred is at prayer, while her husband is on the battle-field, Alfred's wife 'Alswitha' soliloquises:

> How am I torn asunder with my thought;
> To make a scoff at prayer I dare not, yet
> My husband may be slain whilst God Himself
> Is being petitioned for our victory.[34]

Similarly, Eliza Kerr's 1885 novella, *Two Saxon Maidens*, attests that 'old chroniclers' attribute the victory at Ashdown to the piety of Æthelred, but also suggests that the Saxons would have been defeated 'had not Alfred been in his proper place at the right time'.[35]

Kerr's book was published by the Wesleyan Methodist Sunday School Union, so she had good reason to not discount entirely the power of prayer. Most nineteenth-century writers, however, seem to have had few qualms about unambiguously presenting the practical Alfred as the hero of the conflict and Æthelred as a deplorably feeble figure. Indeed, Catholic piety was so castigated for much of the nineteenth-century that the king's ostensibly pious reasons for delaying his arrival at the battlefield were typically presented as a mere cover for cowardice or apathy. In Alfred Engelbach's 1878 novel, *The Danes in England*, the 'heroic valour' of Alfred is harshly compared to the 'indifference' of Æthelred', while in Edmund Hill's 1901 *Alfred the Great: A Drama*, the king is charged with 'sloth' and 'idleness'.[36]

The negative reading of Æthelred's conduct at Ashdown became so dominant during the nineteenth century that it bled into general accounts of the king who, according to Asser, 'vigorously and honourably ruled the kingdom in good repute, amid many difficulties, for five years'.[37] So, for instance, although Tom Bevan's 1902 novel, *A Lion of Wessex*, does not portray the Battle of Ashdown, it nevertheless depicts Æthelred as a cowardly and ineffectual figure who – fearing that the Danes will invade

Wessex – commands his warriors only to 'call earnestly upon the name of God' and must be begged by them to 'Ask God to succour our fleshly arms, rather than . . . pray and wait for him to put forth his own hand to do a man's work for us'.[38]

Ashdown was also typically seen by Victorian writers as the decisive moment when Alfred by his valour had first demonstrated that he was a worthy heir to the throne of Wessex – indeed more deserving of the position than the current monarch. This point was often dramatised – particularly in Alfredian plays. Attenborough's *Alfred the Great: A Drama* opens the night before Ashdown, with the king's fears, Alfred's chiding 'away with fear!' and Æthelred's subsequent expressions of shame and inadequacy.[39] The most politically radical nineteenth-century rewriting of Ashdown, however, was Edmund Hill's three-act drama of 1901, in which Alfred effectively seizes the kingship from his brother during the battle. Hearing that his brother is dawdling at Mass, he announces to the assembled Saxon troops, 'Then take I here the kingship of the King,/ And I command you all in England's name/ To follow me'. When the troops hesitate, Alfred demands:

Who is the King?
What word is King?
. . . if among you any would be King
In its best meaning as a man who dares,
And can do what he dares, then I for one
Will follow him, and here upon my knees
I'll yield up my heirship to the throne.[40]

The troops follow him into battle, and Æthelred briefly follows suit before (in a conflation of separate incidents) he is killed on the battlefield. His last breaths are used to gasp the question, 'Am I but king in name and thou in deeds?' and the implied answer is clearly affirmative.

The scene perhaps draws on Asser's claim that Alfred could have taken the throne while still regent had he wished to, 'with the consent of all'.[41] But the closeness with which Alfred's rhetoric echoes the Carlylean demand for 'doughtiness, courage and the faculty *to do*' highlights the necessity of reading nineteenth-century depictions of Ashdown in relation to the calls for valorous and worthy monarchs that were increasingly made in the wake of the political revolutions of 1789, 1830 and 1848.[42]

Alfred the warrior and Alfred the peacemaker

One of Carlyle's most emphatic statements in his 1843 volume *Past and Present* was 'man is created to fight'.[43] King Alfred could readily be used to illustrate such martial ideals of masculinity in the nineteenth century – as well as cataloguing his military victories, Asser's *Life* had explicitly stated that he was 'a great warrior and victorious in virtually all battles'.[44] Thus, Carlyle's disciple Hughes introduced his biography of Alfred by claiming that the Saxon king illustrated his belief that 'man was sent into this world for the express purpose of fighting'.[45] Alfred's military character was also particularly stressed around the time of the Winchester Millenary, which coincided with the Boer War. Military ineffectiveness and poor-quality recruits meant that Britain was largely unsuccessful in this conflict, and popular concern about this failure seems to have been expressed in a revival of Carlylean interest in the military prowess of historical British heroes. Besant claimed in his 1900 essay 'The Heritage of King Alfred' that the Saxon king was 'first and above all, a soldier', while Hardwick Drummond Rawnsley's poem, 'The Millenary of King Alfred', begins with the line: 'Thou famous, warlike, and victorious king'. Alfred was also, of course, depicted as a great military hero in Hamo Thorneycroft's statue.[46] Views and definitions of military heroism were not hegemonic throughout the nineteenth century, however. Tracing the shifting depictions of Alfred as a military figure can therefore cast an interesting light upon competing Victorian conceptions of male heroism. In order to understand to what extent these were derived from earlier models and in what ways they were specifically products of the nineteenth century, it is worth returning briefly to earlier rewritings of Alfred as a warrior.

The first writer to develop Asser's claim about Alfred's prowess in battle was William of Malmesbury. His *History of the Kings of England* states that at the Battle of Edington, Alfred:

> was present in every emergency, daunting the invaders, and at the same time inspiriting [*sic*] his subjects with the signal display of his courage: he would oppose himself singly to the enemy; by his own personal exertions he would rally his declining forces.[47]

The claim clearly owes much to the chivalric culture of the twelfth century, when the display and ritual of single combat was crucial to the stability of the social order. This late medieval conception of Alfred the warrior was revived in the eighteenth century. William of Malmesbury's stress upon the king's zealous and pre-eminent personal participation in battle was reiterated in Blackmore's 1723 *Alfred: An Epic Poem*, for instance, which describes how the Saxon king 'on the right and left at every Stroke/ Kill'd or dismember'd Heroes, till the Slain/ With ghastly Heaps deform'd the reeking Plain'.[48] Similarly, in Fuller's *The Son of Ethelwolf*, when Alfred fights Guthrum, we are told 'Those who were fighting near, forgot their own employment. Impressed with admiration, and labouring with suspence [*sic*], they stopped as if by one consent, and turned the points of their weapons to the earth'.[49] In particular, the twelfth-century notion that Alfred took part in single combat seems to have appealed to the eighteenth-century imagination – especially to dramatists, although this was doubtless partly due to considerations of dramatic economy. In both John Home's 1778 *Alfred: A Tragedy*, and Ebenezer Rhodes's 1789 *Alfred: An Historical Tragedy*, Alfred repeatedly challenges the leaders of the Danes to duels.

Alfred as a physically pre-eminent warrior and Alfred as a duellist both continued as motifs in early nineteenth-century texts. One of the last in which they appear is John Fitchett's gargantuan epic poem on Alfred, written between 1798 and his death in 1838. Fitchett's Alfred is conspicuous at the Battle of Edington as the bravest, most feared and most physically skilled soldier on the battlefield. The concluding section of the poem (written posthumously by Fitchett's friend and executor, Robert Roscoe) relates that:

> through the ranks
> Burst the irresistible might
> Of England's King . . .
> Through densest press the sword of Alfred hew'd
> Wide access. Terror shouted in his van;
> Mute in the rear stalk'd death. His dreadful path
> He wrought through direst slaughter.[50]

This Alfred also fights numerous duels. However, *King Alfred: A Poem* was the last text to use the device. The shift was probably partly due to an increasing commitment to historical accuracy. But it also perhaps reveals changing definitions of heroic leadership and altering attitudes to the duel, which began to attract increasing moral criticism around the start of the nineteenth century.[51] Indeed, early murmurings of this opposition are perhaps heard long before Fitchett's text was published – in Rhodes's play, when Alfred beats the Danish leader Guthrum in a duel he determines that to take him as a captive would make him 'the victim of blind chance, and not of valour'.[52]

Early nineteenth-century literature does not just make Alfred less prominent on the battlefield – some texts display an anxiety to extenuate or deny Alfred's violent involvement in warfare at all. The account of the Battle of Edington in Joseph Cottle's 1800 *Alfred: An Epic Poem*, states that King Alfred did not fight but 'Sped through the fallen ranks, upheld the faint/ Relieved the dying, succour'd those who bled.[53] Henry James Pye's 1801 king does kill, but in *Alfred: An Epic Poem* his bloodshed is sanctioned on the grounds that it represents his duty to his people. A dying warrior reminds the blood-shy Alfred on the battlefield that 'The widows, orphans, of yon slaughtered band/ Implore, demand, redress, from Alfred's hand'.[54] Similarly, in Thomas Dibdin's 1813 poem 'Alfred the Great', the Saxon leader fights but any bloodshed is suppressed – we are told that 'His aim in battle sought no other plan/ But to convince, then bless, his fellow man'.[55] Such reluctance to tarnish the king's image by the act of killing was perhaps fostered by an increasing public awareness of the violence of warfare – an awareness that was facilitated in the nineteenth century by the emergence of war correspondents. Certainly, Dibdin's poem was composed during the long, expensive and casualty-heavy Napoleonic wars.

Until the middle of the nineteenth century, images of Alfred tending the wounded coexisted with those of him hacking down enemies, but after that they received an additional impetus from the emergence of the doctrine of 'muscular Christianity' – which asserted that tenderness, especially to male comrades, was a natural expression of masculinity.[56] One of the finest examples of the influence of this dogma upon literature is to be found in Richard Kelsey's 1852 *Alfred of Wessex*, in which Alfred is 'strong of arm and of softest palm' and spends the Battle of Edington tending to wounded soldiers and baking barley-cakes for them. Towards the end of the nineteenth century, however, a new way of imagining Alfred's role on the battlefield seems to have emerged. The most striking examples are found in the boys' novels written by G.A. Henty and Charles Whistler – both authors with military interests. In Whistler's 1899 novel *King Alfred's Viking*, several chapters are allotted to describing how Alfred's troops are trained to form shield walls, while Henty's *The Dragon and the Raven* meticulously relates how the Saxon king tactically positioned phalanxes of his best men around the battlefield and planned their movements.[57] This emphasis doubtless owes much to conventions of genre – the epic poem calls more for swashbuckling than for strategy, however admirable. The shift can also perhaps be related however to the fact that after the Battle of Dettingen in 1743, when George II had headed the field, no British monarch had seen active service, and conceptions of military leadership had therefore increasingly excluded the notion that personal risk was a virtue.[58]

Whistler also effectively disguised the brutalities of warfare in *King Alfred's Viking*. The best example is found in the chapter where Alfred's followers discuss how the Saxons will attack the Danes at Edington:

> 'How shall we attack?' said Ethelnoth.
> 'Why, run through the enemy's camp in silence first and cut the tent lines, and then raise a war-shout and come back on them. Then we may slay a few, and the rest will be scared badly enough'. Thereat we both laughed under our breath, for it seemed like a schoolboy's prank.[59]

Such jolly images of battle represent part of the sub-genre of military adventures for boys which flourished in the late Victorian period, and demonstrate how Alfred – alongside Arthurian knights, Elizabethan mariners and gun-toting frontiersmen – was used to nurture idealised images of combat in the generation that was to fight in the trenches of the First World War.

Those late Victorian authors who did not rewrite Alfred either as a tactical soldier or a schoolboy prankster instead often justified his involvement in warfare by applying the reasoning that, since the Vikings were pagan, it had constituted a holy conflict. In his 1899 essay on Alfred, for instance, Charles Oman asserted that for the Saxon king, Edington was 'a religious war'.[60] This interpretation gained strength from Anglo-Israelism – the pervasive nineteenth-century belief that the British were God's newest chosen people, the modern Jews, whom He had always protected and destined for global greatness.[61] So in William Watson's short play, *King Alfred*, for instance, Asser assures an anxious Alfred with an Anglo-Judaic parallel:

He is on thy side who was of old
On Hezekiah's, when Sennacherib's host
With thunder of chariots was come up against
Judah[62]

Paradoxically, although nineteenth-century Alfredianists clearly wrestled with the notion of Alfred as a king who might have killed on the battlefield, they also seem to have struggled with the issue of his peace-treaties. Asser's *Life of King Alfred* states that in 871 (the first year of Alfred's reign) 'the Saxons made peace with the Vikings, on condition that they would leave them'. And again, in the entry for 876, it records, 'King Alfred firmly made a treaty with the army, the condition being that they should leave him'.[63] In the nineteenth century, writers dealt with these peace-treaties in one of two ways. Some presented them as foolish and ignoble mistakes. In Attenborough's *Alfred the Great: A Drama*, Alfred's wife complains:

Now, with much gold he barters for our peace –
Peace here, peace there – Oh, I am sick of it!
The Northmen laugh, I doubt not, and rejoice
That whilst Sire Alfred pays, they're getting fit,
To pounce upon their prey with such effect
As shall bring dreadful ruin to ourselves.[64]

Other writers sought rather to vindicate the treaties. In her 1885 novel, *Two Saxon Maidens*, for the benefit of her juvenile audience Eliza Kerr staged an illuminating discussion between two young Saxon nobles, in which they discuss why Alfred bribed the Danes. One explains that it was 'because there were no men to fight under the Golden Dragon', while the other adds, 'The men of Wessex must have time to recover from those last inroads of the Danes, and bribery was the only means by which that time could be gained'.[65] Similarly, this time for an adult readership, in 'Alfred as a Warrior', Oman excused the settlements by arguing that the king paid the Danes only a 'moderate' sum of money, and 'must have been aware that he was only buying a short respite'.[66] Both approaches seem to reveal anxiety that Alfred's pacifism was a weakness. However, Asser also states that after the Battle of Edington, when the vanquished Danish King Guthrum sought peace, Alfred '(as is his wont) was moved to compassion', and this treaty was universally praised in the nineteenth century as evidence of the Saxon king's 'great wisdom and generosity'.[67] The key to understanding this difference in perception lies in the outcome of the treaties: while the earlier ones were only briefly honoured by the Danes, that with Guthrum was a long-lasting success. What nineteenth-century writers found disturbing it

seems, therefore, was not that a heroic king might seek peace rather than
battle, but rather that his judgement might falter and his actions fail. And
this anxiety also throws light on why Alfred's three months in hiding during
878 were the most widely documented, analysed and elaborated period of
the king's life in the nineteenth century – a subject to which we will now
turn.

A king in hiding

Both the *Anglo-Saxon Chronicle* and *Asser's Life of King Alfred* relate that
in 878 the king was forced to retreat from the Danes and spend three months
in hiding.[68] According to the *Chronicle*, Alfred 'with a small troop went with
difficulty through woods and into swamp-fastnesses'.[69] Asser's *Life* offers a
little more detail. Its account states that in 878:

> King Alfred, with his small band of nobles and also certain soldiers and thegns,
> was leading a restless life in great distress amid the woody and marshy places
> of Somerset. He had nothing to live on except what he could forage by frequent
> raids.[70]

What neither source fully explains, however, is exactly how and why Alfred
was driven to become a fugitive. There is, for instance, no description of any
battle in which after an honourable struggle (perhaps with uneven odds) the
king was defeated by the Danes, immediately prior to his retreat. This was
understandably problematic for nineteenth-century Alfredianists keen to
depict Alfred as a model for monarchs, in an age when Carlyle had asserted
that a king should be 'the Noblest Man', 'a true captain', and 'a commander over men', since it left open the possibility that the Saxon might simply
have fled dishonourably from impending trouble.[71] A number of explanations for Alfred's retreat were therefore formulated, which either developed
fleeting hints in the ninth-century sources or claims in late medieval texts,
but which above all speak of the anxieties and priorities of British politics in
the nineteenth century.

Only a few nineteenth-century authors tried to claim that Alfred's
retreat had followed an unsuccessful battle – partly because to do so was
inevitably to detract from the king's prowess as a warrior. One writer who
did so was R. Payne Knight, whose 1823 *Alfred: A Romance in Rhyme*
relates that in the wake of a defeat at Chippenham, Alfred left the battlefield:

> His ensigns lost, his face with blood besmear'd
> No trace of royalty or rank appear'd;
> A private warrior he escaped from view
> And from the field, midst heaps of slain withdrew.[72]

Knight's theory was based upon the late medieval chronicler Brompton's
claim that Alfred lost two battles to the Danes in 871 – one at Chippenham

and another at Abendune.[73] Nineteenth-century historians observed that these battles could not logically have occurred in 871, and hypothesised that Brompton must have meant 878.[74] In the later nineteenth century, however, this theory was influentially attacked by Thomas Hughes.[75] Although Hughes allowed that 'at first sight it seems hard to account for the sudden and complete collapse of the West Saxon power in January 878', he cautioned his readers that 'there does not seem to be the least ground for taking this liberty with Brompton's text, nor even, if there were, is he a sufficiently sound authority to rely upon for any fact which is not to be found in the Saxon Chronicle, or Asser'.[76]

The *Chronicle* itself, however, provided few clues as to what had occurred in 878, besides stating that 'the raiding-army stole away in midwinter after Twelfth Night to Chippenham'.[77] The use of the word 'stole' (also translated as 'went stealthily') did inspire one nineteenth-century explanation, however – the notion that Alfred's Saxons were caught out because the timing of the Danish invasion was somehow in contravention of the unspoken protocols of ninth-century warfare. This theory was first developed in the late eighteenth century by John Home who, for melodramatic effect, had the Danes attack Wessex during Alfred's marriage – a motif that recalls the Robin Hood tradition (begun in the seventeenth century) in which Earl Robert of Huntington has to flee to the forest during his betrothal ceremony. A century later, Eliza Pollard returned to the theory of a 'stealthy' invasion in her novel *A Hero King*, asserting that Alfred had to retreat because the Danes unexpectedly invaded in 'Winter-time, when men fight not'.[78]

Anne Manning also offered a theological interpretation of the Saxon king's withdrawal. Divine providence, she claimed, engineered the temporary victory of the Danes as a punishment for the West Saxons' 'iniquities', ordaining that they should be 'a very scorn unto their foes' until such time as God granted them forgiveness.[79] A similar, explicitly Christian exposition was also suggested by Thomas Hughes, who suggested that the West Saxons were conquered because 'their religion had become chiefly a matter of custom and routine'.[80] There are several late medieval precedents for such Christian interpretations of Alfred's temporary retreat: in William of Malmesbury's twelfth-century *History of the Kings of England* (where St Cuthbert tells the hiding Alfred that England is paying 'the penalty of her crimes'); in the thirteenth-century *Chronicle of John Wallingford* (where the Saxons have fallen prey to 'sloth, and luxurious eating and drinking');[81] and in the preface to Alfred's translation of Gregory's *Pastoral Care*, in which the Saxon king himself seems to present the temporary Viking victory as a punishment for the decline of learning in England, warning his readers: 'Remember what punishments befell us in this world when we ourselves did not cherish learning nor transmit it to other men'.[82]

Hughes's attraction to such an interpretation of Alfred's temporary fugacity seems also to have had a contemporary motivation, however – his desire to allay fears (possibly instigated by the passing of the 1867 Reform Act) about the likelihood of an impending British revolution. Writing of the religious and moral decline of the West Saxon nation, he related:

> When that state comes, men who love their country will welcome Danish invasions, civil wars, potato diseases, cotton famines, Fenian agitations, whatever calamity may be needed to awake the higher life again, and bid the nation arise and live.[83]

Another line in the *Anglo-Saxon Chronicle* also proved the seed for a nineteenth-century theory about Alfred's retreat – the assertion that the Danes 'drove many of the people across the sea, and the greatest part of the others they over-rode – and they turned to them – except for Alfred the king'.[84] While this extract does not explicitly criticise Alfred's populace for 'turning' (or in some versions 'submitting') to the Danes, it does seem to contrast favourably the king's temporary retreat with the defeatism of his subjects. Consequently, it came to provide the basis for the Victorian theory (here articulated by Francis Steinitz, the 1849 editor of von Haller's *Moderate Monarchy*) that 'Alfred was abandoned by his people . . . he had, therefore, no other alternative than to save himself, as with his ruin would fall all hopes of re-establishing the kingdom of the Saxons'.[85] This proved a popular theory at times of social instability throughout the nineteenth century – particularly with politically conservative authors.[86]

The text to develop the notion furthest away from the account in the *Chronicle* was Stratford Canning's 1876 *Alfred the Great in Athelnay*, published in the wake of Napoleon III's defeat and the founding of the third French Republic in 1871 – and at a time when Tory anxieties about the possibility of a British revolution had been increased by the passing of the second Reform Act.[87] In Canning's play, Alfred's subjects do not merely abandon him, they rebel, demonstrating outside his castle, and complaining that he is too 'listless' to meet the Danes in combat. One Saxon objects that Alfred 'courts his ease/ Makes of his throne a couch;/ Is felt but in taxation'. In response, the Saxon king determines that his subjects 'must feel/ How vain their self-reliance, and submit/ To discipline's stern yoke'.[88] He steals away at night, leaving his people to face the threat of the Danes alone. The plan, of course, is successful and Alfred eventually returns to lead a contritely patriotic community to victory.

Canning's descriptions of insurrectionary Saxons outside Alfred's castle are strongly evocative of the 1789 storming of Versailles, and the king's outwitting of them and their final repentant loyalty to him carry a clear, politically conservative message: without kingship, states founder; republicanism can only lead to national disaster.

Another text to present Alfred's seclusion as a political strategy was published two years after Canning's play. Alfred H. Engelbach's *The Danes in England* was published just as Queen Victoria was beginning to re-emerge into the public eye after a protracted and reclusive period of mourning for the death of Prince Albert.[89] During this interval, increasingly frequent denunciations of the monarchy were voiced, with which Engelbach's novel seems to engage.[90] The text's hero Leowulf explains that Alfred went into hiding because:

> The constant worstings he had latterly sustained ... had begun to destroy all that prestige which is so needful to the preservation of even a semblance of authority. On the other hand, his unexplained disappearance ... led men to turn from the recollection of past defeats to vague but gladly-cherished hopes that something great was to come of this mysterious seclusion.[91]

It can thus be read as a defence of Victoria's withdrawal from public life – as an explanation of the wisdom of occasional monarchic retreat.

Henty's *The Dragon and the Raven* provides a final example of how nineteenth-century Alfredianists developed the notion that Alfred's subjects were culpable for their monarch's enforced retreat. His Alfred calls his subjects to arms, but they ignore the appeal, and so the king, 'finding the struggle hopeless', sadly retires to await the time when the Saxons, having 'found out their error' will be 'driven by oppression to take up arms'.[92] Henty was one of the chief voices in the late nineteenth-century campaign to indoctrinate Britain's youth with military values in the wake of the first Boer War of 1880, when Britain's defeat had been attributed by many (Henty included) to poor recruitment.[93] His Alfredian novel should therefore be read in this context. Its allusions to Britain's difficulty in attracting sufficient recruits for the Boer War are numerous, and its message is clear – the necessity of strong enlistment to national security.

Henty's Alfred also offers further justification for his retreat. He avows, 'when defeated in battle I would not throw away my life, for that belongs to our people rather than to myself'.[94] This depiction of Alfred as a martyr-like sovereign devoted to his populace should be read in relation to the commitment of the royal tutor Henty to maintaining a monarchy in Britain, and in terms of the common conviction at the time that if Britain were to avoid republicanism then its monarchy would have to be seen to be a committed and socially responsible institution – 'the true representative of the nation, the embodiment of its national being'.[95] Presenting Alfred as almost physically inseparable from the nation, Henty's text successfully effects such a representation.

In each of the nineteenth-century reworkings discussed thus far, the emphasis has been upon removing from Alfred the responsibility for his retreat. There was another possible approach to the problem, however – the theory that Alfred was to blame for his temporary defeat. This notion derives from the *Life of St Neot* which, as discussed earlier, states that early in his reign King Alfred visited his kinsman Neot in Cornwall; was admonished by the saint for his pride and tyranny; and was warned to change his ways lest disaster should befall him. According to the *Life of Saint Neot*, Alfred was then forced into hiding as punishment for his evil behaviour and 'reflecting patiently that these things had befallen him through God's just judgement, he remained there awaiting God's mercy through the intercession of His servant Neot; for he had conceived from Neot the hope that he nourished in his heart. "Whom the Lord loves", says the apostle, "He chastises; He scourges every son whom he adopts" '.[96]

The above episode was interpolated into most nineteenth-century editions of Asser, and the *Life of Saint Neot* was also translated and published in its own right in 1802, so the above episode was well known to Victorian Alfredianists.[97] It appears, with little alteration or development in several nineteenth-century texts. Agnes Stewart's 1840 children's book *Stories about Alfred the Great* describes Alfred's retreat as 'a just chastisement for his own sins', while in Engelbach's *The Danes in England* it is described as a 'chrysalis state' from which Alfred can emerge only after he has earned 'heaven's blessing'.[98] In 1799, however, in his *History of the Anglo-Saxons*, Sharon Turner had attempted to modernise the *Life of Saint Neot*'s account for an increasingly secular age. Turner agreed with the *Life*'s basic premise that Alfred had been a sinful ruler – instead of accepting simple divine intervention as the mechanics by which the king had become a fugitive. He suggested, however, that 'The inference which seems naturally to result . . . is, that Alfred had offended his people, and in this trying emergency was deserted by them'.[99] Effectively, then, Turner's rewriting combined the idea that Alfred had been abandoned by his people with the notion of a sinful king. He also speculated as to the precise nature of Alfred's sin, suggesting that he had behaved haughtily towards his subjects because of the 'intellectual disparity' between himself and them.[100]

Turner's interest in the fate of a monarch with no sympathy or understanding of his subjects can be related to the prevailing contemporary belief that the French Revolution had been caused by the offensive behaviour of Louis XIV.[101] Certainly, his notion of an Alfred who had offended his people seems to have appealed strongly to those nineteenth-century authors who wrote in a spirit of admonition at times when the British monarchy seemed imperilled.[102] His interest in theorising about the precise nature of Alfred's sins was also echoed in the nineteenth century. During the eighteenth century it had been imagined that the young Alfred had struggled to sublimate his role as husband to his responsibilities as king – a reflection, perhaps, of public discontent about the prioritising of personal concerns over public duties by the Hanoverian line of monarchs.[103] In Mallet and Thomson's 1745 *Alfred: a Masque*, for instance, a stern-voiced hermit must reprimand Alfred 'thou art a king,/ All private passions fall before that name./ Thy subjects claim thee whole'.[104] The last text to develop this idea, however, was Pye's 1801 *Alfred: An Epic Poem*, in which a guilty Alfred confesses:

> though my country's wrongs, with venom'd dart,
> Strike keenest tortures through this wounded heart,

Still must my bosom feel for ties more near,
Still must Elsitha claim her Alfred's tear.[105]

Thereafter, waning interest in Alfred as a romantic hero was accompanied by the disappearance of anxiety about any conflict between his amorous concerns and statesmanship. By 1830, in a play by James Sheridan Knowles, Alfred would unhesitatingly leave his wife a captive in order to deal with more pressing concerns, explaining curtly, 'Paramount of all/ My public function! Husband – father – friend/ All titles, and all ties are merg'd in that!'[106]

Interest in the romantic distractions that might have misled Alfred was displaced by Turner's theory that scholarship had diverted him from his legislative responsibilities. The germ of this idea probably lay in Asser's description of how it was Alfred's 'peculiar and most characteristic habit either to read books to himself or to listen to others doing so – by day and night, amid all other mental and physical ailments'.[107] From this (and Turner's suggestion) George Lewes Newnham Collingwood, for instance, could speculate in his 1836 Alfredian epic poem that 'oft, mid books, and studious cares engross'd,/ Alfred the duties of his state forgot'.[108] While Attenborough, in her play about Alfred, had his wife complain:

He shows neglect
Unto the kingdom, even unto me,
And only sets himself, with all his strength,
To be the scholar
. . . From learning's lordly height
He now looks coldly down upon us all

Such depictions of Alfred engrossed in study demonstrate how the negative image of the scholar as 'a lamentable type of wasted power . . . preoccupied with dead matter and vain of his preoccupation' – had pervaded nineteenth-century popular culture in a stereotype most famously incarnated by the musty academic Edward Casaubon in George Eliot's 1871 novel *Middlemarch*.[109] Indeed, the unease about scholarship in the nineteenth century is also reflected in those texts which seek to defend Alfred's interest in study – such as Mrs Maxwell-Scott's history of Alfred, written in the same year as Attenborough's novel, which stresses that Alfred was 'a scholar without ostentation', and the *Life of Alfred* by 'J.F.R.' which emphasises that the king's 'love for knowledge' made him 'neither effeminate nor slothful'.[110]

Slothfulness or indolence constituted another nineteenth-century theory about the young Alfred's sinfulness. Again this derived in part from Turner's widely read 1799 history, which states that during Alfred's early years on the throne 'we find nothing but inert quietude'.[111] Thus, in Anne Manning's 1861 novel, *The Chronicle of Ethelfled*, Alfred confesses 'The land is full of foemen – what have I done? Nothing The land also is full of misery – what have I done? Nothing? The land also is full of ignorance, and so is its king, and what have I done? Nothing'.[112] Likewise, in Canning's *Alfred the Great in Athelney*, Alfred's subjects complain that he 'courts his ease; makes of his throne a couch' because he seems to prevaricate instead of attacking the Danes. Canning, however, was a staunchly conservative member of the nine-teenth-century aristocracy. In his play, therefore, the king's inaction (like Victoria's much-criticised delay in joining the Crimean War) is later vindi-cated as a wiser course than to 'leap with headlong rage/ Unthinking into waters, where the tide/ Rushes with ruthless force'.[113]

Alfred is similarly defended against charges of sinfulness in Manning's novel. Here, Alfred distributes 'many bushels of grain, many ambra of malt, many wagon-loads of billets and twigs, that the people might be both warmed and fed', but 'nevertheless, as will always be the case, some were dissatisfied. And of these certain complained unto Neot that they were neglected in the daily ministrations'.[114] Manning's female narrator, Ethelfled, relates 'then considered I, and saw that of all men kings are born to trouble . . . and I pitied him in my heart'.[115] The text demonstrates the longevity in popular culture of the eighteenth-century doctrine of '*noblesse oblige*' – the argument that high station entailed terrible responsibilities.[116] Its attack on St Neot, rewrit-ing him as a disseminator of rumour and slander, is also a fine example of the anti-monasticism which was dominant for much of the Victorian period.

Manning was not the only nineteenth-century opponent of the claims about Alfred's transgressions made in the *Life of Saint Neot*. Indeed, the earliest critic of the text seems to have been its first translator and editor, John Whitaker. In his 1809 commentary upon the text, Whitaker angrily demanded:

> Was the good, the great Alfred, the favourite of history, and the idol of tradi-tion, such a man, or such a king as this? No, surely! . . . I have laid this account in all its fullness before my reader, that he may see it in all its falseness.[117]

His sentiment was echoed by both the historian J.A. Froude and the popular author Thomas Hughes, who objected that no-one with any knowledge of the Saxon king's life could possibly believe such allegations.[118] For those nineteenth-century writers who chose to depict Alfred as a sinful king, there-fore, the decision was by no means uncontroversial. And this became more and more the case as the 1901 Millenary celebrations approached and Alfred became increasingly identified with national virtue. By 1901, even Charles Plummer, in his series of dispassionate academic lectures on Alfred, would become heated on the subject of St Neot, pronouncing it 'pitiable that modern writers should lend even half an ear to these wretched tales, which besmirch the fair fame of our hero king'.[119]

In the swineherd's cottage

It was almost unavoidable, however, that many nineteenth-century writers should be influenced by the *Life of St Neot*'s 'wretched tales' of the sinful

Alfred, for that manuscript, as we heard earlier, also contained the most popular and pervasive of all nineteenth-century stories about the Saxon king – the famous tale of how, during his time in hiding in the Somerset marshes, Alfred:

> happened to come unexpectedly [to Athelney] as a lone traveller. Noticing the cottage of a certain unknown swineherd (as he later learned), he directed his path towards it and sought there a peaceful retreat; he was given refuge, and he stayed there for a number of days, impoverished, subdued and content with the bare necessities.[120]

Like the account of Alfred's sinfulness, this tale was incorporated (with minor changes – such as the swineherd becoming a 'neatherd' or cowherd) into the twelfth-century *Annals of St Neots*, interpolated from there into Matthew Parker's edition of Asser, and subsequently included as an integral part of most editions of *The Life of King Alfred*, so it was readily available in the nineteenth century.[121]

Nearly all Victorian Alfredianists described the king's stay in the humble cottage of a neatherd or swineherd – and those, like Thomas Hughes and the novelist Gordon Stables, who were anxious about contradictory sources, had him stay with both, to be on the safe side.[122] By contrast, the incident was omitted by many eighteenth-century authors. This discrepancy suggests that a shift might have taken place in the early nineteenth century – from a view of kings as the extraordinary representatives of God towards a new dominant attitude to monarchs as essentially ordinary individuals with extraordinary responsibilities. Certainly, this is borne out by the very different ways in which a disguise motif is used in accounts of Alfred in the swineherd's cottage deriving from each respective period. The notion that the Saxon king must have worn a disguise during his time in hiding originates in a ballad known as 'The Shepheard and the King', which was first recorded in 1578 as part of the *Roxburgh Ballads*. This describes how Alfred disguised himself as a peasant in a 'rag'd and torne' coat of russet, and a Monmouth cap, in order to hide in a humble cottage.[123] In those eighteenth-century texts which depict Alfred in the herd's cottage, this detail is included, but the disguise invariably fails to conceal the king's innate nobility from his humble hosts – suggesting that the notion of 'the clothes making the king' was an uncomfortable one for writers of that time.[124] In Mallet and Thomson's *Alfred: A Masque*, for instance, the herd who shelters the disguised Alfred confides to his wife:

> Behold him well. Fair manhood in its prime,
> Even thro the homely russet that conceals him,
> Shines forth and proves him noble. Seest thou, Emma,
> Yon western clouds? The sun they strive to hide,
> Yet darts his beams around.[125]

In almost all of the nineteenth-century texts which describe his stay in Athelney, on the other hand, Alfred is successful in camouflaging himself – a fashion which is perhaps related to the general popularity of the motif of disguised monarchs in the early 1800s, when George III was still on the throne and claims about his disguised forays around London proliferated in the popular press.[126] Only in two novels is Alfred's real identity discovered – Alfred H. Engelbach's 1878 *The Danes in England* and Charles Whistler's 1899 *King Alfred's Viking*. However, in both these cases, it is some object or behaviour which betrays Alfred's true identity, rather than his innate nobility: Engelbach's Alfred is betrayed by a golden jewel nestling in his bosom, while in Whistler's novel, an old witch guesses that her guest must be noble because he 'wipes his hands in the middle of the towel'.[127] The nineteenth-century popularity of the tale of Alfred in the swineherd's cottage should maybe also be related to the Victorian penchant for depicting hard work as morally improving – as exemplified by the large number of heroes in nineteenth-century literature who, like Alfred, have a noble birth but must endure temporary penury.[128] Thus, Victorian Alfreds roll up their sleeves to chop wood, mind livestock and fetch water, whereas their eighteenth-century forebears daydream in a pastoral idyll while in hiding, between enjoying the generous, rustic feasts that their humble host serves up.[129] And, typically, in eighteenth-century texts, Alfred's host is not the very lowly figure of a swineherd, but the considerably more romantic character of a shepherd.[130]

All but one of the nineteenth-century Alfredian texts stress that King Alfred went to the swineherd's cottage as a lone traveller.[131] And Alfred is also without followers in all nineteenth-century artwork depicting the episode. This is a notable departure from *Asser's Life of King Alfred* and the *Anglo-Saxon Chronicle*, which both relate that Alfred spent his three months in hiding with a small group of followers. However, Alfred's solitude was an important dramatic device for Victorian Alfredianists: for painters, it provided a strongly iconic image of nobility amid squalor; while for writers, particularly playwrights, it allowed them to portray the lonesome king reflecting (and soliloquising aloud) on his misfortunes. This was a crucial element of the story for those Alfredianists who wished to present Alfred's sojourn with the herd as a rite-of-passage. Equally indispensable to Alfred's soliloquising was the *Life of Saint Neot*'s by now famous tale of how Alfred burnt the cakes. The earliest version of this relates that:

> Now it happened by chance one day, when the swineherd was leading his flock to their usual pastures, that the king remained alone at home with the swineherd's wife. The wife, concerned for her husband's return, had entrusted some kneaded flour to . . . the oven. As is the custom among countrywomen, she was intent on other domestic occupations, until, when she sought the bread from [the oven], she saw it burning from the other side of the room. She immediately grew angry and said to the king (unknown to her as such): 'Look here, man, You hesitate to turn the loaves which you see to be burning, Yet you're quite happy to eat them when they come warm from the oven!'

... the king, reproached by these disparaging insults, ascribed them to his divine lot. Somewhat shaken, and submitting to the woman's scolding, he not only turned the bread but even attended to it as she brought out the loaves when they were ready.[132]

As well as appearing in nineteenth-century editions and translations of Asser's *Life*, this story of the burnt bread was paraphrased in a number of popular histories such as Spelman's 1709 *Life of King Alfred* and Rapin's *The History of England*, so it was well known to Victorian Alfredianists.[133]

The legend of Alfred burning the cakes seized the popular imagination of the nineteenth century. At the unveiling of the Alfred statute in Winchester, Rosebery described the tale as possessing 'those romantic elements which fascinate successive generations'.[134] The tale was just as popular half a century earlier – in 1852, J.A. Froude described it as 'the favourite story in English nurseries'.[135] And the legend was not confined to nurseries alone: it also became a popular subject in Victorian artists' studios. Alfred burning the cakes had been a favourite illustration in eighteenth-century history text-books – painted to most renown by Francis Wheatley in 1792 for the lavishly illustrated *Complete History of England* published by Robert Bowyer.[136] The first nineteenth-century illustration of Alfred burning the cakes, however, was David Wilkie's 1806 *Alfred Reprimanded by the Neatherd's Wife*, which was engraved in numerous histories, and became a sufficiently iconic image for the playwright Robert B. Brough to provide the stage-direction in an 1860 pantomime: 'Alfred discovered, as in Wilkie's picture'.[137] Later versions of the cake-burning included J. Pain Davis's 1842 *King Alfred in the Swineherd's Cottage*, and H. Warren's 1846 *Alfred in the Swineherd's Cottage*, which was engraved for the *Illustrated London News* (see Figure 12). The scene was also used to represent Alfred's reign in the popular 1834 children's book *Little Arthur's History* by Maria Graham, and in the illustrated 1848 edition of Hume's *History of England*. Indeed, during the first half of the nineteenth century, the incident became the most frequently painted scene from Alfred's life– perhaps because of picturesque historical art's favouring of moral exemplars, and its concern to encourage empathy by depicting scenes of failure and dejection.[138]

By 1848, the subject of Alfred burning the cakes had become so familiar in art galleries and exhibitions, that Thackeray was incited to satirise those who painted the incident. The assault formed part of his sustained 1840s attack upon historical literature and painting as genres produced for a bour-geois audience easily impressed by sentimentality, drama and grand scale.[139] Thus, in the short story '*Our Street*', the atrocious history painter George Rumbold depicts the scene on a colossal scale – 'seventy-two feet by forty eight' – making 'the mere muffin, of which the outcast King is spoiling the baking, . . . two feet three in diameter'.[140] And, in 1853, his first attack having done little to dent painterly enthusiasm for Alfred and the cakes,

12 H. Warren, *King Alfred in the Swineherd's Cottage* (engraved for the
Illustrated London News in 1846)

Thackeray took another swipe at the subject in his novel *The Newcomes*, in
which 'the eminent Mr Gandish, of Soho', explains his painting of Alfred to
Colonel Newcome:

> You know the anecdote, Colonel? King Alfred, flying from the Danes, took
> refuge in a neat-erd's 'ut. The rustic's wife told him to bake a cake, and the fugi-
> tive sovereign set down to his ignoble task, and forgetting it in the cares of state,
> let the cake burn, on which the woman struck him. The moment chose is when
> she is lifting her 'and to deliver the blow. The King receives it with majesty
> mingled with meekness. In the background the door of the 'ut is open, letting
> in the royal officers to announce the Danes are defeated. The daylight breaks in
> at the aperture, signifying the dawning of 'Ope. That story, sir, which I found
> in my researches in 'ist'ry, has since become so popular, sir, that hundreds of
> artists have painted it, hundreds![141]

The account, although satiric, could serve to describe the main features of
most nineteenth-century compositions of the burning of the cakes – the
bread just smouldering, Alfred meekly sorry, the wife with arm raised
(although usually to point at the charred remains), and the dark interior of
the cottage serving to mirror the darkness of the king's plight.

In every one of the nineteenth-century paintings of Alfred burning the
cakes, the Saxon king is portrayed as having committed the unfortunate deed

because he is preoccupied with tending to his weapons, thus emphasising his intrinsically warrior-like nature. This is also the case in the *Annals of Asser* – the text interpolated by Matthew Parker into *Asser's Life of Alfred*. What is surprising, however, is that a warlike Alfred appears in only four examples of nineteenth-century Alfredian literature.[142] Instead, most literary texts adopt the contemplative king who, in the *Life of Saint Neot*, allows the cakes to burn because he is meditating on Hebrews XII: 6 and on the example of Job.[143] *The Life of Saint Neot* was published in an English edition in 1809, but the nineteenth-century preference for a contemplative Alfred remains unexpected from the point of view of the sources, since a warlike king not only appears in nineteenth-century editions of Asser, but also in otherwise influential histories like John Spelman's *Life of Alfred the Great*.[144] The tendency is perhaps partly explained by Carolyn Williams's account of how, from the late eighteenth century onwards, intellect and learning came to be depicted in popular literature as 'manly' attributes, so that the hero was 'regarded with suspicion . . . if basing his claim to greatness solely on military prowess'.[145] More importantly, however, the choice of a contemplative Alfred allowed nineteenth-century authors, by secularising his reflections, to use King Alfred as a mouthpiece to discuss the distribution of wealth, the workings of society and the responsibilities of monarchs. Such a politicised use of the king was probably influenced by dramatic depictions of other famous monarchs who experienced social and moral enlightenment – most famously, of course, Shakespeare's King Lear.

Social 'insights' are first afforded to the hiding Alfred in eighteenth-century literary works. Typically, however, in these texts Alfred reflects upon the 'delights' of a simple rural existence, and the onerous burden that inevitably accompanies wealth and high status. In Alexander Bicknell's 1788 play *The Patriot King*, for instance, Alfred ruminates: 'How placid is the senseless peasant's life!/ Unlike the troubled hours of higher ranks'.[146] The same doctrine of '*noblesse oblige*' is advocated even more insistently in some early nineteenth-century Alfredian texts – especially those published in the politically turbulent decade after 1830. The theme emerges, for instance, in Collingwood's 1836 *Alfred the Great: A Poem*, in which Alfred sorrowfully announces:

Nor think ... that pomp and glittering robes
Sceptre and crown, by reverent thanes obey'd,
Make happy him who bears them – On his neck
Presses a death-like yoke.[147]

The unstable 1830s did not just bring forth conservative depictions of Alfred in the swineherd's cottage, however. James Sheridan Knowles's 1831 *Alfred the Great: Or, the Patriot King* was published in the midst of the social unrest that preceded the passing of the Great Reform Act. Knowles wrote for the *Free Press*, a radical Glasgow journal that promoted social reform.[148] In his Alfredian play he used the narrative of Alfred and the cakes in order to employ the Saxon king as a mouthpiece for his own views on the social responsibilities of the monarchy. Sitting before the burning cakes, Knowles's Alfred muses:

> Adversity's the nurse for kings; but then the palace gates
> Are shut against her! –
> They would else have hearts of mercy oft'ner – gems not always dropp'd
> In fortune's golden cup. What thought hath he
> How hunger warpeth honesty, whose meal
> Still waiteth on the hour?
> . . . I will extract
> Riches from penury; from sufferings
> Coin blessings; that if I assume again
> The sceptre, I may be more a king
> By being more a man!'[149]

In particular, the Saxon king's soliloquy in *Alfred the Great: Or, the Patriot King* may have been intended as a didactic message to the recently crowned William IV, who was still enjoying a brief honeymoon of popularity in 1831. That this was indeed the case is suggested by the preface to Knowles's play, which makes dark allusions to England's recent condition under George IV and draws clear parallels between Alfred and William. It is addressed to:

> His Most Gracious Majesty, William the Fourth, a Patriot Monarch, destined, with the blessing of God, to restore the dilapidated fabric of his country's prosperity and to restore a devoted people from the ravages of the worst of invaders – corruption.[150]

One motif that all nineteenth-century versions of the cake-burning narrative share is the censure to which King Alfred is subjected as a result of his ruminations – the sharp chastisement by the neatherd's wife. Whereas in both medieval and eighteenth-century Alfredian texts the wife is merely a rustic stereotype, nineteenth-century writers sometimes explored her character. The middle-class authors Joseph Cottle and G.A. Henty both depicted her sympathetically as an ideal, assiduous wife and a paragon of womanly virtue. Cottle's 1800 *Alfred: An Epic Poem* feelingly relates that she:

> perceived full oft the wayward man
> Pursuing fancies wild, indifferent grown,
> To each accustomed charge of household sort,
> Her great concern.[151]

Similarly, in his 1886 *Dragon and the Raven*, Henty relates with pity that she was:

> driven well-nigh out of her mind by [Alfred's] inattention. She only asks of him that he will cut wood and keep an eye over her pigs . . . in return for his food; and yet, simple as are his duties, he is for ever forgetting them. . . . the dame would not so long have put up with him had he not been so fair and helpless.[152]

Henty's Alfred is deeply chastened after burning the wife's cakes because his mind is fixed on affairs of state, and acknowledges that her domestic role is both as important and as difficult in many ways as his own regal responsibilities. This presentation of the relationship between Alfred and the wife was shared by many female authors – Katie Magnus postulated that Alfred did not hear the wife ask him to watch the cakes 'or it seems pretty certain that his quick sympathy would have made him understand that her cakes were as much to her as his kingdom was to him. One feels sure that it was not on purpose, not from just not caring, that Alfred gave no thought to those cakes.'[153]

By contrast, other nineteenth-century writers, like Canning in his 1876 *Alfred the Great in Athelnay*, developed the wife into a mean and violent shrew. This was particularly the case with playwrights, for whom the encounter between a king and a housewife provided a fine opportunity for burlesque. In Canning, for instance, the wife boxes Alfred's ears – until her husband hits her and the king threatens to roast her on her own fire.[154] Misogyny, carnivalesque tradition and staunchly conservative politics interact in such depictions of Alfred and the wife. The most interesting nineteenth-century portrayal of the neatherd's wife, however, is perhaps found in Martin Farquhar Tupper's 1850 *Alfred: A Patriotic Play*. Here the woman, described in the *Dramatis Personae* as an 'old vixen wife', accuses Alfred of fighting the Danes simply because he is 'glory-craving', complaining 'A plague on that quarrelsome king of ours, says I! Why can't he be peaceably disposed with these brave newcomers, but fights and wars with the worthy gentlemen?'[155] Worst of all, as soon as she discovers Alfred's true identity she goes to the Danes with the information, hoping to be rewarded with gold for her treachery. There is more going on in the play, however, than simply misogyny. Both the woman and her husband are specifically described as Celts. The play therefore provides an example of the way in which, in the hands of a self-confessed 'Anglo-Saxonist' like Tupper, Victorian Alfredianism often dovetailed with denigration of the inhabitants of Britain's Celtic fringe.

The fort at Athelney and the Danish camp

While Asser's *Life* does not refer to Alfred's stay with any swineherd or neatherd, it does state that towards the end of his time in hiding, 'King Alfred, with a few men, made a fortress at a place called Athelney'.[156] The construction of this fort, although lacking the drama of Alfred's cake-burning, seized the imagination of some nineteenth-century Alfredianists. The Royalist Henty used the incident to demonstrate exemplary loyalty to a king.[157] In his *The Dragon and the Raven*, Edmund (the novel's young hero) finds the impoverished and exiled Alfred and loyally uses his own treasure to build a fort for him, to buy iron and hides, and to employ smiths. He also sends messengers all over Somerset, and within a fortnight succeeds in mustering over a thousand soldiers on Athelney. In short, he single-handedly turns a desolate island into the nerve-centre of a concerted war-effort, without the need for King Alfred to lift a royal finger.[158]

Henty's rewriting of the construction of the Athelney fort was perhaps influenced by the tenth-century *Chronicle of Fabius Ethelwerd* (a loose, Latin translation of the *Anglo-Saxon Chronicle*), according to which not 'King Alfred with a few men', but Alfred's retainer Ethelnoth Duke of Somerset and his retinue, were responsible for constructing the fort at Athelney.[159] In using the construction of the Athelney fort as a means of demonstrating exemplary patriotism, however, Henty was in a minority – far more nineteenth-century writers employed it as a way of demonstrating King Alfred's common touch – his empathy with his subjects. Such writers interpreted literally Asser's assertion that 'King Alfred, with a few men, made a fortress', imagining that Alfred had laboured alongside his men.[160] The idea is developed furthest in Whistler's *King Alfred's Viking*, in which the hero Ranald relates:

> [Alfred] and I were horny-handed and clay-stained from the work. I came with spade in hand, and he leaned on a pike. Whereat he laughed. 'Faith . . . now can I speak in comrade's wise to my churls . . . Nor do I think that I shall be the worse ruler for that.[161]

Whistler's labouring Alfred exemplifies the Carlylean view of the king not as a figure with 'divine right', but as merely 'the ablest man'.[162] He also embodies the concern that monarchs be sympathetic, popular and highly visible, which developed in the aftermath of the French Revolutions and was reaffirmed during the much-criticised withdrawal of Victoria from public life following Albert's death. The dominant Victorian belief in the sanctity of work also reveals itself in the text – Whistler's calloused and sweaty king should be read in relation to the Victorian artistic convention which represented moral good – even that of Christ – by depictions of manual labour.[163]

During Alfred's time at the fort on Athelney, Asser states, he and the thegns of Somerset 'struck out relentlessly and tirelessly against the Vikings'.[164] What interested Victorian Alfredianists, however, was William of Malmesbury's claim – discussed above – that while on Athelney, Alfred had entered the Danish camp in disguise.[165] As we have already heard, this story was elaborated in the *Book of Hyde* (where Alfred is dressed as a minstrel) and in the *History of Ingulf* (where he is, more specifically, disguised as a harper).[166] It was this latter version of the story which was most often adopted by nineteenth-century writers, while William of Malmesbury's claim that Alfred was disguised as a jester proved least popular – drawn on only by the playwrights Edmund Hill (who had Alfred pose as Asser's idiot son) and Tom Matthews (whose pantomime Alfred disguises himself as a comic Ethiopian).[167] Nineteenth-century paintings of Alfred in the Danish camp also, without exception, depict the king holding a harp.[168]

This tendency is rather surprising, given the usual authority of William of Malmesbury during the nineteenth century and the influence of Spelman's *Life of Alfred the Great* which incorporated William of Malmesbury's version.[169] It is explained in part by the cult of minstrelsy, which developed in Britain during the late eighteenth and the nineteenth century and which exerted a widespread influence on writers and artists alike.[170] The fact that Thomas Percy included this version of the story in his popular 1765 *Reliques of Ancient English Poetry* also undoubtedly contributed to its dominance. More specifically, the story of Alfred playing his harp before the Danish Guthrum may also have appealed to nineteenth-century Alfredianists, because of its striking similarity to the account in the first book of Samuel which relates how the future King David played his harp before the bad King Saul.[171] Indeed, several nineteenth-century writers explicitly celebrated Alfred as a modern David: Tupper's poem, 'Alfred Born at Wantage' proclaims, 'But Alfred was a David, to scatter every foe,/ The shepherd, psalmist, warrior, king, unblamed in weal and woe',[172] and in Pollard's novel, *A Hero King*, Alfred is told that he is 'a second David, a poet, a soldier, and thou maketh sweet music even as he did'.[173] Alfred the harper thus appealed to Victorian Anglo-Israelism. Indeed, the entire episode of Alfred's three months in hiding probably owed some of its nineteenth-century popularity to this creed, since the king's spell in the Somerset marshes could easily be likened to Christ's time in the wilderness – Pollard's novel, for instance, has Alfred go alone 'into the wilderness like the Christ' because he is instructed to do so by divine command.[174]

In most nineteenth-century texts, King Alfred ventures into the Danish camp alone, and this is also true of all the Victorian paintings that depict the scene. This Victorian tendency, however, represents a decisive break from the medieval sources for the legend, since one of the few things that the *History of the Kings of England*, the *Book of Hyde* and the *History of Ingulf* agree upon is that Alfred was accompanied on the venture by 'one of his faithful adherents' – and this version of the story was also recorded by Percy in the eighteenth century. The reason for the nineteenth-century innovation seems to have been largely aesthetic. The result for painters was a strongly iconic image – the best example is Daniel Maclise's 1852 'Alfred in the Camp of the Danes', in which a solitary, glowering and meditative Alfred is strikingly contrasted with a rabble of intoxicated and debauched Danes (see Figure 13).[175] For authors, too, depicting Alfred's visit as a solo mission was a useful dramatic device, allowing a strong distinction to be drawn between the king's virtue and moderation and the anarchic abandon of his enemies.[176] It also meant that Alfred was very decisively presented as the bravest and ablest man among the Saxons – a veritable hero king. That this was an important concern for Victorian Alfredianists is strongly suggested by those few texts in which Alfred is accompanied on his visit to the camp – in each, the 'faithful adherent' is a character who could not possibly pose any threat to the king's pre-eminence. Martin Farquhar Tupper, for instance, created a fictional

13 Daniel Maclise, *Alfred, the Saxon King, Disguised as a Minstrel, in the Tent of Guthrum the Dane* (first exhibited at the Royal Academy in 1852)

sister, Bertha, who secretly follows Alfred to the Danish camp in his *Alfred: A Patriotic Play*, while in Edmund Hill's 1901 *Alfred the Great: A Drama*, a rotund and inept Asser accompanies the king.[177] And in each text the companion, rather than helping Alfred, comes close to foolishly jeopardising the mission.

By striking contrast, in eighteenth-century texts, the credit for the disguised foray into the Danish camp is often stripped from Alfred and allotted to one of his followers. In Mallet and Thomson's 1740 play, for instance, Alfred offers to go into the Danish camp himself but is prevented from doing so by the Earl of Devon, who argues the inappropriateness of a king undertaking the mission and insists on carrying it out himself.[178] Such reluctance to depict Alfred in the Danish camp (like the eighteenth-century unwillingness to portray him disguised in the neatherd's cottage) can probably again be attributed in part to social discomfort with the notion that, stripped of regal apparel, a king could be indistinguishable from a commoner. That this was a contributing factor is suggested by the fact that in those eighteenth-century texts in which Alfred does disguise himself as a minstrel the enterprise is often a failure – whereas in nineteenth-century texts, it is always a success. In Rhodes's 1789 *Alfred: An Historical Tragedy*, for instance, one of the Danish chiefs quickly sees through Alfred's disguise, jubilantly likening the king to 'th'unpolished diamond encrusted o'er with meaner matter'.[179]

Several eighteenth-century authors also theorised that there must have been some reason, other than observing every 'object of secrecy', behind Alfred's disguised mission into the enemy camp. In John Home's 1778 *Alfred: A Tragedy*, for instance, the king undertakes the mission not to spy on his enemies but rather to rescue his captive wife. Moral concern about the ethics of espionage seems to have lain behind such innovation. This is rather suggested by the play's defensive preface which (apparently alluding to recent debate on the issue) states 'the dramatic and the real Alfred are both involved in the charge of imposture', and responds:

> Is it improbable to suppose that a young hero was in love? . . . If this reasoning is just, there will be no difficulty in vindicating the subsequent conduct of the hero. . . . The conduct of Alfred in the camp of Hinguar; the manner in which he deceives the Dane, is extremely similar to the conduct of Orestes in the Electra of Sophocles, which no critic hitherto has blamed.[180]

Home's motif of the captive Ethelswida does not derive from either a medieval source or an early history of Alfred. On the contrary, earlier texts like Robert Powell's 1634 *Life of Alfred* make no bones about the fact that the Saxon king went to Guthrum's camp to discover his 'martiall counsels and designs'.[181] However, his theory was reworked by several writers until the early nineteenth century.[182] One of the last texts to incorporate it was Joseph Cottle's 1800 *Alfred: An Epic Poem*, in which Alfred proposes to enter the Danish camp so that he can discern 'How stands the enemy; their force how great;/ Their next designs'. But when his follower Oddune points to the 'absence of all meaning' in Alfred, rather than some politically less important figure, going into the Danish camp, the king confesses that he wants to go himself because his queen is held captive there.[183]

Cottle's text seems positioned between different sets of values about leadership and war: a residual concern that kings should only perform tasks befitting their station and warfare should be fair and chivalrous; a new expectation that kings should be active and foremost among their men; and an emergent acceptance of espionage. By the mid-nineteenth century, Alfred's reasons for visiting the Danish camp were unashamedly military and strategic – to assess the weak points of the encampment, or the number of troops possessed by the Danes – and this was even more the case in the last two decades of the Victorian period.[184] In Stables's robustly militaristic *'Twixt Daydawn and Light*, for instance, Alfred's visit to the Danish camp is triumphantly hailed as the 'most perfect system of scouting and espionage', and Stables adds, 'there really was nothing to beat it during even the terrible Franco-German War'.[185] Such proud descriptions perhaps owe something to the renewed British enthusiasm for militarism that arose in the late nineteenth century, along with public approbation of Britain's 1898 war in the Sudan.[186]

Nineteenth-century authors were also attracted by the tale of Alfred's visit to the Danish camp, because it allowed them to develop the character of the Viking king Guthrum who, Asser tells us, was beaten by Alfred at the Battle of Edington and then baptised and received as his adoptive son.[187] In the eighteenth century, authors had typically used Guthrum as a simple foil for Alfred: a bad king, vanquished by the Saxon. So, in Fuller's novel, for instance, Guthrum is a 'volcano' who takes women by force, lives in a tent in which precious ornaments are 'scattered in wild profusion', and is 'reduced to the senseless condition of his followers' at bacchanalian feasts, bereft of 'the power or the inclination to enforce obedience, or establish order'.[188] In the nineteenth century, by contrast, a tendency developed to portray Guthrum as a merely misguided or unenlightened monarch, ripe for education, who is tutored and shown the error of his ways by Alfred, while the king is disguised as a minstrel. This conveniently explained the Dane's sudden conversion to Christianity after Edington, which seems to have concerned many nineteenth-century Alfredianists as far too expedient a change of heart.[189] Fitchett was just one writer to explicitly present Alfred's time in the Danish camp as a preparation for Guthrum's later conversion. The argument to Book XXXVII of his *King Alfred* relates how:

> Alfred, in his character of a minstrel, sings in compliance with Guthrun's request, the revelation of the last day, according to the Christian belief, and afterwards further explains to Guthrun the system of Christianity, thereby laying the foundations of the future conversion of the Danish monarch.[190]

Several nineteenth-century texts went even further, suggesting that a bond of brotherhood developed between Guthrum and the disguised Alfred, a bond which later facilitated their truce. In Sarah Hamilton's 1829 play, Guthrum confides in Alfred the minstrel about his love for a Saxon girl and receives words of advice and comfort. Later the Saxon king muses:

> If Guthrum were not chief of robbers
> Who would with their unhallowed yoke destroy us,
> I could admire his generous sense of honour
> And the rough virtues of his noble heart.[191]

Likewise, in James Sheridan Knowles's play, *Alfred the Great; Or The Patriot King*, Alfred advises Guthrum on how to deal with his petulant daughter, and vows 'Guthrum!/ Where'er I speak of thee I'll give thee out/ Indeed a royal chief!'[192] The motif was doubtless attractive to playwrights simply on grounds of dramatic economy, facilitating a brisk movement from enmity to peace treaty. But such a bond seems also to be suggested in Daniel Maclise's 1852 painting of Alfred in the Danish camp – in which Guthrum is visibly less intoxicated than his own followers, physically very similar to Alfred, and gazes pensively at the disguised Saxon.[193] Maclise's Guthrum also reclines amid turbaned followers, suggesting that one contributing factor to the new nineteenth-century attitude to Guthrum may well have been the influence of British imperial rhetoric, which in the nineteenth century increasingly stressed the value of education and acculturation of the colonised, above conquest.

Alfred and Haesten

Of the large body of nineteenth-century Alfredian texts, many conclude in the immediate aftermath of the Battle of Edington, suggesting that for a great number of authors the Saxon king was primarily to be celebrated as a military hero. 'It were but copying out a page of history' to relate the events of Alfred's reign after Edington, Engelbach for instance asserted, at the end of his 1869 novel.[194] King Alfred ruled Wessex for a further twenty-one years, however. Moreover, in the later years of his reign he fought other wars, and secured victories which were in fact more impressive than that at Edington – most notably against the Danish force under the leadership of Haesten which invaded in 892 and was only conquered in 896.

One explanation for the neglect which the Haesten conflict received perhaps lies in the dominant Victorian conception of history as a narrative of national progress. To depict Alfred's reign as an endless cycle of invasion and defence would undermine such a linear view. And although cyclical models of history were proposed during the nineteenth century (particularly in the wake of Darwin's 1859 *Origin of Species*), these could not be employed in political rhetoric as easily as the progressive model could be used to defend Britain's aggressive colonial expansion, or to inspire confidence in the nation's future. The lack of nineteenth-century enthusiasm for the tale of Alfred's struggles against Haesten was also, however, due to the fact that *Asser's Life of King Alfred* does not mention the war at all (which must have been current at the time when he was writing). And the *Anglo-Saxon Chronicle*'s claim that Haesten's Danes 'had not altogether utterly crushed the English race, but they were a great deal more crushed in those three years by pestilence' may also have been influential.[195] For many nineteenth-century writers this seems to have made the whole episode uninspiring and devoid of real drama – a view epitomised by Frederick Pollock's dismissive 1899 description of Alfred's struggles against Haesten as 'not . . . fights for the life of the kingdom. . . . not critical . . . episodes that . . . may be passed over with a rapid survey'.[196]

One late eighteenth-century Alfredianist – the popular historian Sharon Turner – took a very different view, however. For Turner, the fact that Haesten had failed to seriously afflict Wessex was exciting, evincing 'the energy and wisdom of the regulations by which Alfred had provided for the defence of his people'. In his *History of the Anglo-Saxons*, therefore, Turner asserted that:

> The most brilliant incident in the life of Alfred was his defence of England against the formidable Hastings, which has not hitherto been sufficiently remarked. In his struggles against the Northmen over whom he prevailed at Edington, he had to oppose power rather than ability; but in resisting Hastings, he had to withstand a skilful veteran, disciplined in all the arts of war by thirty years' practice of it. . . . The defence of England against Hastings was a greater

evidence of Alfred's military talents than his triumph over the armies which had harassed the first part of his reign.[197]

Turner's history provides a lengthy account of Alfred's 892–96 war. His absurd Anglicisation of Haesten's name to 'Hastings' also subtly inflated the importance of Alfred's conflict by likening it to the well-known and important battle of 1066. The text was widely read and generally very influential during the nineteenth century – ten editions were published between 1799 and 1900. In spite of this, however, it inspired almost no nineteenth-century Alfredianists to explore imaginatively Alfred's struggle against Haesten (although it did engender a tradition of misspelling the name of Alfred's Danish foe).

Thomas Hughes was a significant exception. Following Turner's lead, the nineteenth-century popular historian was impressed by the account of Alfred's war against Haesten, because it revealed not only the Saxon king's martial vigour but also his intelligence and tactical skills. Writing of Alfred's 893–96 conflict in his history, Hughes asserted 'As we might expect, the tactics and method of defence adopted by him in his mature years offer a marked contrast to the impetuous gallantry of his early campaigns'. The underlying reason for Hughes's enthusiasm, however, seems to have been his identification of a modern parallel in Britain's early nineteenth-century war against Napoleonic France. Hughes imagined that 'on the cliffs of Boulogne, Hasting, like a leader of the same type in the first years of this nineteenth century, planned the invasion of Alfred's kingdom.[198] His interest exemplifies the way in which nineteenth-century Alfredianists were most attracted to those aspects of the Saxon king's life and reign for which they could find parallels in contemporary life – and suggests that Turner, too, may have been drawn to the conflict because of seeming parallels with the Napoleonic wars.

The other nineteenth-century Alfredianists to take an interest in Alfred's conflict against Haesten were fascinated not by the battle itself but by the *Anglo-Saxon Chronicle*'s account of how in 894, Alfred's men 'brought Haesten's wife and his two sons to the king, and he gave them back to him, because one of them was his godson, the other Ealdorman Æthelred's'.[199] Although Alfred's Christianity is clearly presented here as the root cause of his actions, many nineteenth-century writers portrayed the incident as exemplifying the Saxon king's magnanimity, reverence for family values, and gentlemanly respect for femininity – qualities that were highly regarded in the Victorian era.[200] In Pollard's *A Hero King*, for instance, a very gallant Alfred releases Haesten's family, explaining 'I war not with women and children'.[201] The emblematic quality of Alfred's freeing of his enemy's wife and children meant that the incident was also a popular subject for historical painters.[202] The earliest version of the scene was Henry Singleton's 1798 painting 'Alfred liberating the family of Hastings', which became a well-known image of the king after 1806, when it was engraved as the representative image of Alfred's reign in Robert Bowyer's popular illustrated edition of Hume's *History of England*. Like their literary contemporaries, nineteenth-century artists tended to use the event to illustrate the Saxon king's moral qualities – his gentleness and generosity. In 1842, for instance, James and George Foggo submitted a cartoon for the Westminster competition, an illustration that they entitled 'Alfred the Great generously releases the wife and children of Hastings, the Danish invader'.[203]

Alfred the wise king

Besides the few Alfredianists interested in Alfred's conflict against Haesten, those who took an interest in his later years as king generally did so because they were concerned with depicting the Saxon as the archetypal wise old monarch: a native Solomon. Indeed, Alfred is literally hailed as 'the Saxon Solon' in Winthrop Mackworth Praed's 1888 poem 'King Alfred's Book', and in Tupper's poem 'Alfred Born at Wantage' he is celebrated as 'A Solomon for wisdom's choice'.[204] Among the nineteenth-century writers who celebrated the wisdom of King Alfred in more general terms, G.A. Henty hailed him as 'learned, wise, prudent', while Maria Graham called him 'the wisest king we ever had'.[205] The most developed celebration of Alfred as a wise monarch, however, was probably John Stuart Blackie's 1890 poem, 'Alfred' – a lengthy eulogy to the mature king's wisdom and scholarship. Part of this relates:

> O'er the scholar's book of learning
> He with pious patience pored.
> Well he knew that of all noble
> Doing Thought is rightful lord
> And the pen indites the wisdom
> That gives honour to the sword.
> . . . As a wise physician gathers
> Healing herbs from field and shore
> So from Saxon books and Latin
> Alfred swelled his thoughtful store.[206]

The nineteenth-century notion that the mature Alfred was particularly wise drew upon a strong medieval tradition, beginning with Asser, who described him as 'judicious' and 'extremely astute', as well as relating how the king summoned scholars to his court (Asser included) to satisfy his strong 'desire for knowledge'.[207] It must also have been encouraged by the translations of Latin texts into the vernacular – translations which Alfred allegedly completed and which are alluded to in Blackie's poem. And several late medieval texts which celebrate Alfred as a sagacious monarch also seem to have encouraged the Victorian conception – above all the twelfth-century *Proverbs of Alfred*.[208] This text, which is composed of a collection of precepts for good conduct, allegedly uttered by the Saxon king, declares 'Wise the sayings Alfred said' and 'Wise was he and choice in speech'.[209] However, there is no evidence that the *Proverbs* has any connection with Alfred whatsoever.[210] However, it was published in a modern translation in 1852, as part of *The Whole Works of Alfred the Great*, and was also excerpted in Spelman's *The Life of Alfred the Great*, so it was known to nineteenth-century Alfredianists and was accepted by many as representing the mature king's deepest thoughts.[211] The Catholic historian Mrs Maxwell Scott, for instance, prefaced her biography of Alfred with a quotation from the *Proverbs*, while in 1855, E.L. Hervey produced a poetic paraphrase of them addressed – not as the *Proverbs* are, to Alfred's son – but instead to 'the children of his land', and accompanied by an engraving of *Alfred the Great Teaching the Anglo-Saxon Youth*'.[212]

The nineteenth-century emphasis upon Alfred's wisdom should also be read in the context of the Carlylean dictum that an ideal ruler should be one capable of expressing 'the wisest' ideas that one could 'anywhere or anyhow learn'.[213] In fact, during the nineteenth century, the conception of Alfred as one of history's most sagacious monarchs became so influential and popular that some of those writers who ended their texts with the Battle of Edington opted to ignore chronology in order to depict Alfred as a shrewd old monarch at a time when he was actually only thirty years old. In Alfred Austin's *England's Darling*, for instance, Alfred inexplicably has adult children who fight in the battle of Edington, while he himself functions as a source of wisdom and inspiration – a stark contrast to the Alfred of many eighteenth-century texts, who is the pre-eminent warrior on the battlefield.[214]

Alfred the royal reformer

For some nineteenth-century writers there was one reason, in particular, why the later years of Alfred's reign were the most fascinating – and why the Saxon king should indisputably have been celebrated as the most outstandingly wise of English monarchs. This was the belief that in his mature years on the throne, Alfred had made positive and significant changes to England's political structure. Various apologists and parties made very different claims about the nature of this innovation. In 1899, Harrison asserted that the Saxon king had been an elected monarch, chosen to rule 'almost against his will' – a claim evidently connected to his own stance as a self-proclaimed 'republican conservative' in search of a compromise between outright republicanism and monarchy.[215] By contrast, in an 1852 article, Froude used Alfred to bolster his opposition to proposed increases in the powers of local government, depicting the king as a monarch who had centralised power and drawn 'the rein of government tighter than before'.[216]

Most often, however, nineteenth-century conceptions of Alfred as a politically reforming monarch bestowed upon him opinions that would now be classified as 'left-wing'. Besant claimed in his *The Story of King Alfred* that Alfred:

> began the custom, which has been of incalculable advantage to the country, of recruiting continually into the ranks of the noble class. ... It will be one of the great glories of the nineteenth century that it effected the breaking-down of this caste; that it ... created every year new nobles.[217]

Similarly (although less laudatory about contemporary affairs), Stables complained in his 1898 *'Twixt Daydawn and Light* that 'nowadays the bravest and best are sometimes permitted to languish in obscurity and poverty', whereas Alfred had never neglected to 'honour and recognise bravery and worth quite irrespective of birth. Education and mental ability were, in Alfred's eyes, far higher than the accident of a man's being born of high degree'.[218] Both egalitarian Alfreds should be read in the context of the increasingly common calls, voiced in the late nineteenth century, to eradicate hereditary peerages.[219]

The most common discourse of all, however, presented Alfred as the first chapter in a national narrative of gradual constitutional progress, by claiming that he had instituted the earliest British parliament, to become the country's first limited monarch. This idea is alluded to in the many early nineteenth-century texts, which hail Alfred as a champion of liberty. In Pye's 1801 *Alfred: An Epic Poem*, the Saxon king dramatically denounces unlimited monarchy as 'a charge too fast for mortal man to wield', while George Dyer's 1802 poem praises Alfred as 'The Prince, whose bosom glows with freedom's flame'.[220] It is in mid- and late nineteenth-century texts, however, that the notion is more explicitly developed. Hughes's 1869 history claims that Alfred could 'do no imperial act . . . could not make a law, impose a tax, call out an army, or make a grant of folkland, without the sanction of his witan'.[221] And Albert Savage's 1901 essay asserts 'The England of Alfred, like the England of today, was a limited constitutional monarchy . . . The king was not absolute'.[222]

The idea of Alfred as a limited monarch was particularly popular among defenders of Britain's Hanoverian royal family, since it endowed the country's model of constitutional monarchy with an ancient heritage and effectively distanced it from the absolute monarchies that were tumbling across Europe during the first half of the nineteenth century. Thus, the vehemently pro-Hanoverian Tupper alluded to the Saxon king's 'constitutional' reign and 'parliament' in several of his works.[223] And in 1832, when a Sunderland mug and commemorative plate were issued to celebrate William IV for his supposed contribution to the passage of the Great Reform Act, they hailed him, respectively, as 'the only royal reformer since Alfred', and 'the first radical monarch since Alfred'.[224]

The nineteenth-century conception of Alfred as a limited monarch seems to have been ultimately based on a reference to 'the councillors of the West Saxons' and two references to 'assemblies' being held, in the Saxon king's will.[225] There is nothing in the will, however, or indeed in any other ninth-century manuscript, to suggest that Alfred's assemblies were the equivalent of a modern parliament, or that his councillors wielded any real independent political power. Rather, Tupper's notion of Alfred's 'parliament' should probably be traced back to Spelman's *The Life of Alfred the Great*, which asserts that the Saxon king 'Often heard the Opinion of his Council, whom, although they were not yet known by that Name, yet may we properly call his Council of State'. In fairness, it must be acknowledged that Spelman does further qualify this statement, explaining that Alfred's assembly was not 'of one and the same Form and Solemnity with our later Parliaments'.[226] However, until the late nineteenth century (by which time many more ninth-century manuscripts had been published and translated) writers seem to have overlooked this qualification and to have assumed that Alfred's 'council of state' was virtually identical with their own parliament.

Certainly a large number of nineteenth-century Alfredianists explicitly presented Alfred's parliament as the direct ancestor of their own. In so doing, they competed with contemporary claims that the ancient Druids, Boudicca, or Simon de Montfort had established Britain's first parliament, and, along with those assertions, formed part of a general swell of nationalistic fervour which sought to forge an ancient history for the British parliament which would rival those of classical institutions. In 1888, Praed prefaced his poem on Alfred with a quotation avowing that the king did 'no less than to new model the Constitution, to rebuild it on a plan that should endure for ages'.[227] And Bowker, similarly, prefaced his 1901 *Alfred the Great* with a claim that the commemoration of Alfred's death should be viewed as 'veri-tably that of one thousand years . . . of our government'.[228] It was perhaps this conception which lay behind the marked success of Alfredian subjects in the 1840s' painting competitions for the decoration of the new Houses of Parliament – in particular, John Bridges' 'Alfred submitting his laws for the approval of the witan', depicting the king surrounded by his 'parliament', which was awarded a £100 prize.[229] The notion may also have dictated the choice of the retired Whig prime minister Lord Rosebery to unveil the Alfred statue in Winchester. Certainly, Rosebery did not let any sense of connection between himself and Alfred pass by the crowds assembled for the unveiling ceremony. The 'striking' speech which he delivered drew an explicit parallel between Alfred's councillors – or witan – and the modern British parliament, calling upon his audience to imagine how wondrous it would be if the Saxon king could be shown 'the palace where the *descendants of his Witan* conduct a system of government which . . . is the parent of most constitutions in the civilised world'.[230] The speech also provides an instance of the way in which claims of Alfredian origin were often drawn upon in the nineteenth century as justification for Britain's colonial ventures.[231]

Those nineteenth-century Alfredianists who accepted that Alfred had instituted some form of parliament disagreed on one crucial issue – whether it had been democratically elected. This issue, more than any other debate about Alfred's government, was intimately related to contemporary con-cerns: the Franchise Act, the Municipal Act, and two reform bills gradually increased male suffrage during the nineteenth century, but nevertheless, it was not until 1918 that all men over the age of 21 could vote. A few Tory writers argued that Alfred – like all Saxon kings – had sat at the head of a strictly hierarchical society whose population for the most part had lived in a servile state, bereft of all civil rights. Thus George Godfrey Cunningham's

1834 *Lives of Eminent and Illustrious Englishmen* praises Alfred for his 'great council of the nation', but insists that it was not a 'representative government'.[232]

More popular, however, was the Whiggish project to incorporate Alfred into the theory of the 'Norman Yoke'. This position argued that as the greatest Saxon ruler, Alfred had undoubtedly been responsible for establishing the primitive democracy which it was imagined had been in operation in Saxon England until it was abolished by the tyrannical Normans.[233] This idea filtered all the way through nineteenth-century culture from historians like Dugald Macfayden to the level of children's literature.[234] Maria Graham's influential children's book *Little Arthur's History of England*, written only a year after Cunningham's *Lives*, clearly depicts Alfred's parliament as representative, relating:

> When [Alfred] wanted to make a new law, he sent word to all the towns in his kingdom, and as many of the men as could, used to go to the king to hear what the new law was to be . . . But it would have been troublesome for all the men to go to the king . . . so the men in one town said, it will be better to send two or three of the cleverest of our neighbours . . . we call this a parliament in English.[235]

Graham's conception has no basis in any Saxon or even late medieval manuscripts: the trail appears to stop, once again, with John Spelman's history of Alfred. The 1709 English translation of this text asserts that twice a year in London Alfred held 'an assembling of the *Representative* Body of the State'.[236] The use of the word 'representative' here was probably not intended to be politically specific. However, in the nineteenth century, the word was sufficiently loaded with topical signification for Spelman's use of it to seize the attention of numerous writers who imagined that Alfred's councillors were chosen by ballot – in short, that they were the equivalent of the representative members of a nineteenth-century parliament.[237] This popular idea was also undoubtedly encouraged by the work of eighteenth-century political radicals like Obadiah Hulme, whose *Historical Essay on the English Constitution*, as we have seen above, confidently asserted that King Alfred's 'parliament' was attended by 'representative' burgesses who were 'elected by every resident inhabitant'.[238]

The question of monarchies, republics and democracies was just one contemporary issue in which Alfred became involved in the nineteenth century. This chapter has discussed the many ways in which Victorian rewriters portrayed the Saxon as an ideal king – whether that meant an absolute monarch, a limited sovereign, a warrior-hero, or a wise and aged ruler. Nineteenth-century artists and authors did not base their acclaim of Alfred as king purely on his personal qualities and behaviour, however. Part of the reason why he was celebrated more than any other early monarch in the nineteenth century was the belief that he had created many of the institutions of which Victorian Britain was most proud – and which were viewed as pillars of the nation, inseparable from national identity – including the country's navy, education system and legal apparatus. This belief will be the subject of the next chapter.

Notes

1 *The Times* (21 Sep. 1901), p. 10; Bowker, *The King Alfred Millenary*, p. vii.
2 Herbert, 'Lessons of the French Revolution', p. 265. See also Herbert's reference (p. 274) to 'an essential identity between the spirit of 1789 and that of 1870'.
3 These included rebellions in Paris, Berlin, Vienna, Warsaw, Prague, Budapest and Rome, as well as Chartist uprisings in London.
4 See *ODNB*; Hibbert, *Queen Victoria*, pp. 222–223, 307–310.
5 Carlyle, *On Heroes and Hero Worship*, p. 184.
6 Carlyle, *On Heroes and Hero Worship*, pp. 187, 182.
7 Carlyle, *On Heroes and Hero Worship*, pp. 182, 181, 192, 201, 206.
8 See Chandler, *A Dream of Order*, p. 48.
9 Hughes, *Alfred the Great*, p. 7.
10 Hughes, *Alfred the Great*, pp. 9, 4.
11 See Herbert, 'Lessons of the French Revolution', pp. 279, 292–294.
12 Hughes, *Alfred the Great*, pp. 13, 27, 5.
13 Hughes, *Alfred the Great*, pp. 27, 86
14 *The Anglo-Saxon Chronicles*, p. 64.
15 *Asser's Life of King Alfred*, p. 69. See also *The Anglo-Saxon Chronicles*, p. 43.
16 Æthelwulf is presented as a great warrior in Camden, *Britannia*, p. cxlii; and Fuller, *The Son of Ethelwolf*, p. 5.
17 Pauli, *The Life of Alfred the Great*, p. 46; Stables, *'Twixt Daydawn and Light*, p. 250. See also Henty, *The Dragon and the Raven*, p. 21.
18 Carlyle, *On Heroes and Hero Worship*, p. 199.
19 *Asser's Life of King Alfred*, p. 70. Stables could have been directly influenced by Rapin, *The History of England* (p. 102), in which Æthelwulf is described as 'naturally of a slothful, inactive temper'; or Bicknell, *The Life of Alfred the Great*, p. 75, which claims that he was 'too inactive to command his army in person'.
20 *Asser's Life of King Alfred*, p. 71.
21 Giles, *Six Old English Chronicles*, p. 46.
22 See, for instance, Thomas Love Peacock, *Maid Marian* (London, 2002 [1822]), p. 125.
23 *The Anglo-Saxon Chronicles*, p. 66.
24 *Asser's Life of King Alfred*, p. 73.
25 *The Annals of Roger de Hoveden*, p. 38. Hoveden's account is reiterated in Roger of Wendover, *Flowers of History*, p. 187; and the *Book of Hyde*, p. 493.
26 Colley, *Britons: Forging the Nation*, pp. 46–53.
27 Bicknell, *The Life of Alfred the Great*, p. 75. See also Rapin, *The History of England*, p. 103.
28 Tappan, *In the Days of Alfred the Great*, pp. 103, 94. See also Hughes, *Alfred the Great*, p. 33.
29 *Asser's Life of King Alfred*, p. 79.

30 *The Chronicle of Pierre de Langtoft*, p. 315; William of Malmesbury, *The History of the Kings of England*, p. 99.
31 See Spelman, *The Life of Alfred the Great*, p. 42, for a reference to this claim. Curiously, I have been unable to find it in Gibson's 1695 English translation of *Britannia*. It is perhaps possible that, considering the notion to be wrong, the translator removed it from the text.
32 See Spelman, *The Life of Alfred the Great*, p. 42.
33 'J.F.R.', *Lives of Alfred the Great, Sir Thomas More, and John Evelyn*, pp. 5–6.
34 Attenborough, *Alfred the Great*, p. 7.
35 Kerr, *Two Saxon Maidens*, p. 127.
36 Engelbach, *The Danes in England*, p. 121; Hill, *Alfred the Great*, p. 6.
37 *Asser's Life of King Alfred*, p. 80.
38 Bevan, *A Lion of Wessex*, p. 188. See also Henty, *The Dragon and the Raven*, p. 75; Creswick, *In Ælfred's Days*, p. 18; Tappan, *In the Days of Alfred the Great*, p. 188.
39 Attenborough, *Alfred the Great*, p. 2.
40 Hill, *Alfred the Great*, p. 6. See also Fitchett, *King Alfred*, III, p. 100.
41 *Asser's Life of King Alfred*, p. 80.
42 Carlyle, *On Heroes and Hero Worship*, p. 201. See also Lilly, 'British Monarchy and Modern Democracy', pp. 853–864.
43 Carlyle, *Past and Present*, p. 220
44 *Asser's Life of King Alfred*, p. 80.
45 Hughes, *Alfred the Great*, p. 69.
46 Besant, 'The Heritage of Alfred the Great', p. 531; Rawnsley, 'The Millenary of Alfred the King', p. 19. See also Oman, 'Alfred as Warrior', p. 115.
47 William of Malmesbury, *The History of the Kings of England*, p. 103.
48 Blackmore, *Alfred: An Epick Poem*, p. 313. See also Bicknell, *The Patriot King*, p. 59.
49 Fuller, *The Son of Ethelwolf*, p. 121.
50 Fitchett, *King Alfred*, III, p. 426.
51 Richard Cohen, *By the Sword* (London, Macmillan, 2002), pp. 167–171.
52 Rhodes, *Alfred*, p. 119.
53 Cottle, *Alfred: An Epic Poem*, p. 168.
54 Pye, *Alfred: An Epic Poem*, p. 25.
55 Dibdin, 'Alfred the Great', p. 66. See also Cottle, *Alfred: An Epic Poem*, p. 198. Cottle's presentation of a peace-loving Alfred was certainly a conscious choice. In the introduction to his poem (p. xxxvii), he theorises about the pernicious psychological effects of reading epic poems about violent battle.
56 Kelsey, *Alfred of Wessex*, II, p. 67; Hall, *Muscular Christianity*, p. 32.
57 Whistler, *King Alfred's Viking*, p. 227; Henty, *The Dragon and the Raven*, p. 209.
58 *ODNB*.
59 Whistler, *King Alfred's Viking*, p. 200.
60 Oman, 'Alfred as Warrior', p. 82.
61 See Colley, *Britons: Forging the Nation*, pp. 20–35.
62 Watson, 'King Alfred', p. 27.
63 *Asser's Life of King Alfred*, pp. 81–82.
64 Attenborough, *Alfred the Great*, p. 22.
65 Kerr, *Two Saxon Maidens*, pp. 155–156.

66 Oman, 'Alfred as Warrior', p. 134.
67 *Asser's Life of King Alfred*, p. 85; Abbott, *Alfred the Great*, p. 36. See also Hamilton, *Alfred the Great*, p. 48.
68 On the dates of Asser's *Life* and the *Chronicle*, see Keynes and Lapidge, *Alfred the Great*, pp. 53, 39.
69 *The Anglo-Saxon Chronicles*, p. 74.
70 *Asser's Life of King Alfred*, p. 83.
71 Carlyle, *On Heroes and Hero Worship*, pp. 181–182, 199.
72 Knight, *Alfred*, p. 2; See also Collingwood, *Alfred the Great: A Poem*, p. 53; Tupper, *Alfred: A Patriotic Play*, p. 5.
73 Hughes, *Alfred the Great*, p. 101, paraphrases Brompton, and cites him as the source of the nineteenth-century belief about Alfred's retreat. I have been unable to locate Brompton's original text.
74 See, for instance, Giles, *The Life and Times of Alfred the Great*, p. 188.
75 Hughes, *Alfred the Great*, p. 100, dismisses the suggestion outright.
76 Hughes, *Alfred the Great*, p. 101.
77 *The Anglo-Saxon Chronicles*, p. 74.
78 Pollard, *A Hero King*, p. 291.
79 Manning, *The Chronicle of Ethelfled*, p. 192.
80 Hughes, *Alfred the Great*, p. 129.
81 William of Malmesbury, *The History of the Kings of England*, p. 100; John Wallingford, *The Chronicle of John Wallingford*, p. 541.
82 *Pastoral Care*, p. 125.
83 Hughes, *Alfred the Great*, p. 129.
84 *The Anglo-Saxon Chronicles*, p. 74. For Asser's almost identical account, see *Asser's Life of King Alfred*, p. 83.
85 Von Haller, *The Moderate Monarchy*, p. 14.
86 It was first expressed in Fuller, *The Son of Ethelwolf*, p. 49.
87 See Herbert, 'Lessons on the French Revolution', pp. 279, 292–294.
88 Canning, *Alfred the Great in Athelnay*, pp. 18, 13, 52.
89 See *ODNB*; Hibbert, *Queen Victoria*, pp. 285–359.
90 On public reactions to Victoria's seclusion, see *ODNB*; Cannadine, 'The Context, Performance and Meaning of Ritual', pp. 120–123.
91 Engelbach, *The Danes in England*, p. 160.
92 Henty, *The Dragon and the Raven*, pp. 92, 203, 126.
93 See Peck, *War, the Army and Victorian Literature*, pp. 141–142.
94 Henty, *The Dragon and the Raven*, p. 60.
95 Henty was a loyal supporter of the monarchy. In 1875, he accompanied the Prince of Wales (the future Edward VII) on a tour through India (see *ODNB*). Hughes, *Alfred the Great*, p. 13. See also Harrison, 'The Monarchy', pp. 613–641; Hill, 'The Future of the English Monarchy', pp. 187–205.
96 *Life of Saint Neot*, p. 198.
97 It also perhaps influenced William Blake to include Alfred on a list of tyrants (including Cain, Satan and Pharaoh) in his 1810 poem *Jerusalem*. This unusual, negative use of the Saxon king seems not to have influenced any later texts.
98 Stewart, *Stories about Alfred the Great*, p. 38; Engelbach, *The Danes in England*, p. 160.
99 Turner, *The History of the Anglo-Saxons*, pp. 323, 328.
100 Turner, *The History of the Anglo-Saxons*, p. 326.

101 See, for instance, Russell, *The Causes of the French Revolution*, p. 9.
102 See for instance 'J.F.R.', *Lives of Alfred the Great, Sir Thomas More, and John Evelyn*, p. 12.
103 On the discontent about George I and George II, see *ODNB*; Lilly, 'British Monarchy and Modern Democracy', p. 860.
104 Mallet and Thomson, *Alfred: A Masque*, p. 26.
105 Pye, *Alfred: An Epic Poem*, p. 13.
106 Knowles, *Alfred the Great*, p. 70. See also Cottle, *Alfred: An Epic Poem*, p. 74; Von Haller, *The Moderate Monarchy*, p. 35.
107 *Asser's Life of King Alfred*, p. 97.
108 Collingwood, *Alfred the Great: A Poem*, p. 107. See also Kelsey, *Alfred of Wessex*, I, p. 260; Attenborough, *Alfred the Great*, p. 21; Fitchett, *King Alfred*, III, p. 100.
109 Reed, *Meditations on the Hero*, p. 94.
110 Maxwell-Scott, *Alfred the Great*, p. 31; 'J.F.R.', *Lives of Alfred the Great, Sir Thomas More, and John Evelyn*, p. 4. See also Austin, *England's Darling*, p. 5.
111 Turner, *The History of the Anglo-Saxons*, p. 329.
112 Manning, *The Chronicle of Ethelfled*, p. 135.
113 Canning, *Alfred the Great in Athelnay*, pp. 13, 20.
114 Manning, *The Chronicle of Ethelfled*, p. 69.
115 Manning, *The Chronicle of Ethelfled*, p. 135.
116 See Colley, *Britons: Forging the Nation*, p. 155.
117 Whitaker, *The Life of Saint Neot*, p. 144. See also Giles, *The Life and Times of Alfred the Great*, p. 307.
118 Hughes, *Alfred the Great*, p. 104.
119 Plummer, *The Life and Times of Alfred the Great*, p. 58.
120 Whitaker, *The Life of Saint Neot*, p. 197.
121 *Annals of Saint Neots*, pp. 197–200. Matthew Parker, *Aelfredi regis res gestae*, p. 15. Examples of nineteenth-century editions include: J.A. Giles, *Six Old English Chronicles*, p. 60; Joseph Stevenson, *The Church Historians*, II: ii, p. 457.
122 See Hughes, *Alfred the Great*, p. 107; Stables, *'Twixt Daydawn and Light*, pp. 319–328.
123 'The Shepherd and the King, and of Gillian the Shepherd's Wife, with her Churlish Answers: Being Full of Mirth and Merry Pastime', p. 504.
124 See, for instance, Mallet and Thompson, *Alfred: A Masque*, p. 8.
125 Mallet and Thomson, *Alfred: A Masque*, p. 8.
126 See Macalpine and Hunter, *George III and the Mad-Business*, p. 11.
127 Engelbach, *The Danes in England*, p. 157; Whistler, *King Alfred's Viking*, p. 185. See also Henty, *The Dragon and the Raven*, p. 200.
128 See Rose, 'The Disappearing Pauper: Victorian Attitudes to the Relief of the Poor', p. 57.
129 Compare G.A. Henty, *The Dragon and the Raven*, p. 200, with Pye, *Alfred: An Epic Poem*, p. 42.
130 See, for instance, Mallet and Thomson, *Alfred: A Masque*, p. 5.
131 The only exception is Stables's *'Twixt Daydawn and Light*, where he is accompanied by his wife and children.
132 Whitaker, *The Life of Saint Neot*, p. 198.
133 Spelman, *The Life of Alfred the Great*, p. 54; Rapin, *The History of England*, p. 109.

134 *The Times* (21 Sep. 1901), p. 10.

135 Froude, 'King Alfred', p. 82.

136 See Mitchell, *Picturing the Past*, p. 58; Keynes, 'The Cult of King Alfred the Great', p. 314.

137 Brough, *Alfred the Great*, p. 21.

138 See Mitchell, *Picturing the Past*, pp. 67, 24, 15–16.

139 On Thackeray's satirising of historical painting and literature, see Mitchell, *Picturing the Past*, pp. 205–215. In the 1840s, Thackeray also produced a series of lampoons on the many popular histories of the Anglo-Saxons appearing around that time – on this, see Melman, 'Claiming the Nation's Past', p. 583.

140 Thackeray, 'Our Street', XII, p. 54.

141 Thackeray, *The Newcomes*, p. 221.

142 See Magnus, *Alfred the Great*, p. 89; Attenborough, *Alfred the Great*, p. 31; Whistler, *King Alfred's Viking*, p. 190; Pollard, *A Hero King*, p. 297.

143 Whitaker, *The Life of Saint Neot*, p. 198.

144 Spelman, *The Life of Alfred the Great*, p. 54.

145 Williams, *Pope, Homer and Manliness*, p. 30.

146 Bicknell, *The Patriot King*, p. 24.

147 Collingwood, *Alfred the Great*, p. 108.

148 *ODNB*.

149 Knowles, *Alfred the Great*, p. 26.

150 Knowles, *Alfred the Great*, p. i.

151 Cottle, *Alfred: An Epic Poem*, p. 100.

152 Henty, *The Dragon and the Raven*, p. 200.

153 Magnus, *First Makers of England*, p. 123.

154 Canning, *Alfred the Great in Athelnay*, p. 80.

155 Tupper, *Alfred: A Patriotic Play*, p. 9.

156 *Asser's Life of King Alfred*, p. 84.

157 Henty was the editor of the 'Union Jack' and also accompanied the Prince of Wales on a tour of India in 1875 (see *ODNB*).

158 Henty, *The Dragon and the Raven*, pp. 204–207. See also Stables, *'Twixt Daydawn and Light*, p. 324; Tappan, *In the Days of Alfred the Great*, p. 272.

159 *The Chronicle of Fabius Ethelwerd*, p. 431.

160 This notion is first seen in Fuller, *The Son of Ethelwolf*, p. 165.

161 Whistler, *King Alfred's Viking*, p. 198.

162 Carlyle, *On Heroes and Hero Worship*, pp. 181, 184.

163 See McLaurin, 'Reworking "work" ', pp. 32–39.

164 *Asser's Life of King Alfred*, p. 84.

165 William of Malmesbury, *The History of the Kings of England*, p. 101.

166 *The Book of Hyde*, p. 509; *The History of Ingulf*, p. 603.

167 Hill, *Alfred the Great*, p. 45; Matthews, *Harlequin Alfred the Great!*, p. 19.

168 See Marshall Claxton's 1842 *Alfred in the Camp of the Danes* (reproduced in Keynes, 'The Cult of King Alfred the Great', pl. XIV*b*); and Daniel Maclise's 1852 *Alfred in the Camp of the Danes*.

169 On Spelman's popularity, see Simmons, *Reversing the Conquest*, p. 40. William of Malmesbury is cited as a reliable authority in, for instance, Kelsey, *Alfred of Wessex: A Poem*, I, p. liii; Hughes, *Alfred the Great*, p. 275; Draper, *Alfred the Great*, p. 129.

170 See Jackson-Houlston, *Ballads, Songs and Snatches*, pp. 1–5.

171 I Samuel 16.16–23

172 Tupper, *Alfred: A Patriotic Play*, p. 249.

173 Pollard, *A Hero King*, p. 133.

174 Pollard, *A Hero King*, p. 102.

175 See Figure 13 for a reproduction of Maclise's painting.

176 See Tupper, *Alfred: A Patriotic Play*, p. 23; Linton, 'King Alfred', p. 56; Knight, *Alfred*, p. 230.

177 Tupper, *Alfred: A Patriotic Play*, p. 29; Hill, *Alfred the Great*, p. 45.

178 Mallet and Thomson, *Alfred: A Masque*, p. 13.

179 Rhodes, *Alfred*, p. 86. See also Fuller, *The Son of Ethelwolf*, p. 63.

180 Home, *Alfred*, p. vii.

181 Powell (*The Life of Alfred or Alvred*, p. 14), for instance, makes no bones about the fact that Alfred went to Guthrum's camp to discover his enemy's 'martiall counsels and designs'.

182 Knight (*Alfred*, p. 230) was the last writer to depict a disguised Alfred rescuing a captive Ealhswith. However, his poem replicates so many eighteenth-century traditions that it should perhaps be viewed not as representative of nineteenth-century Alfredian texts, but as a remnant of eighteenth-century trends – as an example of what Williams (*Marxism and Literature*, p. 121) calls a 'residual discourse'.

183 Cottle, *Alfred: An Epic Poem*, p. 34.

184 For instance, Linton, 'King Alfred', p. 56; Tappan, *In the Days of Alfred the Great*, p 275; Whistler, *King Alfred's Viking*, p. 204.

185 Stables, *'Twixt Daydawn and Light*, p. 367.

186 See Peck, *War, the Army and Victorian Literature*, pp. xi, 128–136.

187 *Asser's Life of King Alfred*, p. 85.

188 Fuller, *The Son of Ethelwolf*, pp. 33, 43, 62.

189 See, for instance, Pauli, *The Life of Alfred the Great*, p. 108; Tappan, *In the Days of Alfred the Great*, p. 277; Hughes, *Alfred the Great*, p. 120.

190 Fitchett, *King Alfred*, V, p. 242.

191 Hamilton, *Alfred the Great*, pp. 9, 19, 25. See also Magnus, *Alfred the Great*, p. 127.

192 Knowles, *Alfred the Great*, p. 58.

193 See Figure 13 of this volume for a reproduction of Maclise's painting.

194 Engelbach, *The Danes in England*, p. 194.

195 *The Anglo-Saxon Chronicles*, p. 89.

196 Pollock, 'Alfred the Great', p. 277. See also Freeman, *Old English History*, p. 54.

197 Turner, *The History of the Anglo-Saxons*, pp. 351, 343, 355.

198 Hughes, *Alfred the Great*, pp. 252, 243.

199 *The Anglo-Saxon Chronicles*, 1996, p. 86.

200 This emphasis probably partly derived from Turner (*The History of the Anglo-Saxons*, p. 350), who states that Alfred's 'generosity' and 'magnanimity' led him to release Haesten's family.

201 Pollard, *A Hero King*, p. 418.

202 Such as Henry Pierce Bone, who in 1814 painted *The wife and sons of Hastings the Danish chief, brought as prisoners before Alfred the Great* (see Keynes, 'The Cult of King Alfred the Great', p. 318).

203 Keynes, 'The Cult of King Alfred the Great', pp. 316, 335.

204 Praed, 'King Alfred's Book', p. 140; Tupper, 'Alfred', p. 250.

205 Henty, *The Dragon and the Raven*, p. 5; Graham, *Little Arthur's History of England*, p. 54; Tappan, *In the Days of Alfred the Great*, p. 278.
206 Blackie, 'Alfred', pp. 98–99.
207 See *Asser's Life of King Alfred*, pp. 93, 109–110.
208 In the tenth-century *Chronicle of Fabius Ethelwerd*, Alfred is described as 'learned in speech' (p. 436). Supposedly Alfredian words of wisdom are quoted in the thirteenth-century poem *The Owl and the Nightingale* (published in 1838), and in the twelfth-century English fables translated by Marie de France (published in 1819), while an alleged writ of Æthelred the Unready also stresses the mature Alfred's wisdom (see Keynes and Lapidge, *Alfred the Great*, p. 47).
209 Tupper, 'King Alfred's Poems', p. 250.
210 See Keynes and Lapidge, *Alfred the Great*, p. 47.
211 Scholarly Alfredianists denied Alfred's connection to the text (see, for instance, Earle, 'Alfred as a Writer', p. 202; Plummer, *The Life and Times of Alfred the Great*, p. 150).
212 Maxwell Scott, *Alfred the Great*, p. 1; Hervey, 'Alfred the Great Teaching the Anglo-Saxon Youth', p. 658.
213 Carlyle, *On Heroes and Hero Worship*, p. 182.
214 Austin, *England's Darling*, p. 69. Austin was perhaps influenced by the anonymous *Alfred the Great: Deliverer of his Country*, p. 63, where Alfred has adult children. See also Knowles, *Alfred the Great*, p. 43, for an Alfred who ages prematurely.
215 Harrison, 'Alfred as King', p. 45. On Harrison's political stance see Harrison, 'The Monarchy', p. 630.
216 Froude, 'King Alfred', p. 83.
217 Besant, *The Story of King Alfred*, p. 116.
218 Stables, *'Twixt Daydawn and Light*, p. 348.
219 See Kidd, *City, Class and Culture*, pp. 1–17; Pilbeam, *The Middle Classes in Europe, 1789–1914*, pp. 23–74, 173–210.
220 Dyer, 'Alfred', p. 214; Pye, *Alfred: An Epic Poem*, p. 159.
221 Hughes, *Alfred the Great*, p. 27.
222 Savage, 'The Anglo-Saxon Constitution and Laws in the Time of Alfred the Great', p. 46.
223 Tupper, *King Alfred's Poems*, p. 32; Tupper, 'Alfred: Born at Wantage', in *Ballads for the Times*, p. 250; Tupper, 'Alfred', p. 297.
224 Keynes, 'The Cult of King Alfred the Great', p. 333.
225 *The Will of King Alfred*, pp. 174–175.
226 Spelman, *The Life of Alfred the Great*, p. 156.
227 Praed, 'King Alfred's Book', p. 140.
228 Bowker, *Alfred the Great*, p. x.
229 Keynes, 'The Cult of King Alfred the Great', pp. 334–341.
230 Bowker, *The King Alfred Millenary*, p. 111. The speech is described in Thurston, 'Alfred the Idolator', p. 425.
231 This will be discussed in more depth in Chapter Five of this volume.
232 *Lives of Eminent and Illustrious Englishmen*, p. 33.
233 On the Norman Yoke theory, see Simmons, *Reversing the Conquest*, pp. 34–37, 76–91.
234 Macfayden is referred to in Plummer, *The Life and Times of Alfred the Great*, p. 6.

235 Graham, *Little Arthur's History of England*, pp. 42–43.
236 Spelman, *The Life of Alfred the Great*, p. 157.
237 This belief was also probably encouraged by eighteenth-century political texts like Obadiah Hulme's *An Historical Essay on the English Constitution*, which asserts that King Alfred's parliament was attended by 'representative' burgesses who were 'elected by every resident inhabitant' (p. 28).
238 Hulme, *An Historical Essay on the English Constitution*, p. 28. See also Von Haller, *The Moderate Monarchy*, pp. 101, 118.

5

'The root and spring of everything we love in church and state': Alfred and Victorian progress

At the second planning meeting for the Alfred Millenary celebrations, Conan Doyle asserted, 'What we are commemorating is not merely the anniversary of the death of King Alfred, but the greatness of those institutions which he founded'.[1] The institutions to which he was alluding included the navy, the British Empire, Oxford University and a free education system. In the 1901 commemorations, as we have seen, these claims were represented by processions of academics, ambassadors and naval officers; by the launch of the *HMS King Alfred*; and by the assembling in Winchester of the National Home Reading Union. Alfred was also hailed as the founder of these institutions in numerous Victorian texts and in works of art. And he was equally credited at different times during the nineteenth century with attempting to abolish slavery; with establishing the English law-code and trial by jury; and with forging a proto-union of the British Isles.

Each of these notions can ultimately be traced to an over-reading or misreading of an Anglo-Saxon source, or to an unreliable late medieval chronicle.[2] Their interest, however, lies in what they reveal about the anxieties and values of nineteenth-century Britain. On the one hand, in claims about Alfredian origins, made by writers keen to aggrandise the Saxon king, we can identify those institutions of which Victorian Britain was most proud and which served as the bedrock of national identity. On the other hand, in the use of Alfred to legitimate nineteenth-century institutions, by bestowing upon them an ancient and prestigious founder, we gain glimpses into contemporary concerns about the criticism, competition or opposition that those establishments might have been facing. And in all of the nineteenth-century conceptions of the intense cultural change that was believed to have taken place during Alfred's reign, we discern both the dominance of Victorian narratives of social progress and hints about the anxieties that underlay the rapid social development of nineteenth-century Britain.

Alfred and the law

Legislation was one area of British society which saw unprecedented growth and development in the nineteenth century, with far more laws being passed or amended than in any preceding age.[3] In the popular fiction of the period, the fascination with legal processes demonstrates that awareness of (and anxiety about) this sudden escalation in the complexity of the law extended throughout Victorian society. Hailing King Alfred as the source of much of Britain's law was therefore a means of giving a reassuring aura of stability and permanence to a fast-changing area of modern life. So, in his *Child's History of England*, for instance, Charles Dickens asserted that Alfred's spirit 'still inspires some of our best English laws'.[4] More specifically, the barrister and historian Warwick Draper claimed that the property law of 'entail', introduced during the nineteenth century, had been foreshadowed in the forty-first law of Alfred's law-code which restricted men from disposing of inherited 'bookland' outside of their immediate family.[5] And another historian, J. Lorimer, asserted that Alfred was the first king to introduce custodial sentences – an assertion without any historical foundation, but merely his evident anxiety to legitimate the Victorian trend from capital to custodial punishment.[6]

Pro-imperial Victorian rhetoric often cited the dissemination of Britain's law as a prime justification for its aggressive colonial expansion.[7] Hailing a respected ninth-century king as the founder of that law-code, therefore, effectively confirmed its antiquity and nobility and consequently its precedence over the laws of seemingly 'younger' countries. Thus, in 1899, Conan Doyle asserted that Alfred, 'Inaugurated that respect for law and order which is now the distinguishing mark of every British colony'.[8] The association between Alfred and British law could work both ways, however. Earlier in the century, when Alfred's reputation was less firmly established, Tupper celebrated Alfred as the originator of 'half the best we boast in British liberties and *laws*', in order to increase the Saxon king's prestige and encourage participation in the proposed celebrations for the millennial anniversary of his birth.

The pervasiveness and popularity of the nineteenth-century association between Alfred and Britain's law-code is reflected in the considerable quantity of artwork which commemorates him in this role. In the 1820s, a design by John Flaxman entitled 'Alfred publishes his laws' was chosen by George IV for a new frieze for the garden front of Buckingham Palace, and in 1821 E. Taylor's *Historical Prints* series included 'Alfred Framing the Laws' as the illustration chosen to represent the Saxon period.[9] But it was in the early 1840s, when competitions were held to choose works of art for the new Houses of Parliament, that 'Alfred the legislator' really made an impact in the art world. One of the prizes in the 1842 competition for preparatory cartoons for frescos was won by John Bridges' design 'Alfred submitting his code of laws for the approval of the witan' (see Figure 14). The cartoon was exhibited to the public in Westminster Hall in the summer of 1843, and was later published as an engraving.[10] Its subject apparently impressed a number of other artists. When a second Westminster competition was held in 1843, two 'cartoons' and two statues of Alfred as a legislator were entered – although none enjoyed Bridges' success.[11]

14 John Bridges, *Alfred submitting his Laws to the Witan* (cartoon for a fresco, exhibited at Westminster Hall in 1843)

The nineteenth-century celebration of Alfred as a great legislator did not derive from either *Asser's Life of King Alfred* or the *Anglo-Saxon Chronicle*, neither of which refers to any particularly outstanding laws that the king instituted. Neither did it draw on any established eighteenth-century tradition.[12] The source was probably Alfred's own law-code, which was drawn up in the late 880s or early 890s; was first published in 1720; and appeared in a modern English edition in 1840. Very few of the laws in the code are actually of Alfred's own invention, however. The text mainly represents a compilation of earlier laws – Old Testament law, New Testament law, and the laws of earlier Anglo-Saxon kings. Indeed, Alfred unashamedly acknowledges this derivative element in his introduction to the law-code, relating 'Then I, King Alfred, gathered [the laws] together and ordered to be written many of the ones that our forefathers observed . . . For I dared not presume to set down in writing at all many of my own'.[13]

Prior to the publication of the 1840 translation of Alfred's laws, nineteenth-century Alfredianists were obviously aware of the existence of Alfred's law-code, but had no knowledge of the precise nature of its content and so celebrated the king in very generalised terms as a great legislator. In his 1813 'Alfred the Great', for instance, Dibdin vaguely claims 'Of thirty years in which the land he sway'd,/ Not one elaps'd but some good laws he made'.[14] After 1840, however, as popular histories began to disseminate more accurate information about the limited extent of Alfred's legislation, writers had to reconcile with their desire to hail Alfred as a legislator the fact that the king had produced few original laws.[15] Some responded to this dilemma by presenting Alfred's lack of originality as in itself a positive trait. Besant celebrated the Saxon king as 'a conservative reformer who desired to rebuild the past, to restore the past, to present the past on new foundations and with a view to possible developments in the future. . . . He did not put his trust in new laws; he did, however, put his trust in old laws newly edited'.[16] In other words, his values bore a striking similarity to the neo-feudally inspired philanthropy of Besant himself. The conservative-reformer Hughes also admired this cautious quality in Alfred's law-code. In his biography of the Saxon king he observed darkly, 'It would be instructive to inquire carefully how much of the trouble and misery which has come upon this land since [Alfred's] time has been caused by the want of Alfred's spirit in this matter of law-making'.[17]

Hughes was not the only nineteenth-century writer to present Alfred's legislation as infinitely wiser than that of the present. The most extended and politically conservative treatment of Alfred's law-code was attempted by Praed in his 1888 poem 'King Alfred's Book'. Praed's poem begins by imagining the modern discovery of Alfred's laws:

I saw in a dream, on a summer day,
The tomb where the Saxon Solon lay;
And thither the prince of the land was led,
With the robe on his shoulder, the crown on his head;
And they bade him draw from its secret nook
The volume of law, King Alfred's Book.
He held the tomb in his feeble grasp;
He broke the seals, and he snapped the clasp.
Long years had marred the dim, dim page
The treasured truth of the Chief and Sage;
And whose were the hands that undertook
To write new words in the holy book?

Praed presents an enfeebled modern world which is both unable and unworthy to supplement or improve upon Alfred's ninth-century laws. The rest of the poem describes how, in an almost Grail-like sequence, a series of characters attempt to add to the laws, but each of them either feels unequal to the task and turns away, or undertakes it badly – like the 'sallow penman' who 'had learned of the cunning scribes of France:/ 'Might' for 'right' his haste mistook,/ And 'treason' for 'reason' he wrote in the book'. The poem ends with a nightmarish image of anarchic, social uprising:

'Oh, write what ye may, or write what ye will',
Said the cry of a mob from a cotton mill;
The words may be grave, and the wit may be good;
But we're building the gallows, and lighting the wood:
The bird to the snare, and the fish to the hook,
And a rope for the clerks, and a fire for the book!

Praed's poem, with its allusions to French corruption, should perhaps be read in the context of the defeat of Napoleon III and the founding of the third French Republic in the 1870s. More immediately, it may also be read as part of the conservative anxiety about social instability that was ignited in Britain by the passage of the third Parliamentary Reform Bill in 1884.

Such explicitly political use of Alfred as a legislator was more common in the earlier decades of the nineteenth century – before the publication of the Saxon king's law-code, and when the content of Alfred's laws could be more freely speculated upon. In Henry James Pye's 1801 *Alfred: An Epic Poem*, a druid prophetically proclaims to the Saxon king, 'Thy code, arranged by Nature's purest plan/ Shall guard the freedom and the rights of man'. But he carefully qualifies this by adding, 'Man's real rights – not Folly's maniac dream,/ Senseless Equality's pernicious theme'.[18] On the other hand, in his 1831 *Alfred the Great: Or the Patriot King*, the radical journalist James Sheridan Knowles asserted that a spirit of equality had imbued Alfred's laws, which 'put the peasant and/ The king himself on equal footing'.[19] Of the two conceptions, Pye's is actually the most historically accurate.[20] Neither, however, was historically informed, but rather reflects its author's own politics: Pye's staunch Royalism, versus Knowles's ardent support for an extension to the British franchise. Knowles's conception may have been based on Asser's description of how Alfred 'used . . . to sit at judicial hearings for the benefit both of his nobles and of the common people'.[21] But it is just as likely that the radical journalist was influenced by the widely held Georgian and Victorian dictum that one of the principal causes of the 1789 revolution had been the inequality of the French legal system.

Alfred's reputation as Britain's first limited monarch also, undoubtedly, affected early nineteenth-century conceptions like Knowles's about his law-code. From being hailed as the institutor of an early parliament, the Saxon king became celebrated, more generally, as a champion of freedom: in 1802, George Dyer praised him as 'the Prince, whose bosom glows with freedom's flame'; in 1813, Thomas Dibdin asserted that Alfred 'built, on freedom's basis, England's throne'; while in Sarah Hamilton's 1829 *Alfred the Great: a Drama*, Alfred himself declares 'freedom is the right of Englishmen/ (Free be they as each thought which fills their breasts!)'.[22] This dominant image of Alfred influenced interpretations of one of his laws in particular – that which states that all slaves in Wessex must be given 'the four Wednesdays in the four Ember weeks . . . to sell to whomsoever they please anything of what anyone has given them in God's name, or of what they can earn in any of their spare time'.[23]

The issue of slavery was prominent among British social concerns in the first half of the nineteenth century – the slave trade was banned in the British Empire in 1807, but it was 1865 before it was abolished in the Southern states of America, and its spectre hovered for the rest of the century in the use of anti-slavery rhetoric by campaigners for women's rights.[24] References to slaves in Alfred's laws clearly caused discomfort among many British writers who wished to hail him as a champion of freedom. The children's writer Jesse Page was clearly anxious to extenuate the existence of slavery in ninth-century Wessex, insisting in her 1900 *Alfred the Great: The Father of the English*:

> It must be remembered that in Alfred's day slavery was a recognised institution . . . no surprise may be occasioned by the fact that the enlightened Alfred permitted this system of fettering humanity to exist, seeing that it took many years to teach the English that slavery was wrong.[25]

The law about the four Ember weeks was seized upon by those writers less able to accept slavery in Alfred's kingdom, and interpreted as evidence that the Saxon king had been a proto-abolitionist who in his legislation had pre-empted the reforms of the nineteenth century. Henty in his 1886 novel used it as the basis of his claim that during Alfred's reign, 'Serfdom, although not entirely abolished, had been mitigated and regulated'.[26] For the historian Warwick Draper, the law was evidence of Alfred's 'cautious but effective treatment of the slave question, whereby he first practically created a decent and respectable middle-class of society'.[27]

The law about Wessex's slaves also seems to have caught the attention of Katie Magnus, who approvingly claimed in her children's history of England that Alfred was 'beforehand with Sir John Lubbock (Lord Avebury) in seeing how important it is for all ranks of people to have holidays'.[28] And it was also perhaps that law which inspired the Chartist and factory reformer Samuel Kydd to use the pseudonym of 'Alfred' when calling for shorter working hours as part of his 1857 study of the Factory Reform Movement.[29] Such assertions demonstrate how tiny details in Alfredian source material could become the foundation of elaborate Victorian myths – if they could be made of relevance to contemporary concerns.

This was certainly the case with the nineteenth-century reception of the legend that King Alfred had been responsible for the institution of trial-by-jury. This practice was not introduced to England until the fifteenth century. In his early seventeenth-century *The Life of Alfred the Great*, however, Spelman alleged that Alfred had created 'the Law of Tryal by the Verdict of 12 of our Peers or Equals'.[30] Spelman's claim seems to have been derived from 'The Treaty between Alfred and Guthrum' – copies of which the Cambridge scholar of Anglo-Saxon would have been able to read in both the Cotton Library and the library of Corpus Christi College.[31] The treaty states that 'if anyone accuses a king's thegn of manslaughter, if he dares to clear himself he is to do it with twelve king's thegns'.[32] Clearly, the twelve men mentioned in the passage are not fulfilling the role of a modern jury, but more that of witnesses to the accused's character or recent activity. However, Spelman seems to have seized upon the coincidence of numbers and to have assumed that the king's thegns were equivalent to a modern jury of twelve jurors. Certainly, that was the mistake of Hughes, who in his 1869 *Alfred the Great: A Biography* (having perhaps been influenced by Spelman) misquoted the treaty so that it read 'And if a king's thane be accused of manslaughter, if he desire to clear himself let him do so *before* twelve king's thanes'.[33] Hughes's substitution of 'before' for 'with' subtly but crucially altered the meaning of the statement. Suddenly, the twelve thegns are no longer speaking on behalf of the defendant, but are evidently sitting in judgement upon him.

Spelman's *The Life of Alfred the Great* was the best-known biography of Alfred for the first half of the nineteenth century, and Hughes's was the most popular in the latter decades of the Victorian period.[34] However, not all of the Alfredian legends related in these two texts – or even all of their historical anecdotes – were reiterated in nineteenth-century popular culture with anything like the same enthusiasm as Alfred's association with trial-by-jury. Several writers even dramatised the scene in which the Saxon king was imagined to have bestowed the institution upon his people. At the finalé of James Magnus's 1838 play, *Alfred the Great*, the Saxon king announces 'From Alfred shall fair England take her law/ Of JURY TRIAL; and from her the world!'[35] In Paul Creswick's novel, *In Ælfred's Days*, the scene of Alfred's treaty with his Danish enemy Guthrum is depicted, in which the Saxon commits to parchment the law about the twelve king's thegns, and a footnote adds: 'the origin of our present jury system'.[36] And in Knowles's play, *Alfred the Great: Or the Patriot King*, Alfred proclaims his invention of trial-by-jury with a lengthy soliloquy in which he stresses the practice's egalitarian qualities:

> Thus to a people faithful to their king
> A faithful king an institution gives
> That makes the lowly cottage lofty
> As the regal dome . . .
> Which, when you'd name, you'll call
> Trial by Jury![37]

The particular fascination with Alfred's alleged introduction of trial-by-jury seems to have been due to a general interest in the practice in the nineteenth century – besides the Saxon king, a range of Viking and Celtic rulers were credited with instigating its use.[38] This interest was probably partly due to the passage in the first quarter of the nineteenth century of a number of British laws which specifically concerned the use of juries.[39] And the fact that trial-by-jury was often cited in Victorian rhetoric as a beneficial export to the colonies (just as England's law-code was), also no doubt increased concern to establish an early, native origin for the practice. Above all, however, the interest in Alfred's alleged founding of trial-by-jury should probably be related to the dominance of the Norman Yoke theory in nineteenth-century Britain, which, as we have seen above, maintained that (among their many outrages) upon their arrival in England the Normans had replaced a fair, Saxon system of trial-by-jury with the superstitious trial-by-combat and trial-by-ordeal.[40] The notion enjoyed wide popularity because it tapped into both anti-French feeling and radical opposition to the House of Lords (which was claimed to be of Norman descent). And as Alfred was the best known of Saxon monarchs, it was only natural that he should become part of the scheme, as the originator of the fair, and wrongly displaced, Saxon trial.

Towards the end of the nineteenth century, a late medieval myth about the efficiency of Alfred's laws also began to attract popular interest. In 1890, John Stuart Blackie proclaimed in his poem 'Alfred':

> If you hung a golden bracelet
> By the road in Alfred's time,
> No rude hand might dare remove it,
> Such sure vengeance followed crime.[41]

The claim, as we have seen above, derives from William of Malmesbury's early twelfth-century *History of the Kings of England*, which states that Alfred:

> Diffused such peace throughout the country, that he ordered that golden bracelets, which might mock the eager desires of the passengers while no one durst take them away, should be hung up on the public causeways, where the roads crossed each other.[42]

This account was paraphrased in Spelman's popular *Life* and was published in translation many times during the nineteenth century – the first English edition of the *History of the Kings of England* appeared in 1815 – but, for most of the period, it attracted little interest.[43] Reinhold Pauli dismissed it in 1857 as simply 'the repetition of an old tradition which has been already told by Bede . . . of the happy reign of Edwy of Northumbria, and at a later period was related as occurring in the times of Frothis the Dane and Rollo the Norman'.[44] Blackie's background in law perhaps provides the best clue to the tale's sudden appeal towards the end of the century.[45] High rates of crime – especially theft – prevailed throughout much of the nineteenth century. More specifically, however, it was in the late Victorian period that a shift took place in Britain from deterrent to detective policing.[46] Whereas at the start of the nineteenth century it was believed that crime would vanish entirely if a deterrent police presence could be consolidated throughout the country, by the end of the period it had become clear that the roots of crime were too complex for such a simple strategy to succeed.[47] Blackie's image of Alfred's England as a crime-free society can therefore perhaps be read as nostalgia for the naïve faith in preventative policing that had by 1890 been discredited – and as another example of the way in which the nineteenth century developed those aspects of Alfredian narrative which most closely related to contemporary concerns and interests.[48]

This is also seen in the nineteenth-century treatment of William of Malmesbury's claim that Alfred:

> appointed centuries, which they call 'hundreds', and decennaries, which they call 'tythings'; so that every Englishman, living according to the law, must be a

member of both. If any one was accused of a crime, he was obliged immediately to produce persons from his hundred and tything to become his surety; and whosoever was unable to find such surety must dread the severity of the laws. If any who had been impleaded made his escape, either before or after he had found surety, all persons of the hundred and tything paid a fine to the king.[49]

As discussed above, this idea was perhaps based upon the general references to communal liability in Alfred's laws and in 'The Treaty Between Alfred and Guthrum', and it probably derived from the Norman historian's desire to seek acceptance of the new system of frankpledge.[50]

The *History of Ingulf*, as we have seen, added to William of Malmesbury's notion the idea that Alfred had also developed shires.[51] Both this text and the *History of the Kings of England* were available in print by the nineteenth century. And, like the golden bracelet story, Alfred's creation of the shires was also paraphrased in Spelman's biography of Alfred – where it was hailed as having pre-empted and inspired the *Domesday Book*.[52] But, despite this, there was almost no interest in the subject in the nineteenth century. The general Victorian indifference to Alfred's shires, hundreds and tithings differs dramatically from the contemporary fascination with his alleged institution of, say, trial-by-jury or the English law-code. And it also contrasts with seventeenth- and eighteenth-century writers' interest in the tradition.[53] Once again, it illustrates the way in which it was those of Alfred's achievements which seemed to have contemporary relevance that were celebrated by writers in each successive age. So, for instance, the Royalist historian Robert Powell celebrated Alfred's shires, hundreds and tithings in 1634, because Charles I had just dissolved parliament, leaving only *local* government in England. And, in 1777, likewise, the historian and playwright Alexander Bicknell acclaimed those institutions because he considered them a likely system, if reintroduced, to solve the social problems of eighteenth-century England.[54]

In contrast, by 1869, Hughes was remarking upon the difficulty of seeing in Alfred's shires, hundreds and tithings any relevance for 'an age of electric telegraphs and railways'.[55] On further consideration, he suggested:

> At the same time, unless the world is essentially different from the world in which Alfred lived and reigned . . . there must be something answering, or analogous, to this custom or institution of frank-pledge . . . English life has become more and more disjointed . . . What we want is something which shall bind us more closely together. . . . The study of the modern statesman must be [to ensure that . . .] men cannot divest themselves of responsibility for their neighbours.[56]

The Tory politician remained almost alone, however, in seeing any modern significance in the tradition. Only Warwick Draper, in his 1901 *Alfred the Great*, also took a passing interest, on the grounds that Alfred's invention of shires could be viewed as having 'anticipated the principles of the County Council legislation of ten centuries later', which had put the jurisdiction for public health, sewerage, buildings and highways into the hands of local authorities.[57]

Alfred and education

While shires, hundreds and tithings may not have seemed particularly pertinent to nineteenth-century life, educational reform was an important preoccupation in Victorian Britain. It was not until 1902 that a free primary and secondary education was provided for all English children but, as early as 1816, voices were raised in condemnation of the country's widespread illiteracy and lack of schools.[58] This concern increased as the century progressed. It was encouraged by the European revolutions of 1830 and 1848, and by rising levels of crime at home – since education was argued by many to be the best means of suppressing both criminal and radical tendencies.[59] Britain's rapidly growing population (which meant that as the years went by there were proportionally fewer and fewer schools) also intensified worries. And so too did the fact that, towards the close of the century, Britain began to lose ground in the industrial race – a decline that was widely attributed to the superior literacy rates in other European countries.[60]

Alfred became effectively embroiled in the debate surrounding these anxieties, because of two brief passages in *Asser's Life of King Alfred* and a part of the king's own introduction to his translation of Gregory's *Pastoral Care*. One of the Asser passages states that the Saxon king never ceased 'from personally giving, by day and night, instruction in all virtuous behaviour and tutelage in literacy' to the sons of his clergy and nobles who were being brought up in the royal household. The other claims that he decreed that all of his 'ealdormen and reeves and thegns (who were illiterate from childhood)' should learn how to read, or else 'relinquish their offices of power'.[61] Neither of these accounts attracted any particular attention until the start of the nineteenth century. In the Victorian period, however, with the subject of education commanding such widespread public attention, they possessed sufficient relevance to be dramatised in both art and literature. In 1885, John Gilbert painted *King Alfred the Great teaching the Anglo-Saxon youth*, in which the Saxon monarch sits surrounded by young, attentive nobles. It was engraved for the *Illustrated London News* later that year, and a poem was composed by E.L. Hervey to accompany it (see Figure 15).[62]

Two other nineteenth-century authors depicted Alfred teaching rather different pupils to read. In his 1898 novel *'Twixt Daydawn and Light*, Gordon Stables described how the Saxon king spent his time in hiding instructing Denewulf, his famous swineherd-host, while the Poet Laureate Alfred Austin, in his 1896 play, *England's Darling*, claimed that Alfred gave lessons to Edgiva, daughter of the swineherd.[63] In an age when there was much debate as to the levels of education appropriate for working-class children, and when various schemes were being launched to educate the many illiterate working-class adults in Britain, it was unavoidable that images of a king

15 John Gilbert, *King Alfred teaching the Anglo-Saxon Youth* (engraved for *The Illustrated London News* in 1885)

instructing the most humble of his subjects would be seen as politically charged – effectively claiming Alfred as an early champion of educational reform. Alfred's association with democratic government, fair legal processes, and general rights and freedoms, probably influenced both writers to depict him instructing such lowly pupils. However, they may also have drawn on Asser's account of how Alfred's youngest son was 'given over to training in reading and writing . . . in company with all the nobly born children of virtually the entire area, and a good many of lesser birth as well'.[64]

It was not *Asser's Life of King Alfred*, however, but a passage from Alfred's own introduction to his translation of Gregory's *Pastoral Care* that really endeared the Saxon king to those nineteenth-century authors in favour of educational reform. In it, he states his desire that:

> all free-born young men now in England who have the means to apply themselves to it, may be set to learning (as long as they are not useful for some other employment) until the time that they can read English writings properly. Thereafter one may instruct in Latin those whom one wishes to teach further and wishes to advance to holy orders.[65]

The document was readily accessible in the nineteenth century. It had appeared in both Latin and modern English translations in Parker's 1574 edition of *Asser's Life of King Alfred*, and thereafter was often appended to other editions. More influentially, it was also paraphrased by Spelman.[66] His account of Alfred's educational initiatives rather overstates the king's plans to educate his populace. It reads 'In sundry Parts of the Kingdom (as it seemeth) he erected Schools for Youth, ordaining . . . that every Freeman of Ability sufficient should bring up their Children to Learning'.[67] In asserting that Alfred educated the children of every 'Freeman of Ability', Spelman entirely overlooked the Saxon king's provisos that only those youths with 'the means' (and furthermore only those 'not useful for some other employment') should be educated – in other words, only the sons of nobles.

This over-interpretation proved influential in the nineteenth century. It was reiterated and embellished with particular enthusiasm by the authors of children's literature, keen to encourage learning in their young audiences. In her 1835 children's book *Little Arthur's History of England*, Maria Graham asserted that Alfred 'determined to encourage all the young people of England to love learning'. And, even as late as 1885, Eliza Kerr's story for Sunday-school children, 'Two Saxon Maidens', dispensed with Spelman's single specification of 'ability sufficient' to state that Alfred had caused 'all the freeborn youth of his people' to be educated.[68] For some authors, Alfred's supposed educational improvements paralleled those of their own times. Hughes likened Alfred's scheme to educate his 'ealdormen and reeves and thegns' to 'the schools started near some great railway work in our time for the navigators'.[69] And in an 1862 article, 'Anglo-Saxon and Anglo-Norman Christianity', the historian John Tulloch argued that Alfred's court school had pre-empted 'what has proved so great a benefit to England, its public school system'.[70]

On the other hand, those more critical of the current state of education in Britain used the apparent universality of Alfred's educational schemes as a foil for what they considered the insufficient progresses of their own times. In his 1852 *Child's History of England*, Charles Dickens proclaimed:

> Let you and I pray that [Alfred's spirit] may animate our English hearts, at least to this – to resolve, when we see any of our fellow creatures left in ignorance, that we will do our best, while life is in us, to have them taught; and to tell those rulers whose duty it is to teach them, and who neglect their duty, that they have profited very little by all the years that have rolled away since the year nine hundred and one, and that they are far behind the bright example of King Alfred the Great.[71]

Conan Doyle echoed these sentiments at the 1899 planning meeting for the Alfred Millenary, praising Alfred as 'an educationalist on a scale to which we have hardly yet attained'.[72]

By the time of the Winchester anniversary, the foundations were being laid for the 1902 Education Act, which would answer such criticisms by making primary education ubiquitous throughout Britain. Alfred's reforms were thenceforth increasingly celebrated as the starting point in a narrative of gradual progress. At a planning meeting for the Winchester celebrations, G. Shaw-Lefevre asserted that Alfred had 'desired that every child in this country should be instructed, and that education should be compulsory, and in that way he preceded by nearly 1,000 years the final conclusion at which this country has arrived.[73] In 1901, the historian James Bryce celebrated the Saxon king as 'the founder of education in England' in an article for the *Independent*.[74] And, in his 1901 *The Story of King Alfred*, Besant claimed that Alfred 'desired universal education. . . . he thought also of the poorer class. . . . Unhappily he was unable to carry out this wish. Only in our own days has been at last attempted the dream of the Saxon king – the extension of education to the whole people'.

In June of the Millenary year, the National Home Reading Union chose to hold their summer assembly in Winchester, in order to associate their work with the educational reforms of the Saxon king. A series of lectures was given on 'Alfred as a Man of Letters, 'Alfred as Statesman and Lawgiver', and – most importantly – 'Links between Alfred and Ourselves'.[75] And, in the wake of the 1849 celebration of Alfred's birth in Wantage, the city's grammar school was re-launched as 'King Alfred's College'.[76] The nineteenth century's most interesting Alfredian educational initiative, however, was perhaps the founding of the 'King Alfred School Society'. Initially, this was a small group of radicals, opposed to the narrowly utilitarian Victorian education system which concentrated on delivering basic, standardised, and moralised instruction to large numbers of pupils. It founded the progressive 'King Alfred School' in Hampstead, North London, in 1898 (which survives to the present day, as a small independent school) but the society's aim (never realised) was for this to be just one of a chain of co-educational day schools in urban areas, all of which would stress the cultivation of character and individuality, and aim to counter the prevailing materialism and collectivism of late Victorian society. The society also promoted its reformist views on education through a programme of public lectures.

It is not recorded exactly how or why Alfred was chosen as the society's figurehead. However, it appears that he was closely identified with its aims: the King Alfred School seems to have had a tradition of dramatising the life of the king, and when a logo was designed for the society by the architect Charles Voysey (whose children were among the first pupils at King Alfred's School) it took the form of a heart with a tree growing out of its top and a seated Alfred in the centre. Voysey's account of the logo explained that the king's crown and sceptre were modelled on those depicted upon the Alfred Jewel; that the Saxon letters and monograms surrounding him had been taken from coins of his reign; and that the book held in one hand was a bible, open at Proverbs II: 6 – 'For the Lord giveth wisdom: out of his mouth cometh knowledge and understanding'.

The schools and institutes that associated themselves with Alfred in the nineteenth century followed in the footsteps of a far earlier precedent. As discussed above, in the fourteenth century, Ralph Higden's *The Polychronicon* had proclaimed Alfred as the founder of the University of Oxford.[77] Higden asserted that, 'On the advice of Neot the abbot, whom he visited often, he was the first person to establish a common school at Oxford teaching diverse arts and sciences'.[78] This claim (which bestowed upon their twelfth-century institution a more venerable founder and a greater antiquity than the University of Cambridge) was restated and elaborated by a series of Fellows of the university, and was popularised through being interpolated into *Asser's Life of King Alfred* and paraphrased in Spelman's history.[79] We have already considered its consequent importance in the seventeenth and eighteenth centuries. However, the notion also appeared in a few early nineteenth-century texts. Thomas Dibdin's 1813 poem 'Alfred the Great', for instance, proclaims, 'thy venerable turrets, Oxford, rose/ From him'.[80] By the Victorian period, the myth was in decline, but one of the last uses of it is also one of the most interesting. At the inauguration of the University of Sydney on 11 October 1852, the historian John Wooley gave a lecture in which he associated the institution's foundation with Alfred's supposed establishment of Oxford University. It now seems an unlikely pairing, but for Wooley there were obvious parallels: while the Saxon king had dared to choose 'the furthest Place, in which, with any reasonable Security, an university could be placed' (that is, the edge of Wessex), Sydney could likewise be viewed as an outpost of Western culture in the modern day.[81] He proclaimed:

> Nine hundred and eighty years have passed since our glorious Alfred provided . . . a home of union and refuge for the poor and scattered scholars . . . Did his imagination dare her flight beyond the limits of his island-home, and picture in the remotest corners of the earth the children of his race, nurtured in his institutions, bearing forth the spirit and the form which he loved into a yet wilder solitude, and a more inaccessible wilderness?[82]

For Wooley, Alfred's founding of Oxford was 'a struggle more arduous than against the invading Dane, a conquest more glorious than the subjugation of a kingdom'. His lecture concluded by asserting 'I have invoked the spirit of Alfred; and I hope, without presumption or exaggeration; it *is* in his spirit that the founders of this University seek to be partakers of his success'.[83] In effect, then, Wooley hailed Alfred not only as the originator of the University of Oxford, but also as the spiritual founder of Sydney University.

This sentiment was perhaps echoed at the Winchester Millenary in the decision to make a meeting of representatives from universities worldwide central to the celebration.[84] Ironically, however, in scholarly circles by this time, Alfred's association with the University of Oxford had been entirely discredited.[85] By 1899, 'the story that he founded the University, or schools of any kind, at Oxford' could be dismissed by Frederic Pollock as 'a late and gross fiction, which it would be too polite to call a legend'.[86] And such scepticism had even taken root at Oxford University itself. In 1872, the millennium of Alfred's alleged foundation of University College was marked by a grand dinner, but whereas in the seventeenth and eighteenth centuries such an event would have been attended with deference and pride, this was a signally ironic affair at which the charred embers of a burnt cake was presented to the Master of the college.[87]

Nevertheless, the story of Alfred's foundation of Oxford retained much affection at the university. In 1901, the Oxford historian Warwick Draper wrote:

> The best-known story connected with the educational work of Alfred the Great is concerned with his alleged creation of the University of Oxford . . . Although this myth has long since been entirely explained, yet it will always possess a certain historical value as belonging to that sacred praise of legendary fame which Alfred's personality has continuously won.[88]

And, a year later, his colleague, Charles Plummer, announced:

> We may not, here in Oxford, claim Alfred as our founder; but surely our hearts may be uplifted at the thought that in all that we do here in the cause of true learning and of genuine education, we are carrying on the work which Alfred left us to do.[89]

Alfred and the Union of Great Britain

Another popular seventeenth- and eighteenth-century Alfredian legend which had some limited currency in the nineteenth century – particularly at the start of the period – was the claim that it was King Alfred who had begun the process of uniting the separate kingdoms of Great Britain.[90] The origins of this tradition perhaps lie in the *Anglo-Saxon Chronicle*'s account that in the year 894, King Alfred's forces were joined by 'a certain part of the Welsh race', and in Asser's claim that in the 880s much of Wales submitted to King Alfred's overlordship. Asser also claimed that in 886 'All the Angles and Saxons – those who had formerly been scattered everywhere and were not in captivity with the Vikings – turned willingly to King Alfred and submitted themselves to his lordship'.[91] And, more importantly, he dedicated his *Life of King Alfred* to 'Alfred, ruler of all the Christians of the island of Britain'.[92] These last two claims were probably part of a propagandist attempt to encourage Welsh acceptance of Alfred as the overlord of Wales, by exaggerating the extent of the king's power – which never in fact extended into the northernmost parts of Britain. They were from the outset, then, tied to unionist ambitions. And when they were revisited and reinvented in later centuries, this often seems to have coincided with projects to unite the disparate elements of what is now Great Britain.

In the thirteenth-century, when Edward I was engaged in aggressive campaigns to annex both Wales and Scotland to England, Asser's claim that Alfred had united all of the Angles and Saxons (not in captivity to the Vikings) caught the attention of two Anglo-Norman chroniclers, Roger of Wendover and Matthew Paris, who both claimed (ignoring any Danish control) that the Saxon king had been the sole ruler of a united England.[93] This notion (probably bolstered by the reference to 'the island of Britain' in Asser's dedication) was then further developed in the seventeenth century. Although Spelman's *The Life of Alfred the Great* was not published until much later, it was written in the early 1640s. In it Spelman celebrated Alfred not just as ruler of all the Angles and Saxons, or even of all the Christians, but simply as 'sole Sovereign of the whole Island' – thus effectively implying that he acted as overlord to all of England, Scotland and Wales.[94] The history was composed thirty-nine years after the union of the English and Scottish crowns by James I, and at a time when the merging of the two kingdoms was still the object of much discontent on both sides of the border. Since Spelman was a staunch supporter and close follower of Charles I, his effective claim that Alfred had united England to Wales and Scotland may have been an attempt to vindicate the union forged by that monarch's father – by endowing it with an ancient prototype. However, at the time when Spelman was writing, during the tumult of the Civil War, Scotland had sided with the English parliamentary forces. It seems more likely, therefore, that his decision to celebrate Alfred as 'sole Sovereign' may have merely formed part of a sustained attempt to associate the Saxon monarch with Charles I (who was also sole sovereign of the island) and thus enhance the esteem of that contemporary monarch.

During the eighteenth century, Spelman's assertion, however, certainly did inspire attempts to enlist Alfred to promote the idea of union– despite the fact that by then scholarly historians had begun to contest the claim that Alfred was 'sole Sovereign of the whole Island'. In the wake of the 1707 union of the parliaments of England and Scotland, the Saxon king was celebrated by pro-union popular authors keen to forge a sense of Britishness.[95] As a historical monarch believed to have forged a proto-union and also to have successfully overcome the risk of foreign invasion, Alfred suited the agenda of unionist writers perfectly, since one motivating factor behind the 1707 union had been the fear that France and an independent Scotland might combine forces in an attempt to restore a Jacobite monarchy.[96]

One such writer was James Thomson, a lowland Scot who has been described as 'a child of the Union, and perhaps the first important poet to write with a British, as distinct from a Scots or English outlook'.[97] The 1740 *Alfred: A Masque*, which Thomson composed with David Mallet, concludes, as we have seen above, with the song now known as 'Rule, Britannia' – perhaps the most famous expression ever of British, as distinct from English, national pride. In its original context in the play, it also effectively suggested that the 1707 Act was ordained, predestined and inevitable, and implicitly presented the respected Alfred as an apologist for that union – an association made even more forcefully in the 1754 revision of the play, in which the song is performed as a duet by Alfred himself and his queen.

Alfred is also a spokesman for union in the anonymous 1753 play *Alfred the Great: Deliverer of his Country*, in which the Saxon king plans to establish a standing navy 'when we become a People so united,/ As by one Faith, I hope, we soon shall be/ Free from intestine Wars'. He goes on to predict that 'we may defy/ The Danes, or any other potent Neighbours:/ So we preserve the Scotch, and Welch our friend'.[98] The play was published only a few years after the 1745 Jacobite rebellion and the plotted Jacobite invasion of 1750. In the aftermath of these threats to the fragile cohesion of Great Britain, there was a renewed attempt to promote a sense of British identity: to reduce the risk of any Jacobite revival in Scotland, and to soothe anti-Scots resentment in England.[99] *Alfred the Great: Deliverer of his Country* can be best understood as part of this project.

Debate about the rights and wrongs of the 1707 Act of Union was still current over a hundred years later – it is discussed, for instance, in Walter Scott's 1817 novel, *Rob Roy*.[100] The 1801 *Alfred: An Epic Poem*, by the Poet Laureate Henry James Pye, can also be read as a late vindication of the union with Scotland. In this poem, when King Alfred goes into hiding from the Danes he flees not to Athelney but to Scotland, where the Scottish king Gregor vows loyally to him, 'Thy country's wrongs are ours, thy wrongs are mine'. The poem ends with the institution of a proto-union – Alfred proclaiming, 'be Britain's nations join'd', and the Scottish monarch swearing 'eternal friendship' and 'homage to Alfred'. Gregor also predicts:

> So, at the eve of some victorious day,
> When in mix'd folds the British ensigns play,
> Either unconquer'd nation shall embrace,
> In deathless amity, a kindred race,
> Each shall protecting Alfred's glory claim,
> And hail him monarch in Britannia's name.[101]

The mixed ensigns to which Gregor alludes include not just the standards of Wessex and Scotland, however, but also those of Ireland and Wales (according to Pye, a harp and a griffin), since in this poem Alfred is joined in his battle against the Danes by Scottish, Welsh and also Irish troops. And the final proto-union is forged between all four nations.

Pye's poem was published in 1801, the year of another Act of Union – between the kingdoms of Great Britain and Ireland. It should, therefore, be read in this context: as a celebration and vindication of the new union. The contemporary allusions and parallels in it are numerous. Alfred's unions with Scotland and Wales precede that with Ireland, and the Irish union is only cemented after that nation has been persuaded to break its alliance with the invading Danes. One of Alfred's knights is entrusted with this diplomatic task, and presents the Saxon king with a full account of how he met with the brave but 'artless' Irish and:

> in mild speech, with gentle chidings fraught,
> I shew'd of broken faith the foul disgrace,
> And base submission to an alien race.
> I saw the glow of shame ingenuous rise,
> Paint the flush'd cheek, and bend to earth the eyes.[102]

One of the most important motives for the 1801 union with Ireland was the threat that the country would serve as a springboard for a French invasion of

England: the Irish rebellion of 1798 had been inspired by the French Revolution of 1789, and the uprising was supported by Napoleon, who landed an army at County Mayo in the August. The similarities between this late eighteenth-century anxiety and Pye's account of Ireland's ninth-century 'submission to an alien race' are inescapable – as are the poem's attempts to contain the contemporary threat.

The ensigns attributed to each nation in Pye's poem also have contemporary resonances. On Alfred's battlefield:

> The snow-white steed in Saxon banners flies,
> There Cambria's griffin on the azure field,
> In snaky volumes writhes around the shield;
> And Scotia's lion, proud, erect and bold,
> Rears high his irritable crest in gold.
> Gold too her harp, and strung with silver wire,
> Erin her arms displays with kindred fire.[103]

When Pye wrote, popular antiquaries had long known that the standard of Alfred had been the golden dragon. However, the four symbols chosen by Pye – white horse, griffin, lion and harp – together formed the Hanoverian coat of arms. The poem, therefore, creates a ninth-century myth of origin for George III's armorial bearings; implicitly presents that monarch as the direct descendant of the Saxon king; and provides his unionist project with a venerable ninth-century precedent.[104]

Pye's poem also alludes to the creation of the new union flag, whose design was announced in 1800, and which was first raised on New Year's Day 1801.[105] Near the end of the poem, a druid prophesies to Alfred:

> Now learn events, yet unrevealed that lie
> In the dark bosom of futurity –
> As my delighted eyes, in yon firm line,
> With friendly folds see Albion's banners join,
> I view them, in prophetic vision shewn,
> United subjects of a mighty throne;
> See Cambria's, Caledonia's, Anglia's name
> Blended, and lost in Britain's prouder fame.
> And ye, fair Erin's sons, though Ocean's tide
> From Britain's shores your kindred shores divide,
> That tide shall bear your mingled flags unfurl'd,
> A mutual barrier from an envying world;
> While the same waves that hostile inroad awe,
> The sister isles to closer compact draw,
> Waft friendship's intercourse, and Plenty's stores,
> From Shannon's brink, to Humber's distant shores.
> Each separate interest, separate right shall cease,
> Link'd in eternal amity and peace,
> While Concord blesses, with celestial smiles,
> THE FAVOUR'D EMPIRE OF THE BRITISH ISLES.[106]

Pye's Alfred, then, looks approvingly forward to the union of 1801, and is effectively claimed as part of Britain's (as opposed to just England's) history. It has been widely remarked in recent cultural histories that the nineteenth century saw the substitution of the term 'England' as an umbrella term for 'Britain. Thus, in 1805 a Scottish MP remarked that 'we commonly when speaking of British subjects call them English, be they English, Scotch, or Irish'.[107] The linguistic development also signalled a more profound process – the creation of an 'Anglo-British' national identity, by which English history was substituted for that of the other constituent parts of Great Britain. Pye's poem suggests that Alfred was already part of this process of substitution by 1801 – the very year that the United Kingdom itself was formed.

The druid's prophecy about the future union of Great Britain links that alliance intrinsically to the growth and success of the British Empire. This proved to be a prediction on Pye's part too, for, as the nineteenth century progressed, the Union was crucially cemented by the success of British overseas commerce and colonisation. The need for Alfred as a spokesperson for the virtues of union largely disappeared; however, it seems to have revived briefly, amid the Welsh nationalist furore that arose in the wake of the 1870 Government Education Act (which effectively threatened the future of the Welsh language, by making English the medium of communication in all Welsh schools).[108] In Alfred Austin's play *England's Darling*, the Welsh, who are described as 'dark outlandish men/ That hang upon your heel as though afeard', come to Alfred's court to 'crave' his overlordship. Alfred instructs Asser to teach the men English, proclaiming 'In this Island there must be one lord,/ One law, one speech, one bond of blood between/ Saxon and Briton'.[109]

The depiction of Alfred as part of an English history that could stand proxy for all of Great Britain continued throughout the nineteenth century. The notion was particularly stressed in the years around the Alfred Millenary, by popular historians who hoped to encourage all the nations of Britain to join together in celebrating the thousandth anniversary of Alfred's death. Frederic Harrison's 'Alfred as King' formed part of the 1899 volume *Alfred the Great: Containing Chapters on his Life and Times*, a book written specifically to promote participation in the commemorations. In his essay, Harrison claimed, 'Neither Welshman, nor Scot, nor Irishman can feel that Alfred's memory has left the trace of a wound for his national pride'. He continued:

> He never attempted to conquer or annex them in the mass . . . His wise, firm, and victorious government impressed the smaller and more backward tribes on all sides; so that, without demanding any formal subjection, his paramount authority was recognised over the island.[110]

The Scottish novelist Gordon Stables similarly sought to encourage his fellow peripheral Britons to view the Alfred Millenary as part of their own cultural property. His 1898 novel *'Twixt Daydawn and Light* is perhaps the most interesting example of Alfred's role in the creation of an Anglo-British identity. Dedicated to 'all true-hearted Britons', the novel asserts – in a chapter entitled 'What Britain Owes to Alfred' – 'Although this king was English, Scotland, England and Ireland are now as one, and united we are able to carry the pen, the sword and the spade into the uttermost regions of the globe'.[111] 'British' and 'English' are used interchangeably, as in many Alfredian texts. In Stables's case, however, this is a self-conscious usage. Stables contests the possibility of any narrowly English identity, stressing the equally hybrid ancestry of Scots, Irish and English. Alluding to Defoe's poem, he protests, 'We often hear the expression "A true-born Englishman". . . . But by descent there is no such being as your true-born Englishman'.[112]

Stables himself no doubt had a vested interest in these issues of national identity: Scottish by birth, he spent much of his adult life as an inhabitant of Berkshire. He was also a naval officer, and thus part of a distinctly Anglo-British institution. King Alfred, national identity and the navy are inextricably bound together in *'Twixt Daydawn and Light*. The novel is organised around a framing narrative in which a Scottish naval officer persuades his Irish comrade that each possesses a cultural heritage deriving from King Alfred, and that the Saxon king should be recognised as the spiritual father of the modern shipping capital of Glasgow. Tying together both themes is Stables's confession in the preface: 'Between you, me and the binnacle, reader, I love [Alfred] all the more because at last he became a sailor, and, we may almost say, was the first to hoist that bit of bunting which Campbell has called the flag that "Braved a thousand years/The battle and the breeze" '.[113] The quotation is from 'the Scottish Milton' Thomas Campbell, whose highly popular and oft-paraphrased 1801 poem 'Ye Mariners of England' begins by celebrating:

> Ye Mariners of England
> That guard our native seas,
> Whose flag has braved a thousand year
> The battle and the breeze.[114]

The claim, referred to by Stables, and alluded to more obliquely by Campbell, is the belief that towards the end of his reign, and exactly a thousand years before the late Victorian period of naval pre-eminence, King Alfred the Great of Wessex had first launched the British navy.

Alfred and the English navy

The Poet Laureate Alfred Austin chose to celebrate King Alfred in his 1896 play, *England's Darling*, because, he declared, the Saxon king had 'laid the foundation, in days of distracting trouble, of our society, our language, and our naval power.[115] Similarly, in his epic poem on Alfred, published sixty years earlier, G.L. Newnham Collingwood opined:

Not for other cause
Does England dearer hold her Alfred's name,
Than that he first gave to the island-queen
Dominion o'er the waters.[116]

Both statements demonstrate the high status of the navy in nineteenth-century Britain: it was a crucial pillar of national identity, and it was acknowledged as the backbone of the vast and lucrative British Empire and thus essential to national prosperity.[117] In the preface to his 1865 ballet *Sketch of Alfred the Great*, therefore, M. Lonsdale asserted that, in creating a navy, Alfred had 'laid the foundation of his Country's future Fame and Greatness'.[118]

In a period characterised by a fascination with the past and the desire to construct narratives of national progress, such an institution of course called for a venerable founder – and attracted rival attributions. These can be roughly grouped by geography, and understood in terms of provincial pride. In the South of England – especially in those areas with some connection to the Saxon king – Alfred was most often hailed as the origin of Britain's naval force. In his 1849 poem 'The Order of Alfred', for instance, Tupper, asserted 'Sailors, ten centuries our British boast,/ He sent you first afloat on every coast'.[119] In Winchester, during the 1901 Alfred Millenary celebrations, Alfred's foundation of the navy was represented, as we have seen, by the conspicuous presence of the Portsmouth naval brigade, which was chosen to head the procession through the city to the Alfred statue. And, in Portsmouth itself, a month later, Alfred's connection with the British navy was grandly asserted when Countess Lathom launched the *HMS King Alfred* before a crowd of thousands of spectators (see Figure 4 for the invitation card to this event).[120]

In northern Britain, on the other hand, notable Viking figures tended to be hailed as the founders of the navy (particularly in those areas which had once formed 'the Danelaw').[121] These rival claims were obviously taken seriously, as witnessed by the attempts made by some King Alfred enthusiasts to absorb them into Alfredian narratives of naval origin. Whistler, for instance, suggested that although a Norwegian might have taught the West Saxons how to build boats and sail, the Viking in question (innocuously named 'Saga') had in fact been a follower of Alfred.[122] And likewise, Henty theorised that while the British navy might have been inspired by the Viking mastery of the sea, it had been created by one of Alfred's Saxon followers, Edmund, who had lived as a hostage among the Danes, and learned seamanship from them in Denmark.[123]

That there should have been non-Alfredian theories about the origin of the navy in the nineteenth century is hardly surprising when the grounds for the Alfredian claim are considered. Sea-borne defences were carried out off England's coasts before Alfred's reign. During the sovereignty of his father, Æthelwulf, for instance, Alfred's elder brother Æthelstan 'fought in ships, and struck a great raiding army at Sandwich, and captured 9 ships and put the others to flight'.[124] Moreover, Alfred's reign was not particularly marked by naval successes. *Asser's Life of King Alfred* makes just three brief references to occasions on which Alfred engaged the Danes in naval encounters. The first relates that, in 875, Alfred captured one out of six Viking ships 'and the others escaped'; the second (more positive) records that, in 882, Alfred captured two Viking ships and had a further two surrender to him; and the last states that, in 885, Alfred managed to destroy several Danish ships – before their comrades arrived and 'the Vikings had the victory'.[125]

The origin of the Alfredian claim to the navy, however, seems to have been the account in the *Anglo-Saxon Chronicle* of how in the year 897:

> King Alfred ordered long-ships to be built to oppose the 'askrs'; they were well-nigh twice as long as the others, some had 60 oars, some more; they were both swifter and less flexible, and also more responsive than the others; they were neither of Frisian design nor of Danish, but as it seemed to himself that they might be most useful.[126]

Certainly, this passage was echoed in Bowker's report of the launch of *HMS King Alfred*. 'It cannot be gainsaid', he asserted:

> that the launch of that mighty cruiser, H.M.S. *King Alfred*, was a fitting commemoration of the Millenary of King Alfred's association with the navy of England. Alfred caused ships to be built which were swifter and larger than those of the Danes; and to this day the ships of England are larger, swifter, and more numerous than those of her enemies. The first-class armoured cruiser is the highest developed type of warship yet built, for she combines within herself the power of an ordinary battleship with the fleetness of the fastest ocean greyhound, thus embodying the same ideal which animated King Alfred 1000 years ago in the formation of his fleet.[127]

The *Anglo-Saxon Chronicle*'s account seems to have particularly appealed to writers in the nineteenth century because of its insistence that Alfred had boats built 'as it seemed to *him himself* that they could be most useful'. Such an apparent insistence upon the king's personal involvement in the scheme chimed well with Carlylean calls for leaders to be talented and skilled individuals – 'the ablest man'. Thus, in his 1852 epic poem, Richard Kelsey stressed that the West Saxon fleet owed its entire creation to 'Alfred's workmanship,/ Alfred's conception', and in her 1900 novel, *In the Days of Alfred the Great*, Eva March Tappan dramatised a scene in which Alfred persuades his councillors to establish a navy, assuring them that he can teach men both how to build ships and how to sail them – knowledge that he gained from his reading of classical texts.[128] Even the historian George Eayrs claimed in his essay on Alfred that 'Britain's maritime supremacy began when his sharp eye saw that the sea might be a highway to sovereignty'.[129] And it was perhaps the notion that Alfred had been personally involved with establishing a navy that, in Victorian times, also led to the Victorian formation of the friendly society known as 'The Royal Alfred Aged Merchant Seamen's Institute'.

Eayrs' claim that Alfred established British 'maritime supremacy' represents a significant imaginative leap from the *Anglo-Saxon Chronicle*'s account that the Saxon king built ships that were merely swifter, higher and steadier than those of his enemies. The springboard for his notion, however, was probably the assertion in Spelman's *The Life of Alfred the Great* that Alfred 'was the first that put to sea such a Navy as was awful unto Strangers, begun the first Mastery of the Seas.[130] It was Spelman, then, who first associated Alfred's new ships with the highly successful modern British 'navy'. His claim almost certainly had more direct influence in the nineteenth century than the passage in the *Anglo-Saxon Chronicle* – as witnessed by the number of nineteenth-century writers who explicitly refer to Alfred's ships as a 'navy'.

An eighteenth-century text was also highly influential upon the nineteenth-century celebration of Alfred as the founder of the British Navy. In the last lines of Mallet and Thomson's 1740 *Alfred: A Masque*, a hermit prophesies:

> Britons proceed, the subject Deep command
> Awe with your navies every hostile land
> In vain their threats, their armies all in vain
> They rule the balanc'd world, who rule the main.[131]

As has already been discussed, the hermit also performs a 'Grand Ode in Honour of Great Britain' – now better known as 'Rule, Britannia'. As well as being a celebration of British union, the song is one of the most famous expressions ever of British naval pride. Its chorus resounds 'Rule, Britannia, rule the waves' and in performance, as was stated earlier, it was accompanied by a shadow-play of King Alfred's new ships conquering those of the Danes.[132]

Lines from 'Rule, Britannia' found their way into several nineteenth-century plays and poems about Alfred. Lonsdale's 1865 ballet, *Sketch of Alfred the Great*, for instance, ends with the triumphal line 'Britannia rules the waves!' Mallet and Thomson's play had also been reworked in 1854 as an oratorio, in which both the song and the hermit's prophecy were given to Alfred himself, thus implying that in designing his new ships, the Saxon king was conscious that his actions represented the beginnings of what would become British naval pre-eminence. This suggestion that their navy had not only had an early originator but, more importantly, one who had been strategic and far-seeing, clearly appealed to Victorian Alfredianists. In a number of nineteenth-century plays, in particular, Alfred therefore speaks prophetically and proudly of England's great naval future.[133] Knowles's King Alfred, for instance, prophetically announces:

> My countrymen!
> Sons of the sea – henceforth her restless plain
> Shall be your battlefield! There shall you meet
> The threat'ning storm of war!

There shall it burst
Its rage unfelt at home.[134]

Alfred also predicts Britain's future maritime strength in Canning's 1876 play, *Alfred the Great in Athelnay*. In this play, however, the Saxon king foresees not only the future need for fleets as a defensive measure, but also the necessary role that shipping would play in British imperialism. He announces 'Girt by the seas, we must have fleets to guard/ Our naked coasts, and line them with the gold/ Of wealthier lands'.[135] Tupper also viewed Alfred as the founder of Britain's foreign commerce. His poem, 'The Order of Alfred', proclaims 'Merchants, who waft your venture on the breeze,/ He gave you first the freedom of the seas'.[136] Alfred's new ships were thus invoked not merely in celebration of him as the founder of the British Navy, but also in relation to another prevalent nineteenth-century legend – that the West Saxon king had sown the first seed of the British Empire.

Alfred and the Empire

At an 1898 planning meeting for the Alfred Millenary in Winchester, Walter Besant recalled the previous year's Jubilee celebrations – 'that memorable day when we were all drunk with the visible glory and the greatness of the Empire'. On that day, he continued:

> there arose in the minds of many a feeling that we ought to teach the people the meaning of what we saw set forth in that procession – the meaning of our Empire; not only what it is, but how it came – through whose creation, by whose foundation. Now so much is Alfred the founder that every ship in our navy might have his name, every school his bust, every Guildhall his statue. . . . We want a monument to Alfred, if only to make the people learn and remember the origin of our Empire.

As Besant wished, King Alfred was publicly celebrated as the founder of the Empire at the Millenary celebrations in 1901. Unveiling the Winchester statue, Lord Rosebery asked the assembled crowds to imagine that a seer could have led the Saxon king:

> to the banks of the Thames, and had shown him the little Saxon fort developed into a world-capital and a world-mart . . . Suppose that he could have seen in an unending procession the various nations which own the free fatherhood of the British Crown . . . Suppose in a word, that he could have beheld, as in an unfolded tapestry, the varying but superb fortunes of that indomitable race by whose cradle he had watched: would he not have seen in himself one of those predestined beings, greater than the great, who seem unconsciously to fashion the destinies and mark the milestones of the world?[137]

The sense of racial and national destiny which is so striking in this speech was a common feature of the rhetoric used to justify and exalt British imperialism in the late nineteenth century. The dogma that the English were the world's new chosen race made it desirable to trace the workings of fate by identifying prophecies, precursors and the very earliest prelude of the country's ultimate imperial success. This need seemed to be answered in the life of Alfred the Great.

Two passages in the ninth-century sources for Alfred's life provided the ultimate basis for his connection with the British Empire in the nineteenth century. In *Asser's Life of King Alfred*, it is stated that Alfred had 'daily involvement with the nations which lie from the Mediterranean to the farthest limit of Ireland'.[138] This 'involvement' was typically interpreted by nineteenth-century writers as the earliest instance of British overseas trade. Writing in 1901, for instance, Walter Besant claimed that Alfred 'endeavoured to remove the separation of his island from the rest of the world . . . he created commercial relations with foreign countries'.[139] More important, however, was the *Anglo-Saxon Chronicle*'s account of how, in 883, Alfred sent two of his men, Sigehelm and Athelstan, with alms to the shrine of St Thomas.[140] According to versions B and C of the chronicle, this shrine was in Judaea. In manuscripts D, E and F of the text, however, 'Judaea' is mistranscribed as 'India'.[141]

The corrupted, Indian version of the account became dominant in the nineteenth century. In part this was simply because of India's economic importance to Britain during this period – with the loss of North America, it represented the most lucrative, extensive and established of Britain's colonial territories. The slightest suggestion that Alfred had sent men there a thousand years earlier was thus inevitably seized upon as an event laden with portentous significance – indeed, as proof that England had always been ordained by God to rule over the subcontinent.[142] Thus, Hughes described the mission of Sigehelm and Athelstan as 'the first intercourse between England and the great empire which has since been committed to her in the East', and Sir Clements Markham, in his essay 'Alfred as a Geographer', described how they visited a country 'which was *destined*, in after ages, to become the brightest gem in the diadem of the descendants of Alfred the Great'.[143]

The reiteration of the Indian (rather than the Judaean) version of Alfred's alms-giving in Spelman's history also probably helped to guarantee that story's ascendancy in the nineteenth century. Spelman also claimed that Alfred designed new ships not only for warfare but for 'traffic' – and that, having carried the king's alms to the East Indies, they came back with 'a fair return of precious stones, perfumes, and other Eastern rarities'.[144] This rewriting of the incident with its mercantile stress upon 'fair returns' clearly needs to be understood in the context of burgeoning Anglo-Indian trade. It was developed enthusiastically in the eighteenth century. Paul Rapin's *History of England* (translated into English in 1732), for instance, further secularised Spelman's account by omitting all mention of Alfred's alms and presenting the Indian voyage purely as the dispatch of 'merchants' wishing to 'traffik'.[145] Some early Victorian writers also adopted the idea. The anonymous historian 'J.F.R.'

stated in his 1845 life of Alfred that 'Swithelm' brought 'precious stones, perfumes and other valuables' back from India to King Alfred.[146]

However, in Britain the nineteenth century saw increasing moral examination of the country's colonialism. This intensified after the 1857 Indian uprising and the founding of the Indian National Congress, when increasing numbers of British critics began to denounce the acquisitiveness and violence of British control in India.[147] Pro-imperial discourse responded by stressing that Britain's occupation of India was motivated not primarily by profit, but by a desire to disseminate Christianity among the subcontinent's supposedly benighted Hindu and Muslim populations. From the mid-nineteenth century onwards, therefore, Alfred's supposed interaction with India tended to be drawn upon not as an early example of British trade (as Spelman had celebrated it), but rather to demonstrate the longevity of Britain's Christian concern for the country. All mention of merchants disappeared and, instead, the claim that a Saxon king had sent alms to an Indian shrine was once again stressed. Writing of Alfred's venture in his 1862 article, 'Anglo-Saxon and Anglo-Norman Christianity', for instance, John Tulloch asserted: 'It is interesting to be able to trace back the first intercourse between England and Hindastan [sic] to the year 883, and to know that it consisted in an interchange of Christian feeling'.[148] And, likewise, in his 1890 poem, 'Alfred', John Stuart Blackie described Alfred's mission to India as the delivery of a Christian 'greeting'.[149]

It was not only Christianity that was drawn upon as a means of defending British colonialism in the nineteenth century. The Empire was also endorsed as a mechanism to facilitate the dissemination of culture, law and constitutionalism.[150] Alfred's reputation as the venerable founder of Britain's law-code and democracy meant that he was often invoked in such rhetoric. Thus Conan Doyle celebrated Alfred as having 'inaugurated that respect for law and order which is now the distinguishing mark of every British colony'.[151] The earliest example of Alfred's use in this context returns us to Pye's 1801 epic poem, in which a druid character prophetically assures Alfred 'By British arms and British virtues borne,/ Shall arts of cultured life the waste adorn'.[152] Pye's pro-imperial view of non-European countries as cultureless wastelands is expressed in many later Victorian texts. His allusion to 'British arms' was another matter, however, and marks the poem as an early nineteenth-century work. As the Empire came under increasing scrutiny, later writers were more diplomatic. Tupper's 1849 poem 'The Alfred Medals' presents King Alfred's progeny not as a conquering army, but as 'Ambassadors of truth to every coast/ And mercy's messengers from pole to pole'.[153]

In a number of nineteenth-century literary texts – particularly plays – Alfred himself speaks prophetically in support of British colonialism. In Stratford Canning's 1876 *Alfred the Great in Athelnay*, the Saxon king speaks of Britain's future colonial venture in terms of a cure or service to the colonised:

Our social customs and our Saxon laws,
Dating from eld, retain such healthy seeds
That taking root, and spreading o'er the land,
Our race in after-years may heal the world,
And render boundless service to mankind.[154]

It is in Edmund Hill's 1901 play *Alfred the Great*, however, that Alfred is most explicitly appropriated as a spokesman for imperialism. Hill's play ends in the wake of the battle of Edington, with Alfred looking forward proudly to the many peoples whom his institutions will 'make free', and prophesying:

I see an Empire stretching o'er the seas,
Of many lands, of many races knit,
And held together in the bonds of love,
Whose mother is this English land of ours,
Free and unfettered, free and making free.[155]

As a supremely malleable figure, Alfred could also be enlisted to criticise British activity in the colonies. In the same year that Hill's play was published, Charles Stubbs, the Dean of Ely, addressed the National Home Reading Union in Winchester, using Alfred's life to criticise British treatment of the Boers.[156] Stubbs's criticism was one voice of dissent amid the chorus of imperial celebration that formed an intrinsic part of King Alfred's millennial celebrations in Winchester. Soldiers freshly returned from the Transvaal received honours as part of the grand unveiling ceremony, and in the procession through the city to the foot of the statue were dignitaries from 'all lands controlled by the English-speaking race' – invited as part of a conscious initiative to use the Saxon king to 'strengthen and consolidate' Britain's Empire, and bring about 'that good understanding which we are led to believe will secure for the world a perpetual peace'.[157]

In particular, it had been hoped from the outset that the Alfred Millenary might be used to cement a special relationship between Britain and one former colony – America. As we heard earlier, this had also been an aim of the earlier Alfredian anniversary in Wantage, for which two commemorative medals were minted, both celebrating Alfred as a bond between America and Britain. Lest the meaning of the medals was not entirely apparent, Tupper also composed a poem, 'The Alfred Medals', which proclaimed:

Then, Brothers, be at peace and love each other,
Let us contend for mastery no more,
Britain! Columbia! Let the name of brother
Echo with tenderness from shore to shore.[158]

Trans-Atlantic guests were certainly present at the Wantage celebrations, and at the grand dinner at the Alfred's Head Inn the Stars and Stripes was prominent among the decorations, while Tupper further invoked America in a toast to 'the Anglo-Saxon Race all over the World'.[159]

Tupper's concern to involve Americans in the commemoration of Alfred was outdone, however (like so much else), by Bowker. His record of the Winchester Millenary noted that the organising committee had early hoped that it would be 'an occasion when Americans might wish to unite with Englishmen in doing honour to the memory of the great man who should be regarded as their common ancestor. Letters had therefore been written to America. A reply had been received from President McKinley, stating that he naturally felt an individual interest in a celebration of this character.'[160] This theme of Alfred as the common ancestor and shared heritage of both America and Britain was replayed over and again in the preparations for, and during the course of, the Winchester commemorations. In an article published early in 1901 in the *Independent*, James Bryce declared 'Englishmen have rejoiced to hear that great interest is taken in America in the approaching celebration of the thousandth anniversary of the death of King Alfred. For Alfred is a hero who belongs to the whole English or Anglo-Saxon race, wherever it may dwell'. Bryce further stressed Alfred's connection to America by likening the Saxon king to 'another hero far removed from him in time and place, tho' of the same stock, George Washington'.[161] Alfred was also linked to Washington by Arthur Conan Doyle. Speaking of the king's strength in adversity, at a planning meeting for the Winchester celebrations, Doyle proclaimed:

> Such was Washington in America. Such was Alfred in England. It is not the conqueror in his blaze of glory which appeals in the highest degree to our mind, but it is Alfred, beaten and fugitive, but indomitable, amongst the marshes of Sedgemoor, or Washington undaunted with his rustic soldiers among the snows of Valley Forge.[162]

It was another American figure, however, who came to be most intimately connected with Alfred during the days of the Millenary itself. On 6 September 1901 – just before the Winchester celebrations began – the American president McKinley was assassinated. Initially, this tragedy threatened to overshadow the anniversary, diverting the desired American interest in the event. McKinley's funeral was arranged for the Thursday of the proceedings, obliging the American ambassador to Britain to withdraw his acceptance to attend the Millenary, and necessitating the respectful postponement of the Earl of Northbrook's Alfredian garden party. The Winchester committee was not to be beaten, however. Instead of giving up on America, it successfully turned the country's tragedy to its advantage. On Wednesday 18 September (the day before McKinley's funeral), Henry Irving introduced the tone that was to be assumed for the rest of the celebrations. Concluding his reading of Tennyson's *Beckett*, he announced:

> All the race which looks up to King Alfred and knows his memory as a common heritage, all that race is to-day united in bitter grief for one who to-morrow a

mourning nation is to lay at rest. President McKinley was at once the advocate
and emblem of noble conduct, of high thought and patriotism. He, like his pre-
decessor of a thousand years ago, worked not only for his own country, but for
all the world, and his memory shall be green for ever in the hearts of our loyal
and expansive race, in the hearts of all English-speaking people.

At the commemorative Alfred luncheon, Rosebery also connected the
deaths of Alfred and McKinley to promote Anglo-American solidarity, proclaiming 'King Alfred wrought immortal work for us and for our sister
nation over the sea, which in supreme moments of stress and sorrow is irresistibly joined to us across the centuries and across the seas'. And, at the same
luncheon, the Bishop of Winchester announced that there was 'a singular
appropriateness' in commemorating Alfred at the time of McKinley's death,
when both branches of the Anglo-Saxon race were united in sorrow.[163]
In the absence of the American ambassador, General Rockwell attended
the Alfred Millenary. He too highlighted the similarities between the Saxon
monarch and the deceased president, speaking at length of a 'fundamental
Anglo-Saxon character' uniting both Britons and Americans and ensuring
them a future as 'the dominant race of the world'. 'Our late, lamented
President was a true son of the race', he asserted, 'in his public life we see the
same high sense of duty and devotion to what he conceived to be the best
interests of his country, which distinguished his great prototype'.[164] The connection between McKinley and Alfred – as a union drawing together
America and Britain – was reiterated in both the US and the British press in
the days following the Millenary. Reporting Irving's oration on McKinley,
the Boston-based *National Magazine* pronounced, 'And so it was that, at the
end of a thousand years of English history, the man first in the thoughts and
hearts of all English-speaking peoples – first even in the thoughts and hearts
of the men assembled to honour the founder of the race – was an
American'.[165] But it was in the elegy which appeared in *The Times*, the
morning after the unveiling of the Alfred statue, that McKinley's bond with
Alfred was most memorably immortalised:

Ave Atque Vale
Praise we the Dead! where once his grave
Received to peace the Saxon King,
Do honour to the wise and brave,
And let the world-wide nation sing
The memory of a thousand years –
Then hush! and think of others' tears!

Beyond the western sea they fall
From eyes that yet with joy behold
The kingly ancestor of all,
The glory of the years of old;
But o'er th'Atlantic water-ways,
A mist of sorrow dims their gaze.

Again, with his city's bound, truth-teller Alfred stands in fame –
Beyond the sea, a mournful sound
Re-echoes to the glad acclaim:
We listen to the passing-bell –
True child of Washington, farewell!

Up with our hearts! And over sea
Swift be the word of friendship sped –
You praise our hero-king, and we
Lament with you your patriot dead:
In Sorrow's name, one boon we crave –
Lay England's wreath upon his grave.[166]

Alfred in the colonies

As the elegy in *The Times* suggests, Alfred was praised in America in 1901 just as he was celebrated in Britain. The Alfred committee in Winchester had been concerned that this should be the case. In 1900, Besant wrote articles on Alfred for American publications and, early in 1901, Frederic Harrison was dispatched on a lecture tour of the United States to promote the approach of Alfred's anniversary as an occasion on which America and Britain should join together in celebration. What is not clear is whether the Winchester committee was aware of America's native cult of King Alfred when they looked to the 1901 Millenary as a means of drawing America and Britain closer together. Certainly they were 'surprised and gratified' to discover that President Roosevelt, when they met him, already possessed 'not only a full, but a detailed knowledge of King Alfred's career', so they were perhaps unaware of the role that Alfred had played in America as a hero of constitutional freedom in the late eighteenth century. Soon after the outbreak of the War of Independence, in 1775, a twenty-four-gun American ship named the *Black Prince* had been renamed *Alfred* and had proceeded to distinguish herself in battle against the British.[167] And, when Thomas Jefferson had drafted the Declaration of Independence in 1776, and later divided the American West into states, he had apparently been recalling the political liberties, and the system of shires, hundreds and tithings, which tradition attributed to Alfred.[168]

America then was readily receptive to suggestions that Alfred should be commemorated in 1901. However, it did so very much on its own terms, celebrating not 'England's hero king', but an Alfred who was also the property of the United States. At the Winchester commemorations, General Rockwell pointed out that Alfred's name was 'a household word on the other side of the Atlantic, quite as much as here in England, and with good reason, for he was our king just as much as yours'.[169] This sentiment was also voiced by the editor of the New York magazine *Outlook* in a footnote to Besant's article on 'The Heritage of King Alfred'. In response to Besant's suggestion that the magazine's readers might be interested in Alfred's life because of 'a certain similarity of mind between the American and the Englishman', the editor added rather archly:

> As many of our readers probably know, the year 1901 is the thousandth since King Alfred's death. The anniversary will be observed in November next with public addresses and memorials in England, and probably also by Americans, who are certainly equal sharers in the heritage about which Sir Walter Besant here writes so earnestly.[170]

Those invited from America to the commemorations in Winchester certainly seem to have gone with the sense that they were there to celebrate their own heritage. 'It stirs the blood', said the President of Columbia University, discussing the apparent brevity of American history, 'to realise that the roots of much that is best in our national life can be traced by direct descent to a period so remote and to a man so noble as King Alfred the Great'. He was accompanied at the Winchester Millenary by representatives from Yale, Harvard and California University. Far more Americans celebrated Alfred's anniversary at the commemorations held in North America itself, however. These took place in New York on the two days following the actual anniversary of Alfred's death (26 October), and included an exhibition (displaying books, manuscripts, and engravings relating to Alfred's time); the opening of a new annex of the New York Public Library (called the 'Alfred Memorial Library' and dedicated to the Anglo-Saxon period); a grand banquet; and a commemorative service.[171]

The service was held at St Paul's Chapel – a building strongly associated with American independence. It had been the parish church of George Washington, and as the Reverend Henry Lubeck announced during the Alfred commemoration service, 'it was to this church that General Washington came in procession immediately after his inauguration, on 30th April 1789, as our first President . . . and as the great Alfred and the great Washington resembled each other in their characters, their vicissitudes, and their final success, it is peculiarly fitting that we should commemorate the one while surrounded by memories of the other'. The New York Alfred Millenary was, then, a distinctly American event. At the same time, however, like the Winchester celebration, it looked towards conciliation and fraternity. Invitations to the proceedings stressed that Alfred's achievements were 'the common heritage of the English-speaking race', and St Paul's chapel, it was stressed, had not only been Washington's church, but was 'the only church left in this city that was standing in colonial days, when these two nations, the United States and the United Kingdom, were one'.[172]

The celebrations in America were not just local to New York. On Monday 28 October, memorial exercises were held at schools and colleges throughout the country, and in Portland the Maine Historical Society was just one of many historical organisations across America that in the latter months of 1901 marked Alfred's Millenary with a series of lectures stressing the Saxon king's affiliation with Washington and presenting him as 'a man whom every American, however high his ideal, may imitate with profit'.[173] A flurry of articles on King Alfred also filled the American press in the wake of the Millenary. Arthur McIlroy's 'A Thousand Years of English', published in Boston's *National Magazine* is representative of their tone. 'Alfred is and will always remain, the typical man of our race – call him Anglo-Saxon, call him American, call him Englishman, call him Australian', it asserted. And, insisting yet more forcefully on America's Alfredian heritage, it demanded, 'What think you would have been the ultimate result to America, to Australia, to all the lands where the sons of England have brought the light of civilization, had the Danes . . . been permitted to trample out the last spark of Christianity from England?'[174]

North America was not the only English-speaking country beyond British shores to claim a share of Alfred's heritage in the nineteenth century. The Canadian poet J.B. Mackenzie marked Alfred's Millenary with a long ballad in praise of the king – a ballad which was to lend its title to his next anthology of verse (but which contains little of interest beyond the by-then-traditional cycle of Alfredian legends, and an evident desire for a shared cultural identity with Britain). More interesting, however, in 1853, the Saxon monarch had been celebrated by the Australian poet Clement C. Elrington, in his 1853 'Alfred the Great: A Poem Addressed to the Youth of Australia'. Elrington's poem is prefaced by two quotations. The first is unattributed: ''Tis a glorious title, deny it who can,/ That's contained in the words 'I'm an Englishman'. The second is taken from Thomas Dibdin's 'Alfred the Great' (part of his 1813 *A Metrical History of England*):

> Replete with soul the Monarch stood alone
> And rear'd on Freedom's basis England's throne;
> The Patriot, Legislator, Parent, Sage,
> He died the light of a benighted age.

The stress on the virtues of Englishness that emerges from both prefaces intimates that the poem represented an attempt to employ Alfred to reinforce Australian loyalty to the British throne. And this is further suggested by the didactic tone of its title, and by the poem's opening, which introduces an account of Alfred's most famous deeds by asserting:

> We of his race, still boastful of our blood,
> Ever had merit to esteem the good;
> Tho' lowly still, tho' humble be our fate,
> When weighed with mighty nations in their state,
> We honour, reverence, the truly great.[175]

The poem should therefore perhaps be read in the context of the Australian nationalism that began to emerge in the mid-nineteenth century, partly as a result of anger at the British export of felons and cheap labour to Australia, and partly because of dissatisfaction with British policy in the Pacific.

Alfred was also invoked to assuage colonial dissatisfaction in India. Jacob Abbott's biography of the king, *Alfred the Great*, was published in 1898 in

Madras by the Christian Literature Society for India, as part of a cheaply produced series called 'The Anna Library'. The volume was clearly intended for Indian (rather than Anglo-Indian) readers – it begins by explaining: 'Britain is the largest island belonging to Europe. It is more than thrice the size of Ceylon'. In this context, then, Alfred is presented as 'the founder of the British Monarchy', and depicted as the exemplary English leader. Abbott describes that he was:

> mild and gentle towards every one, instead of acting haughtily like a proud king. In India the so-called high castes often treat with rudeness and contempt the classes regarded as lower than themselves. Indians sometimes justly complain of the rudeness of low Europeans; but no Englishman treats the people of this country with the contempt and insolence which high caste Hindus habitually display towards their low caste brethren.[176]

Most interesting, however, is Abbott's celebration of Alfred's peace-treaty with the Danes in 878. Explaining the desirability of this, he relates that:

> There were two races in the same island that had been engaged for many years in a fierce and bloody struggle, each gaining at times a temporary victory. The Danes had for many years settled in Britain. Large numbers had quietly settled on agricultural lands. They had become peaceful inhabitants. They had inter-married in some cases with Saxons. Alfred determined to . . . allow those peaceably disposed to remain in quiet possession of such lands.[177]

Abbott's depiction of the Danes contrasts strikingly with the general nineteenth-century stereotype of them as debauched, plundering invaders, and his language – with its references to 'settlement', 'two races', and 'inter-marriage' – would clearly have contained a strong subtext of contemporary allusion in a colonial context at the end of the nineteenth century. His biography of Alfred may therefore be read as a plea for peace and inter-racial tolerance in the wake of Indian uprisings, and at a time when the Indian National Congress was gaining in influence.

Abbott's biography not only presents Alfred as an exemplary king, but also as a model for the average Indian reader to emulate. His narrative of Alfred's life ends by asserting:

> The foregoing account of Alfred should be read, not merely for amusement, but chiefly to learn how we may profit by his example. It is true that we are not kings, but the same spirit may be shown in whatever position we may be placed.

And the book ends with a section entitled 'Review: Lessons from Alfred's Life'. Among this list of pronouncements is 'His efforts to benefit his Countrymen by Translation' (which explains, 'Educated Indians who have acquired a knowledge of English should make the knowledge which it contains accessible to their countrymen in their own vernacular'). Another virtue endorsed is 'His Piety', which relates, 'It was Christianity that gave birth to such a noble character as Alfred. Cordially embraced, it would have similar effects upon the people of India').[178]

The lessons gleaned from Alfred's life in Abbott's biography are undisguisedly geared towards the author's aim of securing and safeguarding British colonial rule in India. Alfred was also employed as a moral example in Britain, however, by other writers with different agendas. It is this use and image of Alfred, neither as an ideal king nor the source of great institutions, but as a paradigm for all men – as 'the typical man of our race at his best and noblest' – that will be considered in the next chapter.[179]

Notes

1 Bowker, *The King Alfred Millenary*, p. 20.
2 The claim about Alfred's navy is based on a reference in *The Anglo-Saxon Chronicles* to Alfred designing boats (p. 90). Alfred's connection with the origins of the British Empire derives from a reference to his sending alms to Judaea in *The Anglo-Saxon Chronicles*, which in three manuscript copies of the text is mistranscribed to read 'India' – see Abels, *Alfred the Great*, p. 190. Alfred was first hailed as the founder of Oxford University in Ralph Higden's fourteenth-century *The Polychronicon*. The notion that Alfred instituted a system of free education originates in Asser's statement that he taught the children of his clergy and nobles to read – see *Asser's Life of King Alfred*, p. 91.
3 See *The Public General Acts of the United Kingdom of Great Britain and Ireland* (London: The Law Society, series).
4 Dickens, *A Child's History of England*, p. 24.
5 Draper, 'Alfred the Great as a Man of Letters', p. 598.
6 Lorimer, 'King Alfred', p. 162. On Victorian legal change, see Midwinter, *Victorian Social Reform*, pp. 14–20.
7 Mill asserts, for instance, 'It is a noble work to . . . diffuse over a new created world the laws of Alfred' ('Principles of Political Economy', p. 61). On this subject, see also Eldridge, *England's Mission*, pp. 142–171, 235–255.
8 Quoted in Bowker, *The King Alfred Millenary*, p. 21.
9 See Keynes, 'The Cult of King Alfred the Great', p. 322; Mitchell, *Picturing the Past*, p. 65.
10 Keynes, 'The Cult of King Alfred the Great', p. 336.
11 Harold John Stanley submitted *Alfred Compiling His Laws*; Henry C. Selous entered *Alfred Submitting His Code of Laws to the Witena-gemot*. The sculptors Frederick S. Archer and Edward B. Stephens respectively entered *Alfred the Great with the Book of Common Law* and *Alfred the Great Propounding His Code of Laws* (see Keynes, 'The Cult of King Alfred the Great', p. 336).
12 The only eighteenth-century text to depict Alfred as a legislator is Bicknell, *The Life of Alfred the Great*, pp. iii, xi.
13 *The Laws of King Alfred*, p. 163.
14 Dibdin, 'Alfred the Great', p. 67.
15 One popular history to disseminate this information was Pauli, *The Life of Alfred the Great*, p. 128.
16 Besant, *The Story of King Alfred*, p. 161.
17 Hughes, *Alfred the Great: A Biography*, p. 159.
18 Pye, *Alfred: An Epic Poem*, p. 61.
19 Knowles, *Alfred the Great*, p. 84.

20 Although Alfred's laws protected the poor as well as the noble, at the heart of his law-code is a firm belief in social hierarchy: the compensation payable to victims of crime, for instance, is always specified with reference to the social rank of the afflicted – see Keynes and Lapidge, *Alfred the Great*, p. 166.

21 See *Asser's Life of King Alfred*, p. 109.

22 Dyer, 'Alfred', p. 214; Dibdin, 'Alfred the Great', p. 66; Hamilton, *Alfred the Great*, 7. See also Pye, *Alfred: An Epic Poem*, p. 159; Graham, *Little Arthur's History of England*, p. 4.

23 *The Laws of King Alfred*, p. 170.

24 See Colley, *Britons: Forging the Nation*, pp. 323, 354, 359.

25 Page, *Alfred the Great*, p. 181.

26 Henty, *The Dragon and the Raven*, p. 352. See also Hughes, *Alfred the Great*, p. 306.

27 Draper, 'Alfred the Great', p. 34.

28 Magnus, *First Makers of England*, p. 131.

29 'Alfred' [pseud. Samuel Kydd], *The History of the Factory Movement, from the Year 1802 to the Enactment of the Ten Hours' Bill in 1847* (London, 1857).

30 Spelman, *The Life of Alfred the Great*, p. 106.

31 See Aarsleff, *The Study of Language in England*, p. 169.

32 'The Treaty Between Alfred and Guthrum', p. 171.

33 Hughes, *Alfred the Great*, p. 123.

34 Simmons, *Reversing the Conquest*, p. 40.

35 Magnus, *Alfred the Great*, p. 155.

36 Paul Creswick, *In Aelfred's Days*, p. 292.

37 Knowles, *Alfred the Great*, p. 84.

38 See, for instance, Barnes, 'The Rise and Progress of Trial by Jury in Britain', pp. 412–420; Kneeland, 'The Vikings and What We Owe to Them', pp. 259–261.

39 Laws to do with juries were passed in 1815 and 1825 (see *The Statutes of the United Kingdom of Great Britain and Ireland*).

40 See, for instance, Walter Scott, *Ivanhoe: A Romance* (London: J.M. Dent, 1906 [1819]), pp. 142, 323; 'The Anglo-Normans', p. 439.

41 Blackie, 'Alfred', p. 97.

42 William of Malmesbury, *History of the Kings of England*, p. 104.

43 Spelman, *The Life of Alfred the Great*, p. 114.

44 Pauli, *The Life of Alfred the Great*, p. 142.

45 Blackie studied for three years at the Scottish bar (see *ODNB*).

46 The CID was established in 1842. On the shift from preventative to detective policing in Britain, see Midwinter, *Victorian Social Reform*, p. 43.

47 See Midwinter, *Victorian Social Reform*, pp. 19–24.

48 Since Blackie was born in 1809, he would have been able to remember the period when the theory of preventative policing was promoted (see *ODNB*).

49 William of Malmesbury, *History of the Kings of England*, p. 104.

50 See Keynes, 'The Cult of King Alfred the Great', p. 230.

51 The notion could have developed from Henry of Huntingdon's *English History*, which claims that it was the kings of Wessex who first divided England into shires (see Keynes, 'The Cult of King Alfred the Great', p. 232).

52 *The History of Ingulf* was first published in 1596 and was first translated in 1854. William of Malmesbury's text was first published in 1596 and first translated in 1815.

53 For instance, Powell, *The Life of Alfred or Alvred*, 1634, p. 70; Bicknell, *The Life of Alfred the Great*, 1777, p. 197; and Rapin, *The History of England*, p. 113. On this subject, see also Keynes, 'The Cult of King Alfred the Great', p. 243; Yorke, 'The Most Perfect Man in History', p. 12.

54 Powell, *The Life of Alfred or Alvred*, p. 70; Bicknell, *The Life of Alfred the Great*, p. 197.

55 Hughes, *Alfred the Great*, p. 185.

56 Hughes, *Alfred the Great*, p. 185.

57 Draper, 'Alfred the Great', p. 12.

58 For a more detailed account of the lack of schools in the nineteenth century, see Midwinter, *Nineteenth-Century Education*, pp. 77–78.

59 On the high rates of crime in Victorian England, see Midwinter, *Victorian Social Reform*, pp. 14, 44. On the Victorian association between crime and illiteracy, see Brantlinger, 'How Oliver Twist Learned to Read', p. 65. Thomas Hughes explicitly linked Alfred's educational reforms to the suppression of civil revolt (*Alfred the Great*, p. 161).

60 See Midwinter, *Nineteenth-Century Education*, pp. 40–41.

61 *Asser's Life of King Alfred*, pp. 91, 110. The 'school' is referred to again by Asser when he states that Alfred gave one-eighth of his revenues to its running (*Asser's Life of King Alfred*, p. 107).

62 See Hervey, 'Alfred the Great Teaching the Anglo-Saxon Youth', p. 658. Gilbert's painting is reproduced next to Hervey's poem.

63 Austin, *England's Darling*, p. 21; Stables, *'Twixt Daydawn and Light*, p. 328. See also Brough, *Alfred the Great*, p. 3.

64 *Asser's Life of King Alfred*, p. 90.

65 Pope Gregory, *Pastoral Care*, p. 126.

66 See Parker (ed.), *Aelfredi regis res gestae*, sig. folio ii recto [43], sig. folio iii verso [47]. It was also paraphrased in Powell, *The Life of Alfred or Alvred*, p. 47.

67 Spelman, *The Life of Alfred the Great*, p. 143.

68 Graham, *Little Arthur's History of England*, p. 51; Kerr, *Two Saxon Maidens*, p. 220.

69 Hughes, *Alfred the Great*, p. 178.

70 Tulloch, 'Anglo-Saxon and Anglo-Norman Christianity', p. 52.

71 Dickens, *A Child's History of England*, p. 24.

72 Bowker, *The King Alfred Millenary*, p. 20.

73 Bowker, *The King Alfred Millenary*, p. 26.

74 See Bryce, 'Alfred the Great', p. 1538.

75 Bowker, *The King Alfred Millenary*, p. 32.

76 Hudson, *Martin Tupper*, pp. 96, 100.

77 See Chapter Three of this volume for a longer discussion of this subject. Higden's text was translated into English by John de Trevisa in 1398 and printed by William Caxton in 1480.

78 Higden, *The Polychronicon*, p. 355 [spelling and syntax modernised by the present author].

79 See Camden, *Britannia*, p. 272.

80 Dibdin, 'Alfred the Great', p. 66. See also Pye, *Alfred: An Epic Poem*, p. 150; Tupper, 'The Order of Alfred', p. 253, in *Ballads for the Times*.

81 Spelman, *The Life of Alfred the Great*, p. 145.

82 Wooley, *Lectures Delivered in Australia*, pp. 4–5.

83　Wooley, *Lectures Delivered in Australia*, pp. 5–6.

84　See Bowker, *The King Alfred Millenary*, p. 48.

85　See, for instance, Stewart, *Stories about Alfred the Great*, p. 53; Giles, *The Life and Times of Alfred the Great*, p. 298.

86　Pollock, 'Alfred the Great', p. 280. See also Eayrs, *Alfred to Victoria*, p. 11.

87　See Keynes, 'The Cult of King Alfred the Great', 261–263, 265–266.

88　Draper, 'Alfred the Great', p. 91.

89　Plummer, *The Life and Times of Alfred the Great*, p. 193.

90　See, for instance, Pye, *Alfred: An Epic Poem*, p. 138; Fitchett, *King Alfred: A Poem*, II, p. 412; Austin, *England's Darling*, p. 49; Harrison, 'Alfred as King', p. 59.

91　*The Anglo-Saxon Chronicles*, p. 87; *Asser's Life of King Alfred*, pp. 96, 98.

92　See *Asser's Life of King Alfred*, p. 67.

93　See Keynes, 'The Cult of King Alfred the Great', p. 231. They were published together in 1571, and Roger of Wendover's text was also translated into modern English by Giles in 1849.

94　Spelman, *The Life of Alfred the Great*, p. 92.

95　See, for instance, Rapin, *The History of England*, p. 112

96　See Groom, *The Union Jack*, pp. 162–169.

97　Sambrook, *James Thomson*, p. 53.

98　*Alfred the Great: Deliverer of his Country*, p. 66.

99　See Groom, *The Union Jack*, pp. 155–158.

100　See Groom, *The Union Jack*, p. 153.

101　Pye, *Alfred: An Epic Poem*, pp. 13, 138, 37.

102　Pye, *Alfred: An Epic Poem*, p. 78.

103　Pye, *Alfred: An Epic Poem*, p. 100.

104　Groom, *The Union Jack*, p. 172–173

105　Groom, *The Union Jack*, p. 172.

106　Pye, *Alfred: An Epic Poem*, p. 153.

107　Colley, *Britons: Forging the Nation*, p. 162.

108　On this subject, see Davies, *Education in a Welsh Rural Community*, pp. 19–27.

109　Austin, *England's Darling*, pp. 48–49.

110　Harrison, 'Alfred as King', pp. 65, 59.

111　Stables, *'Twixt Daydawn and Light*, p. 354.

112　Stables, *'Twixt Daydawn and Light*, p. x.

113　Stables, *'Twixt Daydawn and Light*, p. xi.

114　Campbell, 'Ye Mariners of England', p. 128.

115　Austin, *England's Darling*, p. xi.

116　Collingwood, *Alfred the Great: A Poem*, p. 138.

117　See Gat, *The Development of Military Thought*, p. 205.

118　Lonsdale, *Sketch of Alfred the Great*, p. 3. See also E.A. Freeman, *Old English History*, p. 55.

119　Tupper, 'The Order of Alfred', p. 253. See also Dibdin, 'Alfred the Great', p. 65.

120　*The Times* (28 Oct. 1901), p. 7.

121　On this subject, see Wawn, *The Victorians and the Vikings*, p. 131.

122　Whistler, *King Alfred's Viking*, pp. 60–68.

123　Henty, *The Dragon and the Raven*, p. 345.

124　*The Anglo-Saxon Chronicles*, p. 65.

125　See *Asser's Life of King Alfred*, pp. 82, 86–87.

126 *The Anglo-Saxon Chronicles*, p. 90.

127 Bowker, *The King Alfred Millenary*, p. 147.

128 Kelsey, *Alfred of Wessex*, I, p. 262; Tappan, *In the Days of Alfred the Great*, p. 256.

129 Eayrs, *Alfred to Victoria*, p. 27.

130 Spelman, *The Life of Alfred the Great*, p. 150.

131 Mallet and Thomson, *Alfred: A Masque*, p. 44.

132 Mallet and Thomson, *Alfred: A Masque*, p. 42.

133 See, for instance, Hill, *Alfred the Great*, p. 22; Collingwood, *Alfred the Great*, p. 120.

134 Knowles, *Alfred the Great*, p. 85.

135 Canning, *Alfred the Great in Athelnay*, p. 172.

136 Tupper 'The Order of Alfred', p. 253, in *Ballads for the Times*. See also Tupper, *Alfred*, p. 297.

137 Bowker, *The King Alfred Millenary*, pp. 9, 111.

138 *Asser's Life of King Alfred*, p. 101.

139 Besant, *The Story of King Alfred*, p. 192. See also Harrison, 'Alfred as King', p. 59.

140 *The Anglo-Saxon Chronicles*, p. 79.

141 Abels, *Alfred the Great*, p. 190. This claim is repeated in William of Malmesbury's *History of the Kings of England* (p. 104).

142 On India's importance in the nineteenth century, see Eldridge, *England's Mission*, p. 209.

143 Markham, 'Alfred as a Geographer', p. 166.

144 Spelman, *The Life of Alfred the Great*, p. 152. It is interesting to note that Spelman here substitutes the East Indies for India. This change probably reflects the fact that in the seventeenth century when he was writing, the former region was of greatest consequence to Britain, in terms of overseas trade. No nineteenth-century writers reiterated or remarked upon Spelman's innovation, however.

145 Rapin, *The History of England*, p. 113.

146 J.F.R., *Lives of Alfred the Great, Sir Thomas More, and John Evelyn*, p. 40.

147 See for instance Engelbach, 'The English in India', pp. 331–346; Carnarvon, [Untitled], p. 63.

148 Tulloch, 'Anglo-Saxon and Anglo-Norman Christianity', p. 52. See also Besant, 'Introduction', p. 60; Freeman, *Old English History*, p. 49.

149 Blackie, 'Alfred', p. 98. See also Wordsworth, 'Alfred', in *The Poetical Works of William Wordsworth*, p. 70

150 On this subject, see Eldridge, *England's Mission*, p. 239; Thornton, *The Imperial Idea and its Enemies*, p. ix.

151 Bowker, *The King Alfred Millenary*, p. 21.

152 Pye, *Alfred: An Epic Poem*, p. 153.

153 Tupper, 'The Alfred Medals', p. 258, in *Ballads for the Times*. See also Stables, *'Twixt Daydawn and Light*, p. 354; Pollard, *A Hero King*, p. 426.

154 Canning, *Alfred the Great in Athelnay*, p. 171. See also Rapin, *The History of England*, I, p. 338.

155 Hill, *Alfred the Great*, p. 86.

156 See Yorke, *The King Alfred Millenary*, p. 20.

157 Bowker, *The King Alfred Millenary*, p. 189.

158 Tupper, *Alfred*, p. 259.

159 Hudson, *Martin Tupper*, p. 100.
160 Bowker, *The King Alfred Millenary*, p. 11.
161 Bryce, 'Alfred the Great', p. 1534.
162 Bowker, *The King Alfred Millenary*, p. 22.
163 Bowker, *The King Alfred Millenary*, pp. 75, iii.
164 Bowker, *The King Alfred Millenary*, p. 120.
165 McIlroy, 'A Thousand Years of English', p. 103.
166 Bowker, *The King Alfred Millenary*, p. 94.
167 Bowker, *The King Alfred Millenary*, p. 155; Keynes, 'The Cult of King Alfred the Great', p. 288.
168 Keynes, 'The Cult of King Alfred the Great', p. 288.
169 Bowker, *The King Alfred Millenary*, p. 121.
170 Besant, 'The Heritage of Alfred the Great', p. 531.
171 Bowker, *The King Alfred Millenary*, pp. 144, 155.
172 Bowker, *The King Alfred Millenary*, p. 156.
173 *In Commemoration of the Millenary Anniversary*, p. 4.
174 McIlroy, 'A Thousand Years of English', 101, 103.
175 Elrington, 'Alfred the Great', p. 3.
176 Abbott, *Alfred the Great*, pp. 5, 46.
177 Abbott, *Alfred the Great*, p. 36.
178 Abbott, *Alfred the Great*, pp. 45–46.
179 Besant, *The Story of King Alfred*, p. 206.

6

'The most perfect character in history': Alfred and Victorian morality

As he unveiled the King Alfred statue in Winchester, Lord Roseberry presented the Saxon monarch to the assembled crowds not merely as 'the highest type of kingship', but as 'a man, a complete man', whose greatness was 'in the first place, a question of personality'.[1] Likewise, in his opening address to a 1901 Alfredian conference in the United States, the President of the Maine Historical Society, James Phinney Baxter, stressed that 'we today honour Alfred not because he was a king, or a successful ruler of a great people, but as a wise and noble man'. Whereas eighteenth-century Alfredianists celebrated Alfred as an ideal king and a paradigm for rulers, through the nineteenth century the Saxon monarch became increasingly promoted as a moral role-model for everyone, and his personal achievements, accomplishments and character were investigated and discussed as much as his civic institutions and establishments.

The notion of some quintessential affinity between Alfred and the average British man was manifested in late nineteenth-century descriptions of the king as 'a man of science', 'an engineer', a 'captain of enterprise', and an 'industrial foreman'.[2] Such descriptions proliferated particularly around the time of the Winchester Millenary, whose supporters had a vested interest in encouraging large numbers of the public to identify closely with the Saxon king. The origins of Alfred's role as a moral paradigm are, however, complex. The invention of cheaper printing methods during the nineteenth century probably played the most important role. Once Alfredian texts could be published by major publishers for mass consumption, Alfredianists began to write texts specifically aimed at the new reading classes. Besant, as discussed earlier, determined that he 'would rather write a book for the people than anything else', so his *The Story of King Alfred* was sold for just a shilling, while Thomas Hughes's popular biography of Alfred, first published in 1869, ran to five editions.[3] The nineteenth century's three reform acts also, however, probably contributed to the period's interest in Alfred as an exemplar for the common man – by gradually devolving the responsibility for England's social policy, they incited many writers to realign their interest from improving kings to developing the social conscience of the average voter. In his 1869 *Alfred the Great*, Thomas Hughes asserted that in response to the growth of democracy, writers must strive 'to develop to the utmost the sense of personal and individual responsibility'.[4]

The development of Alfred's role from regnal to moral exemplar may also have owed something to the growth of publishing for children during the nineteenth century. In history textbooks aimed at juvenile readers, historical heroes were typically used as a means of advocating the sort of virtues that would be relevant to a child's immediate domestic circle rather than public responsibilities.[5] The rise of the historical novel was probably influential, too, since its plot inevitably needed to be driven partly by character. Certainly, Thomas Carlyle praised the form for having taught the public 'that the bygone ages of the world were actually filled by living men, not by . . . abstractions of men'.[6] And Carlyle's own definition of a king as merely 'the ablest man . . . the truest-hearted, justest, the Noblest Man' also opened the way for Alfred to be presented as a moral ideal for men of all stations. Ironically, the emergence around the middle of the nineteenth century of 'scientific histories' focusing on political economy and laws at the expense of human relationships also perhaps heightened the drive to re-imagine Alfred as an individual man, by engendering a backlash among popular historians and authors. Charles Kingsley, for instance, devoted his inaugural lecture as Regius Professor of History to an assertion that 'History is the History of men and women and of nothing else'.[7]

One text above all, however, can be identified as having influenced the late Victorian fascination with Alfred's character. The first part of Edward Augustus Freeman's multi-volume *History of the Norman Conquest* was published in 1867. Widely read during the late nineteenth century (six editions were published between 1867 and 1900), it allotted a mere ten pages to Alfred's reign, but within that narrow scope it dwelt upon the exceptional nature of the Saxon king's character as never before. Alfred, Freeman asserted (twice in three pages) was 'the most perfect character in history'.[8] This claim was frequently quoted by later Alfredianists, particularly around the time of the Alfred Millenary – for instance, by the Dean of Ely, addressing the National Home Reading Union in Winchester that very year, and by Besant who asserted that, 'among all who have written of Alfred . . . there is no tribute so entirely satisfactory in its expression as that of Freeman: "Alfred . . . is the most perfect character in history" '.[9]

Freeman went on to compare the Saxon king's virtues to those belonging to a wide range of other historical luminaries, but found that no rival could match the perfection of Alfred's character. 'There is no other name in history to compare with his' he claimed:

> The virtue of Ælfred, like the virtue of Washington, consisted in no marvellous displays of superhuman genius, but in the simple, straight-forward discharge of the duty of the moment. But Washington, soldier, statesman, and patriot, like Ælfred, has no claim to Ælfred's further characters of saint and scholar. . . . The same union of zeal for religion and learning with the highest gifts of the warrior and the statesman is found, on a wider field of action, in Charles the Great. But even Charles cannot aspire to the pure glory of Ælfred. . . . Among our later princes, the great Edward alone can bear for a moment the comparison with his

glorious ancestor. And, when tried by such a standard, even the great Edward fails. Even in him we do not see the same wonderful union of gifts and virtues which so seldom meet together; we cannot acquit Edward of occasional acts of violence, of occasional recklessness as to means; we cannot attribute to him the pure, simple, almost childlike disinterestedness which marks the character of Ælfred.

This formula also proved popular around the time of the Winchester Millenary, when it was frequently recited, or adapted to include more contemporary figures.[10] In his 1897 speech at the Midland Institute, for instance (at which he first proposed the idea of a Millenary celebration), Frederic Harrison declared that compared with Alfred, 'Aurelius was occasionally too much of the philosopher; Saint Louis usually too much of the saint; Godfrey too much of the Crusader'.[11] And in his introduction to the 1899 volume of essays, produced to prepare the nation for the Winchester celebrations, Besant likewise compared the Saxon king with Francis of Assisi and Joan of Arc – finding, again, that neither equalled the 'god-like' Alfred.[12] Freeman's celebration of Alfred's moderation was also plundered by those involved in the Winchester celebrations. Alfred was, he claimed, 'a saint without superstition, a scholar without ostentation, a warrior whose wars were all fought in the defence of his country, a conqueror whose laurels were never stained by cruelty, a prince never cast down by adversity, never lifted up to insolence in the days of triumph'. This paean was to provide the inspiration for much of Rosebery's rousing speech at the unveiling of the Alfred statue. 'Alfred', the former prime minister informed the crowds, was 'a man, a complete man. What strikes one most is his completeness; complete is, I think, his distinctive epithet'. He then reworded Freeman's account for a popular audience, suggesting that 'though profoundly pious he was no anchorite; though a king, not a pompous and mysterious phantom; though a passionate seeker after knowledge, not a pedant or a prig'.[13]

Part of the reason why Freeman's stress upon Alfred's character seems to have been drawn upon so enthusiastically in the late nineteenth century probably lies in the development of racialist theories which sought to identify a distinct English 'type' or 'national character'. In the preface to her 1901 children's book *First Makers of England* (which included a chapter on Alfred), Katie Magnus stated that 'the seeds of our national character are to be sought in the lives of the heroes of early England, from whom we trace our best habits'.[14] And, in his 1900 history *Alfred to Victoria*, George Eayrs claimed that Alfred and his line 'must be acknowledged the strongest of the several strains which have combined to produce that distinctive type, the Englishman'.[15] Freeman's notion of Alfred's equanimity, in particular, became associated with the idea that English national character was typified by moderation – a notion which paralleled, and probably owed much to, popular views of the English constitution (and Alfred's reign) as the ideal *compromise* between absolute monarchy and outright democracy. Thus at the Winchester unveiling, Rosebery also praised the moderate

Alfred as 'the ideal Englishman . . . the embodiment of our civilization . . . the highest and best type of the qualities which we cherish in our national character'.[16]

Other aspects of Alfred's character were also identified by nineteenth-century Alfredianists as components of the English racial type. The Bishop of Winchester, speaking at the Millenary, claimed that the Saxon king 'embodied the distinctive characteristics of our race – deep-rooted love of straightforwardness, and of absolute fairness between man and man'. And Conan Doyle described Alfred as 'the man who combined in his person all the virtues which go to make up the best type of Englishman. He was sturdy, resolute, persevering, and formidable in action'.[17] Such racialist rhetoric was often used to provide a justification for British colonialism in the late nineteenth century – the British, it was argued for instance, were aggressive colonisers simply because it was in their inherent nature to behave thus. A glimpse of this may be discerned in Conan Doyle's description of the English as 'formidable in action', while the notion of an inherent English 'fairness' (invoked at the Millenary by the Bishop of Winchester) was often used to justify the imposition of English trade and legislature in the colonies. The most explicit use of Alfred's character in relation to British imperialism, however, was made by General Rockwell, who at the commemorative Alfred luncheon proposed a toast to 'Alfred and the modern Anglo-Saxon race', proclaiming that the race's characteristics were 'wonderfully persistent. It has been less changed than most by contact with other races . . . it has succeeded when others have failed, and thriven when others have wasted away. And why? . . . because it has carried everywhere with it those principles of self-reliance and individual freedom inherent in the race . . . is it too much to say that the Anglo-Saxons will be, if they are not already, the dominant race of the world?'[18]

Victorian authors, artists and orators interested in the character of Alfred looked to different periods of the king's life, depending upon the personal qualities they sought; the particular lessons which they aimed to illustrate; or the specific audience they wished to identify with the Saxon monarch. Those interested in encouraging education, for instance, were drawn to tales about his childhood love of reading, while those concerned about moral standards among Britain's youth looked to make an example of Alfred's wayward years as a young man. Although the earliest years of Alfred's life provided rich pickings for such specific agendas, however, they were not commonly appealed to in texts that sought to cast the king as a more general moral paradigm – and as such they will be treated later in this chapter. Before that it is important to consider the period of Alfred's life which was most often invoked by those Alfredianists who wished, like Rockwell and Conan Doyle, to make of the king a broad exemplar of the 'English' qualities of self-reliance, resolution and perseverance. That episode of the king's life was his three months in hiding from the Danes – a time when he must have developed not just as a king, but also as a man.

Alfred's rite of passage

'Alfred', Lord Rosebery announced, speaking of the king's time in hiding to the crowds assembled for the Winchester Millenary, 'was the first Englishman of whom it is recorded that he never knew when he was beaten'.[19] Likewise, in his letter to *The Times* in January 1901, one J.G. James hailed Alfred as having 'taught Englishmen for all future time never to know when they are beaten'.[20] The claim represents just one example of the Victorian belief in the value of obstacles to individual development which permeated nineteenth-century society – affecting everything from poor laws to imperial strategy, from economic policy to education. It was a doctrine most infamously championed by Samuel Smiles, who in his 1859 manual *Self-help* proclaimed: 'It is not ease, but effort – not facility, but difficulty, that makes men . . . Without the necessity of encountering difficulty, life might be easier, but men would be worth less'.[21] It was reflected in the popularity of the *Bildungsroman* and quest narratives like Bunyan's *Pilgrim's Progress* during the period.[22] And it was an ideology which rendered Alfred's humbling period of defeat before his great victory at Ethandune peculiarly attractive – and which almost certainly contributed enormously to the king's general growth in popularity during the nineteenth century. Indeed, in attempting to encourage support for an Alfred Millenary celebration in Winchester, Arthur Conan Doyle explicitly invoked Alfred as one who had triumphed over hardship, asserting:

> The ideal man has never been the man who has been brilliantly and easily successful, the Napoleon Bonaparte man, but it has been the man who has been beaten, and who has refused to take his beating, who has struggled on through years of adversity, until by sheer doggedness he has attained his end. Such was Washington in America. Such was Alfred in England.[23]

Late Victorian depictions of Alfred's temporary defeat as a personal rite of passage during which he gained resilience and patience were probably encouraged by the publication in the first half of the nineteenth century of King Alfred's Old English translation of Boethius's *Consolations of Philosophy* – the contrite and long-suffering sentiments of which the editors typically interpreted in terms of Alfred's own biography, rather than in relation to the Roman prisoner Boethius.[24] One example from Tupper's 1852 edition of Alfred's translation may stand as an example of the way in which the text as a whole was treated. In Book II, Boethius laments:

> Worldliness brought me here
> Foolishly blind,
> Riches have wrought me here
> Sadness of mind.

'This', Tupper writes, 'may fairly be regarded as a picture of Alfred's own mind in the dark times of his adversity'.[25]

Alfred's time of adversity, and the personal improvement that he derived from it, proved to be a theme particularly popular among those late Victorian authors whose work formed part of the burgeoning sub-genre of adventure fiction 'for boys' – designed to inculcate those 'manly' virtues into its young readers which would best fit them for a life of service to Queen and Country. In Whistler's 1899 novel *King Alfred's Viking*, Alfred's time in hiding is a period during which he learns to rise above despair.[26] Likewise, in Stables's 1898 *'Twixt Daydawn and Light* Alfred loses trust 'in the mercy and goodness of God', but his opportune dose of hardship quickly requires him to 'resume his manhood' – to 'arise, exert himself, believe' – and he emerges from his time in hiding 'strengthened in body and mind'. 'If he had not as yet conquered his enemies', Stables observes approvingly, 'he had done an even more difficult deed, he had conquered himself'.[27]

Alfred is assisted to conquer himself in Stables's novel by the appearance of St Cuthbert in a dream. Since Stables derived from a naval background, it should perhaps occasion little surprise that the rationale for this celestial visitation is in order to suggest to the king that a standing navy might be the key to overcoming Danish invasion.[28] This is a rewriting of the narrative that began life in the eleventh-century *History of Saint Cuthbert*, in which Alfred 'encouraged by St Cuthbert in an obvious revelation, gave battle to the Danes, and at the very place and time which the saint had ordered; he obtained the victory; and ever after . . . held St Cuthbert in especial honour'.[29] As discussed above, this story was then reworked in both William of Malmesbury's *History of the Kings of England* and the fourteenth-century *Polychronicon*. This latter version relates that:

> One day when [Alfred's] companions were fishing . . . a pilgrim came to him and asked alms in God's name. The king held up his hands to heaven and said, 'I thank God who visits his poor servant this day in the form of a poor man . . . the king had only one loaf and a little wine but he told his servant to give half to the poor man. The poor man thanked him and vanished suddenly. The half loaf of bread and the remaining wine became whole again. Alfred's men who were fishing brought in a great quantity of fish. Later when the king was asleep, a man in bishop's clothes appeared to him and said . . . 'Alfred, Christ knows your good conscience and your wishes, and will put an end to your sorrow and care, for tomorrow powerful helpers will be with you and by their help you will overcome your enemies'. 'Who are you?' asked the king. 'I am Cuthbert', he answered, 'the pilgrim that was here yesterday with you, to whom you gave bread and wine: I am busy for you and your people; remember this when all is well with you'.[30]

This didactic version of the Cuthbert legend played well with the late Victorian agenda to portray Alfred's temporary defeat as a period of self-improvement and moral growth. And in particular it appealed to explicitly religious writers – keen to make a native parable of the Saxon king's life.

From its opening line, in which the invading Danes are described as locusts which 'covered the face of the earth, so that the land was darkened', Eliza

Pollard's 1896 novel *A Hero King* is replete with Christian allusion. Unsurprisingly, then, when Pollard's Cuthbert appears to Alfred (divested of his disguise) he explicitly informs the king that his moral virtue has been tested: 'God sent me to thee, so that I might try thy faith, and lo! Thou hast not been found wanting; and now thy afflictions are well nigh ended'.[31] The archaism of Cuthbert's language intensifies the sense of biblical parallel. John Stuart Blackie also seems to have had gospel analogies in mind when he confusedly described Alfred's meeting with Cuthbert in an 1890 poem, relating not that the king gave alms to the disguised saint but that, conversely, Cuthbert, 'Came and filled with bread his basket,/ Filled his scanted cup with wine'.[32] More than any other period in his life, Alfred's three months in hiding attracted religious similes in the nineteenth century as part of the moral rewriting of the episode. In Pollard's novel, Alfred goes 'into the wilderness like the Christ', while in Anne Manning's 1861 novel *The Chronicle of Ethelfled*, St Neot appears to Alfred on Athelney, urging the king, 'Up, why sleepest thou? Behold, the set time is come'– echoing the words of Christ to his disciples on the Mount of Olives.[33]

Cuthbert's trial of Alfred's virtue could also accommodate secular reworkings in the nineteenth century, however. The generosity of the impoverished king to the disguised saint proved a popular subject for Victorian visual artists. Tableaux were painted in 1841 by Alexander Chisholm; in 1842 by William Simpson; and in 1850 by William Cave.[34] None of these artists chose to identify the beggar as an undercover Cuthbert, but rather depicted the scene merely as an exhibition of Alfred's charity to a poor beggar. The most interesting rationalist rewriting of the story, however, was undertaken by the novelist Charles Whistler. In Whistler's *King Alfred's Viking*, three Norwegian followers of Alfred come upon the king's thanes as they are unsuccessfully trying to catch fish in the frozen rivers around their hideout in Athelney. The Norwegians show the Saxons (who have never known such a severe winter) their native method of ice-fishing, and using this technique the thanes catch a huge basketful. Meanwhile, Alfred has a dream in which he is bidden by Cuthbert to 'look for a sign that out of hopelessness should come help and victory'. When his thegns arrive with their haul of fish, Whistler relates that 'Alfred rose up and stared, crossing himself. "Deo Gratias" he said under his breath, and then said aloud, "Lo, this is the sign" '.

At this point in the narrative, Whistler's interpretation of the Cuthbert story seems to teeter on the edge of parody. Alfred's naïve faith is not, however, either undermined or ridiculed, for not only are the Saxons awed by the sight of the laden fishermen, but one of the Norwegians also feels 'feared', for it seems to him that he is 'most truly under a power stronger than that of the old gods'.[35] *King Alfred's Viking* therefore successfully fuses medieval marvel and modern rationalism in retelling the Cuthbert tale. By rationalising the cause of the great catch of fish the novel takes away the mystery surrounding St Cuthbert, but it replaces this with a sense of wonder at Alfred's faith in God and with a celebration of what can be achieved by humankind's industrial advance and international cooperation. Indeed, in Whistler's version of the Cuthbert story, the wonderful catch of fish becomes a token of the fact that Alfred will later only manage to defeat the Danes because of the assistance of Norwegian allies.

Alfred the sickly youth

In the medieval texts, the visitations of Cuthbert and Neot to Alfred during his time in hiding were not the Saxon king's only brushes with divine intervention. According to *Asser's Life of King Alfred*:

> in the first flowering of his youth before he had married his wife, he realised that he was unable to abstain from carnal desire, fearing that he would incur God's disfavour if he did anything contrary to His will, he very often got up secretly in the early morning at cockscrow and visited churches and relics of saints in order to pray . . . that Almighty God through His mercy would more staunchly strengthen his resolve in the love of His service by means of some illness. . . . When he had done this frequently with great mental devotion, after some time he contracted the disease of piles through God's gift.[36]

Like his temporary defeat, this image of Alfred as a young man struggling against his passions became widely popular in the nineteenth century as an instance of the difficulty overcome in the lives of great men. The historian J.A. Froude praised it in glowing terms in his 1852 article for *Fraser's Magazine*, averring that 'there is no more beautiful instance in history of a young boy's unassisted efforts at self-mastery'.[37] And in his 1869 biography of the Saxon king, Thomas Hughes stressed the contemporary relevance of the story of Alfred's battle against 'the young man's foes', despite its 'language and clothing of a far-off time, with which we are little in sympathy'. 'Wherewith shall a young man cleanse his way?' Hughes asked his readers, and presenting Alfred's struggles as a parable for the contemporary youth, answered, 'he who has the word of the living God to rule himself by . . . may even in this strange disjointed time of ours carry his manhood pure and unsullied through the death-grips to which he must come with the lust of the flesh, the lust of the eye, and the pride of life'.[38] Asser does not specify the precise practice by which Alfred's 'carnal desires' manifested themselves. However, the language of both Froude and Hughes, which presents the vice very specifically as an affliction of youth, suggests that they might have been interpreting and implicitly presenting it as masturbation – a social 'problem' which, as Thomas Lacqueur has discussed, caused much concern in paediatric medicine and the governance of public schools for much of the Victorian period.[39]

   The nineteenth-century fascination with Alfred's youthful vices contrasts starkly with eighteenth-century authors' apparent embarrassment about the subject. Almost no eighteenth-century accounts of the king's life refer to them – despite the fact that Spelman's *The Life of Alfred the Great* had made the material readily accessible. Those that do allude to Alfred's problems do so in the most delicate terms. In Fuller's *The Son of Ethelwolf* the youthful Alfred is merely overcome with shame because his love for his fiancée occasionally distracts him from affairs of state.[40] If Victorian authors were not diffident about Alfred's lust, however, there was some reservation about the miraculous aspect of his subsequent affliction – perhaps because it was considered to savour too strongly of Catholicism. Froude, while an admirer of the story's moral framework, objected that 'with the miraculous part of it we have nothing to do', and concluded by interpreting the account in psychosomatic terms.[41] And Hughes also voiced scepticism about a divinely inflicted disorder, but concluded that for the purposes of retelling the story 'it seems better, however, to leave it as it stands. Any attempt to remove what we should call the miraculous element out of it would probably take away all life'.[42] Many nineteenth-century authors also retreated from specifying the precise nature of Alfred's complaint – in so doing revealing much about Victorian relationships with the body. Such evasiveness is unsurprising in a children's author like Alfred H. Engelbach, who relates in his 1878 story *The Danes in England* only that Alfred endured 'the almost intolerable agony of an incurable malady'.[43] However, texts for an adult audience, like Alfred Austin's play *England's Darling*, also describe only that Alfred suffered from 'some sickness'.[44] And even nineteenth-century translators of Asser avoided detailing the Saxon king's affliction. Joseph Stevenson's 1854 edition states elusively that Alfred suffered from 'a certain disease which prevailed from infancy'.[45]

In Eliza Pollard's *A Hero King*, Alfred's piles are replaced by a dermatological condition – the young prince awakes one morning to discover that his skin 'which had been fair and clean before, was blotched and marked'.[46] Rather than squeamishness, however, Christian traditions of making sin physically manifest may have prompted this adaptation, for the novel is suffused with religious allegory. In some ways, Pollard's novel is the most *risqué* nineteenth-century rewriting of the young Alfred's carnal desire. It is the only text to consider precisely what form his lust might have taken – and suggests that that was a near-incestuous flirtation with his stepmother, Judith. As such, it should probably be read as part of the *fin de siècle* fascination with all forms of moral transgression.[47] Ultimately, however, the text is one of the most morally conservative investigations of Alfred's lust – for it transfers all responsibility for the transgression from Alfred himself to the actively seductive Judith who, Alfred afterwards concludes, 'was mad for a short time'.[48]

In Pollard's novel, Alfred's rebuttal of Judith is set against depictions of his father and brother Æthelbald, both of whom are portrayed as having submitted to their lust for her. Indeed, the neatness of this moral contrast probably played no small part in determining Pollard's decision to involve Judith in the young Alfred's carnal desires. According to Asser, Æethelwulf married Judith on his return from Rome in 855. Just two years later, after his death:

Æthelbald his son, against God's prohibition and Christian dignity, and also
contrary to the practice of all pagans, took over his father's marriage-bed and
married Judith, daughter of Charles, king of the Franks, incurring great disgrace
from all who heard of it.[49]

Both marriages to Judith met with censure during the late nineteenth century.
In part, this perhaps simply reflects the currents of anti-French feeling that
existed in popular British culture at the time – certainly, the Anglo-Saxonist
J.A. Giles postulated that Æthelwulf's union with Judith must have met with
resentment in ninth-century Wessex, because in marrying a French woman
he had 'lightly esteemed all the women of England'.[50] The nineteenth-
century reception of the marriages also reveals, however, something of
contemporary attitudes to marriage. Æthelwulf's union was principally
lamented on the grounds of disparity in age. Thus Gordon Stables's reflection upon the marriage – 'to his shame be it spoken, for sixty years and fourteen are but poorly matched' – should be read alongside the attacks upon
child brides voiced by Dickens, Eliot, and others, in the late nineteenth
century.[51]

Æthelbald's union with Judith, on the other hand, illustrates the dominant
Victorian tendency to apportion any blame for sexual 'malpractice' to the
female party involved (a tendency most notoriously manifested in the
passing of the Contagious Diseases Act of 1864). The *Pictorial History of
England* published in 1837 by Charles Knight, for instance, does not in any
way criticise Æthelbald for marrying his father's widow, but adjudges that
'our Alfred' must have been 'we may be sure, much shocked in early years
at the doings of his young stepmother'.[52] It was late Victorian female authors
who were most severely critical of Judith, however – presumably for reasons
of both didacticism (since their readership was young and female) and personal repute. In Eva March Tappan's *In the Days of Alfred the Great*, Judith
is a capricious figure, described as 'a careless, trivial' child queen who stamps
her feet, cries when thwarted, and sets her sights upon Æthelbald long before
his 'brief and determined wooing'.[53] The most negative portrayal of the
young queen, however, is in Pollard's *A Hero King*, in which (after being
rejected by Alfred) Judith seduces an unsuspecting Æthelbald:

> 'Thou wouldest not even grant me the golden bauble of a crown', and she
> pouted her rosy lips and tossed back her head with its mass of golden hair . . .
> as she spoke, she drew herself up to her full height, and looked at him with eyes
> which seemed to say, 'Wilt thou let me go?'[54]

With her voluptuous lips and luxuriant locks, she is the very image of the
ambitious temptresses who adorn Pre-Raphaelite art and the Gothic novels
of the *fin de siècle*. And although Judith did not elicit sympathy from
authors, like those women she clearly was fascinating – both Tappan and
Pollard devoted pages to her misdoings. Such portrayals of the young queen,
therefore, need to be read in the context of the complex fascination with sex-
ually dominant women that developed in the late nineteenth century. The

fact that Pollard has Judith end her days repenting in a convent also suggests that the nineteenth-century interest in King Arthur's Guenevere may have played some role in increasing Judith's attraction for writers of the time.

Such curiosity about Judith's misdeeds contrasts with the suppressed treatment of her story in Fuller's *The Son of Ethelwolf*. Here, Æthelbald does not actually marry his stepmother but rather – in the typically displaced mode of Gothic fiction – imprisons her when she virtuously repulses his 'licentious passion', and then repentantly releases her after a bishop has represented to him 'in soul-piercing language, the heinousness of the crime he was about to commit'.[55] Eighteenth-century authors also tended to omit any reference to the second affliction by which, Asser tells us, Alfred was affected. According to his *Life of King Alfred*, Alfred could finally tolerate his piles no longer and, during a hunting trip to Cornwall, he went into a church and prayed:

> that the almighty God in his bountiful kindness might substitute for the pangs of the present and agonizing infirmity some less severe illness, on the understanding that the new illness would not be outwardly visible on his body, whereby he would be rendered useless and contemptible.[56]

Shortly after this, the king was cured of his piles, but instead was struck down with 'another more severe illness' during his wedding feast. This complaint then:

> plagued him remorselessly by day and night from his twentieth year until his forty-fifth; and if at any time through God's mercy that illness abated for the space of a day or a night or even an hour, his fear and horror of that accursed pain would never desert him, but rendered him virtually useless – as it seemed to him – for heavenly and worldly affairs.

According to Asser, Alfred's new illness was:

> a sudden severe pain that was quite unknown to all physicians. Certainly it was not known to any of those who were present on that occasion, nor to those up to the present day who have inquired how such an illness could arise and – worst of all, alas! – could continue so many years without remission.[57]

Ignoring this lengthy account of Alfred's mysterious illness, eighteenth-century authors typically depicted the king as a paragon of strength and rude health – presenting this as indicative of his moral goodness.[58] Some nineteenth-century authors, similarly, seem to have been unable to reconcile Alfred's many achievements with his ill-health and so to have down-played the latter. Tappan claimed that, far from being 'remorseless' and rendering him 'virtually useless', Alfred's disease attacked only 'sporadically', and that it 'seemed to have little effect upon his health and strength';[59] Besant insisted that 'it had no weakening effect';[60] while Charles Plummer objected, 'It seems to me quite inconceivable that Alfred could have accomplished what he did under the hourly pressure of incapacitating disease'.[61]

For most nineteenth-century Alfredianists, however, the Victorian veneration of difficulty meant that the idea of his physical weaknesses only augmented their admiration of Alfred. The 1837 *Pictorial History of England* published by Charles Knight enthused that 'our admiration of this wonderful man is increased by the well-established fact, that all these exertions were made in spite of the depressing influences of physical pain and constant bad health', while Charles Whistler claimed that Alfred 'made up for want of strength by quickness and mastery of his weapons'.[62] And the development of psychiatry in the nineteenth century meant that another way of reconciling Alfred's achievements with his disease was to postulate that it had been psychiatric in nature. The novelist Charles Whistler suggested that it was 'neuralgic, as it seems to have been violent pain without lasting effect', while the historians Pauli, Besant and Lorimer concurred that it must have been epilepsy.[63]

Alfred the lover and husband

Alfred's second, mysterious illness struck during his wedding feast. All Asser relates about King Alfred's marriage is that in 868 he 'was betrothed to and married a wife from Mercia, of noble family'.[64] Nothing more is divulged about the woman herself, the manner of their meeting, or the character of their marriage. This proved a lacuna which eighteenth-century Alfredianists were keen to fill, and many postulated that the wedding must have been preceded by a romantic courtship. The most ridiculously elaborate of such narratives was Fuller's, in which Alfred falls in love with 'Ethelswitha' at the age of five, but even as a young man he does not disclose his true feelings to her, wrongly believing that she is enamoured (Guenevere-like) with his right-hand man 'Oddune'.[65] For page after page, the reader must then endure Alfred's lamentably blind misinterpretations of Ethelswitha's maidenly shyness as indifference, before the king finally manages to marry his true love after his conquest of Guthrum – and a good decade later than Asser dates the wedding.[66] Indeed, Fuller's novel so entirely rewrites Alfred's life as romantic comedy that the marriage displaces Alfred's triumph over the Danes as the true climax of the novel. Several other eighteenth-century texts also inject romance into Alfred's biography by blithely presenting the king as a wooing suitor when historically he was already married.[67] As the nineteenth century dawned, however, and marriage – as well as historical accuracy – became increasingly valorised, this emphasis shifted to an interest in considering the perfect marriage which might have been enjoyed by Alfred and his queen.

In Joseph Cottle's 1801 *Alfred: An Epic Poem* we seem to see the turning point between the dominant eighteenth-century tendency to depict Alfred as a wooing lover, and the burgeoning nineteenth-century desire to portray him as the ideal husband. The preface to Cottle's poem defends his decision to break with tradition and depict Alfred as happily married, declaring 'I believe by exhibiting the conjugal affection in its purity, I have had a more dignified passion to develop than could result from any display of the earlier and more romantic attachments'.[68] Indeed, although the poem lacks the excitement of courtship, it takes pains to portray marriage as not incompatible with romance. Despite being married with a child, Cottle's Alfred and 'Alswitha' are mutually besotted; Alfred addresses his wife as the 'Joy of my heart'; and, when he must temporarily separate from her, speaks of 'the bitter pang/ Of separating from that holiest friend –/ A dear-loved wife'.[69]

Many later Victorian writers – both historians and literary authors – similarly idealised Alfred as a devoted young husband.[70] Pauli stated in his 1857 history that the king 'remained attached through his whole life with true conjugal fidelity to his consort Ethelswitha'; while in Edmund Hill's 1901 play, Alfred ardently tells his wife, 'My life is full of joy while I have thee'.[71] In the early sources dealing with Alfred's life there is little to support such suppositions – only the fact that the Saxon king left land at Lambourn, Wantage and Edington to his wife. This was seized upon by the historian Warwick Draper, for one, as evidence of Alfred's 'loving honour' for his wife.[72] What the image of Alfred as dedicated husband indicates more, however, is the extent to which the value of faithful marriage was increasingly stressed in Victorian culture in response to growing awareness of the social problems of the fallen woman, illegitimacy and divorce.

In reality, Alfred's ninth-century marriage would probably have been an arranged, political union. One nineteenth-century Alfredian writer was unique in not only acknowledging but, moreover, developing this notion as part of her portrayal of the youthful Alfred. In Pollard's *A Hero King*, Alfred falls in love with a childhood friend Iris, but is unable to marry her because she is kidnapped by Danes. Instead, he has to reconcile himself to marrying 'Ealhswith' in order to secure a political alliance with the girl's father. Of this marriage we are told, 'they both felt they could pass their days in peace together like Christian man and wife'.[73] However, when Iris returns to Wessex after Alfred's marriage he is heart-broken, confessing that 'Ealswith had never held his soul'.[74] Pollard's rather cheerless presentation of Alfred's politically motivated marriage was probably not, however, motivated by any desire for historical accuracy. Rather, her tragically devoted Alfred should be viewed in terms of the popularity in Victorian literature of the 'Jacob figure' – the ever-constant but unfulfilled lover, named after the Old Testament's Jacob who worked for fourteen years to win his wife.[75] This male type proved popular in the nineteenth century 'partly because the suffering associated with frustrated love had the same value as did other forms of suffering which were viewed as a means to moral improvement'.[76] Pollard, then, seems to have chosen to represent Alfred as unhappily married as part of a design to portray the youthful prince's spiritual and moral progression from boyhood to manhood, and from regency to kingship.

She also seems to have had an interest in locating within Alfred's reign a sociological development in marriage customs. According to a tenth-century Latin version of the *Anglo-Saxon Chronicle* – known as the *Chronicle of Æthelweard* – Alfred sent his daughter Ælfthryth to marry Baldwin II, Count of Flanders.[77] This text formed part of Petrie's 1848 *Monumenta*

Historica Britannica and was also published in English translations in the mid-nineteenth century by both Joseph Stevenson and J.A. Giles. From such editions, the account of Ælfthyth's marriage then probably found its way into Pauli's *Life of Alfred the Great*. Pauli postulated that the Baldwin to whom Ælfthryth was married must have been the son of Judith, who in 862, after Æthelbald's death, married Baldwin of Flanders.[78] His theory was then reiterated and explored by Pollard, who imagined that Judith had returned to Wessex late in Alfred's life with her son to ask for the hand of one of Alfred's daughters. This supposed occasion was used by Pollard to make of Alfred a distinctly modern opponent of enforced marriage. When Judith proposes to the Saxon king that a union be arranged between her son and one of his daughters, the king responds:

> thy son shall dwell among us as long as it pleasures him, and if he finds a wife among my maidens to suit his fancy, and she be willing to go with him, it shall be even so. Now we will speak no more thereof. True love and marriage are threads in our earthly lives, not to be woven by men's hands, but by God's will; so shall it even be with the children He has given me.

As fortune has it, Baldwin is 'speedily enamoured with Elfleda'.[79] Since Pollard's Alfred has himself endured an arranged marriage, her novel effectively dramatises a progression from an age of arranged marriages to a new era (spearheaded by Alfred the Great) of unions based on love. Such interweaving of social history – the history of the people – with national and political history was a technique first popularised by Sir Walter Scott, and it subsequently became characteristic of much nineteenth-century historiography.[80] Of course, there is no indication that any significant changes in marriage customs occurred during the ninth century.[81] But there are ample data to indicate that this change took place during the early decades of the nineteenth century.[82] Pollard's imagined interchange between Judith and Alfred, as two very different models of parent, then, also allowed her to portray the Saxon king as the embodiment of contemporary ideals about liberal parenting.

Alfred the scholar

Part of the reason for Pollard to have selected Alfred as a historical spokesman for free marriage may well have lain in the king's reputation in the nineteenth century as one of the wisest and most learned figures in British history. We have already discussed the ways in which he was celebrated as an astute monarch – in the words of the popular historian Maria Graham, as 'the wisest king we ever had'. Alfred's wisdom and love of learning were also, however, acclaimed by Victorian authors as virtues which could be emulated by anyone. Eva March Tappan celebrated him simply as 'one wise, conscientious man'.[83]

In particular, King Alfred was enthusiastically drawn upon in the nineteenth century as a model scholar for the people, because, according to Asser, until adulthood he had lacked 'knowledge of the liberal arts', and it was not until he was a grown man that he had learned to read and translate Latin.[84] This image of the king as a man who had chosen to pursue learning and self-improvement was highly appealing to an age which venerated the myth of the 'self-made man'; viewed a literate, educated workforce as the key to economic prosperity and political stability; and consequently pioneered continuing education for manual workers – so Alfred became a hero of adult education.[85] As has already been noted, the National Home Reading Union chose to hold their 1901 annual meeting in Winchester and to link the event to the king's Millenary celebrations. Besant, as we have seen, also linked Alfred to adult learning when he dedicated his biography to 'the Continuation Classes' and 'those who spend their evenings over books from the free libraries'.[86] And after the 1849 anniversary of Alfred's birth in Wantage, a mechanics' institute was opened in memory of the Saxon king, as well as the 'Alfred Literary and Scientific Institute'.[87] Whether the students at those institutions empathised with Alfred's struggle for self-improvement remains unknown. However, one Wantage resident certainly did identify closely with Alfred as an adult learner: the Conservative MP Robert Lloyd-Lindsay – a student at a working-man's college and a keen advocate of continuing education – who commissioned, funded and posed for the statue of the Saxon king that was erected in Wantage in 1877.

Once Alfred had acquired his apparently hard-won learning he seems to have used his new abilities to rework and translate a number of Latin texts into the vernacular. Certainly, Anglo-Saxon versions of Pope Gregory's *Pastoral Care*, Boethius's *Consolation of Philosophy*, Augustine's *Soliloquies*, and the *Psalter* survive to the present day, which evince his authorship. These all became available in print (and translated into modern English) during the nineteenth century, and were also alluded to and excerpted in several seminal biographies of the king, so were known to many Alfredianists.[88] The fact that the translations were executed in prose inspired several nineteenth-century authors to hail Alfred as a literary role model – a writer who had eschewed the more élite genre of poetry for a form which had long been denigrated but was now enjoying greater prestige (due to the rise of the novel and the growth of nationalist antipathy to classicism). In 1852, Froude celebrated Alfred's 'invention' of prose as the bequeathing to his people of 'a national literature' – adding that poetry 'would serve but indifferently for the sole spiritual food' of the English nation. And in his 1899 volume *Alfred the Great*, Besant – a firm believer in the value of accessible and popular literature – averred that 'To Alfred we owe the foundations of our literature: the most noble that the world has ever seen . . . Alfred began the prose'.[89]

For both Besant and Froude, Alfred's literary endeavours also demanded particular admiration and emulation specifically because he had translated works, rather than authoring his own texts – a choice which was interpreted as a sign of selflessness and modesty. Froude praised Alfred for having determined 'not to write new books, but to translate good old books', while

Besant averred that the Saxon king's translation project was 'modern in its spirit', acclaiming the desire to undertake it as 'the most human, the wisest, and the most sympathetic' of Alfred's acts.[90] Similarly, writing for the Boston-based *National Magazine* in 1896, Arthur McIlroy described Alfred's translations as, 'the most enduring benefit which he conferred upon his people and upon all posterity'.[91] Such expressions of admiration should almost certainly be read in relation to the dramatic increase in the translation of texts from dead and foreign languages into modern English for consumption by the growing market of middle-class readers who characterised the Victorian age.[92]

The nineteenth century was also an era in which colonial rhetoric presented the translation of English texts into foreign languages as an act of great benevolence, and this impulse also perhaps contributed to the admiration for Alfred as a translator. Certainly, Jacob Abbott, in his undisguisedly pro-imperial life of Alfred published in Madras in 1898, called upon 'Educated Indians' to emulate the Saxon king's 'efforts to help his countrymen' by rendering English literature 'accessible to their countrymen in their own vernacular'.[93] It was not only as a role model for translators, authors and adult learners that Alfred's acquisition of Latin and his subsequent work of translation was celebrated in the nineteenth century, however. The authors of texts for children also drew upon that period in the king's life as a means of encouraging the study of Latin among their juvenile readers. Tappan, for instance, dramatically depicted the actual instance when Alfred first began to translate Latin in order, it seems, to imbue classical studies with a sense of drama and excitement. Her 1900 novel for girls, *In the Days of Alfred the Great*, relates:

> 'Why can't I translate this into Saxon and give it to my people?' asked the king eagerly; and before Asser could answer, Alfred was saying over the Latin to himself and putting it, word by word, into simple, everyday Saxon. . . . So it was that Alfred began to be an author.[94]

It was not to Alfred's late years as a scholar that nineteenth-century children's authors most often turned for exemplars, fables and meaningful incidents for the consumption of their young readers, however. Instead they resorted to the very earliest years of the Saxon king's life – to the childhood, unknown and inaccessible for most British kings of such an early period, yet uniquely described in this case in Asser's ever invaluable *Life of King Alfred*.

Alfred's childhood

Interest in the rearing and early years of famous figures is one of the marked features of Victorian culture. It was doubtless encouraged by the growth of children's literature as a distinct genre and market during the period, but it derived from the Romantic dictum that the 'child is father of the man': that is, that essential character is formed during the earliest years of life.[95] This belief is reflected in those nineteenth-century novels which begin by documenting a character's childhood and then trace the path of that figure through adult life – Charlotte Brontë's *Villette* and Dickens's *Great Expectations* being two of the most notable examples. And it is also manifested in the cult of King Alfred – in the attention which nineteenth-century Alfredianists allotted to the Saxon's early years and in particular to celebrating that period as a model childhood, which had consequently produced the perfect man.

Asser tells us that in his youth Alfred was 'always brought up in the royal court and nowhere else'.[96] For most nineteenth-century writers, however, the ideal start in life was one spent amid rural surroundings. In her 1843 text *The Mothers of England*, the polemicist Sarah Stickney Ellis avowed that 'If I were asked to point out the happiest situation on earth, I believe I should say – that in which children enjoy a free life in the country'.[97] Consequently, many nineteenth-century writers imagined that, far from being raised amidst a military and legislative nerve centre, Alfred's childhood had taken place in a pastoral idyll. Writing of the Saxon king's early years, Pauli, for one, asserted 'What were the first impressions which must have influenced the spirit of this child? Surely they were the invigorating pictures of surrounding nature, the verdant woods and fields'.[98] Such pastoral idealism was in part a reaction to the appalling overcrowding and pollution which blighted so many Victorian cities but it was also heir to the Romantic conviction that childhood amid the beauty of nature could impress a heightened sensitivity upon the soul.[99] Pauli's conception of Alfred's rural childhood was reiterated by George Manville Fenn, in whose 1902 novella *The King's Sons* Alfred grows up surrounded by flocks of sheep on lush hillsides, watched by 'shepherds in their long smock frocks with turn-down collars and pleatings and gatherings on breast and back' – an imagined scene less descriptive of Saxon sheep-farming than a lament for the English pastoral culture which had been lost only in the previous century. And it was also echoed by John Stuart Blackie whose short 1890 poem, 'Alfred', relates:

Mid the leafy wealth of Berkshire
Oak and beech in breezy play
Mid green England's gardened beauty,
Up he shot into the day.[100]

This account, with references to the oak and to the idea of the countryside as a garden, also seems to have been part of an attempt to yoke the figure of Alfred (and the concept of vigorous growth) to a sense of English national identity.

The notion of Alfred's pastoral childhood may have sprung in part from Asser's claim that the young Saxon prince was 'an enthusiastic huntsman'.[101] Both Blackie and Fenn developed this notion, depicting the young prince's prowess at hunting as training for his later eminence in battle – a defence of blood-sports that was frequently invoked during the nineteenth century.[102]

And in Tom Bevan's 1902 novel *A Lion of Wessex*, similarly, Alfred the child astonishes his father's warriors – and first signals his future prowess as a warrior – by single-handedly killing a boar.[103] Far more often, however, Alfred's childhood was imagined in the Victorian period not as a time when the young prince had developed martial skills, but rather when he had first gained the love of learning that would distinguish him as an adult. In Fenn's novella the Saxon prince – charmingly named 'Little Alfred' – is exemplary in many ways. Not only is he a fine huntsman, he is also a paragon of nineteenth-century youthful conduct, who respects his father, adores his mother and is polite to his teachers (in contrast to his rebellious and disrespectful elder brothers). Most importantly, however (and again unlike his brothers) he is a keen reader. This notion derives from Asser's description of how:

> One day . . . when his mother was showing him and his brothers a book of English poetry which she held in her hand, she said: 'I shall give this book to whichever one of you can learn it the fastest'. Spurred on by these words, or rather by divine inspiration, and attracted by the beauty of the initial letter in the book, Alfred spoke as follows in reply to his mother, forestalling his brothers (ahead in years, though not in ability), 'Will you really give this book to the one of us who can understand it the soonest?' Whereupon, smiling with pleasure she reassured him, saying: 'Yes, I will'. He immediately took the book from her hand, went to his teacher and learnt it. When it was learnt, he took it back to his mother and recited it.[104]

This narrative was the most widely recounted story of the king's childhood in the nineteenth century. Besides being included in Fenn's text, it was related in many poems, novels and popular histories, and was evidently loved and cherished by many readers. Freeman described it as 'such a beautiful tale'; the historian S. Harris considered it 'charming'; and at the Winchester Millenary the story was one of just a few scenes, chosen from Alfred's life, to be dramatised as a tableau.[105]

The choice of tableau scenes at the Millenary probably owed much to nineteenth-century artistic conventions: one of the tableaux presented – Alfred burning the cakes – was one of the most popular subjects of Victorian history painting. The young Alfred's love of literature was also a popular subject for artists. Solomon Alexander Hart's painting *Alfred the Great when a youth, encouraged by the Queen, listening to the heroic lay of a minstrel* was exhibited at the British Institution in 1836; Alfred Stevens's *King Alfred and his Mother* was completed in 1848; Thomas Thornycroft's *Alfred the Great encouraged in the pursuit of learning by his mother'* was exhibited at the Royal Academy in 1850, and the subject was also illustrated in numerous novels and popular histories of the period – proving to be particularly favoured by the female authors of 'improving' juvenile texts, such as Maria Calcott, who chose an image of King Alfred learning from his mother to illustrate her 1834 volume, *Little Arthur's History of England* (see Figure 16).[106] The choice suggests not only a desire to encourage reading in her

16 Alfred Stevens, *King Alfred and his Mother* (first exhibited in the
Tate Gallery in 1848)

young audience but, more importantly, an attempt to legitimate historically
her own role as female author – the bestower of wisdom to the nation's
youth. More broadly, it also indicates an interest in celebrating educated
mothers and their beneficial influence upon future generations – a theme that
was to be reiterated by many other writers in favour of female education
later in the century, most famously by John Ruskin in his 1865 *Sesame and
Lilies*.[107]

Veneration of the teaching mother-figure also emerges from nineteenth-
century paintings of the scene of Alfred learning to read, which are without
exception iconographic and deeply sentimental. In the most famous version
today – Alfred Stevens's 1848 *King Alfred and his Mother* – a blond, cheru-
bic Alfred leans eagerly over an open book on his mother's lap, his eyes

locked devotedly upon her admiring gaze, accentuating her role in transmit-
ting learning to him. Clergymen hover in the background, presaging the
revival of monastic learning that this young prodigy's manhood will bring to
pass. The painting was well-known in the nineteenth century, and must have
exerted a significant influence on general conceptions of Alfred the child, as
it was reproduced as an engraving in several popular histories.[108]

Certainly Stevens's painting – or an illustration very like it – seems to have
imparted the strikingly pictorial quality to the depiction of Alfred's childhood in Francis Turner Palgrave's 1891 poem 'Alfred the Great', which
describes:

> The fair-haired boy is at his mother's knee,
> A many-coloured page before them spread,
> . . . But through her eyes alone the child can see,
> From her sweet lips partake the words of song,
> And looks as one who feels a hidden wrong,
> Or gazes on some feat of gramarye.
> 'When thou canst use it, thine the book!' she cried:
> He blush'd, and clasp'd it to his breast with pride.[109]

Again, the emphasis is upon the mother as a channel for the child's learning,
revealing that it was not only the aesthetic appeal of the scene of Alfred
learning to read which rendered it so widely popular in the nineteenth
century. Rather, the story's charm owed much to the nineteenth century's
deep reverence for family life, and its idolisation of the influential and
devoted mother.

Palgrave's poem also indicates the high value placed upon literacy in the
late nineteenth century. During the Victorian period, the development of
more widespread literacy was identified as a high social priority, as the
growing technological complexity of industry made it increasingly apparent
that if Britain were to compete commercially against France, Germany and
America in international markets, then more literate workers would be
required. However, while the importance of literacy was increasingly
acknowledged, the concurrent growth of Britain's population and its cen-
tralisation around industrial centres meant that (until the 1870 Education
Act established board schools throughout the country) places at voluntary
church schools were often few and far between.[110] For late Victorian writers
like Palgrave, then, education was a valuable opportunity and one not to be
unappreciated – so Asser's depiction of the eager young Alfred provided a
useful model of the ideal student.[111]

There was, however, one major problem with Asser's account of Alfred
learning to read.[112] The *Life of King Alfred* states that 'by the shameful
neglect of his parents and tutors he remained ignorant of letters until his
twelfth year, or even longer', yet, confoundingly, it also seems to indicate that
Alfred's mother (who allegedly taught Alfred to read) was dead by the time
that he was seven.[113] In the eighteenth century, the dilemma was easily solved

by suggesting that the 'mother' who gave Alfred the book cannot have been his natural mother, but Æthelwulf's second wife, Judith.[114] This theory found expression not only in literary texts, but also formed the subject of a well-received 1799 painting by Richard Westall – *Queen Judith reciting to Alfred the Great, when a child, the songs of the bards, describing the heroic deeds of his ancestors*. It was also accepted by the nineteenth-century Anglo-Saxonists J.A. Giles and Joseph Stevenson, and by Sarah Stickney Ellis, the author of several Victorian conduct manuals for women. Judith forms the subject of the second chapter of Ellis's 1843 volume, *The Mothers of Great Men*. In her preface to this chapter, Ellis discusses the question of nature versus nurture in the formation of a child's character. She concludes that 'training and cultivation' are the strongest influence upon a child; a fact witnessed by the influence of great stepmothers. Judith is then presented as an example of such a stepmother. Ellis describes her as 'an amiable and interesting lady'; as 'a beautiful princess'; and as 'equally earnest but more educated' than her young stepson Alfred. The queen's positive influence upon Alfred is repeatedly stressed. Ellis argues that 'as the after-life of King Alfred affords such unquestionable evidence of good influence having been derived from some source or other, it is but fair to allow the young queen her full share in the education both of head and heart'.[115]

It seems that Ellis might have been ignorant of Judith's later incestuous marriage to Æthelbald when she selected her as a model stepmother, however, for those nineteenth-century writers who were aware of that part of the queen's story seem to have unanimously denounced the idea of her involvement in Alfred's education. Pauli dismissed the theory, ostensibly on the pragmatic grounds that Judith 'cannot, as some have maintained, have taught Saxon poetry to the boy . . . for she herself was scarcely thirteen years of age at the time of her marriage.[116]

One suspects, however, that his objection to Judith's role in Alfred's education in fact owed much to her later incestuous marriage and to contemporary images of her as an unchaste and ambitious woman. And this was certainly the case with the historian Charles Plummer, who indignantly protested that:

> The mother mentioned is unquestionably Alfred's own mother Osburh. That he should ever have spoken of Judith, who was only some four years older than himself, with all her doubtful after-history, as his mother, is . . . absolutely inconceivable.[117]

It was not only historians who objected to the Judith version of the story. Of the various nineteenth-century paintings of the book incident, only one – W. Philip Salter's 1844 *Queen Judith and the children of Ethelwulph* – followed Westall in depicting Judith as the woman who taught Alfred to read. Moreover, when Salter entered the illustration into a competition to decorate the Palace of Westminster, instead of receiving glowing praise such as Westall's painting had generated, his entry was denounced. The image was deemed 'faulty in treatment' by the judges – a reception indicative of the increasing status of faithful marriage and 'family values' in nineteenth-century Britain.[118]

Although nineteenth-century writers rejected the Judith hypothesis, many were nonetheless reluctant to dismiss outright the popular tale of Alfred winning the book. Other methods of reconciling Asser's contradictions therefore had to be constructed. Plummer argued that 'I believe that "illiteratus permansit" means nothing more than that he was ignorant of Latin', while Pauli drew upon Roger of Wendover's thirteenth-century *Flowers of History*, which states that Alfred recited 'from memory' to his mother – arguing that this was how he had earned the book of poetry, and that he had not learned to read until a much later date. This thesis was accepted and reiterated by many subsequent writers.[119]

While most popular Victorian Alfredianists attempted to find ways around the discrepancies in Asser's account of Alfred winning the book, towards the turn of the twentieth century some historians of the Saxon king began to discredit the story outright. Even in their more scholarly texts, however, an incongruous degree of sentimental attachment to the narrative can still be discerned. In his *Old English History* for children, Edward Freeman described it as 'such a beautiful tale that I am really sorry to have to say that it cannot possibly be true', while Besant (although he described the tale as 'impossible'), equivocated by suggesting that nevertheless 'some such story is possible, that is to say, the strong desire to possess a beautiful book . . . may very well have fired a child's imagination and first inspired him with the love of reading'.[120] Such clear attachment to the narrative – and such anxiety to placate the likely disappointment of readers – provides some indication of the degree of contemporary resonance which the tale carried in the nineteenth century, as does the choice of the scene for one of the tableaux performed at the Winchester Millenary (see Figure 3).

Alfred in Rome

Besides the story of Alfred learning to read, nineteenth-century Alfredian texts tend to describe one other major incident that took place during the childhood of the Saxon king – his journey to Rome. This episode is described in both *Asser's Life of King Alfred* and (more briefly) the *Anglo-Saxon Chronicle*. According to Asser, in 853:

> King Æthelwulf sent his son Alfred to Rome in state, accompanied by a great number of both nobles and commoners. At this time the lord Pope Leo was ruling the apostolic see; he anointed the child Alfred as king, ordaining him properly, received him as an adoptive son and confirmed him.

Asser's *Life* also states that Alfred went to Rome again in 855, this time with his father, and that he 'remained for a whole year'.[121] Few nineteenth-century writers refer in any detail to this second stay in Rome – it was superfluous in terms of narrative progression and they imagined that a return visit could have exercised little formative influence upon the young prince. On the other hand, those writers who described Alfred's original trip to Rome imagined that seeing the holy city for the first time must have had a considerable impact upon him. Pauli speculated that the young Saxon 'must have been struck with astonishment at the sight of the magnificent capital'.[122] Other writers, more specifically, suggested that the formation of Alfred's character must have been deeply influenced by the sight of Rome – a view which doubtless derived in part from Romanticism's regard for the benefits of travel.[123] For the religious historian 'J.F.R.' (whose biography of Alfred, as discussed earlier, was published alongside that of the martyr Thomas More) the visit was envisaged as a beneficial experience. His 1845 history of Alfred asserts 'Much activity of mind and novelty of idea must have resulted from the varying impressions . . . if any place on earth could kindle the intellectual fire in the human mind, it must have been, in that period, Rome'.[124]

Anti-Catholicism was still vigorous in nineteenth-century Britain, however – despite the passing of the Catholic Emancipation Act in 1829 – and by far the majority of Victorian writers to visit Rome described it not as a place of wonder but as a disappointing, depressing or even grotesque city.[125] Such attitudes influenced conceptions of Alfred's visit to Rome. R. Kelsey claimed in his 1852 epic poem *Alfred of Wessex* that the Saxon king's first experience of Rome filled him not with inspiration, but with disdain:

All that golden wealth
Profusely given, rapaciously received,
. . . With the stark penury, the utter want,
The outcast wretchedness, in contrast strong
He places: and at the sordid luxury,
The unfeeling avarice, the recklessness
Of all this useless, cruel magnificence,
Fain could have wept.[126]

On the other hand, Besant (known as a man with 'no love of priests and religious dogma') simply refuted the notion that Rome had exercised any lasting impact upon the young Alfred, arguing that 'An attempt has been made to connect Alfred's love of literature and the arts together with his religious inclination, with the court of the pope, then Leo IV. This seems to me sheer nonsense'.[127] Similarly, in *'Twixt Daydawn and Light*, Gordon Stables related that when Alfred returned to Wessex from Rome:

the stories that he had to tell his humble friend Roderic were not about the splendid buildings he had seen, nor the marvellous palace where dwelt the good pope . . . never a word said he about the grandeur and the majesty of imperial Rome. He was too real a boy for that.

According to Stables, Alfred is more impressed by the Alps than by Rome, and more interested in hearing the vigorous yarns of old sailors on the docks than in listening to 'sages and philosophers'.[128]

Stables's Alfred was not alone in the nineteenth century in showing more enthusiasm for his journey to Rome than for his actual stay in the holy city. For the novelist Eva March Tappan, Alfred's trip was a momentous event in the king's early life – not because of its ultimate destination but more for the sheer length and difficulty of the voyage. Her Alfred survives near-shipwreck, evades Danish naval attack, crosses mountain ranges, treks through dense forests and wades across wide rivers on his way to Rome.[129] The journey itself is presented as a rite-of-passage during which Alfred demonstrates his mental endurance, moral fortitude and physical bravery: Rome is simply the necessary end-point of the young prince's travels. There are obvious parallels between Tappan's portrayal of Alfred's visit to Rome and Blackmore's early eighteenth-century depiction of the same journey, discussed in Chapter Two. In Blackmore's epic, Alfred's stay in Rome is just a small part of a much larger expedition (strongly reminiscent of the Grand Tours undertaken by young noblemen during the seventeenth and eighteenth centuries), during which he visits countless temptress-strewn shores, fights in battles, kills a savage panther, and survives both storms at sea and volcanic eruptions.

It is just possible that Blackmore's poem may partly have influenced the 1900 novel. However, his reasons for privileging Alfred's voyage at the expense of his stay in Rome were very different from Tappan's. Blackmore's version of the story is conspicuously neo-classical, and the author's main motivation for embellishing Asser's account of the young Alfred's travels seems to have been in order to emulate two neo-classical tales of youthful journeys which were published shortly before 1723 and thus to bestow upon England's native history a little of what Blackmore – and so many other eighteenth-century scholars – perceived as the high prestige of Graeco-Roman culture.[130]

Tappan's prime concern, on the other hand, was not the venerable status of ancient literature, but rather the question of Alfred's religion. Her relative disinterest in King Alfred's time in Rome is by no means a sign that she was irreligious – on the contrary, Tappan was an overtly Christian writer keen to present Alfred as a king ordained by God.[131] However, she was not a Catholic.[132] Asser's evidence that Alfred was God's chosen ruler – the fact that Pope Leo peremptorily anointed him – was therefore unacceptable to her. Consequently, in Tappan's account of Alfred's voyage to Rome, the king narrowly escapes death on numerous occasions, thanks to the direct intercession of God.[133] The spiritual element of the story is thus transferred from the Vatican to the high seas, in what is effectively a Protestant rewriting of Asser's account of Alfred's journey to Rome.

Tappan was not the only nineteenth-century writer to have found the notion that Pope Leo anointed Alfred disagreeable. A number of nineteenth-century historians argued that it was quite inconceivable that Alfred could have gone to Rome to be anointed as king. In many cases, such objections derived largely from anti-Catholic sentiment. In his 1852 essay on Alfred, for instance, the notorious anti-monastic polemical historian J.A. Froude argued that the whole story of the anointing 'savours strongly' of the work of late medieval monastic writers.[134] He went on to declare that:

> It is not easy to be too disrespectful to the historical ability of the monastic writers; never did any set of men betake themselves to the recording human affairs who had less power of distinguishing between truth and falsehood, or who were less scrupulous in inventing a useful or an edifying fact, when they did not find one ready to their hand.[135]

Other nineteenth-century writers rejected the anointing story on more scholarly grounds, however – citing the fact that Alfred during his youth had had three brothers before him in succession to the throne.[136] This was a problem that had first been identified during the seventeenth century, when it was negotiated by Royalist historians like Robert Powell and Sir John Spelman by claims that Alfred had been anointed as king in Rome (despite his brothers) because his father was 'warned thereto in a dreame by the voice of an Angell'.[137] By the eighteenth century, however, such recourse to divine intervention was already being mocked by historians like Rapin – so that those nineteenth-century writers who wished to retain the incident in biographies of Alfred's life needed alternative explanations.[138] They turned from mysticism to issues more at the heart of their own culture and society, such as politics and education. For the novelist Agnes Stewart, Alfred was sent to Rome as part of a political scheme devised by his father, who harboured 'a secret wish' that he might one day succeed him.[139] On the other hand, the Anglo-Saxon scholar and professor John Earle speculated that:

> The Saxon Chronicle says that Alfred was sent to Rome in the year 853, at which time he was a little boy. This statement naturally suggests that he was sent to reside at the English College in Rome for the benefit of his education. But this is blurred in Asser by the further statement that he went to Rome a second time in the very next year . . . The second journey to Rome is not in the Chronicle, and it looks rather like an artifice, designed to parry the natural inference that the journey to Rome was for a prolonged and educational residence.[140]

Earle's notion may have derived from the assertion in Roger of Wendover's thirteenth-century *Flowers of History* that Alfred went to Rome in order that 'he might be instructed in morals and religion by Pope Leo'.[141] It would, however, be unusual for him to privilege this late source above Asser. It seems most likely, therefore, that the Anglo-Saxonist was keen to argue that Alfred attended a school in Rome not on the basis of late medieval evidence, but rather because, as an Anglican cleric, an educational visit to the Vatican was simply more acceptable for the English Alfred than a pilgrimage to pay homage to a Roman Catholic figurehead.[142]

Alfred's appearance

Alfred's anointing formed the subject of a 1794 painting by Richard Westall. In this, as in Westall's interpretation of Alfred learning to read, the future king appears as a dutifully kneeling youth with luxuriantly curling dark locks and a strikingly classical profile. The anointing scene was not attempted by any artist in the nineteenth century – presumably owing to the same inherent problems with the subject matter that discouraged Alfredian writers from celebrating the incident. The scene of Alfred learning to read, however, proved a popular tableau for the historical painter. In nineteenth-century versions, such as Alfred Stevens's 1848 painting 'King Alfred and his Mother', Alfred typically retains his curls, but turns blond – so that he becomes strikingly reminiscent of the cherubim that feature in much Victorian artwork, and an embodiment of nineteenth-century ideals of child-ish beauty. This is also true of the descriptions of Alfred the child in literary works from the period. In Agnes Stewart's 1840 children's book, he has 'golden hair in loose curls over his shoulders and dark blue eyes', while in G. Manville Fenn's 1901 novel *The King's Sons* he is a chubby child with 'fair curly locks'.[143]

The nineteenth-century idea that Alfred was a child of singular beauty probably derived partly from Asser's ninth-century claim that 'As he passed through infancy and boyhood he was seen to be more comely in appearance than his other brothers'.[144] The notion should also, however, be related to the popular nineteenth-century conviction that an intimate relationship existed between character and physical appearance. This belief was exemplified in the literary caricatures of Dickens, and was elaborated into a complex system in Lavater's theory of physiognomy – translated into English in 1789 and published a further sixteen times during the nineteenth century.[145] Lavater's chief claim in *Essays on Physiognomy* was that there is a 'visible, demonstrable, harmony and coincidence' between physical appearance and one's morality and intellect.[146] Thus the large blue eyes, round face and blonde ringlets of the young Alfred signified for Victorian audiences the future king's goodness, earnestness and innocence.

Lavater was just one contributory factor to the general fascination with Alfred's appearance that existed in the nineteenth century. The opening of public art galleries in the mid-Victorian period was also influential – result-ing in a new market for paintings of 'national' subjects, particularly native history, and thus the need for more careful consideration and debate about the appearance of historical monarchs. And Victorian racialist theories also played a role towards the end of the century – for if each race had a distinct character (and if physical traits were inextricably linked to character), then it must surely be possible to also identify racial types on the basis of appear-ance. Such logic was suggested in 1902, for instance, by the historian George Eayrs who argued in his history of Alfred that 'modern photography offers us the typical face of doctor, artist or mechanic. It is obtained by photographing one upon another the features of, say, twelve persons of the same occupation. . . . in the composite Englishman, it is the Saxon face . . . that looks at us'.[147] For those who shared Eayrs's outlook, Alfred – as a great Saxon – must represent the epitome of the English physique. Thus Besant claimed that 'I like to think that the face of the Anglo-Saxon at his best and noblest is the face of Alfred'.[148] And, in discussing the head of the Saxon king upon Winchester's 1901 commemorative Alfred medal, its designer R.C. Jackson declared in *The Westminster Review* that:

> Without going into physiognomic details, this portrait is one which clearly demonstrates the noble race from which we Britons spring. The head as represented in this medal, taken from a coin of Alfred . . . is a fairly good representative formation of the cranium of the average Englishman. Most certainly it is otherwise than the type everywhere to be seen in Norfolk and Suffolk. This head of Alfred the Great, of Alfred the 'Truth Teller', is the shape of that of our Chaucer, of our Gower, of our Lord Bacon, of our Shakespeare, of our Browning, and of our Tennyson.[149]

Jackson's association of King Alfred with another Alfred – the poet Tennyson – is particularly interesting for in H. Warren's 1846 painting of *Alfred in the Swineherd's Cottage*, the Saxon king bears a striking resemblance to the future poet laureate (see Figure 12). Although the image slightly pre-empts the dominant association of Tennyson with English national identity, it is possible that the likeness is not accidental. On the other hand, however, the resemblance may simply lie in the coincidence of long hair and a beard.

Nineteenth-century Alfredianists were almost unanimous in conceiving that King Alfred, even as a young man, had been 'bearded and long-haired'.[150] Although there was some debate as to whether the Winchester Alfred statue ought to be bearded or not, in only two nineteenth-century works is the Saxon king clean-shaven: in George Watts's strikingly neo-classical painting of 'Alfred inciting the Saxons to resist the Danes', in which the king is not only beardless but also dressed in Roman sandals and a tunic; and in Henty's novel for boys, in which much effort is taken to ensure that juvenile readers should identify themselves with the young Alfred (for Watts' painting, see Figure 17).[151] This general partiality for a hirsute king perhaps owed something to a desire to make of Alfred a native saint. In Warren's painting of the Saxon king burning the cakes, the figure with its far-away gaze not only has a Tennysonian look about it, but also bears a strong resemblance to the images of Christ in illustrated Bibles and religious story-books from the Victorian period.

The preference also, however, needs to be understood in the context of the wider Victorian tradition that distinguished Saxons from Normans by depicting the former as long-haired and bearded and the latter as cropped and shaven. The Saxon's beard and flowing tresses were considered symbolic of his liberty and manliness, and of the more 'natural' condition of Saxon

17 George Watts, *King Alfred Inspiring the Saxons to Resist the Danes* (winner of
the 1847 oil-painting competition for the decoration of the new Houses of
Parliament)

society – George Eayrs described the Saxon as 'the free-necked man whose
long hair floated over a neck that had never been bent to a lord'.[152] In
Victorian depictions of Alfred as long-haired and bearded, therefore, there
lies a subtext associating the king with democratic and liberal values and
with a robust masculinity. Indeed, the association between Saxons, beards
and noble manhood became so dominant by the mid-nineteenth century that
the growth of public enthusiasm for Alfred and Anglo-Saxon England had
the side-effect of making beards fashionable for all those who wished to
appear 'true Englishmen'.[153]

The nineteenth-century inclination to make Alfred bearded did have
notable historical precedents. The earliest image of the Saxon king, as discussed above, is the drawing in Matthew Paris's thirteenth-century *Major
Chronicle*, in which he sports a beard, and in the next-oldest surviving image
of Alfred – commissioned by the Master of University College in 1661–62 –
he is also bearded. This latter representation (as it was reworked by George
Vertue for Rapin's *The History of England*) dominated painting of the king
throughout the nineteenth century. Its serious gaze, beard, and dark, flowing
locks also became the dominant features of Alfred's appearance in the small
amount of Alfredian art produced during the twentieth century (however,
notably, in the illustrations to the nineteen-fifties Ladybird history of the king,
Alfred would become blond). It is to this modest body of twentieth-century
Alfrediana that the next chapter will now turn. And, inevitably, to the reasons
why the 1901 Millenary proved to be the apex of Alfredianism: four glorious
days of self-congratulatory celebration – succeeded by a century of declining
fame and dwindling popularity.

Notes

1 *The Times* (21 Sep. 1901), p. 10.
2 Markham, 'Alfred as a Geographer', p. 167; Besant, 'Introduction', p. 18; Lord Roseberry, quoted in Markham, 'Alfred as a Geographer', p. 151.
3 *The Times* (22 Aug. 1901), p. 5.
4 Hughes, *Alfred the Great*, p. 333.
5 See Mitchell, *Picturing the Past*, p. 60.
6 Carlyle, quoted in Eayrs, *Alfred to Victoria*, p. 4.
7 Melman, 'Claiming the Nation's Past', p. 588.
8 Freeman, *History of the Norman Conquest*, pp. 51, 54.
9 Besant, *The Story of King Alfred*, p. 196.
10 On adaptations of the formula, see Yorke, *The King Alfred Millenary*, p. 18.
11 Bowker, *The King Alfred Millenary*, p. 4.
12 Besant, 'Introduction', p. 34.
13 Bowker, *The King Alfred Millenary*, p. 109.
14 Magnus, *First Makers of England*, p. vii.
15 Eayrs, *Alfred to Victoria*, p. 19.
16 *The Times* (21 Sep. 1901), p. 10; Bowker, *The King Alfred Millenary*, p. 110.
17 Bowker, *The King Alfred Millenary*, pp. 118, 20.
18 Bowker, *The King Alfred Millenary*, p. 120.
19 Quoted in Bowker, *The King Alfred Millenary*, p. 110.
20 *The Times* (29 Jan. 1901), p. 12.
21 Smiles, *Self-Help*, pp. 207, 209.
22 Unpublished paper by Dr Paul Hardwick.
23 Bowker, *The King Alfred Millenary*, p. 22.
24 Alfred's Boethius was published in modern English by J.S. Cardale in 1829, and by Tupper in 1852.
25 Tupper, 'King Alfred's Poems', p. 173. See also p. 175.
26 Whistler, *King Alfred's Viking*, p. 190.
27 Stables, *'Twixt Daydawn and Light*, pp. 299–300, 331.
28 Stables, *'Twixt Daydawn and Light*, p. 311.
29 *History of Saint Cuthbert*, p. 493.
30 Higden, *The Polychronicon*, p. 373 [spelling and syntax modernised].
31 Pollard, *A Hero King*, pp. 11, 253.
32 Blackie, 'Alfred', p. 95. See also Canning, *Alfred the Great in Athelnay*, p. 143.
33 Pollard, *A Hero King*, p. 102; Manning, *The Chronicle of Ethelfled*, p. 199; Luke 22: 46; Mark 14: 37, 41.
34 See Keynes, 'The Cult of King Alfred the Great', p. 339.
35 Whistler, *King Alfred's Viking*, pp. 187, 192–193.
36 *Asser's Life of King Alfred*, p. 89.
37 Froude, 'King Alfred', p. 80.
38 Hughes, *Alfred the Great*, pp. 46–47.
39 Lacqueur, *Solitary Sex*, p. 258.
40 Fuller, *The Son of Ethelwolf*, p. 172.
41 Froude, 'King Alfred', p. 80.
42 Hughes, *Alfred the Great*, p. 46.
43 Engelbach, *The Danes in England*, p. 11.
44 Austin, *England's Darling*, p. 55.

45 Stevenson, *The Church Historians of England*, II: I, p. 463.
46 Pollard, *A Hero King*, p. 100.
47 See Walder, *The Nineteenth-Century Novel*, pp. 190–192.
48 Pollard, *A Hero King*, p. 177.
49 *Asser's Life of King Alfred*, p. 73.
50 Giles, *The Life and Times of Alfred the Great*, p. 185.
51 Stables, *'Twixt Daydawn and Light*, p. 276. See also Henty, *The Dragon and the Raven*, p. 22.
52 *The Pictorial History of England*, p. 43.
53 Tappan, *In the Days of Alfred the Great*, pp. 92, 103, 120.
54 Pollard, *A Hero King*, pp. 97–98.
55 Fuller, *The Son of Ethelwolf*, p. 184.
56 *Asser's Life of King Alfred*, p. 89.
57 *Asser's Life of King Alfred*, pp. 89, 90.
58 For instance in Blackmore, *Alfred: An Epick Poem*, p. 147; Bicknell, *The Patriot King*, p. 12; Fuller, *The Son of Ethelwolf*, p. 30.
59 Tappan, *In the Days of Alfred the Great*, p. 217.
60 Besant, *The Story of King Alfred*, p. 58.
61 Plummer, *The Life and Times of Alfred the Great*, p. 28.
62 Whistler, *King Alfred's Viking*, p. 92; *The Pictorial History of England*, p. 167.
63 Whistler, *King Alfred's Viking*, p. 120; Pauli, *The Life of Alfred the Great*, p. 73; Lorimer, 'King Alfred', p. 153; Besant, *The Story of King Alfred*, p. 78.
64 *Asser's Life of King Alfred*, p. 77.
65 Fuller, *The Son of Ethelwolf*, pp. 181, 192.
66 Fuller, *The Son of Ethelwolf*, pp. 192–201.
67 See, for instance, Home, *Alfred*, p. 12; Rhodes, *Alfred*, p. 35.
68 Cottle, *Alfred: An Epic Poem*, p. iii.
69 Cottle, *Alfred: An Epic Poem*, pp. 23, 84.
70 See, for instance, Tupper, *Alfred: A Patriotic Play*, p. 17; Hill, *Alfred the Great*, p. 27; Pauli, *The Life of Alfred the Great*, p. 221.
71 Pauli, *The Life of Alfred the Great*, p. 221; Hill, *Alfred the Great*, p. 27.
72 Draper, *Alfred the Great*, p. 19.
73 Pollard, *A Hero King*, pp. 152, 173.
74 Pollard, *A Hero King*, p. 253.
75 Genesis, 29: 18–30.
76 Reed, *Victorian Conventions*, p. 79.
77 *The Chronicle of Æthelweard*, p. 408.
78 Pauli, *The Life of Alfred the Great*, p. 223. Judith's marriage to Baldwin is first recorded in the ninth-century *Annals of St Bertin*, pp. 97, 110.
79 Pollard, *A Hero King*, pp. 403–404.
80 See Mitchell, *Picturing the Past*, p. 113.
81 See Macfarlane, *Marriage and Love in England*, pp. 130–133.
82 See Calder, *Women and Marriage in Victorian Fiction*, pp. 27–44, 68–82.
83 Henty, *The Dragon and the Raven*, p. 5; Graham, *Little Arthur's History of England*, p. 54; Tappan, *In the Days of Alfred the Great*, p. 278.
84 *Asser's Life of King Alfred*, pp. 92, 99.
85 See Fieldhouse, *A History of Adult Education*, pp. 10–45.
86 Besant, *The Story of King Alfred*, p. 10.
87 Hudson, *Martin Tupper*, pp. 96, 100.

88 All of Alfred's writings were translated into English and published in Giles, *The Whole Works of Alfred the Great* (1852). The preface to Alfred's translation of Gregory's *Pastoral Care* was published in Old English as a primer for students in 1597; was translated into Latin and English and published in Parker's 1574 edition of Asser's *Life*, sig. Folio I recto–sig. Folio iiii verso [41–48]; and also formed part of the widely used 1849 textbook *Analecta Anglo-Saxonica* (for details, see Hagedorn, 'Received Wisdom', pp. 91, 98). Alfred's translation of Boethius's *De Consolatione philosophiae* was translated anonymously in 1689 and by Cardale in 1829.

89 Besant, 'Introduction', p. 29.

90 Froude, 'King Alfred', pp. 84–85; Besant, *The Story of King Alfred*, p. 159.

91 McIlroy, 'A Thousand Years of English', p. 101.

92 On this subject, see Fry, *Norse Sagas Translated into English*, pp. 9–10, 104; Whitelock, *The Anglo-Saxon Chronicle*, pp. xxv–xxix.

93 Abbott, *Alfred the Great*, p. 46.

94 Tappan, *In the Days of Alfred the Great*, p. 289. See also Whistler, *King Alfred's Viking*, p. 286; Stables, *'Twixt Daydawn and Light*, p. 349.

95 See Midwinter, *Nineteenth-Century Education*, p. 30. This notion was most famously expressed by Wordsworth. The line 'the child is father of the man' appears in his 1807 poem 'My Heart Leaps Up' (*Poetical Works*, p. 226), and as the preface to the 1815 version of his 'Ode: Intimations of Immortality from Recollections of Early Childhood' (*Poetical Works*, p. 279).

96 *Asser's Life of King Alfred*, p. 74.

97 Ellis, *The Mothers of England*, p. 174.

98 Pauli, *The Life of Alfred the Great*, p. 50. Pauli's description is approvingly quoted in Page, *Alfred the Great*, p. 74.

99 See Midwinter, *Victorian Social Reform*, p. 5. For an example of this Romantic belief see Wordsworth, *The Prelude*, in *The Poetical Works of William Wordsworth*, p. 128.

100 Blackie, 'Alfred', p. 90. See also Fenn, *The King's Sons*, p. 5.

101 *Asser's Life of King Alfred*, p. 75.

102 Blackie, 'Alfred', pp. 91–92; Fenn, *The King's Sons*, p. 6. On pro-hunting rhetoric, see Colley, *Britons: Forging the Nation*, p. 172.

103 Bevan, *A Lion of Wessex*, p. 19.

104 *Asser's Life of King Alfred*, p. 74.

105 Freeman, *Old English History*, p. 115; Harris, in a paper presented to the Hull Literary Club (*Alfred the Great*, p. 15) described the tale as a 'charming story'. See also Lorimer, 'King Alfred', p. 150.

106 See Keynes, 'The Cult of King Alfred the Great', p. 340; Mitchell, *Picturing the Past*, p. 60.

107 On the nineteenth-century interest in influential mothers (particularly among female authors), see Mitchell, *Picturing the Past*, pp. 155–157.

108 For instance, see Page, *Alfred the Great*.

109 Palgrave, 'Alfred the Great', p. 24.

110 See Midwinter, *Nineteenth-Century Education*, pp. 40–41, 77.

111 This attitude is voiced by characters in Dickens's *The Adventures of Oliver Twist* and Brontë's *Jane Eyre* and *Villette* (London, 2004 [1853]).

112 See, for instance, Pauli, *The Life of Alfred the Great*, p. 52; Freeman, *Old English History*, p. 115; Besant, *The Story of King Alfred*, p. 56.

113 *Asser's Life of King Alfred*, p. 74. According to Asser, Æthelwulf remarried in 855 (see *Asser's Life of King Alfred*, pp. 14, 70).

114 Judith teaches Alfred to read, for instance, in Fuller, *The Son of Ethelwolf*, p. 182; Pye, *Alfred: An Epic Poem*, p. 132.

115 Giles, *Six Old English Chronicles*, p. 51; Stevenson, *The Church Historians of England*, II: I, p. 450. Ellis, *The Mothers of Great Men*, pp. 58, 62, 60, 65.

116 Pauli, *The Life of Alfred the Great*, p. 52.

117 Plummer, *The Life and Times of Alfred the Great*, p. 83.

118 See Keynes, 'The Cult of King Alfred the Great', p. 337.

119 Plummer, *The Life and Times of Alfred the Great*, pp. 81–82.

119 Plummer, *The Life and Times of Alfred the Great*, pp. 81–82; Giles, *The Life and Times of Alfred the Great*, p. 204; Pauli, *The Life of Alfred the Great*, p. 52. Pauli's thesis was reiterated by, for example, Draper, 'Alfred the Great', p. 4; Harris, *Alfred the Great*, p. 15.

120 Freeman, *Old English History*, p. 115; Besant, *The Story of King Alfred*, p. 56.

121 *Asser's Life of King Alfred*, pp. 69–70.

122 Pauli, *The Life of Alfred the Great*, p. 57. See also Blackie, 'Alfred', p. 91.

123 See, for instance, Blackie, 'Alfred', p. 92.

124 'J.F.R.', *Lives of Alfred the Great, Sir Thomas More, and John Evelyn*, p. 3.

125 For examples of anti-Catholicism, see Norman, *Anti-Catholicism in Victorian Britain*, p. 61. On the Victorians and Rome, see Praz, *The Hero in Eclipse*, pp. 444–467.

126 Kelsey, *Alfred of Wessex*, II, p. 454.

127 Besant, *The Story of King Alfred*, p. 61. On Besant, see ODNB.

128 Stables, *'Twixt Daydawn and Light*, pp. 272, 270.

129 Tappan, *In the Days of Alfred the Great*, pp. 56–73.

130 François de Salignac de la Mothe-Fénelon's *Télémaque* and Andrew Michael Ramsay's *Les Voyages de Cyrus* (for details, see Williams, *Pope, Homer and Manliness*, pp. 47, 50).

131 Tappan (*In the Days of Alfred the Great*, p. i) praises Alfred for being a 'man who believed in God'.

132 See the hostile depiction of Catholic clerics in Tappan, *Robin Hood*, pp. 227–253.

133 Tappan, *In the Days of Alfred the Great*, p. 56.

134 On Froude's anti-Catholicism, see ODNB.

135 Froude, 'King Alfred', p. 77.

136 See, for instance, Besant, *The Story of King Alfred*, p. 60.

137 Powell, *The Life of Alfred or Alvred*, p. 6. See also Spelman, *The Life of Alfred the Great*, p. 18.

138 Rapin, *The History of England*, p. 103.

139 Stewart, *Stories About Alfred the Great*, p. 13.

140 Earle, 'Alfred as a Writer', p. 171. This theory is reiterated in Draper, *Alfred the Great*, p. 4.

141 Roger of Wendover, *Flowers of History*, p. 184.

142 Earle was rector of Swanswick from 1857 until his death (ODNB).

143 Stewart, *Stories about Alfred the Great*, p. 12; Fenn, *The King's Sons*, p. 27. See also Bevan, *A Lion of Wessex*, p. 50.

144 *Asser's Life of King Alfred*, p. 74.

145 On the influence of Lavater on nineteenth-century writers, see Tytler, *Physiognomy in the European Novel*.
146 See Lavater, *Essays on Physiognomy*, p. 95. For an introduction to this theory, see pp. 9–19 of the same volume.
147 Eayrs, *Alfred to Victoria*, p. 20.
148 Besant, *The Story of King Alfred*, p. 206.
149 Jackson, 'The Alfred Medal of 1901', p. 678.
150 Whistler, *King Alfred's Viking*, p. 92. See also Engelbach, *The Danes in England*, p. 118.
151 On the debate surrounding the Winchester statue, see Chapter One of this volume.
152 See, for instance, Eayrs, *Alfred to Victoria*, p. 21.
153 See Heighway, 'A Few Words Upon Beards', p. 614.

7

'Never to be confused with King Arthur': Alfred after Victoria

By the end of the nineteenth century, King Alfred of Wessex was renowned as one of the bravest of British heroes; as the most perfect of moral leaders; as the wise institutor of trial by jury and democracy; and as the king who burnt the cakes. Writing in 1899, Frederic Harrison could claim that 'every schoolboy' knew the salient facts of the Saxon king's biography.[1] In stark contrast, by the end of the twentieth century the decline of popular Alfredianism was such that less than half of Britain could say in which century Alfred had reigned or against whom he had fought, and the legends of the Saxon king's disguised adventures and alleged inventions were virtually forgotten.[2] Even in Winchester, in the shadow of Bowker's 1901 statue, few schoolchildren knew the famous story of Alfred burning the cakes.[3] 'I know NOTHING about this man, NOTHING', one GCSE history student scrawled on a school test about the Saxon king.[4]

Alfred's dramatic fall from fame as a national icon can be attributed in part to the calibre of author who celebrated him in the Victorian period and the centuries preceding it, and to the literary merit of the Alfredian texts that were produced. Blake, Coleridge and Milton all considered working on Alfred – but their plans never left the drawing-board. William Morris got as far as sketching a romanticised and rather Arthurian-looking Alfred, but no further (see Figure 18). Wordsworth did produce three sonnets on the Saxon king – but these are usually dismissed as numbering among his less significant works. And those authors who were attracted to Alfred are now, by and large, either forgotten figures or objects of derision. Tupper, for all his Alfredian poetry and translations and his almost single-handed efforts to commemorate Alfred's birth, was until recently remembered in the *Dictionary of National Biography* as merely 'a synonym for contemptible commonplace'; Henry James Pye's entry called him 'destitute . . . of poetic feeling'; and Joseph Cottle is still best known as the object of Coleridge and Southey's ridicule.[5] Alfred never found his Tennyson. This failure was recognised early. In 1902, an American thesis on *King Alfred in Literature* analysed twenty-six modern Alfredian texts, to sadly conclude that 'On turning to the treatment of [Alfred. . .] in the literature of his country it is impossible not to feel disappointment'. Its author, Louis Wardlaw Miles, confessed himself mystified by this problem of 'Alfred's worth for poetic

18 Undated preparatory sketch of Alfred by William Morris (no finished version of the design seems ever to have been attempted)

use'.[6] Even now, it is not entirely clear why the Saxon king was rejected as a subject by writers like Scott, Tennyson and Kingsley. In 1981, the Anglo-Saxonist Eric Stanley lamented that 'if Alfred fared badly in poetry, especially epic poetry, he fared even worse in drama, especially poetic drama', but he did not attempt to fully explain this misfortune.[7]

In part, King Arthur may have been so much more attractive than Alfred to such nineteenth-century authors simply because he offered them greater imaginative freedom. The known facts about the historical Arthur – if such a figure had even existed – were so scant as to impose 'the minimum demand for historical accuracy'.[8] And the mythical Arthurs of medieval literature were so many and diverse that he remained a malleable and ambiguous figure for rewriting. On the other hand, Asser's meticulous care in recording Alfred's character, appearance and activities left woefully little space for invention. This failing was recognised early by a critic in *The North British Review*. Lambasting Fitchett's *King Alfred* as 'the most useless production which ever proceeded from the human mind', he mused:

> we are obliged to doubt whether Mr Fitchett was happy in the selection of his theme. It is observable, that while the exploits of Arthur so fired the imagination both of Milton and Dryden, as to lead each to meditate an epic poem of which he should be the hero, and actually warmed the beautiful fancy of Spenser into melodious utterance, the more really grand and patriotically valuable career of Alfred kindled no such flames. This is explicable, it seems to us, on sufficiently obvious grounds. ... the truth of his life, in its great characteristic features, stands on this side of the mists of tradition, or the twilight of legendary reputation, as a solid part of the incontrovertible history of the growth of England's independence and power. ... Within such confines, there is naturally little to attract or excite the epic muse, for ... her song can rise with difficulty above the metrical narrative of a chronicler.[9]

The Saxon king's very success in becoming identified so closely with English national identity also meant that any attempt to disagree with Asser's glowing (indeed, propagandist) account of his life and character – any attempt to make of the Saxon king a more flawed and psychologically interesting figure – was vehemently attacked. Indeed, even those nineteenth-century authors who incorporated late medieval legends about the young Alfred's sins (which he manfully overcame) were decried as 'pitiable' for trying to 'besmirch' the king's memory.[10] Thus the anonymous reviewer of Fitchett complained that any Alfredian poem 'must be heavily imbued with didactic monotony', and suggested that it was moreover 'idle, intrusive, and impossible' to attempt to add any fictitious lustre to 'a name so dear, and a renown so ineffaceable'.[11]

Likewise, Alfred was perhaps unattractive to many of the authors we now most value as commentators upon the nineteenth century because he was so unequivocally aligned with the dominant cultural values of the Victorian age. King Arthur may have been used to glorify the Empire, but he could also be used to critique it; he may have exemplified the best traits of an Englishman, but embedded in the work of Tennyson, Morris, and Swinburne was an increasingly *risqué* examination of the institution of marriage.[12] And whereas the intrinsically tragic trajectory of the Arthurian story (a tale of corruption, decline and dynastic collapse) made it ideal to question and critique Victorian narratives of progress, Alfred's story was purely triumphal – a moral fable of determination and perseverance leading inevitably to success. So Bowker perhaps unwittingly identified a reason why so many authors rejected Alfred as a subject when at the 1901 Millenary he proudly proclaimed that 'King Arthur, even as immortalised by Tennyson, leaves no sure message of hope to be gleaned from his life, but we are left with much uncertainty . . . How much grander is the great king whose memory we venerate'.[13]

The end of the Norman Yoke and the purging of myth

The predominantly conservative politics of Alfredianism almost certainly contributed significantly to Alfred's decline in popularity in a twentieth-century culture determined to throw out 'Victorian values'. And the horrors of two world wars and the demise of a vast empire probably rendered the triumphal structure of Alfredian narrative less suited to the nation's mood than the downfall of Arthur's round table. Many other factors also contributed, however, to Alfred's decline as a popular hero in the decades after his 1901 anniversary. In part, it was just one element of a more general revaluation of the Norman period and devaluation of the Anglo-Saxon. Towards the close of the nineteenth century, the theory of the Norman Yoke was largely superseded by the view that Norman blood had contributed positive qualities like shrewdness and determination to the composite English character, while the publication of scholarly legal histories began to reveal that modern English law owed as much – if not more – to Norman administration as to Saxon culture.[14] And this shift in attitude was then compounded in the first decade of the twentieth century by the establishment of the *triple entente* and the *entente cordiale*, which redefined official Anglo-French relations.

Alongside increasing appreciation of the Norman period, scholarly research towards the end of the nineteenth century also gradually stripped away from King Alfred many of his supposed achievements. Pollock and Maitland's 1895 *History of English Law before the Time of Edward I* destroyed the myth that Alfred had invented trial-by-jury; in 1899, Frederick Pollock argued persuasively that Britain's navy proper dated back only as far as Elizabeth I; and, in 1902, Charles Plummer pointed out that any educational schemes implemented by Alfred would have been restricted to nobles – and that in establishing a court school the Saxon king had merely followed the example of Charlemagne.[15] Increased scholarship also discredited the most popular and appealing legends attached to Alfred. In 1899, Frederic Harrison rationalised that the Saxon king was 'too practical a man to let his own supper get burnt on the hearth'; in his 1901 Ford lectures on Alfred, Charles Plummer insisted that 'Alfred at Athelney was not burning cakes, but organising victory'; while Edward Freeman, even in his history for children, insisted that (although he was 'really sorry' to do so) he was duty-bound to reveal that the story of Alfred learning to read 'cannot possibly be true'.[16]

Ironically, the Millenary in Winchester actually accelerated this process of demythification. A year after the event, Bowker would boast that the commemoration had 'stimulated considerable research by experts . . . in times past King Alfred to the great body of the people was a dim and unrealised figure, occupying a position in the popular mind much as King Arthur does at the present moment. In the future . . . all teachers will make the study of Alfred more real than it has ever been'.[17] This drive to make Alfred 'more real' also rendered him a far less appealing subject for the painters, poets, playwrights and novelists who had contributed so much to maintaining the Saxon king's popularity throughout the nineteenth century.

There was some resistance to the drive to divest Alfred of legend. It was particularly marked, as one might expect, in those geographical areas which had benefited from Alfredian associations during the nineteenth century – either materially (from tourism or endowments) or culturally (in terms of civic pride or local identity). Although Plummer debunked a great many Alfredian legends in his 1901 Ford lectures, as an Oxford man he still displayed a lingering partiality for Alfred's association with the university. While admitting that 'we may not, here in Oxford, claim Alfred as our founder', he nevertheless asserted that 'in all that we do here in the cause of true learning and of genuine education, we are carrying on the work which Alfred left us to do'.[18] And, in the same year, another Oxford historian, Warwick Draper – writing of Alfred's supposed foundation of Oxford, insisted that 'Although this myth has long since been entirely explained, yet it will always possess a certain historical value as belonging to that sacred praise of legendary fame which Alfred's personality has continuously won'.[19]

Deep popular affection for Alfredian legend also survived in those areas of Britain which had made up the old kingdom of Wessex. In 1899, the amateur Somersetshire historian William Greswell, evidently aware of the growing scholarly denigration of Alfredian legend, proclaimed that 'We who live in, or near, "King Alfred's Country" . . . will part with nothing, not even that good old story of the cakes. For what would Athelney be without it?'[20] And, at the 1901 Millenary celebrations, the Bishop of Winchester announced that 'if anyone in the room were so adventurously rash as to discredit on such a day the dear old story of the burned cakes, he ought not to expect to escape from the doors with a whole skin'.[21] The story of the burnt cakes, in particular, was relinquished with general reluctance. Writing of Alfred's time in hiding in 1901, the popular historian Warwick Draper asserted 'To this sojourn is assigned the well-known story of Alfred neglecting the baked cakes and being scolded by the farmer's wife . . . Old and popular, may it long remain in our history books!'[22] More than any other Alfredian legend, the tale did survive in a limited circulation throughout the twentieth century. In 1999, a report of an excavation at Hyde Abbey in the *Express* newspaper bore the title, 'The heat is on to find the king who burnt the cakes'.[23] But one (discredited) story was not sufficient to make Alfred rival a King Arthur who, modern criticism adjudges, continued to 'reverberate in the imagination' of the twentieth century specifically because of the 'elements of myth in the Arthurian stories'.[24] Between 1902 and 2000, fewer than forty Alfredian texts were published – while works of Arthurian literature numbered in the thousands.[25]

G.K. Chesterton

The importance of legend to Alfred's popular appeal was diagnosed – against early attempts to purge that element from the Saxon's biography – by Gordon Stables. Defending his own use of the story of the cakes, the mysterious appearance of Cuthbert, and Alfred's minstrel disguise in *'Twixt Daydawn and Light*, Stables warned his contemporaries, 'Who would read your dry-as-dust history, think you, if there was no ray of romance illuminating its pages here and there?'[26] Ten years after the Alfred Millenary – and in the face of the growing dominance of scholarly Alfrediana – another, more developed appeal to the value of legend was made by G.K. Chesterton. In the preface to his 1911 *The Ballad of the White Horse*, Chesterton proclaimed:

> King Alfred is not a legend in the sense that King Arthur may be a legend . . . But King Alfred is a legend in this broader and more human sense, that the legends are the most important things about him. . . . It is wholly as a popular legend that I deal with him here. I write as one ignorant of everything, except that I have found the legend of King Alfred of Wessex still alive in the land. . . . A tradition connects the ultimate victory of Alfred with the valley in Berkshire called the Vale of the White Horse. I have seen doubts of the tradition, which may be valid doubts. I do not know when or where the story started; it is enough that it started somewhere and ended with me; for I only seek to write upon a hearsay, as the old balladists did. . . . There is a popular tale that Alfred came in contact with a woman and her cakes; I select it because it is a popular tale, because it is a vulgar one. It has been disputed by grave historians, who were, I think, a little too grave to be good judges of it. . . . I am not concerned to prove the truth of these popular traditions. It is enough for me to maintain two things: that they are popular traditions; and that without these popular traditions we should have bothered about Alfred about as much as we bother about Eadwig.[27]

Indeed, Chesterton not only incorporated existing legend into his poem, he also blatantly added new legendary elements. A near-invincible Saxon thane, Eldred, is attacked at Ethandune with seven spears – six of them splinter on him, but the seventh is 'wrought as the faerie blades . . . By the monstrous water-maids' and brings his death. And time is defiantly telescoped so that Alfred's struggle and triumph becomes not a historical narrative but a timeless fable: a Roman, an Ancient Briton and a Saxon lead the three parts of Alfred's army, representing the three periods in which Christian civilisations fought against 'the heathen nihilism'.[28] Chesterton's retelling of the story of Alfred and the cakes is also deliberately elevated from its specific historical context. Instead, it is situated in relation to the tradition of English storytelling – an alternative form of national history and identity: When the swineherd's wife beats Alfred, the king pauses for a moment on the brink of anger and then laughs:

> The giant laughter of Christian men
> That roars through a thousand tales,
> Where greed is an ape and pride is an ass,
> And Jack's away with his master's lass,
> And the miser is banged with all his brass,
> The farmer with all his flails;
> Tales that tumble and tales that trick,
> Yet end not all in scorning –
> Of kings and clowns in a merry plight
> And the clock gone wrong and the world gone right,
> That the mummers sing upon Christmas night
> And Christmas Day in the morning.[29]

The explicit references to Christianity – here and throughout the eight-book poem – suggest Chesterton's aim in rewriting Alfred's life: his project seems to have been to find meaning in history for an age that had rejected the simple Victorian belief in divinely ordained progress, and was increasingly rejecting Christianity itself as scientific knowledge advanced. This threat – the threat of the modern – is alluded to in the final book of the poem which prophesies that 'in some far century':

> The heathen shall return.
> They shall not come with warships,
> They shall not waste with brands,
> But books be all their eating,
> And ink be on their hands.
> Not with the humour of hunters
> Or savage skill in war,
> But ordering all things with dead words,
> Strings they shall make of beasts and birds,
> And wheels of wind and star.[30]

And the poem begins with a dedication in which the modern voice is evoked, questioning the value of history:

> Of great limbs gone to chaos,
> A great face turned to night –
> Why bend above a shapeless shroud
> Seeking in such archaic cloud
> Sight of strong lords and light?

Chesterton's reply is that Alfred 'also looked forth for an hour/On peopled plains and skies that lower'.[31] History does have a value, the poem suggests, but not as part of an attempt to identify an inexorable path of human progress.

Rather, as a source of inspiring examples – individuals in whose very struggles against adversity religious meaning might be found, within the meaningless cycle of time's successes and failures. The poem's central image of an endless succession of weeds encroaching on the Uffington White Horse, and the perpetual scouring needed to keep the chalk figure visible, represents this post-Darwinian, cyclical vision of time. And, whereas Victorian authors typically omitted Haesten's invasion of Wessex in 882 from their accounts of Alfred's reign, to avoid negating the triumph of his victory over Guthrum and endangering linear narratives of progress, in *The Ballad of the White Horse* this second wave of invasion is crucial to the poem's meaning.

Chesterton's poem – while clearly the progeny of Victorian Alfredianism – is also distinctly modern in other ways. Where Henry James Pye had Welsh, Scottish and Irish vowing voluntary loyalty to Alfred, here the different races of the British Isles band together in an uneasy and grudging union, and Alfred is no uncontested icon of Englishness, but 'like the tales a whole tribe feigns/ Too English to be true'.[32] When the Saxon king looks prophetically into the future he sees not the glorious conclusion of his race, but an unending succession of troubles and failure. And whereas Victorian Alfreds were promised victory by either Cuthbert or Neot during their time in hiding, this king's only comfort is an ethereal visitation from the Virgin Mary, who will say nothing more than:

> I tell you naught for your comfort,
> Yea, naught for your desire,
> Save that the sky grows darker yet
> And the sea rises higher.[33]

It is a call for a heroic but blind faith founded on no inherited certainties and no assurances about the future. Thirty years later, in one of the darkest moments of the Second World War, the lines appeared on the front page of *The Times* newspaper – the day after the island of Crete had fallen to German forces, and 17,000 British troops had become prisoners of war.[34]

The Ballad of the White Horse should perhaps be viewed as the climax of the nineteenth-century cult of King Alfred – as much as the 1901 commemoration in Winchester. It certainly has the greatest claim to literary merit of any poem about the Saxon king, and is probably the only lengthy Alfredian work from the period 1800 to 1945 that is still available in print today. Yet, unlike Tolkien's *The Lord of the Rings* or T.H. White's *The Once and Future King* – texts which, like Chesterton's, reacted to modernity by creating myth cycles invested with cosmic significance – it was to spawn no twentieth-century imitators.[35] The reason for its relative neglect (and, more generally, King Alfred's unpopularity in twentieth-century Britain) lies partly in the events which occurred in the three decades following its publication: namely, two wars against a German enemy. In the aftermath of those wars, a distinct wariness developed in Britain about glorifying, celebrating, or locating national identity within anything – or anyone – that might be viewed as

Germanic, as it was perceived that an influential relationship had existed between the nineteenth-century's racialist theories of Saxon superiority and twentieth-century fascism.[36] As a Saxon king, Alfred was, broadly speaking, Germanic – indeed, he was a figure sufficiently agreeable to Nazi ideals for the fascist sympathiser Unity Mitford to present Adolf Hitler with a replica of the Alfred Jewel in the 1930s.[37]

Two world wars

Nothing seems to have been written about King Alfred during the Great War, and just three short texts appeared in the decade following it. One of these – Robinson Jeffers's poem, 'Ghosts in England' – perhaps speaks best for the difficulty which authors experienced in invoking the Saxon king during this post-war period. His Alfred is an enfeebled ghost who wanders the chalk downs and 'Witlessly walks with his hands lamenting, "Who are the people and who are the enemy?" he says, bewildered'.[38] The fact that nineteenth-century Alfredianism had so insistently constructed Alfred as 'English' perhaps saved the Saxon king from utter forgetfulness, however. In 1927, a painting of 'Alfred's fleet defeating the Danes at sea' was selected as part of the new decoration for St Stephen's Hall in Westminster.[39] However, this may well have been a calculated attempt to reclaim Britain's Saxon heritage after the war, and it does not seem to have been representative of any broad, public enthusiasm for the king, such as had existed at the end of the nineteenth century – or in the 1840s, when paintings were chosen for the new Houses of Parliament.

Only a small number of texts about Alfred were also published during the 1930s. One of these – Samuel Walkley's children's novel *When the Vikings Came* – seems to voice a call for acceptance of Alfred as an English, rather than a Saxon or Germanic, king. Walkley's Alfred has a right-hand man who is a Briton. The king tells him, 'Brothers in arms are we. I am a Saxon and you are a Briton. Let us forget the turbulent past, so that we may now fight back to back for this glorious land which is our heritage. Together we will strive to free our race from all her foes'. Walkley's Briton (who searches out King Alfred, and swears undying loyalty to him) claims to be a Pendragon – 'last of the line of Arthur'.[40] The novel thus seems to appeal for acceptance of Alfred through popular enthusiasm for King Arthur. Certainly, it was in this period that the Saxon king was finally overshadowed in the popular imagination by the Celtic hero – particularly after the publication of T.H. White's *Sword in the Stone* in 1938.

Increasing popular confusion between Alfred and Arthur arose in the early twentieth century as the Saxon king became less dominant and his legends gradually faded into forgetfulness. This was parodied to humorous effect by Walter Sellar and Robert Yeatman in their classic 1930 comic-history, *1066 and All That*. The chapter on Alfred – which deliberately confounds him with Arthur – is irreverently entitled 'Alfred the Cake'. It decrees that:

Alfred ought never to be confused with King Arthur, equally memorable but probably non-existent and therefore perhaps less important historically (unless he did exist). There is a story that King Arthur once burnt some cakes belonging to a Mrs Girth, a great lady of the time, at a place called Atheling. As, however, Alfred could not have been an Incendiary King and a Good King, we may dismiss the story as absurd, and in any case the event is supposed to have occurred in a marsh where the cakes would not have burnt properly. Cf. the famous lines of poetry about King Arthur and the cakes: 'Then slowly answered Alfred from the marsh' – Arthur, Lord Tennyson.

The historical romp continues by asserting that the *Anglo-Saxon Chronicle* was published in Arthur's time, and that 'Alfred had a very interesting wife called Lady Windermere (the Lady of the Lake), who was always clothed in the same white frock, and used to go bathing with Sir Launcelot'.[41]

Hayden White has suggested that the final mode in which histories are rewritten is the satiric.[42] Certainly, the first half of the twentieth century seems to have witnessed Alfred becoming the subject of irreverent humour, as he declined from national icon to neglect. Besides his cameo in *1066*, the Saxon king made an appearance in *Punch* on 28 June 1933, unsuccessfully attempting to invent the wristwatch, and again on 23 April 1941, burning the cakes (see Figure 19).[43] And Alfred's memory was derisively evoked in Nancy Mitford's 1945 novel *The Pursuit of Love*, in which (in allusion to her sister's gift to Hitler) a replica of the Alfred Jewel is dismissed as resembling 'a chicken's mess. Same shape, same size, same colour. Not my idea of a jewel'.[44] Alfred also, however, found a twentieth-century niche in the burgeoning genre of children's literature. From 1902, around a quarter of all Alfredian texts published were for a juvenile audience. Such productions concentrated upon making the Saxon king's ninth-century world accessible to a young, twentieth-century audience. So, for instance, the 1956 *Ladybird Book of King Alfred the Great* by Lawrence Du Garde Peach associates the Saxon king with the (still visible and visitable) Uffington White Horse; proclaims that his coronation was 'the same as when our present Queen Elizabeth was crowned'; and asserts that 'wherever you live in England, in town or country, you are in one of the shires into which Alfred divided his kingdom' (see Figure 20 for John Kenney's illustration of Alfred's coronation, for the Ladybird book).[45]

The Ladybird book also informed its young readers that Alfred had been the first to establish 'a sort of Home Guard'.[46] Although the legacy of Victorian racialism made the Saxon a problematic figure for many authors in the decades during and after the Second World War, these cultural politics do not seem to have infected the children's literature of the time. Alfred could thus still find a role as a paragon of national defence and resistance in texts like Jeffery Farnol's aptly titled 1943 novel, *The King Liveth*.[47] Farnol dedicated his text to 'All sons and daughters of England who, blessed with Alfred's ageless spirit, are now fighting, working, striving or suffering for the future welfare of all'. And he ended it with the Saxon king gazing over the peaceful English countryside and pronouncing:

"Well, perhaps they are a SHADE *overcooked, but what does that matter in war-time?"*

19 George Morrow, 'King Alfred Cooking Cakes', *Punch Magazine*

'Look yonder . . . and be glad of our past suffering for what now is and shall be. Here is a comfortable thought . . . that we shall leave behind us a greater England, rising from strength to strength, a bulwark 'gainst Tyranny and sure refuge for all distressed folk'.

It was a powerful message for a generation that had grown up with the threat of air raids and invasion, and the loss of family and friends on Europe's battlefields. And for those almost old enough it was a call to battle too: Farnol's Alfred is celebrated as 'the incarnation of that patient dogged heroism which has (and is) saving England'.[48] In a year when the British publishing industry was a skeleton operation and subject to strict government control, it is perhaps not surprising that *The King Liveth* managed to find its way on to the beleaguered presses.[49]

The restrictions upon the publishing industry during the Second World War also worked in Alfred's favour in another way. With few new books being printed, late nineteenth-century Alfredian texts enjoyed a far longer circulation than they might otherwise have done, and some were still read by adults and children in the 1950s. This in itself was not sufficient, however, to stem Alfred's retreating tide of popularity. And the 'Celtic Revival' of the 1960s – when the music, artwork and folklore of Britain's Celtic fringe

20 John Kenney, the imagined scene of Alfred's coronation (in the 1956 Ladybird book, *King Alfred the Great*)

became increasingly valorised – caused the Saxon king to be further eclipsed by Arthur. As the popular historian and archaeologist Geoffrey Ashe asserted in the introduction to his best-selling *The Quest for Arthur's Britain*, the Celtic world could provide the focus for 'a new and acceptable patriotism' – untainted by any shadow of fascism.

Alfred in the late twentieth century

Another reason why Arthur appealed so much more than Alfred to the 1960s' imagination seems to have been the steamy dose of sexual intrigue and adultery that lay at the heart of the Arthurian myth. Arthur's Camelot, Geoffrey Ashe assured his readers, had been 'the swinging city of its time'.[50] Alfred's story, on the other hand, could offer the free-love generation nothing raunchier than a severe attack of piles. That this deficiency was felt by those who considered Alfred as a potential subject for 1960s' audiences is suggested by the one attempt made to produce an Alfredian feature film.[51] Clive Donner's 1969 *Alfred the Great*, starring David Hemmings as the Saxon king, looks very much like a displaced Arthurian tale. Alfred appears as a priggish and frigid king who wishes he was a priest, views all passion as sinful, and is cold and distant with his queen – consequently losing her, when she is swept off her feet by the passionate Viking, Guthrum (see Figure 21). Essentially, the film is concerned not with the military triumphs of the historical Alfred, but with exploring the differences between Christianity and prudishness, love and lust – and with a pairing of the Saxon and Danish kings as a ninth-century Arthur and Lancelot.

Donner's film can still be viewed occasionally on television – mostly on Sunday afternoons in the height of summer – but while Arthurian film proliferated in the late decades of the twentieth century, *Alfred the Great* engendered no progeny. An increasingly iconoclastic and questioning attitude to the authority and reliability of historical texts, and a popular supplanting of 'top-down' history by social histories probably contributed to the indifference into which Alfred fell (and which Arthur escaped, since he could be rendered as a purely mythical figure). This newly sceptical approach to history marked those few Alfredian texts produced in the late decades of the twentieth century as distinct from Victorian Alfrediana. C. Walter Hodges' 1976 novel *The Marsh King*, for instance, displays a clear awareness of the problematic nature of textual transmission and authorial reliability. Nothing in the book is presented as historical fact: rather, the tale's narrator is a man living decades after Alfred's death, who has merely heard stories about the king from his mother, and read unreliable manuscripts about Alfred, written as exercises in propaganda by the king's scribe.[52]

In the late twentieth-century world of spin-doctors, tabloids, and widespread media-awareness, doubts about Alfred's true greatness even infected the genre of children's literature. The cute 1998 picture book by Stewart Ross, warningly relates:

21 A pious Alfred, in Clive Donner's 1969 film *Alfred the Great*

In Anglo-Saxon times priests were almost the only people who could read and write. There were no newspapers, and, of course, no TV or radio . . . They said a lot of kind things about King Alfred, because he was their hero! We now know that some of what they wrote was untrue.[53]

And scepticism about Alfred also became dominant in academia. In his 1995 study *King Alfred the Great*, Alfred P. Smyth argued that the *Life of King Alfred* was a forgery, written around a hundred years after the death of Asser. Likewise, Barbara Yorke in her article on Alfred – 'The Most Perfect Man in History?' – presented the Saxon king as a wily politician who knew the value of controlling his own image and 'had the foresight to commission his biography'.[54]

Yorke's article was published to mark the eleven-hundredth anniversary of King Alfred's death in 1999. This event was observed on a scale infinitesimal by comparison with the celebrations organised by Alfred Bowker in 1901.

Proceedings consisted of a small academic conference; a modest archaeological dig; and an exhibition at the Museum of London gloomily entitled 'Alfred
the Great: London's Forgotten King', which concluded by stating only that 'it
remains to be seen whether in the next thousand years he will continue to be
London's forgotten king'.[55] More positive was the art installation created in
Winchester in 2001 to mark the anniversary of the erection of the Alfred statue
– although it might be observed that this was less a commemoration of the man
himself than of the local *cult* of Alfred. Directed by Pierre Vivant, the project
used web-cameras to transmit live pictures of five contemporary Alfreds living
in Winchester on to a large screen near the 1901 Alfred statue, thus 'providing a visual echo of it'. The Alfreds ranged from an eighteen-month-old toddler
to a pensioner, and at least one of them was conscious of having been named
with the Saxon king specifically in mind – thus indicating that Alfred continued to possess some potency and relevance at the start of the twenty-first
century, at least in the former heart of his nineteenth-century fan-base.[56]

Alfred and the future

As long as the 1901 statue stands in Winchester, it is probable that Alfred will
continue to attract interest as a focus of local pride in that city. There are also,
however, some indications that the twentieth-century's forgetfulness and
rejection of the Saxon king may see a reversal, and that in the near future he
might find new cultural roles of national significance. With the growing political power of Brussels, there are signs that King Alfred – as one who resisted
European invasion – may be becoming a hero of Euroscepticism. Whether by
coincidence or design, it is the case that the George Watts painting of '*King
Alfred Inciting the Saxons to Resist the Danes* – the winner of the 1847 oil-
painting competition for the decoration of the new Houses of Parliament –
now hangs in Committee Room Ten of the House of Commons, which is the
frequent meeting-room of a European standing committee. Consequently, the
Saxon king has more than once been invoked in political discussion of
Britain's role within Europe. On 26 February 2003, for instance, during discussion of how best to protect the country's financial interests, it was
observed that it was 'particularly appropriate' that *King Alfred Inciting the
Saxons to Prevent the Landing of the Danes* should be hanging on the wall.[57]
Three months later, during debate over a particularly inscrutable European
finance bill, Mark Prisk, Conservative MP for Hertford and Stortford,
commented:

> As this is my first Finance Bill, the prospect of 447 pages, 214 clauses and 43
> schedules seems remarkable and daunting. In facing the challenge, I draw some
> comfort and inspiration from the painting entitled 'Alfred inciting the Saxons
> to prevent the landing of the Danes'.[58]

Such use of Alfred has not been confined to sealed chambers. In the run-
up to the 2001 General Election, the then Conservative leader William

Hague travelled to Winchester to appeal for voters to maintain national identity and reject the Euro from 'the city of the ninth century King Alfred, who laid the foundations for a single English kingdom'.[59]

The limited devolution of Great Britain into its national components, and the growing assertion of independent Welsh, Scottish and Northern Irish identities also seems to be creating an increasing need for new icons of Englishness. Although the national identity that 'English Alfred' embodied during the nineteenth century was really a declaration of Britishness and Union, the malleability of the figure of Alfred throughout his reception history suggests that contrary use of him is by no means ruled out. Certainly, at the close of 1999, the Saxon king was invoked as an emblem of 'Englishness' in more than one popular cultural history seeking to find a new, distinct identity for the English.[60]

Alfred has also recently become the subject of a trilogy by the best-selling novelist Bernard Cornwell – representing the first lengthy popular treatment of the Saxon king for many decades. In the first part of the series, however – *The Last Kingdom*, published in 2004 – he appears a far cry from the iconic hero of the Victorian age. We first see Alfred crouched shamefully outside a tent, like an Irvine Welsh anti-hero, moaning in pain, vomiting and grovelling for God's forgiveness: 'It seemed Alfred had humped a servant girl and, immediately afterwards, had been overcome by physical pain and what he called spiritual torment'.[61] Cornwell's Alfred is also heir to that late twentieth-century academic rewriting of the Saxon king as a politician who had the foresight to commission his biography. A leader cast in a distinctly twenty-first-century mould, he is a subtle, shrewd ruler who plays men like chess pieces, secures the loyalty of his followers as strategically as any option-dispensing corporation, and, above all, knows the value of spin. The book's narrator learns that Alfred 'had never been invested as the future king', but 'to his dying day, insisted the Pope had conferred the succession on him, and so justified his usurpation of the throne'.[62]

Myth-making is central to the novel. Its narrator describes how the self-mutilation of the Saxon nuns of St Abbs, to preserve their chastity under the threat of Viking attack, is sold in Alfred's kingdom 'as evidence of Danish ferocity and untrustworthiness'. He relates, 'I remember one Easter listening to a sermon about the nuns, and it was all I could do not to interrupt and say that it had not happened as the priest described'.[63] Such anatomising of the process by which an invasion in search of land and riches is conceptualised into a 'holy war' can surely be read as an attempt to invest Alfred's times with contemporary relevance for an age which has itself witnessed the blurring of boundaries between foreign policy and religious activism.

That issue of English national identity, with which Alfred recently seems to have become associated, also finds resonance in Cornwell's novel. Its narrator is Uhtred, a Northumbrian boy who is captured and raised by Danes, before granting his allegiance to Alfred's West Saxons. Sitting between cultures, he wrestles throughout with issues of identity: 'Northumbrian or

Dane? Which was I? What did I want to be?' Finally, he swears his sword to the English Alfred. There can be little doubt, however, that Uhtred's heart tugs irresistibly towards the Danes. 'To exchange Ragnar's freedom for Alfred's earnest piety seemed a miserable fate to me', he muses.[64] Indeed, Cornwell's Danes – like many nineteenth-century Vikings – are enticing figures who roar with delight on the battlefield, swear with mouth-filling oaths, revel in the salt-spray soaking their flaxen locks, and feast with carnivorous joy. But Alfred and his Saxons are juxtaposed with them not as models of virtuous Victorian manliness and moral hardihood, but as rule-bound, pale and pious leek-eaters. And a far larger portion of the book is narrated from the camps and ships of the Danes than from Alfred's kingdom. The question must inevitably be raised, therefore, of whether *The Last Kingdom* really can be read as an example of renewed interest in Alfred – or whether it is rather a romance of the now more enticing, pagan Old North.

The Vikings are not Alfred's only rivals for popular interest and affection in Cornwell's novel. Twice, in the first edition of the book, the Saxon king's name accidentally mutates to 'Arthur'. On the face of it, this is merely a sub-editor's oversight, and a mistake entirely excusable in an author who had already completed a successful trilogy on the Celtic monarch. But that ghost of Arthur flitting in the background reminds us of the deliberate confusion between the two kings in *1066 and All That* and of Donner's unsuccessful 1960s' attempt to rewrite Alfred in an Arthurian mould. It remains to be seen whether Cornwell's Alfred will engender further popular rewritings of the Saxon king, or whether – like several of his previous works – it will find its way into either filmic or televised form. But one thing seems certain. If there is to be any sort of revival of the nineteenth-century cult of Alfred, the Saxon king will first have the fiercest of battles on his hands to either overcome or coexist beside that twentieth-century icon of the silver screen, favourite of the fantasy genre, and hero of South-Western tourist boards – the Excalibur-wielding Celt.

Notes

1 Froude 'King Alfred', p. 82; Harrison, 'Alfred as King', p. 42.
2 In a survey of general public knowledge about King Alfred (J.M. Parker, 2000) forty out of 100 adults knew that he had burnt the cakes; 39 per cent of adults knew that he reigned in the ninth century; 38 per cent knew that he fought against the Vikings; 10 per cent had heard of Alfred as the founder of Britain's navy; and just 4 per cent associated him with democratic government.
3 In a survey of secondary-school children in Winchester (J.M. Parker, 2000), only 38 per cent appeared to have heard the tale of Alfred burning the cakes.
4 Comment scrawled on question sheet about Alfred's reign, by anonymous GCSE history student (July 2000).
5 Thomas Seccombe, *Dictionary of National Biography* (hereafter *DNB*), vol. 57, p. 319; Sidney Lee, *DNB*, vol. 47, p. 68.
6 Miles, *King Alfred in Literature*, pp. 125, 117.

7 Stanley, *The Glorification of Alfred*, p. 116.
8 Doel, *Worlds of King Arthur*, p. 168.
9 'Fitchett's *King Alfred*', p. 393.
10 Plummer, *The Life and Times of Alfred the Great*, p. 58.
11 'Fitchett's *King Alfred*', p. 393.
12 On this, see Barczewski, *Myth and National Identity*, pp. 216–219.
13 Bowker, *The King Alfred Millenary*, p. 190.
14 See, for instance, Charles Gibson, 'Some Characteristics of the Normans', *Catholic World*, 65 (1897), pp. 506–513; W.S. Holdsworth, *A History of English Law* (London, 1903); Charles Oman, *England Before the Conquest* (London, 1910).
  On this change in attitude, see Simmons, *Reversing the Conquest*, p. 198.
15 Pollock, 'Alfred the Great', p. 280; Plummer, *The Life and Times of Alfred the Great*, p. 135.
16 Harrison, 'Alfred as King', p. 42; Plummer, *The Life and Times of Alfred the Great*, p. 105; Freeman, *Old English History*, p. 115.
17 Bowker, *The King Alfred Millenary*, p. 186.
18 Plummer, *The Life and Times of Alfred the Great*, p. 193.
19 Draper, *Alfred the Great*, p. 91.
20 Greswell, 'County of Alfred the Great', p. 474.
21 *The Times*, 21 Sep. 1901, p. 10.
22 Draper, *Alfred the Great*, p. 8.
23 Iliff and Rees, 'The heat is on to find the king who burnt the cakes', p. 33.
24 Taylor and Brewer, *The Return of King Arthur*, p. 237.
25 Between 1965 and 1985 alone, over 8,000 books were published concerned with some aspect of the Arthurian legend.
26 Stables, *'Twixt Daydawn and Light*, p. 207.
27 Chesterton, *The Ballad of the White Horse*, p. 123.
28 Chesterton, *The Ballad of the White Horse*, pp. 192, 124.
29 Chesterton, *The Ballad of the White Horse*, p. 175.
30 Chesterton, *The Ballad of the White Horse*, p. 226.
31 Chesterton, *The Ballad of the White Horse*, pp. 125–126.
32 Chesterton, *The Ballad of the White Horse*, p. 126.
33 Chesterton, *The Ballad of the White Horse*, p. 138.
34 Michael W. Perry, in Chesterton, *The Ballad of the White Horse*, p. 120.
35 Perry (in his introduction to *The Ballad of the White Horse*, p. 121) likens Chesterton's project to Tolkien's.
36 See Simmons, *Reversing the Conquest*, p. 202.
37 See Guiness, *The House of Mitford*, p. 280.
38 Jeffers, 'Ghosts in England', p. 124. The other two texts were Browne, *King Alfred's Books*; Monkhouse, *Alfred the Great*.
39 See Keynes, 'The Cult of King Alfred the Great', p. 351.
40 Walkley, *When the Vikings Came*, pp. 56, 53.
41 Sellar and Yeatman, *1066 And All That*, pp. 18–19.
42 White, *Metahistory*, pp. 230–265.
43 Keynes, 'The Cult of King Alfred the Great', p. 351.
44 Mitford, *The Pursuit of Love*, p. 57.
45 Peach, *King Alfred the Great*, pp. 12, 14, 48.
46 Peach, *King Alfred the Great*, p. 40.

47 Another example is perhaps Walkley, *When the Vikings Came*. This tale of espionage and invasion was published in the year that Germany broke the Versailles agreement, and was republished in 1943.
48 Farnol, *The King Liveth*, pp. i, 240, i.
49 Farnol's text had to be published in accordance with 'war economy standards' (Farnol, *The King Liveth*, p. i).
50 Geoffrey Ashe, *The Quest for Arthur's Britain* (London: Pall Mall, 1968), p. 14.
51 The only other attempt was an educational film released in 1996.
52 See Hodges, *The Marsh King*, pp. 9–10.
53 Ross, *Find King Alfred*, p. 59.
54 Yorke, 'The Most Perfect Man in History?', p. 9.
55 The conference was held – appropriately – at King Alfred's College, Winchester; the excavations told place at the site of the former Hyde Abbey, in Winchester. The exhibition was held from 8 September 1999 until 9 January 2000. The quotation is taken from the guide to the exhibition – Clarke, *Alfred the Great: London's Forgotten King*, p. 12.
56 A Winchester pub landlord was named Alfred because his father walked past the King Alfred statue on his way home from Winchester maternity hospital.
57 *The United Kingdom Parliament: Standing Committee Database*, 'Protecting the Community's Financial Interests', Wednesday 26 February 2003, column 7.
58 *The United Kingdom Parliament: Standing Committee Database*, 'Finance Bill', Thursday 15 May 2003, column 011.
59 Quoted in Evans, ' "Save the Pound", Tory Chief Pleads', p. 18.
60 Alfred is presented as an emblem of Englishness in Wood, *In Search of England*, pp. 125–148, and in Paxman, *The English: A Portrait of a People*, p. 135.
61 Cornwell, *The Last Kingdom*, p. 79.
62 Cornwell, *The Last Kingdom*, p. 91.
63 Cornwell, *The Last Kingdom*, p. 125.
64 Cornwell, *The Last Kingdom*, p. 55.

Select bibliography

NB Anonymous texts are listed by the first significant word in the title. Editions of texts are listed by original author rather than by modern editor.

Aarsleff, Hans, *The Study of Language in England, 1780–1860* (Princeton, 1983)

Abels, Richard, *Alfred the Great: War, Kingship and Culture in Anglo-Saxon England* (London, 1998)

Abbott, J., *Alfred the Great* (Madras, 1898)

Acton, William, 'Marriage', in *The Functions and Disorders of the Reproductive Organs in Childhood, Youth, Adult Age, and Advanced Life, Considered in their Psychological, Social, and Moral Relations* (London, 1865)

Alfred the Great: Deliverer of his Country: A Tragedy (London, 1753)

Alfred the Great: Or, England's Darling on the Egyptian Campaign: A Parody of Alfred Austin, in Verse (Bristol, 1898)

Alison, Archibald, 'On Parliamentary Reform and the French Revolution', *Blackwood's Edinburgh Magazine*, 29 (1831)

'Anglicanism and Early British Christianity', *The Dublin Review*, 23 (1890)

'The Anglo-Normans', *The North British Review*, 6 (1847)

The Anglo-Saxon Chronicles, ed. by Michael Swanton (London, 1996)

The Annals of Roger de Hoveden, ed. by Henry T. Riley (London, 1853)

Annals of St Bertin, in Joseph Stevenson, ed., *The Church Historians of England* (London, 1853–55)

The Annals of St Neots with Vita Prima Sancti Neoti, eds David Dumville and Michael Lapidge (Cambridge, 1985)

Anster, John, 'Alfred', in John Anster, *Xeniola* (Dublin, 1837)

Arata, Stephen D, 'The Occidental Tourist', *Victorian Studies*, 33 (1990)

Arnold, Arthur, 'The Indebtedness of the Landed Gentry', *The Contemporary Review*, 47 (1885)

Arnold, James Loring, *King Alfred in English Poetry* (Meiningen, 1898)

Arnold, Thomas, 'Introductory Lectures on Modern History, with the Inaugural Lecture', in Thomas Arnold, *History of the Later Roman Commonwealth* (London, 1849)

Ashe, Geoffrey, *The Quest for Arthur's Britain* (London, 1968)

Asser's Life of King Alfred, in Simon Keynes and Michael Lapidge, eds, *Alfred the Great: Asser's Life of King Alfred and Other Contemporary Sources* (Harmondsworth, 1983)

Attenborough, Florence G., *Alfred the Great: A Drama, The Ballad of Dundee, and Other Poems* (London, 1902)

Atwood, William, *The Superiority and Direct Domination of the Imperial Crown of England over the Crown and Kingdom of Scotland* (London, 1704)

Auerbach, Nina, *Woman and the Demon: The Life of a Victorian Myth* (Cambridge MA, 1982)

Augustine, *Soliloquies*, in Simon Keynes and Michael Lapidge, eds, *Alfred the Great: Asser's Life of King Alfred and Other Contemporary Sources* (Harmondsworth, 1983)

Austin, Alfred, *England's Darling*, 5th edn (London, 1896)

—— *The Passing of Merlin* (London, 1901)

Ayres, Philip J., *Classical Culture and the Idea of Rome in Eighteenth-Century England* (Cambridge, 1997)

Baker, George Edward, *Golden Dragon* (London, 1955)

Bale, John, *The Ymage of Bothe Churches* (London, 1550)

Ball, Nancy, *Educating the People* (London, 1983)

Barczewski, Stephanie L., *Myth and National Identity: The Legends of King Arthur and Robin Hood* (Oxford, 2000)

Baring Gould, Sabine, *Folk Songs of the West Country*, ed. by Gordon Hitchcock (Newton Abbot, 1974)

Barnes, William, 'The Rise and Progress of Trial by Jury in Britain', *Macmillan's Magazine*, 5 (1862)

Belsey, Catherine, 'Disputing Sexual Difference: Meaning and Gender in the Comedies', in John Drakakis, ed., *Alternative Shakespeares* (London, 1985)

Besant, W., 'Introduction', in A. Bowker, *Alfred the Great: Containing Chapters on his Life and Times* (London, 1899)

—— 'The Heritage of Alfred the Great', *Outlook*, 67 (1900)

—— *The Story of King Alfred* (London, 1901)

Bessinger, J.B., ed., *A Concordance to the Anglo-Saxon Poetic Records* (Ithaca, 1978)

Bevan, Tom, *A Lion of Wessex* (London, 1902)

Bicknell, Alexander, *The Life of Alfred the Great, King of the Anglo-Saxons* (London, 1777)

—— *The Patriot King: Or Alfred and Elvida. An Historical Tragedy* (London, 1788)

Billington, Rosamund, 'The Dominant Values of Victorian Feminism', Eric M. Sigsworth, *In Search of Victorian Values: Aspects of Nineteenth-Century Thought and Society* (Manchester, 1988)

Blackburn, John W. Vernon, 'Alfred: A Prize Poem' (n.p., 1853)

Blackie, John Stuart, 'Alfred', in John Stuart Blackie, *A Song of Heroes* (Edinburgh, 1890)

Blackmore, Sir Richard, *Alfred: An Epick Poem. In Twelve Books* (London, 1723)

Boethius, *Consolation of Philosophy*, in Simon Keynes and Michael Lapidge, eds, *Alfred the Great: Asser's Life of King Alfred and Other Contemporary Sources* (Harmondsworth, 1983)

Bogan, 'Where is Alfred Buried?', *Winchester Cathedral Record* 55 (1986)

Boger, C.G., 'Alfred, King in Somerset', *The Antiquarian Magazine and Bibliographer*, 7 (n.d.)

Bolingbroke, Henry, *Letters on the Spirit of Patriotism, On the Idea of a Patriot King, And on the State of Parties* (London, 1749)

Book of Hyde, in Joseph Stevenson, ed., *The Church Historians of England* (London, 1853–55), II:i

Bosworth, G.F., *Alfred the Great: A Paper Read to the Hull Literary Club* (Hull, 1903)

Bowker, A., ed., *Alfred the Great: Containing Chapters on his Life and Times* (London, 1899)

—— *The King Alfred Millenary: A Record of the National Commemoration* (London, 1902)

Brantlinger, Patrick, 1990. 'How Oliver Twist Learned to Read and What he Read', in Patrick Scott, and Pauline Fletcher, *Culture and Education in Victorian England* (Lewisburg, 1990)

—— *Rule of Darkness: British Literature and Imperialism, 1830–1914* (Ithaca, 1998)

Brewer, Derek, ed., *Chaucer: The Critical Heritage* (London, 1978)

Briggs, Asa, 'Victorian Values', in Eric M. Sigsworth, *Aspects of Nineteenth-Century Thought and Society* (Manchester, 1988)

Brontë, Charlotte, *Jane Eyre* (Oxford, 2000 [1847])

—— *Villette* (London, 2004 [1853])

Brooks, Ron, *King Alfred School and the Progressive Movement, 1898–1998* (Cardiff, 1998)

Brough, Robert Barnabas, *Alfred the Great: Or, The Minstrel King. An Historical Extravaganza* (London, 1860)

Browne, George Forrest, *King Alfred's Books* (London, 1920)

Bryce, J., 'Alfred the Great', *Independent*, 53 (1901)

Bryden, Inga, *Reinventing King Arthur: The Arthurian Legends in Victorian Culture* (Aldershot, 2005)

Buchanan, Robert Williams, 'A Song of Jubilee', in Robert Williams Buchanan, *The Complete Poetical Works* (London, 1901)

Bulwer-Lytton, Edward, *King Arthur* (London, 1849)

Burges, J.B., *Alfred's Address to the Ladies of England* (London, 1803)

Byerly, Alison, 'From Schoolroom to Stage: Reading Aloud and the Domestication of Victorian Theatre', in Patrick Scott, and Pauline Fletcher, *Culture and Education in Victorian England* (Lewisburg, 1990)

Calder, Jenni, *Women and Marriage in Victorian Fiction* (London, 1976)

Camden, William, *Anglica, Hibernica, Normannica, Cambrica* (Frankfurt, 1603)

— *Remaines of a Greater Worke: Concerning Britaine, the Inhabitants Thereof, their Languages, Names, Surnames, Empresses, Wise Speeches, Poemes, and Epitaphes* (London, 1605)

— *Britannia, Newly Translated into English with Large Editions and Improvements* (Oxford, 1695 [1586])

Campbell, Thomas, 'Ye Mariners of England', in Chris Brooks and Peter Faulkner, eds, *The White Man's Burden: An Anthology of British Poetry of the Empire* (Exeter, 1996)

Cannadine, David, 'The Context, Performance and Meaning of Ritual: The British Monarchy and the "Invention of Tradition", c. 1820–1977', in Eric Hobsbawm and Terence Ranger, eds, *The Invention of Tradition* (Cambridge, 1983)

Canning, Stratford, *Alfred the Great in Athelnay. An Historical Play* (London, 1876)

Carlyle, Thomas, *On Heroes and Hero Worship and the Heroic in History* (London, 1840)

— *Past and Present* (London, 1843)

Carnarvon, Henry, [Untitled], *Fortnightly Review*, 24 (1878)

Cartwright, John, *The Legislative Rights of the Commonality Vindicated: Or Take Your Choice!* (London, 1777)

— *Take your Choice! Representation and Respect, Imposition and Contempt, Annual Parliaments and Liberty, Long Parliaments and Slavery* (London, 1777)

— *The English Constitution Produced and Illustrated* (London, 1823)

'Celticism, a Myth', *Saturday Review*, 68 (1889)

Champneys, William Weldon, *Alfred the Great* (London, 1852)

Chandler, Alice, *A Dream of Order: The Medieval Ideal in Nineteenth-Century English Literature* (Lincoln NB, 1979)

Chatterton, Thomas, *The Complete Works of Thomas Chatterton: A Bicentenary Edition*, ed. by Donald S. Taylor (Oxford, 1971)

Chesterton, G.K., *The Ballad of the White Horse* (Oxford, 2004 [1911])

Christ, Carol, 'Victorian Masculinity and the Angel in the House', in Martha Vicinus, ed., *A Widening Sphere* (London, 1977)

The Chronicle of Æthelweard, in Joseph Stevenson, ed., *The Church Historians of England* (London, 1853–55)

The Chronicle of Fabius Ethelwerd, in Joseph Stevenson, ed., *The Church Historians of England* (London, 1853–55), II:i

The Chronicle of John Wallingford, in Joseph Stevenson, ed., *The Church Historians of England* (London, 1853–55), II:i

The Chronicle of Pierre de Langtoft, ed. by Thomas Wright (London, 1866)

Clarke, John, *Alfred the Great: London's Forgotten King* (London, 1999)

Cobbett, William, *Selections from Cobbett's Political Works*, ed. by John M. Cobbett and James P. Cobbett (London, 1835)

Cockshut, A.O.J., *The Unbelievers: English Agnostic Thought, 1840–1890* (London, 1964)

Cohen, Richard, *By the Sword* (London, Macmillan, 2002)

Colley, Linda, *Britons: Forging the Nation, 1707–1837* (New Haven, 1992)

Collingwood, George Lewes Newnham, *Alfred the Great: A Poem* (London, 1836)

Conybeare, C.A. Vansittart, *The Place of Iceland in the History of European Institutions* (Oxford, 1877)

Coombe, Elizabeth Jane, *In the Days of King Alfred* (London, 1948)

Corner, Julia, *The Life and Times of Alfred the Great: An Interesting Narrative in Easy Language for Young Children* (London, 1850)

Cornwell, Bernard, *The Last Kingdom* (London, 2005)

Cottle, Joseph, *Alfred: An Epic Poem, in Twenty-Four Books* (London, 1800)

—— *Science Revived: Or, The Vision of Alfred* (London, 1802)

Cox, George W., 'The Origin of the English', *The Fortnightly Review*, 6 (1866)

Craik, Dinah Maria, *A Brave Lady* (London, 1870)

Creasy, E.S., 'Alfred the Great', *Bentley's Miscellany*, 32 (1852)

Creswick, Paul, *In Ælfred's Days* (London, 1900)

—— *Under the Black Raven* (London, 1901)

Cross, Nigel, *The Common Writer: Life in Nineteenth-Century Grub Street* (Cambridge, 1985)

Cunningham, George Godfrey, *Lives of Eminent and Illustrious Englishmen from Alfred the Great to the Latest Times* (Glasgow, 1834).

Curtis, L.P. Jr, *Anglo-Saxons and Celts: A Study of Anti-Irish Prejudice in Victorian England* (New York, 1968)

Daniel, Samuel, *A Panegyrike with a Defence of Ryme* (London, 1603)

Davies, J.A., *Education in a Welsh Rural Community, 1870–1873* (Cardiff, 1973)

Davies, Robertson, *The Mirror of Nature* (Toronto, 1983)

Dellheim, Charles, *The Face of the Past: The Preservation of the Medieval Inheritance in Victorian England* (Cambridge, 1982)

Dibdin, Thomas John, 'Alfred the Great', in Anon., *A Metrical History of England* (London, 1813), vol. I

Dickens, Charles, *The Adventures of Oliver Twist* (Oxford, 1966 [1837])

—— *A Child's History of England* (London, 1852)

Digby, Kenelm Henry, *The Broad Stone of Honour: Or, the True Sense and Practice of Chivalry* (London, 1822)

Doel, Geoff, *Worlds of King Arthur* (London, 1998)

Dollimore, Jonathan, 'Shakespeare, Cultural Materialism and the New Historicism', in Richard Wilson and Richard Dutton, eds, *New Historicism and Renaissance Drama* (London, 1992)

Donne, W.B., 'The Saxons in England', *The Edinburgh Review*, 89 (1849)

Draper, Warwick H., 'Alfred the Great as a Man of Letters', *The Antiquary*, 36 (n.d.)

— 'Legislation and Local Government of Alfred the Great', *Green Bag*, 11 (n.d.)

— *Alfred the Great: A Sketch and Seven Studies*, 2nd edn (London, 1901)

Dusinberre, Juliet, *Shakespeare and the Nature of Women* (London, 1975)

Dyer, George, 'Alfred', in Anon., *Poems* (London, 1802), vol. II

Earle, John, 'Alfred as a Writer', in A. Bowker *Alfred the Great: Containing Chapters on his Life and Times* (London, 1899)

Eayrs, George, *Alfred to Victoria: Hands Across a Thousand Years* (London, 1902)

Egerton, Francis, *Alfred: A Drama, in One Act* (London, 1840)

Eldridge, C.C., *England's Mission: The Imperial Idea in the Age of Gladstone and Disraeli* (London, 1973)

Eliot, George, *Middlemarch* (Edinburgh, 1871)

— *Scenes of Clerical Life* (Oxford, 1985 [1857])

Elley, D., *The Epic Film: Myth and History* (London, 1983)

Ellis, Sarah Stickney, *The Mothers of England: Their Influence and Responsibility* (London, 1843)

— *The Mothers of Great Men* (London, 1859 [1843])

Elrington, Clement C., 'Alfred the Great: A Poem Addressed to the Youth of Australia' (Carthage, 1853)

Elstob, Elizabeth, *The Rudiments of Grammar for the English-Saxon Tongue* (London, 1715)

Engelbach, A.H., 'The English in India', *Bentley's Miscellany*, 42 (1857)

— *The Danes in England: A Tale of the Days of King Alfred* (London, 1878)

Evans, Dominic, ' "Save the Pound", Tory Chief Pleads', *The Ottawa Citizen*, 7 June 2001

Evans, Eric, 'Englishness and Britishness: National Identities, c. 1790–1870', in Alexander Grant and Keith J. Stringer, eds, *Uniting the Kingdom? The Making of British History* (London, 1995)

Faas, Ekbert, *Retreat into the Mind: Victorian Poetry and the Rise of Psychiatry* (Princeton, 1988)

Fairholt, Frederick William, *Costume in England: A History of Dress from the Earliest Period till the Close of the Eighteenth Century* (London, 1846)

Farnol, Jeffery, *The King Liveth* (London, 1943)

Fell, Christine E., 'The First Publication of Old Norse Literature in England and its Relation to its Sources', in Else Roesdahl and Preben Meulengracht Sørenson, eds, *The Waking of Angantyr: The Scandinavian Past in European Culture* (Aarhus, 1946)

Fenn, G. Manville, *The King's Sons* (London, 1902)

Fenton, Richard, *A Tour in Quest of Genealogy, through Several Parts of Wales, Somersetshire and Wiltshire in a Series of Letters to a Friend in Dublin* (London, 1811)

Fieldhouse, Roger, *A History of Adult Education* (Leicester, 1996)

Fisher, T., *Alfred the Great: A Drama* (London, 1901)

Fitchett, John, *King Alfred: A Poem*, ed. by Robert Roscoe, 6 vols (London, 1842)

'Fitchett's *King Alfred*', *North British Review*, 2 (1844)

Fleming, Robin, 'Picturesque History and the Medieval in Nineteenth-Century America', *American Historical Review*, 100 (1995)

Flowers of History, in Joseph Stevenson, *The Church Historians of England* (London, 1853–55)

Foxe, John, *Acts and Monuments of the Christian Church* (Manchester, 1873 [1570])

Frantzen, Allen J., *King Alfred* (Boston, 1986)

—— *The Desire for Origins: New Language, Old English, and Teaching the Tradition* (New Brunswick, 1990)

Frantzen, Allen J. and Niles, John D., *Anglo-Saxonism and the Construction of Social Identity* (Gainesville, 1997)

Fraser, W.R., *Residential Education* (Oxford, 1968)

Freeman, Edward A., *History of the Norman Conquest* (Oxford, 1867)

Freeman, Edward A., *Old English History*, 2nd edn (London, 1871)

Freeman, Kathleen, *Alfred the Great* (Edinburgh, 1958)

Froude, J.A., 'King Alfred', *Fraser's Magazine for Town and Country*, 45 (1852)

Fry, Donald K., *Norse Sagas Translated into English: A Bibliography* (New York, 1980)

Frye, Herman Northrop, *Fables of Identity: Studies in Poetic Mythology* (New York, 1963)

Fuller, Anne, *The Son of Ethelwolf* (London, 1789)

Gale, Thomas, *Historiae Anglicanae scriptores* (Oxford, 1691)

Garnett, Richard, 'English Dialects', *The Quarterly Review*, 55 (1836)

Gat, Azar, *The Development of Military Thought: The Nineteenth Century* (Oxford, 1992)

Gibbon, Edward, *The History of the Decline and Fall of the Roman Empire* (London, 1776–88)

Gibson, Charles, 'Some Characteristics of the Normans', *Catholic World*, 65 (1897)

Giles, J.A., *The Life and Times of Alfred the Great* (London, 1848)

—— ed., *The Whole Works of King Alfred the Great: With Preliminary Essays Illustrative of the History, Arts, Manners, of the Ninth Century* (Oxford and Cambridge, 1852)

Giles, J.A., ed., *Six Old English Chronicles* (London, 1878)

Gill, Thomas H., 'Alfred the Great', in Anon., *The Anniversaries* (London, 1858)

Gilliat, E., *God Save King Alfred* (London, 1901)

Gillis, John R., *For Better, For Worse: British Marriages, 1600 to the Present* (Oxford, 1985)

Gilmour, Robin, *The Victorian Period: The Intellectual and Cultural Context of English Literature, 1830–1890* (New York, 1993)

Glass, Sandra A., 'The Saxonists' Influence on Seventeenth-Century English Literature', in Carl T. Berkhout and Milton McGatch, eds, *Anglo-Saxon Scholarship* (Boston, 1982)

Gordon, Helen C., 'King Alfred's Great Legacy', *The English Illustrated Magazine*, 25 (July 1901)

Gorham, George Cornelius, *The History and Antiquities of Eynesbury and St. Neot's in the County of Cornwall* (London, 1820)

Graham, Maria, *Little Arthur's History of England* (London, 1835)

Greg, Percy, 'The Future of the Peerage', *The Fortnightly Review*, 42 (1884)

Green, J.R., *A Short History of the English People* (London, 1874)

Greswell, W., 'County of Alfred the Great', *Fortnightly Review*, 72 (1899)

Griffiths, Ralph A. and Roger S. Thomas, *The Making of the Tudor Dynasty* (Gloucester, 1985)

Groom, Nick, *The Union Jack: The Story of the British Flag* (London, 2006)

Guinness, Jonathan, *The House of Mitford* (London, 2005)

Gustafson, Ralph Barker, *Alfred the Great* (London, 1937)

Hagedorn, Suzanne, 'Received Wisdom: The Reception History of Alfred's Preface to the Pastoral Care', in Allen Frantzen and John D. Niles, *Anglo-Saxonism and the Construction of Social Identity* (Gainesville, 1977)

Hall, Donald E., *Muscular Christianity: Embodying the Victorian Age* (Cambridge, 1994)

Hamilton, Sarah, *Alfred the Great: A Drama* (London, 1829)

Hardman, Frederick, 'French Conquerors and Colonists', *Blackwood's Magazine*, 65 (1849)

Harris, Richard L., *A Chorus of Grammars: The Correspondence of George Hickes and his Collaborators on the Thesaurus Linguarum Septentrionalium* (Toronto, 1992)

Harris, S., *Alfred the Great: A Paper Read to the Hull Literary Club, 9th March 1903* (Hull, 1903)

Harrison, Frederic, 'The Monarchy', *The Fortnightly Review*, 66 (1872)

—— 'Alfred as King', in A. Bowker, ed., *Alfred the Great: Containing Chapters on his Life and Times* (London, 1899)

Hayward, Abraham, 'Young England', *The Edinburgh Review*, 80 (1844)

Heighway, O.W.T., 'A Few Words Upon Beards', *Tait's Edinburgh Magazine*, 19 (1852)

Henty, G.A., *The Dragon and the Raven: Or, The Days of King Alfred* (London, 1886)

Herbert, H.H.M., 'Lessons of the French Revolution', *The Quarterly Review*, 135 (1873)

Hervey, E.L., 'Alfred the Great Teaching the Anglo-Saxon Youth', *Illustrated London News*, 30 June 1885

Heygate, Frederick William, 'An Elected Peerage', *The National Review*, 5 (1885)

Hibbert, Christopher, *Queen Victoria: A Personal History* (London, 2000)

Higden, R., *The Polychronicon*, ed. by J.R. Lumby (London, 1876)

Hill, Edmund, L., *Alfred the Great: A Drama* (London, 1901)

Hill, Frank H., 'The Future of the English Monarchy', *The Contemporary Review*, 57 (1890)

History of Ingulf, in Joseph Stevenson, ed., *The Church Historians of England* (London, 1853–55), II:i

History of Saint Cuthbert, in Joseph Stevenson, ed., *The Church Historians of England* (London, 1853–55)

Hoak, Dale, 'The Iconography of the Crown Imperial', in Dale Hoak, ed., *Tudor Political Culture* (Cambridge, 1995)

Hodges, C. Walter, *The Marsh King* (London, 1964)

Holdsworth, W.S., *A History of English Law* (London, 1903)

Holmes, Robert, *Alfred: An Ode, with Six Sonnets* (Oxford, 1778)

Home, John, *Alfred: A Tragedy* (London, 1778)

Hudson, Derek *Martin Tupper: His Rise and Fall* (London, 1949)

Hughes, Thomas, *Alfred the Great: A Biography*, 2nd edn (London, 1874)

—— *Tom Brown's Schooldays* (London, 1993 [1857])

Hulme, Obadiah, *An Historical Essay on the English Constitution: Or, An Impartial Inquiry into the Elective Power of the People, from the first Establishment of the Saxons in this Kingdom* (London, 1771)

Hume, David, *The History of England from the Invasion of Julius Cæsar to the Accession of Henry VII* (London, 1762)

Hunt, Frederick Knight, *The Book of Art: Cartoons, Frescoes, Sculptures and Decorative Art, as Applied to the New Houses of Parliament and to Buildings in General* (London, 1846)

Hutton, E.M., *The Grand Tour in Italy in the Sixteenth, Seventeenth and Eighteenth Centuries* (Cambridge, 1937)

Iliff, Jay, and Rees, Alun, 'The heat is on to find the king who burnt the cakes', the *Express*, 20 July 1999

Imrie, *Alfred the Great, and Other Poems* (Toronto, 1902)

In Commemoration of the Millenary Anniversary of the Death of King Alfred the Great, November 12, 1901 (Portland, 1901)

Jackson, R.C., 'The Alfred Medal of 1901', *The Westminster Review*, 156 (1901)

Jackson-Houlston, C.M., *Ballads, Songs and Snatches: The Appropriation of Folk Song and Popular Culture in British Nineteenth-Century Realist Prose* (Aldershot, 1999)

James, G.P.R., *Forest Days* (London, 1843)

Jamieson, John, *An Etymological Dictionary of the Scots Language* (Edinburgh, 1808)

Jeffers, Robinson, 'Ghosts in England', in Robinson Jeffers, *The Collected Poetry of Robinson Jeffers* (Stanford, 1989)

'J.F.R.', *Lives of Alfred the Great, Sir Thomas More, and John Evelyn* (London, 1845)

Jones, Richard Foster, *The Triumph of the English Language* (Stanford, 1952)

Jones, Robert W., *Gender and the Formation of Taste in Eighteenth-Century Britain* (Cambridge, 1998)

Jones, Vivien, *Women in the Eighteenth Century* (London, 1990)

Kelsey, Richard, *Alfred of Wessex: A Poem*, 3 vols (Battle, 1852)

Kemble, John Mitchell, 'Anglo-Saxon Laws and Institutes: Incunabula Juris Anglicani', *The British and Foreign Review*, 12 (1841)

—— *The Saxons in England: A History of the English Commonwealth till the Period of the Norman Conquest* (London, 1849)

Ker, N.R., *Catalogue of Manuscripts Containing Anglo-Saxon* (Oxford, 1957)

Kerr, Eliza, *Two Saxon Maidens. Gytha: A Story of the Time of Baeda. Elgiva: A Story of the Time of Alfred the Great* (London, 1885)

Kershner, R.B., *The Twentieth-Century Novel: An Introduction* (Boston, 1997)

Keynes, Simon, 'The Cult of King Alfred the Great', *Anglo-Saxon England*, 28 (2000)

Keynes, Simon and Lapidge, Michael, eds, *Alfred the Great: Asser's Life of King Alfred and Other Contemporary Sources* (Harmondsworth, 1983)

Kidd, Alan J., *City, Class and Culture* (Manchester, 1985)

Kidd, Colin, *Subverting Scotland's Past: Scottish Whig Historians and the Creation of an Anglo-British Identity, 1689–1830* (Cambridge, 1993)

'King Alfred: A Comic Opera. In One Act and Two Scenes', *Harper's New Monthly Magazine*, 66 (March 1883)

King Alfred's Version of Boethius' De consolatione philosophiae, ed. by J.S. Cardale (London, 1829)

King Alfred's West Saxon Version of Gregory's Pastoral Care, ed. by H. Sweet (London, 1871)

Kingsley, Charles, *Hereward the Wake, the Last of the English* (Boston, 1866)

Kneeland, S., 'The Vikings and What We Owe to Them', *Open Court*, 1 (n.d.)

Knight, Richard Payne, *Alfred: A Romance in Rhyme* (London, 1823)

Knight, Stephen, *Robin Hood: A Complete Study of the English Outlaw* (Oxford, 1994)

Knight, William, *The Philosophy of the Beautiful* (London, 1899)

Knowles, James Sheridan, *Alfred the Great: Or, the Patriot King* (London, 1831)

Kramnick, Isaac, *Bolingbroke and his Circle: The Politics of Nostalgia in the Age of Walpole* (Ithaca, 1992)

Lacqueur, Thomas W., *Solitary Sex: A Cultural History of Masturbation* (New York, 2004)

Laing, Robert, 'The Transition from Medieval to Modern Politics', *The Quarterly Review*, 138 (1875)

Lang, Andrew, 'The Latest Theories on the Origin of the English', *The Contemporary Review*, 57 (1890)
—— 'The Celtic Renascence', *Blackwood's Magazine*, 161 (1897)
—— 'A New History of Scotland', *Blackwood's Magazine*, 165 (1899)
Langenfelt, Per Gosta Lars Magnus, *Historic Origins of the Eight Hour Day* (Stockholm, 1954)
Lavater, J.C., *Essays on Physiognomy: For the Promotion of the Knowledge and the Love of Mankind* (London, 1875 [1789])
The *Laws of King Alfred*, in Simon Keynes and Michael Lapidge, eds, *Alfred the Great: Asser's Life of King Alfred and Other Contemporary Sources* (Harmondsworth, 1983)
Lee, Sidney, *Dictionary of National Biography*, vol. 47, p. 68
Leland, John, *The Itinerary of John Leland*, ed. by Lucy Toulmin Smith (London, 1908)
Lewis, G.C., 'The Celts and the Germans', *The Edinburgh Review*, 108 (1858)
Lilly, W.S., 'British Monarchy and Modern Democracy', *Nineteenth Century*, 41 (1897)
Lindsay, Bart Coutts, *Alfred: A Drama* (London, 1845)
Lingard, John, 'The Ancient Church of England and the Liturgy of the Anglican Church', *The Dublin Review*, 11 (1841)
Linton, William James, 'King Alfred', in *Poems* (London, 1865)
Life of Saint Neot, ed. by Simon Keynes and Michael Lapidge, in *Alfred the Great: Asser's Life of King Alfred and Other Contemporary Sources* (Harmondsworth, 1983)
Lives of Eminent and Illustrious Englishmen, from Alfred the Great to the Latest Times, ed. by G.C. Cunningham (Glasgow, 1834)
The London Hermit's Tour to the York Festival (London, 1826)
Lonsdale, M., *Sketch of Alfred the Great: Or, The Danish Invasion: A Grand Historical Ballet* (London, 1865)
Lorimer, James, 'King Alfred', *The North British Review*, 17 (1852)
Lyell, Charles Bart, *Principles of Geology* (London, 1830)
Macalpine, Ida and Richard Ian Hunter, *George III and the Mad-Business* (London, 1969)
MacDougall, Hugh, *Racial Myth in English History: Trojans, Teutons, and Anglo-Saxons* (Montreal, 1982)
Macfarlane, Alan, *Marriage and Love in England* (Oxford, 1986)
McIlroy, Arthur, 'Alfred the Great and One Thousand Years of English', *National Magazine*, 15 (1896)
Mackay, Charles, 'The Hair and Beard, as Fashioned by Politics and Religion at Various Periods', *Bentley's Miscellany*, 7 (1840)
—— 'King Alfred', in Charles Mackay, *The Collected Songs* (London, 1859)
Mackenzie, J.B., 'Alfred the Great', in J.B. Mackenzie, *Alfred the Great and Other Poems* (Toronto, 1902)
Mackenzie, John M., 'Empire and Metropolitan Cultures', in Nicholas Canny, ed., *The Oxford History of the British Empire* (Oxford, 1999)

McLaurin, Allen, 'Reworking "work" in some Victorian writing and visual art', in Eric M. Sigsworth, *In Search of Victorian Values: Aspects of Nineteenth-Century Thought and Society* (Manchester, 1988)

Macpherson, James, *The Poems of Ossian and Related Works*, ed. by Howard Gaskill (Edinburgh, 1996 [1805])

Macpherson, William, 'Scottish Character', *The Quarterly Review*, 110 (1861)

Magnus, James, *Woloski: A Tragedy; Alfred the Great: A Play; And Poems* (London, 1838)

Magnus, Katie, *First Makers of England: Julius Caesar, King Arthur, Alfred the Great* (London, 1901)

Mallet, David and Thomson, James, *Alfred: A Masque* (London, 1740)

Manners, John, *A Plea for National Holy-Days* (London, 1843)

Manning, Anne, *The Chronicle of Ethelfled* (London, 1861)

Manning, Owen, *The Will of King Alfred* (Oxford, 1778)

Mansfield, Horatio, 'The Biographical Mania', *Tait's Edinburgh Magazine*, 25 (1854)

Mapp, Alfred J., *The Golden Dragon* (La Salle, 1975)

Markham, Clements, 'Alfred as a Geographer', in A. Bowker, *The King Alfred Millenary: A Record of the National Commemoration* (London, 1902)

Marshall, Dorothy, *Eighteenth-Century England* (London, 1962)

Marvin, F.S., *Alfred the Great: His Life and Times* (London, 1901)

Masson, David, 'The Union with England and Scottish Nationality', *The North British Review*, 21 (1854)

Matthews, Tom, *Harlequin Alfred the Great! Or, the Magic Banjo and the Mystic Raven* (London, 1850)

Maxwell-Scott, Mary Monica, *Alfred the Great* (London, 1902)

Mellor, J., *The Curious Particulars Relating to King Alfred's Death and Burial, Never Before Made Public* (Canterbury, 1871)

Melman, Billie, 'Claiming the Nation's Past: The Invention of an Anglo-Saxon Tradition', *Journal of Contemporary History*, 26 (1991)

Midwinter, E.C., *Victorian Social Reform* (London, 1968)

—— *Nineteenth-Century Education* (London, 1971)

Miles, Louis Wardlaw, *King Alfred in Literature* (Baltimore, 1902)

Mill, John Stuart, 'Principles of Political Economy', *The Edinburgh Review*, 91 (1850)

Millett, Kate, 'The Debate over Women: Ruskin vs. Mill', in Martha Vicinus, ed., *Suffer and be Still: Women in the Victorian Age* (Bloomington, 1972)

Milner, J., *The History, Civil and Ecclesiastical, and Survey of the Antiquities of Winchester*, 2nd edn, 2 vols (Winchester, 1809)

The Mirror of Justices, ed. by W.J. Whittaker (London, 1895)

Misra, Udayon, *The Raj in Fiction: A Study of Nineteenth-Century British Attitudes Towards India* (Delhi, 1987)

Mitchell, Rosemary, *Picturing the Past: English History in Text and Image 1830–1870* (Oxford, 2000)

Mitford, Nancy, *The Pursuit of Love* (London, 1945)

Mitford, Sybil C., 'The Palace of King Alfred', *The English Illustrated Magazine*, 25 (July 1901)

Monkhouse, Alan Noble, *Alfred the Great* (London, 1927)

Morris, Kevin L., *The Image of the Middle Ages in Romantic and Victorian Literature* (London, 1984)

Myers, Ernest James, 'Alfred the Great', *Cornhill Magazine*, 84 (1901)

Nead, Lynda, *Myths of Sexuality: Representations of Women in Victorian Britain* (Oxford, 1988)

Nelson, Janet L., 'Myths of the Dark Ages', in Lesley M. Smith, *The Making of Britain: The Dark Ages* (Basingstoke, 1984).

—— ed., *The Annals of St. Bertin* (Manchester, 1991)

Nicol, Henry, 'English Philology', *The Westminster Review*, 98 (1872)

Norman, Edward, *Anti-Catholicism in Victorian Britain* (London, 1968)

O'Keeffe, John, *Alfred: Or the Magic Banner* (London, 1796)

The Old English Orosius, ed. by Janet Bately (London, 1980)

Oldfield, T.H.B., The *Representative History of Great Britain and Ireland* (London, 1816)

Oliphant, Margaret, 'Scottish National Character', *Blackwood's Magazine*, 87 (1860)

Oman, Charles, 'Alfred as Warrior', in A. Bowker, *The King Alfred Millenary: A Record of the National Commemoration* (London, 1902)

—— *England Before the Conquest* (London, 1910)

Oxford Dictionary of National Biography (London, 2005)

Page, Jesse, *Alfred the Great: The Father of the English* (London, 1900)

Palgrave, Francis, *History of England* (London, 1831)

—— 'The Conquest and the Conqueror', *The Quarterly Review*, 74 (1844)

—— *The History of Normandy and of England* (London, 1864)

Palgrave, Francis Turner, 'Alfred the Great', in *The Visions of England* (London, 1891)

Parker, James, *The Early History of Oxford* (Oxford, 1885)

Parker, Matthew, *Aelfredi regis res gestae* (London, 1574)

Paris, Matthew, *Chronica Majora*, ed. by Nigel Wilkins (Stroud, 1984)

Pauli, Reinhold, *The Life of Alfred the Great*, trans. by B. Thorpe (London, 1857)

Paxman, Jeremy, *The English: A Portrait of a People* (London, 1998)

Peach, Lawrence du Garde, *King Alfred the Great* (Loughborough, 1956)

Peck, John, *War, the Army and Victorian Literature* (Basingstoke, 1998)

Penn, John, *The Battle of Eddington, or, British Liberty: A Tragedy* (London, 1792)

Pennie, J.F., *Britain's Historical Drama: A Series of National Tragedies* (London, 1832)

Percy, Thomas, *Reliques of Ancient English Poetry: Consisting of Old Heroic Ballads, Songs and other Pieces of our Earliest Poets* (London, 1765)

Percy, Thomas, ed., *Northern Antiquities: Or, a Description of the Manners, Customs, Religion and Laws of the Ancient Danes, and other Northern Nations* (London, 1770)

Perkin, Joan, *Women and Marriage in Nineteenth-Century England* (London, 1989)

Peterson, Linda H., 'Harriet Martineau's *Household Education*: Revising the Feminist Tradition', in Patrick Scott and Pauline Fletcher, *Culture and Education in Victorian England* (Lewisburg, 1990)

Petrie, Flanders, *Monumenta Historica Britannica: or, Materials for the History of Britain* (London, 1848)

Pevsner, Nikolaus, *The Buildings of England: Berkshire* (Harmondsworth, 1966)

The Pictorial History of England (London, 1837)

Pilbeam, Pamela M., *The Middle Classes in Europe, 1789–1914* (London, 1990)

Pinder, W.H., *Alfred the Great: A Chronicle Play* (London, 1902)

Plummer, Charles, *The Life and Times of Alfred the Great: Being the Ford Lectures for 1901* (Oxford, 1902)

Pocock, Isaac, *Alfred the Great: Or, the Enchanted Standard. A Musical Drama* (London, 1827)

Pollard, Eliza F., *A Hero King* (London, 1896)

Pollock, Frederick, 'Alfred the Great', *The National Review*, 33 (1899)

Pollock, Frederick and Maitland, Frederic, *History of English Law before the Time of Edward I* (Cambridge, 1895)

Pope Gregory, *Pastoral Care*, in Simon Keynes and Michael Lapidge, eds, *Alfred the Great: Asser's Life of King Alfred and Other Contemporary Sources* (Harmondsworth, 1983)

Potter, Andrew, 'Religion, Missionary Enthusiasm, and Empire', in *The Oxford History of the British Empire*, Nicholas Canny, ed. (Oxford, 1999)

Powell, Robert, *The Life of Alfred or Alvred. the First Institutor of Subordinate Government in this Kingdome, and Refounder of the University of Oxford. Together with a Parallell of our Soveraigne Lord, King Charles, untill this Yeare, 1634* (London, 1634)

Praed, Winthrop Mackworth, 'King Alfred's Book', in Winthrop Mackworth Praed, *Political and Occasional Poems* (London, 1888)

Pratt, Lynda, 'Anglo-Saxon Attitudes?: Alfred the Great and the Romantic National Epic', in Donald Scragg and Carole Weinberg, *Literary Appropriations of the Anglo-Saxons* (Cambridge, 2000)

Praz, Mario, *The Hero in Eclipse in Victorian Fiction* (Oxford, 1956)

Prest, John, *Liberty and Locality. Parliament, Permissive Legislation and Ratepayers' Democracies in the Nineteenth Century* (Oxford, 1990)

Psalter, in Simon Keynes and Michael Lapidge, eds, *Alfred the Great: Asser's Life of King Alfred and Other Contemporary Sources* (Harmondsworth, 1983)

Pye, Henry James, *Alfred: An Epic Poem* (London, 1815 [1801])

Quinn, Judy and Ross, Margaret Clunies, 'The Image of Old Norse Poetry and Myth in Seventeenth-Century England', in A. Wawn, ed., *Northern Antiquity: The Post-Medieval Reception of Edda and Saga* (Hisarlik, 1994)

Rance, Nicholas, *The Historical Novel and Popular Politics in Nineteenth-Century England* (London, 1975)

Rapin, Paul, *The History of England*, trans. by John Kelley (London, 1732)

Rawnsley, H.D., 'The Millenary of Alfred the King', in H.D. Rawnsley, *A Sonnet Chronicle* (Glasgow, 1906)

Redlich, Josef and Hirst, Francis Wrigley, *The History of Local Government in England* (London, 1970)

Reed, John R., *Victorian Conventions* (Athens, Greece, 1975)

Reed, Walter L., *Meditations on the Hero* (New Haven, 1974)

Reiman, Donald H., ed., 'Introduction', in Henry James Pye, *Alfred: An Epic Poem* (London, 1979)

—— 'The Republicanism of Young England', *The Contemporary Review*, 5 (1867)

Rhodes, Ebenezer, *Alfred: An Historical Tragedy* (Sheffield, 1789)

Robinson, 'The Preservation of the Monarchy and Empire', *Fraser's Magazine*, 12 (1835)

Roger of Wendover's Flowers of History, ed. by J.A. Giles (London, 1849)

Rogers, Henry, 'History of the English Language', *The Edinburgh Review*, 92 (1850)

Roscoe, Thomas, *Summer Tour to the Isle of Wight* (London, 1843)

Rose, Michael E., 'The Disappearing Pauper: Victorian Attitudes to the Relief of the Poor', in Eric M. Sigsworth, *In Search of Victorian Values: Aspects of Nineteenth-Century Thought and Society* (Manchester, 1988)

Ross, Stewart, *Find King Alfred* (London, 1998)

Round, John Horace, *Feudal England* (London, 1895)

Ruskin, John, 'The Pleasure of Learning: Bertha to Osburgha', in John Ruskin, *The Pleasures of England* (Orpington, 1884)

—— *Sesame and Lillies* (London, 1907 [1865])

—— 'Letter to Henry Ackland', in E.T. Cook and A. Wedderburn, *The Works of Ruskin*, 39 vols (London, 1909), vol. 36

Russell, John, *The Causes of the French Revolution* (London, 1832)

Sambrook, James, *The Eighteenth Century: The Intellectual and Cultural Context of English Literature, 1700–1789* (London, 1986)

—— *James Thomson, 1700–1748. A Life* (London, 1991)

San, Oba, *Alfred the Great: A Drawing Room Play for Children* (Ipswich, 1898)

Sanderson, Michael, *Education, Economic Change and Society in England: 1780–1870* (London, 1983)

Savage, Albert R., 'The Anglo-Saxon Constitution and Laws in the Time of Alfred the Great', in Anon., *In Commemoration of the Millenary Anniversary of the Death of King Alfred the Great* (Portland, 1901)

'Saxon, Alfred' [pseud.], 'My First Campaign', *Ainsworth's Magazine*, 25 (1854)

Science Revived: Or, The Vision of Alfred (London, 1802)

'Scotch Nationality', *The North British Review*, 6 (1846)

Scott, Patrick and Fletcher, Pauline, *Culture and Education in Victorian England* (Lewisburg, 1990)

Scott, Walter, *Ivanhoe: A Romance* (London, 1906 [1819])

Scragg, Donald and Weinberg, Carole, *Literary Appropriations of the Anglo-Saxons from the Thirteenth to the Twentieth Century* (Cambridge, 2000)

Sellar, W.C. and Yeatman, R.J., *1066 And All That: A Memorable History of England* (London, 2005)

Shakespeare, William, *King Lear*, ed. by Kenneth Muir (London, 1972 [1605])

'Shall we Overturn the Peers?', *Blackwood's Edinburgh Magazine*, 38 (1835), 573–586

'The Shepherd and the King, and of Gillian the Shepherd's Wife, with her Churlish Answers: Being Full of Mirth and Merry Pastime', in *The Roxburgh Ballads* (London, 1578), vol. I: II

Shippey, T.A., *Beowulf* (London, 1978)

—— 'The Undeveloped Image: Anglo-Saxon in Popular Consciousness from Turner to Tolkien', Donald Scragg and Carole Weinberg, *Literary Appropriations of the Anglo-Saxons from the Thirteenth to the Twentieth Century* (Cambridge, 2000)

Sigsworth, Eric M., *In Search of Victorian Values: Aspects of Nineteenth-Century Thought and Society* (Manchester, 1988)

Simmons, Clare A., *Reversing the Conquest: History and Myth in Nineteenth-Century British Literature* (New Brunswick, 1990)

—— 'Iron-worded Proof: Victorian Identity and the Old English Language', *Studies in Medievalism*, 4 (1992)

Skeat, W.W., 'On the Study of Anglo-Saxon', *Macmillan's Magazine*, 39 (1879)

Smiles, Samuel, *Self-Help* (London, 1996 [1859])

Smyth, Alfred P., *King Alfred the Great* (Oxford, 1995)

—— *The Medieval Life of King Alfred the Great* (Basingstoke, 2002)

Soane, George, 'King Alfred's Song in the Danish Camp: Sung by Mr Sims Reeves, Written by George Soane, Composed with Accompaniment for Harp or Pianoforte by John Thomas' (London, n.d.)

Speed, John, *The History of Great Britaine Under the Conquests of ye Romans, Saxons, Danes and Normans* (London, 1650)

Spelman, John, *Certain Considerations upon the Duties Both of Prince and People* (London, 1642)

—— *The Life of Alfred the Great from the Manuscripts in the Bodleian Library: With Considerable Additions, and Several Historical Remarks by the Publisher, Thomas Hearne* (Oxford, 1707)

Stables, Gordon, *'Twixt Daydawn and Light: A Tale of the Times of Alfred the Great* (London, 1898)

Stafford, Fiona J., *The Last of the Race: The Growth of a Myth from Milton to Darwin* (Oxford, 1994)

Stafford, Robert A., 'Scientific Exploration and Empire', in *The Oxford History of the British Empire* (Oxford, 1994), vol. III

Stang, Richard, *The Theory of the Novel in England, 1850–1870* (London, 1959)

Stanley, Eric Gerald, 'The Glorification of Alfred King of Wessex (From the Publication of Sir John Spelman's *Life*, 1678 and 1709, to the Publication of Reinhold Pauli's, 1851)', *Poetica*, 12 (1981)

Stephens, J.E.R., 'The Origin and Growth of Trial by Jury in England', *The Westminster Review*, 144 (1895)

Stevenson, Joseph, ed., *The Church Historians of England* (London, 1853–55)

Stevenson, W.H., ed., *Asser's Life of King Alfred Together With the Annals of Saint Neots Erroneously Ascribed to Asser* (Oxford, 1959)

Stevenson, William H., 'The Date of King Alfred's Death', *English Historical Review*, 13 (1898)

Stewart, Agnes M., *Stories about Alfred the Great, for the Amusement and Instruction of Children* (Dublin, 1840)

Stray, Christopher, *Classics Transformed: Schools, Universities, and Society in England, 1830–1960* (Oxford, 1998)

Strong, Roy, *And When Did You Last See Your Father? The Victorian Painter and British History* (London, 1978)

Strutt, Joseph, *A Complete View of the Dress and Habits of the People of England, from the Establishment of the Saxons in Britain to the Present Time* (London, 1796)

—— *Ancient Times: A Drama* (Edinburgh, 1808)

Stubbs, *The Constitutional History of England in its Origin and Development* (Oxford, 1866)

Sullivan, W. K., 'Celtic Ethnology', *The Home and Foreign Review*, 4 (1864)

—— ed., *The Oldest English Texts* (London, 1885)

Tappan, Eva March, *In the Days of Alfred the Great* (London, 1900)

—— *Robin Hood: His Book* (London, 1905)

Taylor, Beverley and Brewer, Elisabeth, *The Return of King Arthur* (Cambridge, 1983)

Textus Roffensis, ed. by Thomas Hearne (Oxford, 1720)

Thackeray, William Makepeace, 'Our Street', in *William Makepeace Thackeray, The Works of William Makepeace Thackeray* (London, 1872)

—— *The Newcomes: Memoirs of a Most Respectable Family*, ed. by A. Sanders (Oxford, 1995)

Thomson, Patricia, *The Victorian Heroine: A Changing Ideal* (Westport, 1978)

Thompson, E.P., *The Making of the English Working Class* (Harmondsworth, 1980)

Thornton, Archibald Paton, *The Imperial Idea and Its Enemies. A Study in British Power* (London, 1985)

Thorpe, Benjamin, ed., *Ancient Laws and Institutes of England* (London, 1840)

— *A History of England Under the Anglo-Saxon Kings, Translated from the German of Dr J.M. Lappenberg* (London, 1845)

— *The Anglo-Saxon Chronicle According to the Several Original Authorities* (London, 1861)

'Thoughts Upon Beards', *Blackwood's Edinburgh Magazine*, 34 (1833)

Three Excellent Old Songs (Falkirk, 1816)

Thurston, Herbert, 'Alfred the Idolator', *The Month*, 98 (n.d.)

The Times

Tracy, Robert, 'Loving You All Ways: Vamps, Vampires, Necrophiles and Necrofilles in Nineteenth-Century Fiction', in Regina Barreca, ed., *Sex and Death in Victorian Literature* (London, 1990)

'The Treaty Between Alfred and Guthrum', in Simon Keynes and Michael Lapidge, eds, *Alfred the Great: Asser's Life of King Alfred and Other Contemporary Sources* (Harmondsworth, 1983)

Troup, George, 'Our Anglo-Saxon Empire', *Tait's Edinburgh Magazine*, 20 (1849)

Tulloch, John 'Anglo-Saxon and Anglo-Norman Christianity', *The North British Review*, 37 (1862)

Tupper, Martin Farquhar, *Alfred: A Patriotic Play* (Westminster, 1850)

— 'The Late Commemorations', in the *Anglo-Saxon* I (1849), 16–21

— *Ballads for the Times* (London, 1851)

— *Three Hundred Sonnets* (London, 1860)

— 'King Alfred's Poems', in J.A. Giles, ed., *The Whole Works of King Alfred the Great: With Preliminary Essays Illustrative of the History, Arts, Manners, of the Ninth Century* (Oxford, 1878)

Turner, Sharon, *The History of the Anglo-Saxons from the Earliest Period to the Norman Conquest* (London, 1799)

Tylor, E.B., 'The Philology of Slang', *Macmillan's Magazine*, 29 (1874)

Tytler, Graeme, *Physiognomy in the European Novel: Faces and Fortunes* (Princeton, 1982)

The United Kingdom Parliament: Standing Committee Database, 'Protecting the Community's Financial Interests', Wednesday 26 February 2003

Verstegan, Richard, *A Restitution of Decayed Intelligence in Antiquities Concerning the Most Noble and Renowned English Nation* (London, 1673)

Von Haller, Albert, *The Moderate Monarchy, or Principle of the British Constitution, Described in a Narrative of the Life and Maxims of*

Alfred the Great and his Councellors, ed. by Francis Steinitz (London, 1849)

Wade, John, *The Black Book: Or, Corruption Unmasked* (London, 1819)

Walder, Dennis, *The Nineteenth-Century Novel: Identities* (London, 2001)

Walkley, Samuel, *When the Vikings Came: A Tale of Adventure in the Days of King Alfred* (London, 1936)

Watson, William, 'King Alfred', in William Watson, *Sable and Purple with Other Poems* (London, 1910 [1901])

Wawn, Andrew, *The Anglo-Man: Thorleifur Repp, Philology and Nineteenth-Century Britain* (Reykjavík, 1991)

—— ed., *Northern Antiquity: The Post-Medieval Reception of Edda and Saga* (Hisarlik, Iceland, 1994)

—— *The Victorians and the Vikings* (Cambridge, 2000)

Westwood, Jennifer, *Alfred the Great* (Hove, 1978)

Whistler, Charles W., *King Alfred's Viking* (London, 1899)

Whitaker, John, *The Life of Saint Neot, the Oldest of all the Brothers of King Alfred* (London, 1809)

White, Donald A., 'Changing Views of the Adventus Saxonum in Nineteenth- and Twentieth-Century English Scholarship', *Journal of the History of Ideas*, 32 (1971)

White, Hayden, *Metahistory* (Baltimore, 1973)

Whitelock, Dorothy, *The Anglo-Saxon Chronicle: A Revised Translation* (London, 1965)

Wildman, W.B., *King Alfred's Boyhood, and the Date of his Death* (Sherborne, 1898)

The Will of King Alfred, in Simon Keynes and Michael Lapidge (eds), *Alfred the Great: Asser's Life of King Alfred and Other Contemporary Sources* (Harmondsworth, 1983)

William of Malmesbury, *History of the Kings of England*, in Joseph Stevenson, *The Church Historians of England* (London, 1853–55), III:i

Williams, Carolyn D., *Pope, Homer and Manliness: Some Aspects of Eighteenth-Century Classical Learning* (London, 1993)

Williams, David, *Lessons to a Young Prince, on the Present Disposition in Europe to a General Revolution* (London, 1790)

Williams, Raymond, *Marxism and Literature* (Oxford, 1977)

—— *The Country and the City* (London, 1993)

Wilson, Richard, 'Historicising New Historicism', in Richard Wilson and Richard Dutton, eds, *New Historicism and Renaissance Drama* (London, 1992)

Wilton, Richard, 'The Priest's Door, Little Driffield Church', in Richard Wilton, *Lyra Pastoralis* (London, 1902)

Winstanley, Gerrard, *The Law of Freedom and Other Writings* (Cambridge, 1983)

Wise, Francis, *Annales rerum gestarum Aelfredi Magni* (Oxford, 1722)

Withycombe, E.G., *The Oxford Dictionary of English Christian Names* (Oxford, 1977)

Wolff, Henry W., 'The Early Ancestors of Our Queen', *The National Review*, 18 (1892)

Wood, Michael, *In Search of England* (London, 1999)

Wooley, John, *Lectures Delivered in Australia* (London, 1862)

Wordsworth, William, *The Poetical Works*, ed. by John Carter (London, 1850)

—— *The Poetical Works of William Wordsworth*, ed. by E. Selincourt (Oxford, 1947)

Wright, Thomas, ed., *Biographia Britannica Literaria: Anglo-Saxon Period* (London, 1842)

Yorke, Barbara, *The King Alfred Millenary in Winchester, 1901* (Winchester, 1999)

—— 'The Most Perfect Man in History?' *History Today*, 49: 10 (1999)

Index